1st Edition

THE
TOOLS
AND
TECHNIQUES
OF

Employee Benefit And Retirement Planning

- Stephan R. Leimberg

- John J. McFadden

NATIONAL UNDERWRITER

The National Underwriter Co. • 420 East 4th St. • Cincinnati, OH 45202

Library of Congress Catalog Card Number: 89-60066

ISBN 0-87218-462-5

published by

NULAW SERVICES

a department of

THE NATIONAL UNDERWRITER COMPANY

Copyright © 1989
The National Underwriter Company
420 East Fourth Street
Cincinnati, Ohio

Printed in the United States of America

DEDICATIONS

Stephan R. Leimberg

*To Dan Hoellering, my 85-years-young friend
who always found the time to
do so much for so many*

John J. McFadden

To Rhoda, Susanna, and Diana

ABOUT THE AUTHORS

Stephan R. Leimberg

Stephan R. Leimberg serves as Professor of Taxation and Estate Planning at The American College. He has been granted the B.A. degree by Temple University, a J.D. by the Temple University School of Law, and holds the CLU designation. Mr. Leimberg is a Lecturer in Law at both the Tax Masters of Temple University School of Law and in its M.B.A. Program, as well as an adjunct professor in the Tax Masters Program at Widener University.

Professor Leimberg is on the Board of Advisors of the Bureau of National Affairs — Tax Management — Financial Planning, and Commerce Clearing House's Financial and Estate Planning Advisory Board as well as Warren, Gorham, and Lamont's new Financial and Estate Planning Service. He is the co-chairman, with Sidney Kess, of the American College-Commerce Clearing House National Conference on Financial Planning.

Professor Leimberg is the author of over 30 books including *The Tools and Techniques of Estate Planning* and *The Tools and Techniques of Financial Planning*, published by The National Underwriter Company. Leimberg is co-creator, with Dr. Robert T. LeClair, of NumberCruncher, TOOLKIT, and GraphPak financial and estate planning software.

Mr. Leimberg is the Editor and Publisher of *Think About It,* a monthly newsletter on income, estate, and gift taxes relating to Insurance, Business, Financial, and Estate Planning, published by many Associations of Life Underwriters, CLU Chapters, and insurance companies, and financial institutions.

Professor Leimberg has been a main platform speaker at both the Million Dollar Round Table annual meeting and the Top of the Table and has appeared before numerous estate planning councils, Life Underwriters Associations, life insurance companies, and study groups. He has also addressed the Advanced Planners meeting of the International Association for Financial Planning, the State Bars of Texas, Wisconsin and Oklahoma, the Pennsylvania Bar Institute Basic Legal Practice Course, numerous CPA societies, and has been a featured speaker at three workshops of the National Aeronautics and Space Administration. He appeared as an expert witness on IRAs before a subcommittee of the House Ways and Means Committee of the United States House of Representatives.

Professor Leimberg has also spoken at the N.Y.U. Tax Institute, The Southern California Tax and Estate Planning Forum, and at the Annual Meeting of the National Association of Estate Planning Councils.

Leimberg has served on the Board of Directors of the Philadelphia CLU chapter, the Philadelphia Estate Planning Council, and was a Director of the Delaware Valley Chapter of the International Association for Financial Planning, Inc.

John J. McFadden

John J. McFadden is a tax lawyer and employee compensation planning consultant. He holds the position of Professor of Taxation at The American College in Bryn Mawr, PA. His undergraduate degree is from Lehigh University, with a master's degree from the University of Rochester, and a J.D. from Harvard Law School. He has been admitted to the Pennsylvania Bar and the United States Tax Court and is a member of the Philadelphia Bar Association.

At the American College Mr. McFadden is responsible for the College's graduate courses in Advanced Pension and Retirement Planning and Executive Compensation.

Mr. McFadden is the author of articles on such subjects as professional corporations, accumulated earnings, stock redemptions, and cafeteria compensation for various tax and professional journals. He is author of *Retirement Plans for Employees* and coauthor of *Employee Benefits*, 2nd edition, both published by Richard D. Erwin, Inc. in 1988. Mr. McFadden also speaks and consults on tax and compensation matters and conducts seminars for financial planners active in those areas.

PREFACE

Tools and Techniques of Employee Benefit and Retirement Planning is intended to serve as an easily accessible, up-to-date guide to creative employee benefit and retirement planning for use by practicing financial planners, insurance agents, accountants, attorneys and other financial services professionals, as well as company managers, personnel departments, and law and graduate school students. It is designed to meet these professionals' needs for timely and accurate introductory, overview, or review information in this area. Such needs are increasing for two reasons. First, the high direct and indirect expenses involved with recruiting, retaining and ultimately retiring employees mandates a careful search for the benefit and compensation package that will accomplish an employer's objectives in the most cost effective way. Second, in recent years there has been a tremendous growth in federal legislation and regulatory activity in the compensation area; this increases the difficulty of designing benefit packages and also the cost (in taxes and penalties to employer and employee) of mistakes in benefit planning.

This book covers all major types of employee benefit arrangements. Although special consideration is given to employee benefit arrangements as applied to smaller, closely held businesses, most of the benefits described here are used by both small and large companies, and the same tax and other rules apply to both.

As is the case with our companion books, *The Tools and Techniques of Estate Planning* and *The Tools and Techniques of Financial Planning*, in this book each individual tool or technique of benefit or retirement planning is discussed in an easy-to-use format that is aimed at answering the planner's major questions:

WHAT IS IT? provides a brief description of the benefit planning tool or technique.

WHEN IS IT INDICATED? summarizes the client situations where the particular technique is most often beneficial.

ADVANTAGES and DISADVANTAGES provides a summary of the advantages and disadvantages of each technique.

DESIGN FEATURES summarizes the characteristic features of the technique and the planning options that are available.

TAX IMPLICATIONS describes the federal income, estate and payroll tax implications of the technique to both employer and employee; some state tax aspects are also noted where appropriate.

ERISA AND OTHER IMPLICATIONS summarizes the ERISA reporting and disclosure, funding, and other non-tax federal regulatory requirements.

HOW TO INSTALL THE PLAN provides a summary of the steps that must be taken for an employer to adopt and implement the plan.

WHERE CAN I FIND OUT MORE ABOUT IT? provides a list of references for further study and information.

QUESTIONS AND ANSWERS discusses some specific problems (and their solutions) that are often encountered by planners in connection with the benefit plan.

Where appropriate, some chapters may deviate somewhat from this format in order to provide the best approach to understanding the material.

The authors wish to acknowledge many members of the benefit planning community for discussions and critiques that over the years have contributed to the perspective taken in this book. Also, in particular the authors are fortunate to have received substantial technical copy editing assistance from Deborah Tabacco, Darlene Chandler, and Alice Fossett of The National Underwriter Company.

INTRODUCTION TO EMPLOYEE BENEFIT AND RETIREMENT PLANNING

A CONTINUING PROCESS

Employee benefit and retirement planning tools and techniques should be designed to solve both general and specific financial planning problems for employees and employers. Before investigating a particular benefit arrangement in depth, the planner must first identify the client's planning objectives and needs — exactly what it is that the client wants to accomplish. Then the planner must determine which particular benefit arrangements can help to meet these objectives most effectively and efficiently.

Step 1 — Meet Client and Gather Data

The planning process begins with fact finding. Only a thorough knowledge of the client's personal and business financial picture can provide the right analysis of benefit plan needs. A fact finder specifically designed for qualified retirement plans is included in Appendix C of this book. Much of the information on that fact finder also is applicable in a more general way and can serve as a useful vehicle for overall benefit plan design.

Step 2 — Identify Corporate and Personal Objectives; Quantify and Prioritize Them

Many clients may have a number of conflicting objectives or have unrealistic expectations as to what can be accomplished or the costs of achieving certain goals. The planner must help the client establish an order of priorities and then give first preference to those the client feels are most important and which the planner considers realistic.

Step 3 — Analyze the Client's Existing Plans to Identify Weaknesses or Gaps

To what extent do the existing plans fail to meet the client's business and personal needs? What needs to be added, removed, or modified?

Step 4 — Formulate and Test New Plan Designs

Once the initial steps are accomplished, the planner must focus on the types of benefit plans that are most appropriate within comfortable risk/reward and cost/benefit considerations. The chapters and appendices of *Tools and Techniques of Employee Benefit and Retirement Planning* deal with specific issues in formulating each type of benefit plan. But before focusing on specific types of plan, some broad questions discussed in the next paragraphs must be addressed. These are

(a) What is the form of business entity?

(b) Does the employer want special compensation arrangements for "executives only," a broader type of plan for a larger group, or a mixture of both? and

(c) Is tax sheltering a major consideration?

(a) What is the "form of business entity?"

Many initial issues can be settled by determining the client's form of business entity — that is, whether the business is organized formally as a sole proprietorship, a partnership, an S corporation, or a regular or C corporation.

The issue is as follows: in most cases, any form of entity can adopt any kind of benefit plan. However, some entity types cannot cover employees with an ownership interest under certain benefit plans. (The restrictions apply to partners, proprietors or S corporation shareholder-employees with a more-than-2% stock interest.) Such plans are thus unattractive in most cases to the business owners. However, it is possible that the business may still want to provide these benefits to regular employees as a method of attracting and retaining employees.

Figure I.1 indicates which types of plan are unavailable to proprietors, partners, or "more-than-2 percent" S corporation shareholder employees, in which types of entity.

Several chapters of this book contain a more thorough discussion of how various plans are affected by the type of business entity involved. These discussions are usually found in the "Questions and Answers" section of the chapter involved.

(b) Does the employer want special compensation arrangements for executives only?

For both small and large companies, there are two distinct types of benefits: (1) *executive benefits*, designed as part of special compensation packages for selected executives, and (2) *group plans*, which are provided to a large group of employees (sometimes because the law requires it). Generally, these are as follows:

Executive Benefits
Bonus Plan — Chapter 1
Death Benefit Only (DBO) Plan — Chapter 5
Incentive Stock Option — Chapter 16
Key Employee Life Insurance — Chapter 18
Nonqualified Deferred Compensation — Chapter 24
Restricted Stock Plan — Chapter 26
Split Dollar Life Insurance — Chapter 31
Stock Option — Chapter 32

Figure I.1

Comparison of Fringe Benefits by Entity Type				
Benefit	**Sole Prop.**	**Partnership**	**S Corp**	**C Corp**
Qualified plan	Yes	Yes	Yes	Yes
Deferred compensation	No	No	No	Yes
Salary continuation	No	Yes	Yes	Yes
Group life	No	No	No	Yes
Group health	Partial	Partial	Partial	Yes
Group disability	No	No	No	Yes
Medical reimb. plans	No	No	No	Yes
Accidental death	No	No	No	Yes
Disability income plan	No	No	No	Yes
Employee death benefit				
-Employer provided	No	No	No	Yes
-Qualified plan	Yes	Yes	Yes	Yes
Group legal plan	Yes	Yes	Yes	Yes
Educ. assistance plan	Yes	Yes	Yes	Yes
Dependent care	Yes	Yes	Yes	Yes
Meals & lodging	No	Yes	Yes	Yes
Cafeteria plan	No	No	No	Yes

Source: Adapted from Jenkins, Gary E., "The Impact of Choice of Entity Selection upon Compensation and Fringe Benefit Planning after Tax Reform," *Journal of American Society of CLU and ChFC,* March 1988.

Group Plans

Cafeteria Plan — Chapter 2
Dependent Care Assistance Plan — Chapter 7
Educational Assistance Plan — Chapter 8
Flexible Spending Account — Chapter 10
Governmental Employer Deferred Compensation (Section 457) Plan — Chapter 11
Group-Term Life Insurance — Chapter 12
Health Insurance — Chapter 13
Health Maintenance Organization — Chapter 14
Legal Services Plan — Chapter 19
Long Term Disability Insurance — Chapter 21
Medical Reimbursement Plan — Chapter 22
Qualified Pension and Profit-sharing Plans
    Cash Balance Pension Plan — Chapter 3
    Defined Benefit Pension Plan — Chapter 6
    ESOP/Stock Bonus Plan — Chapter 9
    HR 10 (Keogh) Plan — Chapter 15
    Money Purchase Pension Plan — Chapter 23
    Profit-Sharing Plan — Chapter 25
    Savings Plan — Chapter 27
    Section 401(k) Plan — Chapter 28
    Target Benefit Pension Plan — Chapter 33
Simplified Employee Pension (SEP) — Chapter 30
Tax Deferred Annuity — Chapter 34

Some of the plans listed above under "group plans" can be designed to benefit a limited class of employees. However, opportunities for discriminatory coverage are generally limited by legal rules that limit or eliminate tax benefits, or impose a penalty, if the plan discriminates excessively in coverage. Often, however, the applicable rules leave some room to provide special benefits to executives within the group plan. These design opportunities are discussed in individual chapters in the book.

(c) Is "Tax Sheltering" a Major Consideration?

The possibility that benefit plans can be used as tax shelters primarily arises in financial planning for owners of closely held businesses where the owners — and members of their families — are the primary employees of the business, with relatively few regular employees. Benefit plans — primarily qualified pension and profit-sharing plans — can often be used as a significant part of the personal financial and tax planning for these employees. The idea is to use the plan to shelter tax deferred retirement savings, which often produces better results than saving money outside the plan.

Analyzing the desirability of a qualified plan instead of personal savings is not an exact science. Calculations are helpful, but because assumptions — and therefore judgment — are involved, an exact answer cannot simply emerge from the right calculations. Calculations, however, provide a necessary starting point. A worksheet from The American College's Advanced Pension and Retirement Planning graduate program will illustrate the basic features of the analysis (see Figure I.2).

As an example using the worksheet, suppose your client Doctor Leberkrank, age 41, and two office employees are the only employees of the Doctor's professional corporation. The Doctor wants to establish a qualified profit-sharing plan that will enable him to contribute the $30,000 annual maximum (as indexed). A preliminary plan design analysis indicates that in order to do this, a total of $3,000 will have to be contributed annually on behalf of the two office employees, in order to meet the qualified plan nondiscrimination rules. Thus, the choice is between $33,000 annually of private savings outside the plan or a $30,000 annual contribution to the plan with the benefit of tax deferral provided under the plan.

The worksheet (Figure I.2) records these facts and other inputs and assumptions necessary to make a preliminary calculation.

The worksheet shows that, based on these facts and assumptions, the plan is a better deal than a private savings program. The plan will provide an annual net income in retirement of $137,000, as compared with only $97,000 under the private saving program.

You'll note that the advantage of the qualified plan depends to a considerable extent on minimizing contributions on behalf of nonowner employees. Obviously, this will be difficult where there are many employees in the business. However, funds used for employee benefits are not actually "wasted" from the business owner's viewpoint. Employee benefits are a valuable form of additional compensation for employees, and they help the owner attract, retain, and eventually retire good employees. The importance of this factor essentially cannot be quantified; it is a matter of the adviser's and client's business judgment.

What are the alternatives if this preliminary analysis turns out unfavorable for the qualified plan? The next step is not simply to abandon the idea of a qualified plan, but rather to consider various alternative plan designs that might improve the client's cost/benefit ratio. Alternative designs can increase the amount allocated under the plan for the owner(s) or decrease the employer's cost to cover regular employees (or both). Some techniques for doing this (explained in more detail in this book) include:

- using a defined benefit plan for an older owner; often more than $30,000 annually can be contributed for the owner under such a plan, and costs can be minimal for younger regular employees.

- service-based benefit formulas that are favorable to key employees with longer service can be used, particularly in a defined benefit plan.

- social security integration can be maximized to provide relatively better cost allocation to key employees.

- plan eligibility and coverage for regular employees can be tightened within the limits of the law. However, excluding employees often creates employee relations problems.

- plan combinations that favor key employees can be investigated. For example, adding a Section 401(k) plan to an existing pension plan often allows some relatively greater benefit for key employees. Also, combinations of defined benefit and defined contribution plans are often used to advantage.

Step 5 — Implement the New or Revised Plan

Once the new plan has been thoroughly tested on paper by the appropriate advisers and the downside risks and indirect costs considered (including the impact on other plans both inside and outside a corporate employer, and the impact on the corporation itself), the planner must help the client compare and then select the specific financial products and services required to implement and administer the plan. A responsibility checklist must be developed to indicate who is responsible for every aspect of the ongoing plan, and who is responsible for overall implementation.

Step 6 — Periodically Review the Plan

Because of the dynamic business and government regulatory climate relating to benefit plans, no tool or technique is likely to be effective indefinitely without revision. A schedule should be established for monitoring the success (or failure) as well as the direct and indirect cost on the plan. A review procedure should be established and followed to assure continuing achievement of the client's objectives.

Figure I.2

WORKSHEET
Qualified Plan vs. Private Savings

for   Dr. Leberkrank, P.C.

Inputs and assumptions

1. Assumed pretax rate of return	8 %
2. Annual plan contribution for owner	$ 30,000
3. Cost for employees if plan provides line 2 contribution for owner	$ 3,000
4. Total cost (line 2 plus line 3)	$ 33,000
5. Preretirement tax rate	28 %
6. Assumed postretirement tax rate	33 %
7. Years until retirement	24
8. Desired number of years of annuity payout (generally no more than single/joint life expectancy at retirement)	20

Calculations	Qualified Plan	Private Savings
9. Accumulation at retirement (future value (FV) of [line 7] years of payments)	$2,002,943	$1,169,253
	• Annual payment = line 2 • Interest rate = line 1	• Annual payment = line 4 - (line 5) % of line 4 • Interest rate = line 1 - (line 5) % of line 1
10. Annual annuity available (amortization [PMT] of line 9 over [line 8] years)	$204,004	$96,709
	• Principal = line 9 • Interest = line 1	• Principal - line 9 • Interest = line 1 - (line 6) % of line 1
11. Income tax* on annuity payment	$67,321 (line 6) % of line 10	-0-
12. Net annuity (line 10 - line 11)	$136,683	$96,709

* The 15% excess distribution tax on annual amounts over $150,000 (or $112,500 as indexed) should also be taken into account.

CONTENTS

Tools and Techniques

Contents

Chapter 1

BONUS PLAN

WHAT IS IT?

A bonus is an addition to regular salary or compensation that is provided, usually near year end, to enable employees to share in profits resulting from a successful year. This chapter discusses the tax and other planning considerations that apply.

WHEN IS IT INDICATED?

1. Bonuses are often used in closely held companies to enable shareholder-employees to withdraw the maximum compensation income from the company each year.

2. Bonuses are used for executives of larger companies as an incentive-oriented form of compensation, based on the attainment of profit or other goals during the year.

3. Bonuses may be used to assist executives in funding cross-purchase buy-sell agreements or in contributing their share of the premium to a split dollar arrangement.

ADVANTAGES

1. For executives of larger companies, bonuses represent an incentive-based form of compensation that is very effective because of the close connection between performance and receipt. Often, the executive uses the bonus to purchase a life insurance policy which provides death benefit protection and tax deferred accumulation of cash value.

2. Bonuses allow flexibility in compensation to reflect company performance, both in closely held and larger corporations.

3. Bonus arrangements are flexible and simple to design, within the tax constraints discussed below.

DISADVANTAGES

1. Bonuses generally do not offer an opportunity for the employee to defer taxation of compensation for more than one year.

2. Bonuses are limited by the requirement of ''reasonableness'' for the deductibility of compensation payments by the employer.

TAX IMPLICATIONS

Bonus payments are deductible under the same rules as other forms of cash compensation. These rules are discussed in detail in Chapter 4, but will be covered in summary here as they apply to bonuses.

A bonus, together with other compensation, cannot be deducted unless it constitutes (a) a reasonable allowance for (b) services actually rendered. Factors indicating reasonableness — the first part of the test — are listed in the general discussion in Chapter 4. Bonuses can be very large if they are based on profits or earnings and the company has a very good year. For example, suppose a sales manager receives a $400,000 bonus in addition to his regular $100,000 base salary, under a sales-target bonus formula. Although $500,000 of compensation might, as a general rule, be considered unreasonably high for this type of sales manager, this arrangement might be sustained by the IRS for two reasons:

- Reasonableness of compensation is often tested in accordance with circumstances existing when the bonus agreement is entered into rather than when the bonus is actually paid.

- In testing the reasonableness of a bonus, both the IRS and the courts will usually take into account the element of risk involved to the employee. That is, an employee presumably had a choice between a relatively lower amount of guaranteed compensation and a higher amount of contingent compensation. So the two should be deemed equivalent for purposes of testing reasonableness. For instance, a sales manager who receives a $100,000 base salary and a bonus of 10% of the gross sales increase in 1990, producing a $400,000 bonus for 1990, probably could not at the beginning of 1990 have negotiated a contract for $500,000 of guaranteed compensation without bonus. The reasonableness of the bonus contract should be based on the reasonableness of the equivalent fixed salary agreement that the sales manager could have negotiated, not on the $500,000 total resulting from taking a chance and then having a good year.

This emphasizes the importance of planning ahead when using bonuses as an employee benefit technique. If reasonableness might become an issue, decide upon a bonus formula well in advance of the time the bonus is paid. (Preferably, in advance of the year in which the bonus will be earned). In other words, a formula for determining a bonus for year end 1990 should be determined in writing before the beginning of 1990 to help support the reasonableness of the amount.

1

Tools and Techniques

The timing of income to the employee and deductions to the corporation are governed by the rules discussed in detail in Chapter 4 with regard to cash compensation. Since bonuses are often payable after the end of the year in which they are earned, the "2½ month safe-harbor rule" is important for bonus planning. Under this rule an accrual method corporation can deduct a compensation payment that is properly accrued before the end of a given year, so long as the payment is made no later than 2½ months after the end of the corporation's taxable year. For example, for a calendar year accrual method corporation, a bonus earned for services completed in 1989 can be deducted by the corporation for 1989 so long as it is paid on or before March 15, 1990. Note, however, that the 2½ month rule does not apply to payments to employees who own or control (50 percent or more) the corporation under Code Section 267(b). For those employees, the corporation must pay the bonus during its taxable year in order to deduct it during that taxable year.

For regular employees who can make use of the 2½ month safe harbor technique, the ability to move taxable income into the employee's next taxable year is a significant advantage of the bonus form of compensation. For example, a bonus might be earned (and deducted by the corporation) in 1989, paid on March 15, 1990, and the employee could defer the payment of tax to April 15, 1991 (the employee's due date for the 1990 tax return.)

ALTERNATIVES

1. As with cash compensation in general, as discussed in Chapter 4, taxation can be avoided or deferred by various types of noncash compensation plans that are discussed throughout this book, including qualified pension and profit-sharing plans, nonqualified deferred compensation plans, and medical benefit plans.

2. A form of deferred compensation with many of the same incentive features as a cash bonus plan is a stock option, incentive stock option (ISO), or restricted stock plan. These are discussed in later chapters.

HOW ARE THESE PLANS SET UP?

Bonus plans can be informal or even oral. There are no tax or other legal requirements for a written plan or for filing anything with the government. However, a written plan is often desirable, and in that case employer and employee might want to consult with an attorney experienced in handling employee compensation matters.

WHERE CAN I FIND OUT MORE ABOUT THESE PLANS?

1. Graduate Course: Executive Compensation (GS 842), The American College, Bryn Mawr, PA.

2. CLU/ChFC Courses: Income Taxation (HS 321) and Planning for Business Owners and Professionals (HS 331), The American College, Bryn Mawr, PA.

3. CFP Course: Retirement Planning and Employee Benefits (CFP V), College for Financial Planning, Denver, CO.

QUESTIONS AND ANSWERS

Question — What are the advantages of a written bonus plan?

Answer — A written agreement has at least two advantages:

First, a written plan, particularly one drafted in advance of the year in which compensation is earned, helps to avoid disallowance of the corporation's deduction on the ground that the amount is unreasonable. Without a written plan, the IRS is likely to claim that a bonus is simply a discretionary payment that is excessive and therefore nondeductible. If this payment is made to a shareholder, the payment may be characterized as a dividend instead of deductible compensation. This means that the corporation will not receive a tax deduction even though the entire distribution will probably be taxable as ordinary income to the shareholder-recipient.

A second reason for a written agreement is that it defines the terms of the bonus and assures the employee of legal grounds to require the corporation to live up to the agreement. The terms of the agreement should be clearly defined for this reason.

Question — If a bonus is based on "profits," is there any specific definition of profits that must be used?

Answer — There is no tax or legal reason for any specific definition of profits in a bonus agreement. The important thing is a clear definition to protect against later misunderstandings. Profits can be defined as the amount shown in financial statements, as taxable income for federal income tax purposes, or some other method of defining profits. If the definition relies on company accounting methods or federal tax laws, the agreement should take possible changes in accounting method or the tax laws into account. Paying a bonus in itself may affect profits. So, the agreement must specify whether profits are determined before or after bonus payments. For a company with more than one division or subsidiary, an executive may want to tie the bonus to profits in one particular unit rather than the company as a whole.

Chapter 2

CAFETERIA PLAN

WHAT IS IT?

A cafeteria plan is one under which employees may, within limits, choose the form of employee benefits from a "cafeteria" of benefit plans provided by their employer. Cafeteria plans include a "cash option" — an option to receive cash in lieu of noncash benefits of equal value.

WHEN IS IT INDICATED?

1. When employee benefit needs vary within the employee group — for example where the employee mix includes young, unmarried people with minimal life insurance and medical benefit needs as well as older employees with families who need maximum medical and life insurance benefits.

2. When employees want to choose the benefit package most suited to their needs.

3. When an employer seeks to maximize employee satisfaction with the benefit package and thereby maximize the employer's benefit from its compensation expenditures.

4. When the employer is large enough to afford the expense of such a plan. Because of administrative costs and complexity, cafeteria plans, in general, tend to be used by larger employers. (However, there is one type of cafeteria plan — the flexible spending account or FSA — that provides very specific tax benefits and is often used even by smaller employers including closely held businesses. FSAs feature benefit funding through salary reductions by employees. FSA plans are discussed in detail in Chapter 10.)

ADVANTAGES

1. Cafeteria plans help give employees an appreciation of the value of their benefit package.

2. The flexibility of a cafeteria benefit package helps meet varied employee needs.

3. Cafeteria plans can help control employer costs for the benefit package because provision of benefits that employees do not need is minimized.

DISADVANTAGES

1. Cafeteria plans are more complex and expensive for the employer to design and administer than fixed, standardized benefit packages.

2. Benefit packages usually include some insured benefits — medical and life insurance benefits, for example — and not all insurers will provide these programs on a cafeteria basis.

3. Complex tax requirements apply to the plan under section 125 of the Internal Revenue Code.

4. Highly compensated employees may lose the tax benefits of the plan if it is discriminatory. Key employees may lose tax benefits if more than 25% of aggregate benefits under the plan are provided to them.

EXAMPLE OF CAFETERIA PLAN

1. All employees receive a "basic benefit package" consisting of

   • Term life insurance equal to 1½ times salary

   • Medical expense insurance for employee and dependents

   • Disability income insurance (long and short term)

2. Each employee receives an additional "credit" based on salary and years of service (3 percent of salary for 0-5 years of service, 4½ percent for 5-10 years of service, and 6 percent for 10 or more years). Each year the employee can elect to apply this credit to one or more of a list of additional benefits specified by the employer such as

   • Cash only

   • Additional term life insurance up to 1 times salary

   • Dental insurance for employee or dependents

   • Up to two weeks additional vacation time

TAX IMPLICATIONS

1. A cafeteria plan must comply with the provisions of section 125 of the Internal Revenue Code. This Code section provides an exception for cafeteria plans from the "constructive receipt" doctrine. Under that doctrine, an employee is taxed on money or property that he has a free election to receive, even if he chooses not to receive it. So, if the terms of Section 125 are not met in a cafeteria plan, an employee is taxed on the value of any taxable benefits available from the plan, even if the employee chooses nontaxable benefits such as medical insurance.

2. Under Section 125 and its regulations, only certain benefits — ''qualified benefits'' — can be made available in a cafeteria plan. Qualifying benefits include cash and most tax-free benefits provided under the Code, except for

   • scholarships and fellowships

   • transportation benefits

   • educational assistance

   • employee discounts (for example, those for department store employees)

   • no-additional-cost services (for example, standby airline travel for airline employees)

   • retirement benefits such as qualified or nonqualified deferred compensation; however, a 401(k) arrangement can be included.

3. A cafeteria plan must meet certain nondiscrimination requirements:

   First, the plan must be made available to a group of employees in a manner that does not discriminate in favor of ''highly compensated'' employees. The definition of highly compensated is the same one applicable to qualified pension and profit sharing plans and most other tax-favored employee benefit plans (see Appendix A).

   Second, the plan's benefits must be nondiscriminatory. Qualified benefits provided to key employees under the plan must not exceed, in value, 25 percent of the aggregate value of plan benefits.

   If these nondiscrimination tests are not met by the plan, the result is that otherwise nontaxable benefits become taxable to highly compensated employees or key employees — but not to regular employees.

   In addition, any type of benefit offered under the plan must meet its own nondiscrimination tests — for example, any group term life insurance offered under the plan would also have to meet the nondiscrimination requirements of Section 89. These requirements are discussed in the chapters of this book covering these plans.

   In many cases it is not difficult to meet the nondiscrimination tests. In other cases, the result of not meeting the tests — some taxation to highly compensated employees only — may not be objectionable in view of the overall advantages of the plan.

4. Code section 89(k) states that all employees, not just those who are highly compensated, must include the value of the benefits received in income if the following requirements are not met:

   — employees must be notified of plan benefits

— the plan must be intended as a permanent plan

— there must be a written plan for the exclusive benefit of employees

— the plan must provide legally enforceable rights for employees

ALTERNATIVES

1. The FSA, or flexible spending account is a cafeteria plan funded through salary reductions. It is not just an alternative but a special type of cafeteria plan design that should be thoroughly investigated whenever cafeteria benefits are considered — see Chapter 10.

2. Fixed benefit programs without employee choice may be adequate where most employees have the same benefit needs or where the employer cannot administer a more complex program.

3. Cash compensation as an alternative to benefits gives up tax advantages in favor of maximum employee choice, and assumes that employees will have adequate income to provide benefits on their own.

HOW ARE THESE PLANS SET UP?

1. First, a plan design must be decided upon. This involves a survey of employee needs and employer costs, and a business decision as to the best alternative.

2. A written plan must be drafted and adopted by the employer. IRS or other governmental approval of the plan is generally not necessary, but an IRS ruling can be obtained if there is any doubt about some aspect of the tax treatment of the plan as designed.

3. Employee election (choice of benefit) forms must be designed and distributed to employees. Generally, employees must make benefit choices in advance of the year in which the benefits are earned. For example, for benefits to be earned and used in 1990, employees should complete and file their election forms with the employer before the end of 1989.

4. Skillful communication with employees is the most important element in the success of a cafeteria plan; these plans are often complicated.

HOW DO I FIND OUT MORE ABOUT THESE PLANS?

1. Beam and McFadden, *Employee Benefits*, Richard D. Irwin Inc., Homewood, Ill., 2nd ed. 1988.

2. Graduate Course: Executive Compensation (GS 842), The American College, Bryn Mawr, PA.

Chapter 3
CASH BALANCE PENSION PLAN

WHAT IS IT?

A cash balance pension plan is a qualified employer pension plan that provides for annual employer contributions at a specified rate to individual accounts that are set up for each plan participant. The employer guarantees not only the contribution level but also a minimum rate of return on each participant's account. A cash balance plan works somewhat like a money purchase pension plan discussed in a later chapter, but money purchase plans do not involve employer guarantees of rate of return.

WHEN IS IT INDICATED?

1. When the employees are relatively young and have substantial time to accumulate retirement savings.

2. When employees are concerned with security of retirement income.

3. When the work force is large and the bulk of the employees are middle-income. (Banks and similar financial institutions find this type of plan particularly appealing.)

4. When the employer is able to spread administrative costs over a relatively large group of plan participants.

ADVANTAGES

1. As with all qualified plans, the cash balance plan provides a tax-deferred savings medium for employees.

2. Plan distributions are eligible for the special 5-year (or 10-year) averaging tax computation available for qualified plans.

3. The employer guarantee removes investment risk from the employee.

4. The benefits of the plan are easily communicated to and appreciated by employees.

DISADVANTAGES

1. The retirement benefit may be inadequate for older plan entrants — see Figure 3.1.

2. Because of actuarial and PBGC aspects, the plan is more complex administratively than qualified defined contribution plans.

3. The shift of investment risk to the employer increases employer costs.

DESIGN FEATURES OF THESE PLANS

A cash balance plan sets up individual accounts for each participant. These accounts are credited by the employer at least once a year with two types of credit — the "pay credit" and the "interest credit."

The pay credit uses a formula based on compensation. For example, the plan might require the employer to credit each employee's account annually with a pay credit of 6 percent of compensation. The pay credit formula may also be "integrated" with social security. With social security integration, employee pay below a level specified in the plan — the "integration level" — receives a lesser credit than compensation above the integration level. This reflects the fact that the employer pays social security taxes to provide retirement benefits through social security. Social security integration for qualified plans is discussed in Appendix A of this book.

The interest credit is an amount of employer-guaranteed investment earnings that is credited annually to each employee's account. The interest credit must follow a formula in the plan and cannot merely be discretionary on the employer's part. For example, the interest credit formula in the plan might provide for each employee's account to be credited annually with a rate of earnings defined as the lesser of (a) the increase in the Consumer Price Index over the preceding year or (b) the one-year rate for U.S. Treasury securities. The plan can allow the employer to credit accounts with actual plan earnings, if these are higher.

In a cash balance plan there are no actual individual accounts, as there are in true defined contribution plans. All amounts are pooled in a single fund. Any plan participant has a legal claim on the entire fund to satisfy his or her claim to plan benefits.

The employer's annual cost for the plan is determined on an actuarial basis because of the employer guarantee feature. Investment risk lies with the employer; if actual plan earnings fall below total interest credits for the year, the employer must make up the difference. Employer costs can be controlled primarily by choosing the right kind of formula for the interest credit, one that does not risk uncontrollable and unforeseeable employer obligations. However, the interest credit formula should not be excessively conservative — if actual plan earnings year after year are more than interest credits, plan participants may resent the employer's enrichment and the positive employee relations value of the plan may be lost.

Tools and Techniques

Figure 3.1

CASH BALANCE PLAN ACCUMULATIONS

Pay credit: 10 percent of compensation
Interest credit: 7 percent annually guaranteed rate

Age at plan entry	Annual compensation	Account balance at age 65
25	$30,000	$640,827
30	30,000	443,739
40	30,000	203,028
50	30,000	80,664
55	30,000	44,349
60	30,000	18,459

TAX IMPLICATIONS

1. Employer contributions to the plan are deductible when made.

2. Taxation of the employee on employer contributions is deferred. Contributions and earnings on plan assets are both nontaxable to plan participants until withdrawn assuming the plan remains "qualified." A plan is qualified if it meets the eligibility, vesting, funding and other requirements explained in Appendix A.

3. Distributions from the plan must follow the rules for qualified plan distributions. Certain premature or excessive distributions are subject to penalties. These distribution rules are discussed in Appendix B.

4. Lump sum distributions made after age 59½ are subject to a limited election to use a special 5-year averaging tax calculation. Not all distributions are eligible. Appendix B has a complete coverage of these rules, including IRS forms.

5. The plan is subject to the minimum funding rules of section 412 of the Internal Revenue Code. This requires minimum contributions, subject to a penalty if less than the minimum amount is contributed in any year. For plan years after 1988, such contributions must be made on at least an estimated quarterly basis. Appendix A discusses these rules further.

6. A cash balance plan is considered a defined benefit plan and is subject to mandatory insurance coverage by the Pension Benefit Guaranty Corporation (PBGC). The PBGC is a government corporation funded through a mandatory premium paid by employer-sponsors of covered plans. The current premium flat rate is $16 annu-

ally per participant. An additional annual premium of up to $34 per participant may be required, depending on the amount of the plan's unfunded vested benefit. If the plan is terminated by the employer, PBGC termination procedures must be followed.

7. The plan is subject to the ERISA reporting and disclosure rules outlined in Appendix D.

ALTERNATIVES

1. Money purchase pension plans and profit-sharing plans build up similar qualified retirement accounts for employees, but without the employer guaranteed minimum investment return.

2. Defined benefit plans provide guaranteed benefits for employees, but are more complex in design and administration.

3. Individual retirement savings is always an alternative or supplement to any qualified plan, but there is no tax deferral except in the case of IRAs.

HOW TO INSTALL A CASH BALANCE PLAN

A cash balance plan follows the qualified plan installation procedure discussed in Appendix C of this book.

WHERE CAN I FIND OUT MORE ABOUT THESE PLANS?

1. McFadden, John J., *Retirement Plans For Employees*, Homewood, IL: Richard D. Irwin, 1988.

2. Graduate course: Advanced Pension and Retirement Planning II (GS 843), The American College, Bryn Mawr, PA.

Chapter 4

CASH COMPENSATION PLANNING

WHAT IS IT?

Although cash compensation — the employee's compensation paid currently (during the year in which it is earned) — is not generally thought of as an employee benefit, actually it is the core of any compensation and benefit package. Any proposed employee benefit has to be compared in effectiveness with equivalent cash compensation. In addition, many employee benefit plans such as pension and life insurance plans have benefit or contribution schedules that are based on the employee's cash compensation. Finally, from a tax point of view, cash compensation is not as simple as it might appear. Financial planners must understand the rules to avoid adverse tax results from inappropriate planning.

WHEN IS IT INDICATED?

Opportunities for planning cash compensation primarily arise for employees, including shareholder-employees, of regular or "C" corporations (not "S" corporations). In an unincorporated business or an "S" corporation, all income and losses pass directly through to the owners' tax returns, so there are few compensation planning opportunities.

ADVANTAGES

1. Compared with noncash benefits or deferred payments, cash compensation provides certainty and, therefore, greater security to the employee.

2. Cash compensation tends to set an employee's status in the company and community; the amount of annual salary must be carefully considered for this reason.

3. Cash compensation is an important part of overall financial planning for shareholder-employees of closely held corporations.

4. For employers, cash compensation is preferable to noncash benefits because it is easier to budget, with no unknown or uncontrollable costs.

5. Cash compensation plans rarely involve design and administrative complexities, including ERISA aspects, that may apply to medical benefits, pensions, and other types of noncash or deferred compensation.

DISADVANTAGES

1. Cash compensation paid currently is generally all taxable currently at ordinary income rates.

2. Cash compensation must meet the reasonableness test for deductibility and other tax issues discussed below.

In some cases, other forms of compensation can avoid or defer these problems.

TAX IMPLICATIONS

Reasonableness of Compensation

Under Section 162 of the Internal Revenue Code an employer who carries on a trade or business is allowed to deduct "a reasonable allowance for salaries or other compensation for personal services actually rendered." This "reasonableness" test is the main tax issue in determining whether an employer's payments for compensating an employee are deductible. If the company's payment does not meet this reasonableness test, its deduction is disallowed.

At a corporate income tax rate of 34 percent, the corporation's deduction saves 34 cents for every deductible dollar. Stated in another manner, the out-of-pocket cost for reasonable (deductible) compensation is $.66 of each $1.00 paid, as opposed to $1.00 for nondeductible payments. Since state income tax deductibility usually follows the federal rules, the true difference between deductibility and nondeductibility can be even more than this.

The IRS does not usually raise the reasonableness issue if salaries are not particularly high. However, as the amount paid and deducted increases, it becomes important for a company to "build a case" that compensation is reasonable. Steps to suggest to a client include:

- Determine compensation levels prior to the beginning of each fiscal year, before salary has been earned, instead of simply determining salaries from year to year on a purely discretionary basis. This avoids the impression that the amount of salary is based simply on the amount that shareholder-employees wish to withdraw from the corporation for a given year.

- Written employment contracts should be provided and signed before compensation is earned.

- The company's board of directors should document in the minutes of directors' meetings how the amount of salary was determined.

- Court cases and IRS publications mention many factors in determining what constitutes reasonable compensation. These factors, listed below, should be reviewed in documenting the amount of salary and other compensation.

7

Factors in Determining Reasonable Compensation

Factors mentioned by the courts in "reasonableness of compensation" cases and by the IRS in its publications include the following:

- Comparison with compensation paid to executives in comparable positions for comparable employers.

- The employee's qualifications for the position.

- The nature and scope of the employee's duties.

- The size and complexity of the business enterprise.

- Comparison of the compensation paid with the company's gross and net income.

- The company's compensation policy for all employees.

- Economic conditions — including the condition of the industry and the local economy as well as the overall national economy.

- Comparison with dividend distributions to shareholders. Abnormally low dividends can create an inference that a so-called salary payment to a shareholder-employee is really a disguised dividend.

Treatment of Disallowed Compensation

A deduction for compensation that is disallowed because it is unreasonable is treated in various ways depending on the circumstances. IRS regulations state that if a corporation makes excessive payments and such payments are made primarily to shareholders, these payments will be treated as dividends. Dividend treatment is the most typical situation for disallowed compensation. Other types of treatment are possible, depending on the facts. For example, if an employee at some point had transferred property to the corporation, excessive compensation payments could be treated as payments for this property, which would be nondeductible capital expenditures to the corporation.

From the recipient's point of view, in the absence of any other evidence, any excessive payments for salaries or compensation will be taxable as ordinary income to the recipient. In other words, from the employee's point of view, the reasonableness issue may not have much tax effect.

However, if the employee is a shareholder in the corporation, the corporation's tax picture and the possible loss of a compensation deduction at the corporate level can be very important. For example, suppose Larry Sharp owns 100% of Sharp Corporation and is its sole employee. Sharp Corporation earns $400,000 in 1989. If the corporation pays all $400,000 of this to Larry as deductible compensation, the only tax burden on the $400,000 is the individual income tax that Larry pays. But if the IRS disallows $100,000 of the compensation deduction and treats it as a nondeductible divi-

dend, then Larry still has $400,000 of taxable ordinary income, but the corporation also has $100,000 of taxable income. The corporation's tax on this — $22,250 — is a direct reduction in Larry's wealth since he is a 100% shareholder.

Reimbursement Agreements

Because of the uncertainty of the reasonable compensation issue, companies often enter into reimbursement agreements with employees under which the employee is required to pay back the excessive portion of the compensation to the corporation if the IRS disallows a deduction for compensation. The employee does not generally have to pay income tax on the amount repaid. These agreements can be useful but they do not necessarily solve the reasonableness problem. In fact they may be a "red flag" to the IRS examiner. The IRS sometimes asserts that such an agreement is evidence that the corporation intended to pay unreasonable compensation. Therefore, such an agreement can make the compensation even more likely to attract a tax audit and more difficult to defend in litigation.

An agreement to reimburse is rarely in the direct financial interest of the employee, since the employee would usually be better off keeping the money rather than returning it. The employee's tax on any excessive portion is treated as a dividend so the tax paid from the employee's perspective is the same as if the entire payment was compensation. Reimbursement agreements are primarily used by shareholder-employees where the corporation's tax status is of indirect financial interest to the employee. In those cases what hurts the corporation hurts the employee as a stockholder.

Timing of Income and Deductions

The tax rules for the timing of a corporation's deduction for compensation are more complicated than one might expect, primarily because the IRS sees potential for abuse in compensation payment situations.

Under the usual tax accounting rules for accrual method taxpayers an item is deductible for an accounting period if that item has been properly accrued, even if not actually paid. Accrual occurs for tax purposes in the taxable year when all events have happened that legally require the corporation to pay the amount — the so-called "all events" test. Usually the all events test is satisfied as soon as the employee has performed all the services required under the terms of the employment contract. Because of the apparent potential for abuse of compensation arrangements, particularly for closely held businesses, there are specific rules for deducting compensation payments that override the usual accrual rules in some cases. These are summarized below.

If the company uses the cash method of accounting, deductions for compensation cannot be taken before the year in which the compensation is actually paid.

No employer, whether using the cash method or the accrual method, can take a deduction for compensation for services that are not rendered before the end of the taxable year for which the deduction is claimed. Any compensation paid in advance must be deducted pro rata over the period during which services are actually rendered.

Timing of Corporate Deductions for Compensation Payments

The tax rules for timing of deductions distinguish between *current compensation* and *deferred compensation*. If the compensation qualifies as current compensation, then the employer can deduct it in the year in which it is properly accrued to the corporation under the tax accounting accrual rules. If the amount qualifies as deferred compensation, then the employer corporation cannot deduct it until the taxable year of the corporation in which, or with which, ends the taxable year of the employee in which the amount is includable in the employee's income. For example, if an employer sets up a deferred compensation arrangement in 1989 for work performed in 1989 with compensation payable in 1996 and taxable to the employee in 1996, the corporation cannot deduct the compensation amount until 1996.

Whether an amount is considered current or deferred compensation depends on the type of employee:

- For a regular employee — an employee who is not a controlling shareholder or otherwise related to the employer corporation — the IRS takes the position that a plan is deferred compensation if the payment is made more than 2 1/2 months after the end of the taxable year of the corporation. In other words, there is a 2 1/2 month *safe harbor rule*. For example, if a calendar year accrual-method corporation declares and accrues a bonus to an employee before the end of 1989, the employer is entitled to a 1989 deduction for the bonus as long as the bonus is paid before March 15, 1990. The employee would include this bonus in income for 1990. However, if the bonus was paid on April 1, 1990 — beyond the 2 1/2 month limit — then, although the employee still must include the amount in income for 1990, the employer's deduction would be delayed until 1990.

- If the employee is related to the corporation — owns more than 50 percent of the corporation, directly or indirectly under Section 267(b) of the Code — then the 2 1/2 month safe harbor rule does not apply. Deductions and income are matched in all cases. So, if a calendar year accrual-method corporation declares and accrues a bonus to its controlling shareholder before the end of 1989, but pays it on February 1, 1990, the corporation cannot deduct the bonus until 1990.

ALTERNATIVES

1. Taxation can be avoided or deferred by various types of noncash compensation plans, which are discussed throughout this book. Some examples of plans that defer taxation, usually until cash is actually received by the employee, are:

   - nonqualified deferred compensation plans

   - qualified pension, profit-sharing, ESOP, 401(k) and similar plans

   - stock option and restricted stock plans

   Compensation options that are completely tax free (no taxation either currently or deferred) include such plans as:

   - health and accident plans (provided that certain nondiscrimination, eligibility, and coverage continuation requirements are met)

   - disability income plans of certain types

   - dependent care and educational assistance plans

   - group term life insurance up to $50,000

   - the pure death benefit amount from any life insurance plan, even if the premium is currently taxable

2. Where the employer may lose a deduction for cash compensation due to a reasonableness of compensation problem, part of the compensation might be provided in a form that is both tax-deferred to the employee and deduction-deferred to the employer. This is discussed further under nonqualified deferred compensation plans. The reasonableness of compensation issue does not arise until the year in which the employer takes the deduction, so deferring the deduction can be helpful.

HOW IS THE PLAN SET UP?

Cash compensation planning is simple and is often not even thought of as a form of employee benefit planning. However, for a complex employment agreement involving cash and other forms of compensation, and in situations where reasonableness of compensation may be an issue, a tax accountant, tax attorney, or financial planner specializing in employee benefits and compensation planning can provide useful guidance.

WHERE CAN I FIND OUT MORE ABOUT IT?

1. IRS publication 334, *Tax Guide for Small Business*, has a simple explanation of the IRS position on the employer's tax treatment of employee pay and benefits. IRS Publication 17, *Your Federal Income Tax*, covers the tax treatment from the employee side. Both these publications are available free from the IRS and are revised annually.

2. Graduate Course: Executive Compensation (GS 842), The American College, Bryn Mawr, PA.

3. CLU/ChFC Courses: Income Taxation (HS 321) and Planning for Business Owners and Professionals (HS 331), The American College, Bryn Mawr, PA.

4. CFP Course: Retirement Planning and Employee Benefits (CFP V), College for Financial Planning, Denver, CO.

QUESTIONS AND ANSWERS

Question — If an executive's compensation is based on profits or sales, will it be deemed unreasonable (and therefore nondeductible) if the company has an unusually good year and the payment is therefore very high?

Answer — The reasonableness of salary is typically tested according to the circumstances existing at the time a profit-oriented compensation agreement is entered into rather than when it is actually paid. Thus, if the percentage or formula itself is not unreasonable at the time the agreement becomes binding on the parties, the actual amount may be deemed reasonable, however high. In addition, the issue of reasonableness can also take into account the element of risk involved to the employee. That is, suppose a company agrees to pay an employee $100,000 plus 25 percent of profits for the upcoming year. The company has an extremely good year and the employee receives $600,000. While a $600,000 guaranteed salary might be deemed unreasonable, the fact that the executive took some risk in accepting a contingent type of compensation may bring the $600,000 amount within the limits of reasonableness.

Question — What is the significance of cash compensation planning for an employee of a S corporation?

Answer — An S corporation is a corporation that has made an election under federal tax law to be taxed essentially as a partnership. In an S corporation, all corporate income and losses are passed through to stockholders in proportion to their stock ownership. Corporate income is taxable to shareholders whether or not it is actually distributed as dividends. For S corporation shareholder-employees, there is no opportunity to defer taxation of their share of current income except through a qualified retirement plan, which is discussed in later chapters of this book.

When S corporation shareholders are also employees of the corporation, as is often the case, it is important to distinguish between compensation for services to the shareholder employees, as opposed to their share of corporate earnings passed through to them from the corporation. This distinction between compensation and dividend income has a significant effect on the various qualified and nonqualified employee benefit plans discussed later in this book. For example, pension plans and group term life insurance plans often base their benefits on the employee's compensation income, which does not include any element of income from the corporation that is characterized as a dividend.

Chapter 5

DEATH BENEFIT ONLY (DBO) PLAN

WHAT IS IT?

A death benefit only plan, or DBO plan, (sometimes referred to as an "employer-paid death benefit" or a "survivor's income benefit plan") is a plan by which an employer defers employee compensation and pays it to the employee's designated beneficiary at the employee's death. No benefit is payable in any form to the employee during his or her lifetime.

WHEN IS IT INDICATED?

1. The DBO type of plan is most valuable in the case of a highly compensated employee who (1) expects to have a large estate and (2) faces significant federal estate tax liability because the estate will be payable to a non-spouse beneficiary (i.e., will not be able to fully use the estate tax marital deduction). If the covered employee owns 50 percent or less of the corporation's stock and the plan is properly designed, the benefit from a DBO plan is not subject to federal estate tax.

2. The plan can be used for selected employees as a supplement to qualified retirement plan benefits.

3. The plan can be used to replace a split dollar plan (Chapter 31 of this book) where the cost to the employee (the P.S. 58 table cost) is increasing rapidly because of age — usually after age 60.

4. A DBO plan can be used for deferring compensation of younger employees with families and a need for insurance; the DBO plan can be converted to full nonqualified deferred compensation with lifetime benefits when the employee's value to the employer has increased to the point where this is indicated.

5. A limited employer-paid death benefit plan can be provided to any employee to fully utilize the $5,000 income tax exclusion that is available.

ADVANTAGES

1. If the covered employee is not a controlling (more than 50%) shareholder, properly designed DBO benefits can be kept out of the deceased employee's estate for federal estate tax purposes.

2. The plan's death benefit provides valuable estate liquidity and a source of immediate and continuing cash to the beneficiary upon the employee's death.

3. The benefit is not taxable to the employee during lifetime.

4. The plan can be financed by the employer through the purchase of life insurance, which provides funds to pay the death benefit and avoids current tax on investment returns under the policy. (Some alternative minimum tax — AMT — on the death proceeds may be payable at the corporate level.)

DISADVANTAGES

1. The entire benefit (except for a $5000 exclusion, if applicable) is income taxable to the beneficiary — as ordinary income. This applies even if the benefit is financed using life insurance.

2. Avoiding estate tax requires very careful plan design and avoidance of technical tax traps, thus limiting flexibility in plan design.

3. The employer-corporation's tax deduction for the plan is deferred until the benefit is paid and the beneficiary includes the payments received in income. The employer must wait to take the deduction even if it sets funds aside in advance (such as through the purchase of a life insurance contract).

DESIGN FEATURES

The plan's benefit formula can take many forms:

1. The simplest formula is a fixed dollar amount — for example, $50,000 for each employee covered under the plan or $10,000 a year for 5 years.

2. Benefits can be based on average compensation over a period of years — for example, the death benefit might be equal to a year's salary averaged over the five years prior to death.

3. Benefits are often related loosely to the death benefit under an insurance policy on the employee's life that is owned by and paid for the employer in order to finance the plan. For example, suppose the employer and employee agree that the employee's salary will be reduced by $100 per month — or agree to extra employer payments of $100 per month — that will be used toward the premiums on an insurance policy. If the $1,200 per year will buy approximately a $50,000 life insurance policy for that employee, given his age and health, then the death benefit under the plan will be $50,000. Note, however, that most planners recommend against tying the benefit directly, dollar for dollar, to a life

insurance policy. The plan should be designed to avoid any inference that it is simply the purchase of life insurance for the employee.

TAX IMPLICATIONS

1. The death benefit from the plan will not be included in the deceased employee's estate so long as (1) the plan does not provide any benefits payable during the employee's lifetime and (2) the employee does not have the right to change the beneficiary, once the plan is established.

   In determining whether the plan pays lifetime benefits, the IRS will look beyond the DBO plan itself. Another plan that provides benefits during lifetime can be taken into account for this purpose, even if the employee never actually lives to collect those benefits. Thus, a DBO plan will not be excluded from an employee's estate if the employer also maintains a nonqualified deferred compensation plan providing lifetime benefits. The two plans will be linked together for this purpose and the estate tax exclusion will be lost. However, a *qualified* pension or profit-sharing plan is not taken into account for this purpose, so those plans can be provided in addition to DBOs. After several court cases on the issue, the IRS also now agrees that an employer's long-term disability benefit plan will not "taint" a DBO unless the disability plan requires that the employee be "retired on disability" to receive benefits.

2. Benefits paid to the employee's beneficiary are taxable in full to the beneficiary as ordinary income, except for an exclusion of the first $5000 under Code section 101(b) if the benefit was forfeitable by the employee during lifetime — that is, could be lost because of some event such as quitting before retirement.

3. The benefit payments are deductible to the corporation when paid, so long as they constitute "reasonable compensation" for the services of the deceased employee in prior years. See Chapter 4 of this book for a detailed discussion of the "reasonableness" test. The reasonableness issue is most likely to be raised by the IRS when the decedent was a major or controlling stockholder, particularly if the beneficiary is also a stockholder.

   The IRS may also question whether the death benefit payment was "for services actually rendered" by the employee, as required for deductibility under Code section 162. This issue is most likely to be raised where (1) the deceased employee was a majority shareholder or (2) where there was no written agreement to pay the benefit prior to the employee's death. If the corporation's deduction is disallowed for this reason, the amount could be treated as a nondeductible dividend, or in unusual cases as a gift by the corporation, with

deductibility limited to $25 under Code section 274(b).

ERISA REQUIREMENTS

1. If the plan is limited to a "select group of management or highly compensated employees," it is exempt from all the provisions of ERISA, except that a simple notification of the Department of Labor is required. A form for this notification is provided in Chapter 24, Nonqualified Deferred Compensation.

2. If the plan covers a broader group of employees, the ERISA vesting, funding, and reporting and disclosure requirements applicable to pension plans may apply. The vesting and funding requirements are discussed in Appendix A of this book and the reporting and disclosure requirements are summarized in Appendix D.

ALTERNATIVES

1. Group-term life insurance.

2. Life insurance in a qualified plan.

3. Split dollar life insurance.

4. Individually-owned life insurance (perhaps paid for through additional bonus compensation from the employer).

HOW TO INSTALL A PLAN

There should always be a written plan adopted under a corporate resolution by the board of directors, in advance of the time that payments are to be made under the plan. The plan document can be simple, but it should specify (a) the amount of the benefit, (b) what employee or group of employees is entitled to it, and (c) should indicate that the benefit is intended as compensation for services to be rendered by the employee. Nothing has to be filed with the government, except for the possible ERISA requirements listed earlier.

WHERE CAN I FIND OUT MORE ABOUT IT?

1. Leimberg, Stephan R., et al., *The Tools and Techniques of Estate Planning,* 7th ed. Cincinnati, OH: The National Underwriter Co., 1988.

2. Stoeber, Edward A., *Tax Planning Techniques for the Closely Held Corporation*, 3rd ed. Cincinnati, OH: The National Underwriter Co., 1987.

QUESTIONS AND ANSWERS

Question — Should an employer finance its obligations under a death benefit plan in advance?

Answer — These plans, if provided to a select group of management or highly compensated employees, do not come within the funding requirements of ERISA. However, if they are formally funded, many ERISA requirements come into effect. This is discussed in detail in Chapter 24, Nonqualified Deferred Compensation. Therefore "formal" funding — funding where the employee has rights to the fund ahead of corporate creditors — is undesirable.

Many plans are "informally funded" — a better term to use is "financed" — through the corporation's setting aside an asset or combination of assets that is designed to grow to the point where benefit payments can be made from it. The amount, however, must be available to corporate creditors. The IRS and Department of Labor (which administers parts of ERISA) do not consider this type of arrangement a "fund" for either tax or ERISA purposes.

One of the most common types of investment for this type of fund is life insurance, since the insurance guarantees that adequate amounts will be available even if the employee dies at a relatively young age.

Question — How is life insurance used in a DBO plan?

Answer — As an example, suppose the plan provides a $100,000 death benefit to a key executive. If the employer corporation expects to be in a 34% tax bracket when the benefit is paid, it purchases a $66,000 policy on the employee's life. The corporation is owner and beneficiary of the policy and pays the premiums. The corporation's premium payments are nondeductible. If the employee dies, the corporation pays out $100,000 to the beneficiary and it deducts $100,000 as compensation, which saves $34,000 in taxes. The $66,000 death proceeds from the policy are tax-free to the corporation, assuming no AMT tax. These proceeds reimburse the corporation for its out-of-pocket cost.

If the benefit is to be paid to the beneficiary over a period of years rather than in a lump sum, the amount of life insurance needed by the corporation is further reduced. This is because investment earnings received by the corporation on the policy death proceeds are available to help fund the benefit payments.

Question — What mistakes in plan design or other circumstances would cause an employer death benefit to be included in the employee's estate?

Answer — The promise of the employer to pay a death benefit to a specified beneficiary in return for the employee's promise to continue working for the employer is considered a transfer by the employee of a property right. If the agreement gives the employee the right to change the beneficiary, that retention of the power to designate who will enjoy the "transfer" has been held by the IRS to cause estate tax inclusion.

If the beneficiary's right to receive the death benefit is conditioned on surviving the employee and the employee retained a right to direct the disposition of the property (for example, where the death benefit is payable to the employee's spouse, but if the spouse does not survive the employee, the death benefit is payable to the employee's estate), that reversionary interest may cause inclusion.

If the beneficiary is a revocable trust established by the employee, the right to alter, amend, or revoke the transfer by changing the terms of the trust would cause inclusion. Another problem relates to an employee who is also a controlling shareholder (more than 50 percent). The IRS argues that such an individual, by virtue of his or her voting control, has the right to alter, amend, revoke, or terminate the agreement. Therefore, the benefit should be includable in the estate of such an individual.

If the employee already has postretirement benefits, such as a nonqualified deferred compensation agreement that pays a retirement benefit, the IRS could claim that the preretirement death benefit plan and the postretirement deferred compensation plan should be considered as a single plan. This would cause the present value of the death benefit to be treated for estate tax purposes as if it were a joint and survivor annuity; the present value of the death benefit would be includable in the deceased employee's estate.

If the death benefit is payable to a trust over which the employee had a general power of appointment, the IRS might argue that he had a power of appointment over the death proceeds, which would result in inclusion for estate tax purposes.

If the death benefit is funded with life insurance on the employee's life and the employee owned the policy or had veto rights over any change in the beneficiary, the IRS would probably attempt to include the policy proceeds because of the employee's incidents of ownership.

13

Chapter 6

DEFINED BENEFIT PENSION PLAN

WHAT IS IT?

A defined benefit pension plan is a qualified employer pension plan that guarantees a specified benefit level at retirement.

WHEN IS IT INDICATED?

1. When the employer's plan design objective is to provide an adequate level of retirement income to employees regardless of their age at plan entry.

2. When the employer wants to allocate plan costs to the maximum extent to older employees — often key or controlling employees in a closely held business.

3. When an older controlling employee in a small business — for example a doctor or dentist in a professional corporation — wants to maximize tax-deferred retirement savings.

ADVANTAGES

1. As with all qualified plans, employees obtain a tax-deferred retirement savings medium.

2. Retirement benefits at adequate levels can be provided for all employees regardless of age at plan entry.

3. Benefit levels are guaranteed both by the employer and by the Pension Benefit Guaranty Corporation (PBGC).

4. For an older highly compensated employee, a defined-benefit plan generally will allow the maximum amount of tax-deferred retirement saving.

DISADVANTAGES

1. Actuarial and PBGC aspects of defined benefit plans result in higher installation and administration costs than for defined contribution plans.

2. Defined benefit plans are complex to design and difficult to explain to employees.

3. Employees who leave before retirement may receive relatively little benefit from the plan.

4. The employer is subject to a recurring annual funding obligation (that must be paid in quarterly or more frequent installments) regardless of whether, in a given year, it has made a profit or incurred a loss.

5. The employer assumes the risk of bad investment results in the plan fund.

DESIGN FEATURES

Defined benefit plans provide a specified amount of benefit to the plan participant at the plan's specified retirement age — the "normal retirement age."

There are many types of formulas for determining this benefit. The most common formulas can be summarized as the "flat amount," the "flat percentage" and the "unit credit" types.

Flat amount formula. A flat amount formula provides simply a stated dollar amount to each plan participant. For example, the plan might provide a pension of $500 per month for life, beginning at age 65, for each plan participant. Such a plan might require some minimum service to obtain the full amount — perhaps 10 or 15 years of service with the employer — with the benefit scaled back for fewer years of service.

A flat amount formula does not differentiate among employees with different compensation levels, so it would be appropriate only when there is relatively little difference in compensation among the group of employees covered under the plan.

Flat percentage formula. Flat percentage formulas are very common; they provide a retirement benefit that is a percentage of the employee's average earnings. For example, the formula might provide a retirement benefit at age 65 equal to 50 percent of the employee's average earnings prior to retirement. Under this formula, a participant whose average earnings was $100,000 prior to retirement would receive an annual pension of $50,000.

Typically a plan will require certain minimum service — such as 10 or 15 years — to obtain the full percentage benefit, with the percentage scaled back for fewer years of service. For example, if the plan provides a benefit of 50 percent of average compensation for an employee who retires with at least 10 years of service, it might provide a benefit of only 25 percent of average compensation for an employee who retires at age 65 with only 5 years of service for the employer.

Unit credit formula. A unit credit formula is based on the employee's service with the employer. For example, the formula might provide 1.5 percent of earnings for each of the employee's years of service, with the total percentage applied to the employee's average earnings. Under this formula, a participant with average annual compensation of $100,000 who retired after 30 years of service would

     Tools and Techniques

receive an annual pension of $45,000 (that is, 1.5 times 30, or 45 percent of $100,000).

There are two methods generally used to compute average earnings for these formulas, the "career-average" and the "final average" methods.

Under the *career average* method, the formula uses earnings averaged over the employee's entire career with the employer. The career-average method takes early and often low-earning years into account, and thus the total benefit may not fully reflect the employee's earning power at retirement.

Under the *final average* method, earnings are averaged over a number of years — usually the 3 to 5 years immediately prior to retirement. The final average method usually produces a retirement benefit that is better matched to the employee's income just prior to retirement.

In either a career average or final average formula, only the first $200,000 of each employee's compensation is taken into account. In other words, an employee earning $275,000 annually is treated as if compensation was $200,000.

In most plans, these formulas are further modified by "integrating" them with social security benefits. Integrating the formula gives the employer some credit for paying the cost of employee social security benefits. It helps to provide a reasonable level of retirement income for all employees by taking social security benefits into account. The rules for integrating formulas are complex; they are discussed in more detail in Appendix A.

Employers must fund defined benefit plans with periodic deposits determined actuarially to insure that the plan fund will be sufficient to pay the promised benefit as each participant retires. The objective is to accumulate a fund at the employee's retirement age that is sufficient to "buy an annuity" equal to the retirement benefit. (In some plans, annuities are actually purchased at retirement age, but this is not required.)

For example, suppose the actuary hired by the employer estimates that an annuity of $50,000 per year beginning at age 65 is equivalent to a lump sum of $475,000 at age 65. In other words, for a given interest rate and other assumptions, the amount of $475,000 deposited at age 65 will produce an annuity of $50,000 per year for the life of an individual aged 65. For a participant aged 45 at plan entry, the employer has 20 years to fund this benefit — that is, to build up a fund totaling $475,000 at age 65.

The actuary will use various methods and assumptions to determine how much must be deposited periodically. As an illustration, a "level annual premiums" method (equal annual payment method) with a 6 percent interest assump-

tion would require the employer to deposit $12,180 annually for 20 years in order to build up a fund of $475,000. (As discussed below, the law actually requires deposits to be made at least quarterly; annual deposit illustrations are used here for simplicity.) This shows how investment return works for the benefit of the employer; the 20 deposits of $12,180 total only $243,600, but at age 65 the fund will actually total $475,000 if all annual deposits are made and the fund actually earns a 6 percent investment return annually.

Actuarial methods and assumptions are chosen to provide the desired pattern for spreading the plan's cost over the years it will be in effect. The actuarial method and assumptions often have to be adjusted over the years to make sure that the fund is adequate. It is even possible for a defined benefit plan to become overfunded, in which case employer contributions must be suspended for a period of time.

The actuarial funding approach for defined benefit plans means that, for a given benefit level, the annual funding amount is greater for employees who are older at entry into the plan (see table below), since the time to fund the benefit is less in the case of an older entrant.

AGE/CONTRIBUTION LEVEL FOR DEFINED BENEFIT PLAN

Age at Plan Entry	Annual Benefit at Age 65	Years to fund	Annual Employer Contribution
30	$25,000	35	$ 1,971
40	25,000	25	4,309
50	25,000	15	10,847

This set of calculations assumes (1) that money deposited before retirement will earn a 7 percent investment return (2) no mortality (no discount for the possibility that some plan participants may die before retirement) and (3) a unisex annuity purchase rate of $1,400 per $10 monthly at age 65 (i.e., it will take a deposit of $1,400 at age 65 to purchase a lifetime annuity of $10 per month beginning at age 65, for any plan participant, male or female).

This makes defined benefit plans attractive to professionals and closely held business owners; they tend to adopt retirement plans for their businesses when they are relatively older than their regular employees. A large percentage of the total cost for a defined benefit plan in this situation goes to fund these key employees' benefits.

Example: Doctor Retractor, aged 48, is a sole practitioner with two office employees, a nurse aged 35 and a receptionist aged 25. The doctor earns $200,000 annually and the nurse and receptionist earn $30,000 and $20,000 respectively. Compare the 1988 cost allocation for a maximum defined benefit plan for the doctor (45% of final average salary at age 65, providing $94,023 for the doctor) with that for a maximum defined contribution plan (annual contribution of 15% of salary for all employees — an annual contribution of $30,000 for the doctor):

	Annual cost for Defined Benefit Plan	Annual cost for Defined Contribution Plan
Doctor	$31,819	$30,000
Nurse	1,558	4,500
Receptionist	491	3,000
Total	$33,868	$37,500
Percent for Doctor	94%	80%

Assumptions: 7 percent investment return, no mortality, unisex annuity purchase rate of $1,400 per $10 monthly at age 65 (equivalent to a lump sum of $1,096,935 at age 65 for a benefit of $94,023 per year).

To back up the employer's funding obligation and safeguard employees, defined benefit plans are insured by the federal Pension Benefit Guaranty Corporation (PBGC) up to specified limits. The employer must pay annual premiums to the PBGC to fund this insurance. Furthermore, the employer is liable for reimbursement to the PBGC for any guaranteed payments the PBGC must make to employees.

TAX IMPLICATIONS

1. Employer contributions to the plan are deductible when made.

2. Taxation of the employee on employer contributions is deferred. Contributions and earnings on plan assets are nontaxable to plan participants until withdrawn, assuming the plan remains "qualified." A plan is qualified if it meets the eligibility, vesting, funding and other requirements explained in Appendix A.

3. Under Code section 415, there is a maximum limit on the projected annual benefit that the plan can provide. For a benefit beginning at age 65 (or the social security retirement age, which is later than 65 for persons born after 1938), the maximum life annuity or joint and survivor benefit is the lesser of (a) $90,000, as indexed for inflation ($94,023 in 1988), or (b) 100% of the participant's compensation averaged over his three highest-earning consecutive years.

   For example, if Foxx retires in 1988 at age 65, and his high three-year average compensation was $60,000, his employer's defined-benefit plan can't provide a life or joint and survivor annuity of more than $60,000 per year. For employee Sharp, who retires in 1988 at age 65 with high 3-year average compensation of $250,000, the limit is $94,023 annually.

4. Distributions from the plan must follow the rules for qualified plan distributions. Certain premature or excessive distributions are subject to penalty taxes. The distribution rules are discussed in Appendix B. Lump sum distributions made after age 59½ are subject to a limited election to use a special 5-year averaging tax

calculation. Not all distributions are eligible. Appendix B covers these rules, with illustrations of IRS forms.

6. The plan is subject to the "minimum funding" rules of section 412 of the Code. This requires minimum periodic contributions by the employer, with a penalty if less than the minimum amount is contributed. The employer must make plan contributions at least quarterly (although this requirement will not be fully phased in until 1992). Appendix A discusses the minimum funding rules further.

7. A defined benefit plan is subject to mandatory insurance coverage by the Pension Benefit Guaranty Corporation (PBGC). The PBGC is a government corporation funded through a mandatory premium paid by employer-sponsors of covered plans. The current premium flat rate is $16 annually per participant. An additional annual premium of up to $34 per participant may be required, depending on the amount of the plan's unfunded vested benefits. If the employer wants to terminate the plan, the PBGC must be notified in advance and must approve any distribution of plan assets to participants.

ERISA REQUIREMENTS

The plan is subject to all the ERISA requirements for qualified plans (participation, funding, vesting, etc.) described in Appendix A and the ERISA reporting and disclosure requirements outlined in Appendix D.

ALTERNATIVES

1. Money purchase pension plans provide retirement benefits, but without employer guarantees of benefit levels, and with adequate benefits only for younger plan entrants.

2. Target benefit pension plans may provide adequate benefits to older entrants, but without an employer guarantee of the benefit level.

3. Cash balance pension plans provide an employer guarantee of principal and investment earnings on the plan fund, but provide adequate benefits only to younger plan entrants.

4. Profit-sharing plans, simplified employee pensions (SEPs), stock bonus plans, and ESOPs provide a qualified, tax-deferred retirement savings medium, but the benefit adequacy is tied closely to the financial success of the employer.

5. Section 401(k) plans and savings plans provide a qualified, tax-deferred savings medium in which the amount saved is subject to some control by employees themselves.

17

6. Private retirement savings without a qualified plan does not have the same tax benefits as a qualified plan, except to the extent that IRAs can be used.

HOW TO INSTALL A PLAN

Defined benefit plans are installed according to the qualified plan installation procedure outlined in Appendix C.

WHERE CAN I FIND OUT MORE ABOUT IT?

1. Gee, Judith Boyers, *Pensions in Perspective*, 2nd ed. Cincinnati, OH: The National Underwriter Co. 1987.

2. McFadden, John J., *Retirement Plans for Employees*, Homewood, IL: Richard D. Irwin, 1988.

3. Graduate Course: Advanced Pension and Retirement Planning II (GS 843), The American College, Bryn Mawr, PA.

4. CLU/ChFC Course: Pensions and Other Retirement Plans (HS 326), The American College, Bryn Mawr, PA.

5. CFP Course: Retirement Planning and Executive Benefits (CFP V), College for Financial Planning, Denver, CO.

QUESTIONS AND ANSWERS

Question — At what age is a defined benefit plan more advantageous than a defined contribution plan for tax-deferring the maximum amount of retirement savings?

Answer — Somewhere between age 45 and 50 approximately, depending on the actuarial method and assumptions used in the defined-benefit plan.

For example, suppose a doctor, a sole practitioner, aged 46, wants to adopt a plan providing maximum deductible contributions. Under Code section 415, the maximum contribution to a defined contribution plan is $30,000 annually (or 25 percent of compensation up to $200,000 (as indexed after 1988) if this is less than $30,000). Can the doctor put more into a defined benefit plan with the maximum benefit allowed by Section 415 ($90,000 annually at age 65, as indexed for inflation — $94,023 in 1988)? That depends on the actuarial assumptions. The following table shows the annual contribution level for a given set of actuarial assumptions and method, varying only the assumed investment return.

DEFINED BENEFIT FUNDING BY ENTRY AGE AND INVESTMENT RETURN

Age at Entry	Level funding amount at		
	6%	7%	8%
44	$24,768	$21,872	$19,281
45	26,928	23,937	21,245
46	29,341	26,253	23,457
47	32,051	28,863	25,960
48	35,110	31,819	28,806
49	38,585	35,187	32,060
50	42,557	39,051	35,807
51	47,136	43,516	40,150

Assumptions: $90,000 annual benefit at age 65, equivalent to lump sum at age 65 of $1,050,000. No mortality assumption. These figures can be converted to their post-1987 values by multiplying them by

$$\frac{\text{Current Section 415 dollar limit}}{\$90,000}$$

For example, for 1988 they would be multiplied by 94,023/90,000.

This indicates that at age 46, based on the assumptions in this table, a defined contribution plan would allow a larger contribution, unless an investment return assumption lower than 6% can be used. Of course, this example is oversimplified; in actual cases a careful study of all the possible actuarial methods and assumptions should be made. Also, the maximum allowable contribution may depend on the doctor's coverage under other qualified plans in the past; see the next question.

Question — Can an employee be covered under both a defined benefit plan and a defined contribution plan of the same employer?

Answer — Yes, but the Section 415 limitations for one or both plans must be cut back. It is not possible for an employer to contribute $30,000 annually to a defined contribution plan for an employee and at the same time provide a defined benefit plan with an age 65 benefit of $90,000 per year, as indexed for inflation ($94,023 in 1988). The maximum allowed benefit under one or both plans must be cut back, under a complex formula in section 415 of the Code.

The combined plan formula requires a cutback even if one of the plans has been terminated, so long as a benefit is still due to the employee from the terminated plan. So, in designing qualified plans, all past plans must be taken into account.

Question — If the retirement age is less than 65 in a defined benefit plan, can the annual funding level be increased because of the shorter time left to fund the benefit?

Answer — Yes. However, the tax benefits of this for highly compensated employees are minimized by the fact that the maximum Section 415 limitation on benefits is cut back for retirement earlier than 65 (or the social security retirement age, if that is greater). The maximum annual benefit for various retirement ages is

Retirement age	Maximum annual benefit
55	$42,400
60	61,419
62	72,000
65	90,000

This cutback limits the deductible annual funding and thus the amount of extra tax deferral available through an accelerated retirement age.

Another factor that has to be taken into account if accelerating the funding is desired is that the maximum benefit limit is also cut back proportionately if a participant has participated in the plan for less than 10 years. For example, suppose Dr. Drill, a self-employed dentist, aged 57 wants to start a defined benefit plan. If the retirement age is 65 in the plan, Dr. Drill will have only 8 years of participation at retirement. Assuming that the maximum benefit would be $90,000 for 10 years of service, the benefit for Dr. Drill will be cut back to $8/10$ of that amount, or $72,000 annually. In order to receive the full benefit in this situation, the plan would have to define normal retirement age as the later of age 65 or the age after 10 years of plan participation. This would eliminate the cutback, but it would also require funding of the plan to be stretched out to 10 years.

Chapter 7

DEPENDENT CARE ASSISTANCE PLAN

WHAT IS IT?

A dependent care assistance plan reimburses employees for day-care and other dependent care expenses or provides an actual day-care center or similar arrangement. If the program is properly structured the day-care expenses are deductible to the employer and non-taxable to the employee under Code section 129. The dependent care plan can be funded using employee salary reductions under a flexible spending account (FSA) described in Chapter 10.

WHEN IS IT INDICATED?

1. When the employer wants to attract and keep employees who need help in caring for small children or other dependents during working hours.

2. To provide an attractive tax benefit to all employees who have dependent care expenses.

ADVANTAGES

1. The plan can be helpful in recruiting and keeping relatively low-paid employees who have dependent care needs.

2. The employer gets more benefit for each dollar spent on this form of compensation as opposed to cash compensation since benefits paid under a properly structured dependent care assistance program are tax-free to the employees.

3. The plan can be funded partially or entirely through FSA salary reductions.

DISADVANTAGES

1. A fully-subsidized day-care or other dependent care program can be expensive while a partially-subsidized program may not be helpful in attracting and keeping employees.

2. A substantial day-care program may be seen by nonparticipating employees as discriminatory in favor of participating employees.

DESIGN FEATURES

1. Dependent care can be provided in kind. For example, the employer can provide a day-care and after-school center for employees' children right on the business premises or contract with a nearby center to provide day-care.

2. Alternatively, the benefit can be provided through full or partial reimbursement of qualifying employee expenses for dependent care. This is the approach usually taken when the plan is funded through employee salary reductions as part of an FSA plan.

TAX IMPLICATIONS

1. The costs of the plan are deductible to the employer as employee compensation.

2. If the plan meets the requirements of Code section 129, the benefits are non-taxable to participating employees.

3. Section 129 imposes a variety of nondiscrimination rules summarized as follows:

   • Contributions or benefits must not discriminate in favor of highly compensated employees, as defined in Code section 414(q) (See Appendix A)

   • The plan must cover a group that the IRS finds nondiscriminatory. The following may be excluded

      — employees who have not completed 1 year of service, or attained age 21

      — employees who work less than 17½ hours per week or 6 months or less during any year

      — employees in a collective bargaining unit if there has been good faith bargaining on dependent care

      — nonresident aliens

   • benefits for all employees who own more than 5 percent of the employer, and their spouses and dependents, cannot be more than 25 percent of the total benefits each year

   • the average benefits provided to employees who are not highly compensated must be at least 55 percent of the average benefits provided to highly compensated employees. In applying this benefit test the employer can elect to exclude employees earning less than $25,000 (or a lower specified amount) if the plan is funded through salary reductions.

   As an alternative to the above nondiscrimination tests, the employer can elect to use Section 89 nondiscrimination tests. (See Chapters 12 and 13 and Appendix F.)

4. Dependent care assistance eligible under Section 129 can be provided only to (a) a child under 13 for whom

the employee-taxpayer is entitled to take a dependency deduction on the income tax return or (b) a taxpayer's dependent or spouse who is physically or mentally unable to care for himself.

5. The amount of benefits excluded annually by the employee — the value of the services provided directly plus any employer reimbursements of expenses paid by the employee — cannot be more than the employee's earned income or, if the employee is married, the lesser of the employee's or spouse's earned income. Furthermore, the total amount excluded by the employee is limited to $5000 annually, or $2500 if the employee is married and files a separate return.

6. Qualifying expenses must be for care alone, not for education above the kindergarten level. Following are items that qualify as care:

   • full preschool and kindergarten expenses (full tuition and fees for these programs)

   • after-school programs for children under 13

   • summer camp for children under 13 (however, expenses for overnight summer camp do not qualify)

   • cost of a housekeeper/sitter for children or other dependents cared for at home. (However, payments to a relative or child under 19 do not qualify.)

7. A dependent care assistance plan, like almost all tax-favored benefit plans, must meet the requirements of Code section 89(k). The plan must be in writing, the employees' rights must be enforceable, the employees must be notified of the plan benefits and the plan must be maintained for the exclusive benefit of the employees and have been established with the intent of continuing for an indefinite length of time. Some of these requirements overlap with the ERISA and other requirements described below. If the plan does not meet the Section 89(k) requirements the employees must include the value of the benefits received in income.

8. In order to claim the exclusion for dependent care assistance benefits under Section 129 the taxpayer must report the correct name, address and taxpayer identification number of the care provider on his tax return.

ERISA AND OTHER REQUIREMENTS

The plan is considered a "welfare benefit plan" for ERISA purposes. This requires a written plan document, a summary plan description (SPD) explaining the plan that is provided to employees, a designated plan administrator and a formal claims procedure. (Appendix D details these requirements more fully.) Section 129 requires further that the employer provide each employee with an annual statement of the expenses incurred in providing the prior year's benefits by January 31 of each year.

ALTERNATIVES

One alternative to dependent care assistance programs is the informal coverage of these expenses for selected employees through extra compensation or bonuses. However, this extra compensation is fully taxable to the employee.

HOW TO INSTALL A PLAN

ERISA requires a written plan and an SPD but no governmental approval. Some employers may want to obtain an IRS ruling stating that the plan complies with Section 129 if there are plan features, such as liberal benefits or limited employee eligibility, that raise compliance questions.

WHERE CAN I FIND OUT MORE ABOUT IT?

1. IRS Publication 334, *Tax Guide for Small Business* (annual IRS publication available at local IRS office).

2. Beam, Burton T., Jr. and John J. McFadden, *Employee Benefits*, 2nd ed. Homewood, IL: Richard D. Irwin, 1988.

3. *The Financial Services Professional's Guide to the State of the Art/1989*, The American College, Bryn Mawr, Pennsylvania 19010, 1-800-841-8000, Ext. 19.

QUESTIONS AND ANSWERS

Question — Can an unincorporated business have a dependent care plan covering partners or proprietors as well as regular employees?

Answer — Yes. Section 129 allows self-employed individuals — partners or proprietors — to be treated as employees under the plan. As with regular employees, dependent care benefits are excluded from the income of partners or proprietors who are covered by the plan.

Question — Can employees who receive tax-free benefits under a dependent care plan also use the dependent care tax credit of Code section 21?

Answer — Only if the employee receives benefits from the plan that are taxable to the employee or makes additional expenditures not paid for by the plan. Tax-free benefits from an employer dependent care plan are not eligible for the Section 21 tax credit. Additionally, the amount of expenses eligible for the dependent care credit must be offset dollar for dollar by the amount of expenses that the taxpayer excludes from income under the dependent care plan. For example, if a taxpayer has $2,400 of eligible dependent care expenses during the year and the employer's plan reimbursed him for $1,000 of the expenses only the remaining $1,400 would be eligible for the dependent care credit.

Question — How can an employee decide between using the employer's dependent care assistance plan and using the dependent care tax credit (Section 21)?

Answer — In the past, employees could get a tax break on as much as $9,800 of child care expenses by combining the child care credit with a company's dependent care assistance plan. However, the Family Support Act of 1988 contains a provision effective January 1, 1989, that disallows "double dipping" by taxpayers who pay child care expenses qualifying for the child care credit and who participate in a company sponsored dependent care assistance program.

An employee's tax benefit from the child care credit is reduced to the extent he or she uses a company plan to cover expenses. Specifically, the maximum amount of qualifying expenses ($2,400 for one child; $4,800 for two or more children) a taxpayer may use for the child care credit is reduced dollar-for-dollar by amounts paid through a company plan. For example, if a company plan reimburses an employee with two children $4,000 for child care expenses, only $800 ($4,800 - $4,000) of additional child care expenses paid by the employee will qualify for the child care credit.

As a result, all employees who have child care expenses exceeding $4,800 and who may participate in a company sponsored dependent care assistance program must choose between the company plan and the child care credit.

The choice depends on the employee's tax rate and whether or not amounts that would otherwise be allocated to child care under the company plan can be allocated to other benefits. For example, if the company dependent care assistance plan is part of a cafeteria plan or FSA salary-reduction plan where the employees can choose to allocate the amount that would otherwise go to child care expenses to fund other benefits such as medical expenses, health insurance premiums, or life insurance, the employees will generally be better off if they elect benefits other than child care reimbursements from their company plan. In this way they still get the full benefit of the company plan and may take the child care credit for the child care expenses they pay with after-tax dollars separately from the plan.

However, if the company plan does not allow the employees to use the amount that would otherwise go to child care expenses to fund other benefits, or for those employees who cannot fully use the other benefits that may be elected, the choice between the company plan and the child care credit depends on their tax rate (taxable income), filing status, and adjusted gross income.

The child care credit is equal to 30 percent of qualified expenses for persons with adjusted gross income (AGI) of $10,000 or less. The credit is reduced by one percentage point for each $2,000 of AGI above $10,000 with a floor of 20 percent for persons with income over $28,000. Therefore, for each dollar of qualifying child care expenses the tax savings range from 30 cents to 20 cents for AGIs ranging from $10,000 to $28,000 and above.

In contrast, if child care expenses are reimbursed through a company salary-reduction plan, the tax savings will depend on the person's tax rate, which depends on his or her taxable income and filing status. Employees whose taxable income falls in the 15 percent tax bracket will save only 15 cents on each qualifying dollar of child care expenses reimbursed through a company plan. Consequently, they should clearly opt out of the company plan and use the child care credit since they will save between 5 and 15 cents on the dollar. However, if taxable income falls in the 28 percent or 33 percent bracket, the employees will save either 28 cents or 33 cents on each qualifying dollar of child care expenses reimbursed through the company plan. For these levels of taxable income the tax savings with the company plan will always equal or exceed the tax savings from the child care credit. Figure 7.1 shows the taxable income levels at which employees should choose either the child care credit or the company plan for each filing status.

Figure 7.1

Child Care Choice — Company Plan or Child Care Credit		
Filing Status	**Elect Company Plan (Child Care Credit) if Taxable Income Exceeds (Is Below)**	
	1988 Tax Rates	**Projected 1989 Rates***
Married filing jointly	$29,750	$30,940
Married filing separately	14,875	15,470
Heads of households	23,900	24,856
Single	17,850	18,564

*Assumes 4 percent inflation adjustment in 1989 for inflation.

Chapter 8

EDUCATIONAL ASSISTANCE PLAN

WHAT IS IT?

An employer's educational assistance plan pays or reimburses employees for expenses incurred in educational programs aimed at improving job skills. Some broader plans provide assistance for education even if not job-related, or for education for children or dependents of employees.

ADVANTAGES

1. Employers benefit from improvement in employee skills through education that the employee might not be able to afford otherwise.

2. Properly structured job-related educational benefits are not taxable income to employees.

DISADVANTAGES

1. A program that is too broad may simply train an employee for a job with another employer.

2. Educational benefits beyond certain limits are taxable as compensation to the employee.

TAX IMPLICATIONS

1. An individual can deduct educational expenses — including not only tuition but incidental expenses such as transportation, books, and supplies, if the education:

    (a) maintains or improves a skill required in the individual's employment, or

    (b) is expressly required by the individual's employer as a condition of keeping the individual's job.

Educational expenses are not deductible if they do not meet these requirements. The IRS specifies that the costs for two types of education are not deductible: (a) education required to meet the minimum qualification requirements for an individual's present employment and (b) education that qualifies the individual for a new trade or business.

Some examples will illustrate this:

 • Suppose an individual who has not completed a law degree accepts a position as a lawyer and begins working with a law firm on the understanding that the degree will be completed. Expenses for completing the law degree are nondeductible, because they are incurred simply to meet the minimum qualification requirements of the individual's current job.

 • For a tax accountant in an accounting firm, law school expenses could be deductible if the accountant can prove to the IRS that the education will maintain or improve the accountant's skills as a tax expert.

 • For an English teacher, expenses for law school probably would not be deductible since they would not maintain or improve skills in the teacher's existing job and would be seen as training to qualify in a new trade or business.

2. Employer reimbursements to employees for educational expenses are deductible by the employer as compensation.

3. If the employer's deduction for reimbursements is matched by a corresponding deduction at the employee level, the educational assistance plan provides the employee with a form of tax-free income.

Usually an employer's educational assistance plans are designed to reimburse only the deductible expenses, both to provide the tax benefit and because the deductible expenses will be the ones that the employer will be most interested in subsidizing. For example, it does not make sense for an employer to pay for education that qualifies an employee for a career with a different company.

4. Section 127 of the Code allows an employer to provide a broader range of educational reimbursements to employees on a tax-free basis. Congress has allowed Section 127 to expire several times in the past, then revived it. The Technical and Miscellaneous Revenue Act of 1988 extended Section 127 through the end of 1988.

Section 127 plans- "qualified educational assistance plans"- currently have the following characteristics:

 • Under the plan, an employer can make payments up to a maximum of $5,250 annually for tuition, fees, books, supplies, and equipment for educational programs for an employee. Payments under the plan are deductible by the employer and excluded from the employee's gross income. The employer may pay these expenses directly, provide the education directly, or reimburse employees for expenditures they make.

 • Courses taken by employees and covered under the plan need not be job related. However, course benefits may not involve sports, games, or hobbies unless they relate to the employer's business.

- Section 127 does not cover graduate level courses leading to a law, business, medical or other advanced academic or professional degree.

- Section 127 provides no tax benefits for tools or supplies retained by the employee after completion of the course or for meals, lodging, or transportation.

- A Section 127 plan must be in writing. However, it need not be funded in advance and does not have to be approved in advance by the IRS.

- A Section 127 plan must not discriminate in coverage in favor of highly compensated employees. In addition, there is a nondiscrimination rule for benefits: not more than five percent of the total amount paid or incurred annually by the employer for educational assistance under the plan may be provided for employees who are shareholders or owners of at least five percent of the business.

5. Employer reimbursements of employee expenses for educating children or other dependents are taxable income to the employee and deductible as compensation by the employer. For a highly-compensated employee, such payments may create a question as to whether the overall compensation meets the reasonableness of compensation test for deductibility. This test is discussed in Chapter 4.

ERISA REQUIREMENTS

An employer's educational assistance plan may be considered a "welfare benefit plan" for ERISA purposes, which means that the plan should be in writing, with a written claims procedure, and a Summary Plan Description (SPD) must be furnished to employees. If the plan is funded (most plans are not) additional requirements may apply. The ERISA rules are summarized in Appendix D.

HOW TO INSTALL A PLAN

There should be a written plan, especially if the plan covers more than a few employees, but the document can be a simple one. An SPD should be drafted and distributed to meet ERISA requirements. No government approval is required, nor is it usually recommended. A request for an IRS ruling can be made if there are any tax questions.

WHERE CAN I FIND OUT MORE ABOUT IT?

1. IRS Publication 17, *Your Federal Income Tax*, covers the deduction for educational expenses. It is revised annually and available from the IRS.

2. Beam, Burton T., Jr. and John J. McFadden, *Employee Benefits*, 2nd ed. Homewood, IL: Richard D. Irwin, 1988.

QUESTIONS AND ANSWERS

Question — What is an "educational benefit trust" and how is it used?

Answer — An educational benefit trust is an arrangement under which an employer creates a trust fund to pay educational expenses for dependents of employees covered under the plan. Typically, this is used as an executive benefit, but it can also be provided to a larger group of employees or all employees.

As a result of recent changes in the tax law, there is little, if any, tax advantage to this type of plan. The employer can deduct amounts paid into the trust fund for plan purposes. However, under Code Section 419, the deduction is limited to the amount of benefits provided during the year. In other words, the employer cannot accelerate deductions by setting up the trust fund rather than paying benefits directly.

To the employee, benefits are taxable when they are paid to dependents for educational expenses. The amount paid to an employee's dependent is considered additional compensation income to the employee.

Chapter 9

ESOP/STOCK BONUS PLAN

WHAT IS IT?

A stock bonus plan is a qualified employer plan — similar to a profit-sharing plan — in which participants' accounts are invested in stock of the employer company. An ESOP is a stock bonus plan that the employer can use as a conduit for borrowing money from a bank or other financial institution.

WHEN IS IT INDICATED?

1. To provide a tax-advantaged means for employees to acquire company stock at low cost to the employer.

2. When estate and financial planning for shareholders would benefit from the additional market for company stock. An ESOP not only creates a market but provides estate tax benefits for sale of stock to the ESOP.

3. In the case of an ESOP, to provide an advantageous vehicle for the company to borrow money for business needs.

ADVANTAGES

1. Employees receive an ownership interest in the employer company, which may provide a performance incentive.

2. A market is created for employer stock, which helps improve liquidity of existing shareholders' assets or estates.

3. Employees are not taxed until shares are distributed. Furthermore, unrealized appreciation of stock held in the plan is not taxed to employees at receipt of a distribution from the plan. Taxation of the unrealized appreciation is deferred until shares are sold by the employee.

4. The employer receives a deduction either for a cash contribution to the plan or a noncash plan contribution in the form of shares of stock.

5. The cost of corporate borrowing can be reduced by using an ESOP.

6. A deceased shareholder's estate can obtain a reduction in federal estate tax by selling stock to the plan.

DISADVANTAGES

1. Since the plan is qualified, all the qualified plan requirements apply — coverage, vesting, funding, reporting and disclosure, and others.

2. Issuing shares of stock to employees "dilutes" (reduces the relative value of) existing shareholders' stock and their control of the company.

3. Company stock may be a very speculative investment. This can create employee ill will either because the plan is not considered very valuable by employees or because employees expect too much from the plan.

DESIGN FEATURES

ESOPs and stock bonus plans are qualified defined contribution plans similar to profit-sharing plans. However, participants' accounts are stated in terms of shares of employer stock. Benefits are distributable in the form of employer stock. Dividends on shares can be used to increase participants' accounts or can be paid directly in cash to participants. (If dividends are paid directly in cash, the employer gets a tax deduction, and employees are currently taxable.)

Employer contributions are either shares of stock, or cash that the plan uses to buy stock.

Plan allocation formulas must not discriminate in favor of highly compensated employees, and are typically based on employee compensation. For example, if total payroll of participating employees is $500,000 and the employer contributes stock worth $50,000, an employee earning $10,000 is allocated $1,000 worth of stock under a compensation-based allocation formula. The formula for a stock bonus plan can be integrated with social security, but this is rarely done. An ESOP formula cannot be integrated.

If shares of the employer company are closely held — that is, not publicly traded on an established securities market — then plan participants must be given the right to vote on certain specific corporate issues: (a) approval or disapproval of any corporate merger or consolidation, recapitalization, reclassification, liquidation, or dissolution; (b) sale of substantially all assets of the trade or business; or (c) a similar transaction as prescribed in IRS regulations.

If employer stock is publicly traded, plan participants must be allowed to vote the stock on all issues.

Distributions from stock bonus plans and ESOPs are subject to the same rules applicable to all qualified plans, as described in Appendix B. For example, distributions prior to age 59½, death, or disability are subject to a 10 percent penalty, with some exceptions. Note, however, that a stock bonus plan or ESOP is generally not required to provide a joint and survivor annuity or other spousal death benefit.

Tools and Techniques

Distributions from a stock bonus plan or ESOP must generally be made in the form of employer stock. However, if the participant receives stock that is not traded on an established market, the participant has a right to require the employer to repurchase the stock under a fair valuation formula. This requirement is referred to as the "put option."

To protect employees against unrealistic expectations of stock value, if the stock or securities used in the plan are not traded on an established market, stock valuations used for all plan purposes must be made by an independent appraiser.

Another protective feature is a requirement that participants in ESOPs who have reached age 55 and have at least 10 years of service are entitled to an annual election to diversify investments in their accounts. For a 6-year period after becoming eligible for this election, the participant can elect annually to diversify 25 percent of the account balance. In the last year, diversification of 50 percent of the account balance can be elected. (A plan may offer higher percentages of diversification, if desired.) The plan must offer at least three options other than employer stock for diversification.

ESOP Loans

An ESOP is distinguished from a regular stock bonus plan primarily by the "leveraging" feature of an ESOP that enables the employer company to borrow money on a favorable basis. The transaction works like this:

(a) The ESOP trustee borrows money from a lending institution such as a bank (with the loan guaranteed by the employer corporation).

(b) The trustee uses the loan proceeds to purchase stock of the employer from the employer corporation (or from principal shareholders of the corporation).

(c) The employer makes tax deductible contributions to the ESOP in amounts sufficient to enable the trustee to pay off the principal and interest of the loan to the bank or other lender.

The net effect of this is that the corporation receives the loan proceeds and repays the loan, both principal and interest, with tax deductible dollars.

The Code allows an even further advantage — the lending institution is permitted to exclude from tax 50 percent of the interest income from a loan to an ESOP used to acquire employer securities.

TAX IMPLICATIONS

1. Employer contributions to the plan are deductible when made, up to an annual limit. For a stock bonus plan, the limit is 15 percent of payroll of employees covered under the plan. For an ESOP, higher limits apply — up to 25 percent of covered payroll for amounts used to repay loan principal, with no limit on amounts used to pay interest.

2. Taxation to the employee on employer contributions is deferred, as with any qualified plan. An additional tax benefit to employees with a stock bonus plan or ESOP is deferral of tax on unrealized appreciation of stock received in a plan distribution. For example, suppose an ESOP buys stock for $1,000 and allocates it to participant Farley's account. At retirement 20 years later, the stock is worth $5,000. If Farley receives this stock in a distribution from the plan, he pays tax only on $1,000. The $4,000 of unrealized appreciation is not taxed until Farley sells the stock. Farley could, however, elect out of this deferred treatment.

The taxable amount of any lump sum distribution from a stock bonus plan or ESOP may be eligible for the special 5-year (or 10-year) averaging tax treatment for qualified plans.

3. The plan is subject to the eligibility and vesting rules applicable to all qualified plans (see Appendix A).

ERISA REQUIREMENTS

The plan is subject to the usual ERISA eligibility, vesting, and funding requirements for qualified plans discussed in Appendix A, and the reporting and disclosure requirements summarized in Appendix D.

HOW TO INSTALL THE PLAN

Plan installation follows the qualified plan installation procedure described in Appendix C. In addition, if the employer's stock is subject to securities regulation requirements and the employer issues new stock for the plan, a registration statement may have to be filed with federal or state securities regulatory agencies.

WHERE CAN I FIND OUT MORE ABOUT IT?

1. Leimberg, Stephan R., et al. *Tools and Techniques of Estate Planning*, 7th ed. Cincinnati, OH: The National Underwriter Company, 1988.

QUESTIONS AND ANSWERS

Question — How is an ESOP or stock bonus plan used for estate planning for shareholders of closely held businesses?

Answer — The existence of the ESOP or stock bonus plan as a potential buyer for stock can be very valuable in planning the estate of a shareholder of a closely held business. Such estates are often illiquid because of a lack of a market for the stock, while at the same time the estate may be liable for substantial death taxes because of the inherent value of the stock.

In most small companies, owners typically expect the company to buy stock from their estate at the shareholder's death. However, for a number of reasons this plan may be difficult to carry out:

(a) Accumulation of corporate funds can be difficult. Funds to purchase stock must be accumulated by the corporation out of after-tax income, which is burdensome particularly since current corporate tax rates may be higher than individual rates.

(b) The corporation can purchase life insurance to provide assured funding, but the premiums are not deductible to the corporation, so this is also an accumulation from after-tax income.

(c) An accumulation of funds at the corporate level may result in exposure to the accumulated earnings tax, particularly if the shareholder is a majority shareholder.

(d) Receipt by the corporation of otherwise income-tax-free life insurance proceeds may trigger the corporate alternative minimum tax (AMT).

(e) If insurance is owned by the corporation to fund a buy out, corporate value is increased, which in turn increases the federal estate tax.

Use of an ESOP or stock bonus plan as the purchaser avoids these problems. The corporation gets a deduction for amounts contributed to the plan, and the plan is a tax-exempt entity so its income is not taxed. Thus, funds accumulate in the plan on a before-tax basis. And, the plan is not subject to the accumulated earnings tax or the alternative minimum tax. Furthermore, life insurance held in the ESOP will not increase corporate value for purposes of the federal estate tax.

While it may be difficult to accumulate a large amount of cash in the plan, particularly in a short time, the plan can purchase insurance on the shareholder's life as an investment that will provide funds to purchase stock from a shareholder at the shareholder's death.

Should there be a formal plan to carry out this type of stock purchase? Probably not. A shareholder can give the ESOP or stock bonus plan an option to buy his or her shares, but requiring the plan to do so would probably violate the ERISA fiduciary requirements.

One potentially serious tax problem with this type of plan should be noted — the possibility that the IRS will treat the sale of stock as a dividend paid to the estate by the corporation rather than a sale to the ESOP. Taxwise, this would greatly increase the cost of the transaction. As a sale, little or no capital gain would be realized by the estate because its basis for the stock would be stepped up to the date of death value. However, if the proceeds from the sale was treated as a dividend, all of it would be taxable.

Dividend treatment on a sale of stock to an ESOP is not a serious possibility unless the decedent was a major shareholder. However, the IRS will probably consider all stock held by the decedent and related family members together in determining whether the decedent was a controlling shareholder. In such cases, despite the apparent policy of Congress to encourage stock sales to ESOPs, the IRS may ignore the ESOP and treat the transaction as a dividend paid directly from the corporation to the shareholder, the decedent's estate.

It is advisable in doubtful situations to apply to the IRS for a ruling that the transaction is not a dividend. The IRS has announced, however, that it will not issue such a ruling unless the combined beneficial interest of the selling shareholder and all related persons in the stock held in the plan does not exceed 20 percent. It may be possible to meet this condition in certain cases by amending the ESOP or stock bonus plan to reduce the stock in the selling stockholder's account below this 20 percent limit.

A final and important incentive for the use of ESOPs in estate planning relates to the special tax benefits provided to estates for sales or stock to these plans. These benefits are discussed in the next question.

Question — What are the special tax benefits provided for sales of stock to an ESOP?

Answer — First, under Code section 2057 there is a special estate tax deduction if a shareholder's estate sells employer stock to an ESOP. The deduction is equal to 50 percent of the proceeds resulting from the qualified sale of stock to the ESOP. The deduction can't be greater than $750,000, however, nor can it reduce the taxable estate by more than 50%. Generally, to be eligible for the deduction, the stock sold must have been owned by the decedent immediately before death. Stock sold to the ESOP must be allocated to plan participants; there are penalties if the ESOP resells the stock too soon. The stock cannot be allocated to the account of a more than 25 percent owner of the corporation, however.

Another tax benefit (Code section 2210) allows the executor to transfer estate tax liability to an ESOP with respect to employer stock sold to the ESOP. For example, if the estate holds employer stock worth $100,000 creating an estate tax liability of $50,000, the estate can sell the stock to the ESOP in return for the ESOP's agreement to pay the $50,000 of estate tax liability, plus whatever additional cash is appropriate. This provision can only be used by a shareholder of a closely held business that is eligible to pay estate tax in installments under Code section 6166.

The third major tax benefit allows nonrecognition of gain for income tax purposes when a shareholder sells nonpublicly traded employer stock to an ESOP (Code section 1042). To qualify for this provision, the shareholder must use the proceeds from the sale to purchase "replacement securities" — that is, stock or securities of another corporation. The replacement securities take the same basis as the stock sold to the ESOP, and the shareholder does not pay tax until the replacement securities are sold. Many requirements apply; in particular, after the sale, the ESOP must own at least 30% of the employer corporation for the shareholder to take advantage of Section 1042.

Question — Are there any problems in a shareholder's selling stock to an ESOP or stock bonus plan during the shareholder's lifetime as a means of obtaining cash?

Answer — This is often a good planning technique.

The dividend problem mentioned in the first question also applies to a lifetime sale of stock to an ESOP. However, it may be a less important factor in a lifetime sale. If the shareholder's stock has a low basis — as is often the case in closely held companies — then the capital gain under a "sale" treatment will cost almost as much in taxes as dividend treatment. For example, if a shareholder sells stock with a basis of $20,000 to an ESOP for $500,000, the taxable capital gain is $480,000. Dividend treatment would result in taxable ordinary income of $500,000, a relatively small difference so long as capital gain tax rates are the same as those for ordinary income.

Question — Can any type of stock or securities be used in an ESOP?

Answer — Stock used in an ESOP must be either (a) common stock traded regularly on an established market or (b) common stock having a combination of voting power and dividend rights equal to or greater than that of the employer's class of common stock having the greatest voting rights and the class of stock having the greatest dividend rates. If there is only one class of stock, as is often the case with closely held companies, the second test is met.

Question — Can any type of business organization have an ESOP or stock bonus plan?

Answer — Only a regular or "C" corporation can adopt a stock bonus plan or ESOP. In an S corporation, transferring stock to the plan would cause the Subchapter S election to terminate, because the plan is not a permitted shareholder in an S corporation. Unincorporated businesses — partnerships or proprietorships — cannot have ESOPs or stock bonus plans because they have no stock.

Finally, a professional corporation may not be able to establish an ESOP or stock bonus plan because state corporate law may require all shareholders of a professional corporation to be licensed professionals.

Question — How can an ESOP or stock bonus plan be used to carry out a corporate buy-sell agreement among shareholders?

Answer — For illustration, take a very simple situation with only two major shareholders, Alf and Ben, each owning about half of the corporation's stock, with a relatively small amount held in a stock bonus plan for participants other than Alf and Ben.

The simplest type of arrangement is for the plan trustee to purchase insurance on the lives of Alf and Ben. This insurance is held as key person insurance, since the trust has an insurable interest in the lives of the two business principals. On the death of one shareholder — suppose it is Alf — the trustee collects the insurance proceeds and uses that money to purchase stock from Alf's estate. The stock is reallocated to plan participants. Ben's account will probably receive most of this stock eventually and Ben will retain majority ownership. However, some stock may also be allocated to other participants.

Another arrangement, slightly more formal, makes use of "participant investment direction" or "earmarking," which is permitted under ERISA. With participant investment direction in a qualified plan, a participant is given the right to direct the trustee to invest his or her plan account in specified property. In this case, Alf directs the trustee to invest in insurance on Ben's life. Ben directs investment in insurance on Alf's life. The insurance proceeds on the death of one owner are therefore used to purchase stock directly for the account of the other owner, with no allocation of stock to other plan participants.

Chapter 10
FLEXIBLE SPENDING ACCOUNT

WHAT IS IT?

A flexible spending account, or FSA, is a cafeteria plan — a plan under which employees can choose between cash and specified benefits — that is funded through salary reductions elected by employees each year.

WHEN IS IT INDICATED?

1. When an employer wants to expand employee benefit choices without significant extra out-of-pocket costs (or possibly realize some actual dollar savings). Some situations where benefit choices are desirable:

    • Where many employees have employed spouses with duplicate medical coverage

    • Where employees contribute to health insurance costs

    • Where the employer's medical plans have large deductibles or coinsurance (co-pay) provisions

    • Where employees are nonunion (collective bargaining units prefer uniform benefit packages)

    • Where there is a need for benefits that are difficult to provide on a group basis, such as dependent care.

2. Where costs of an employee benefit plan such as health insurance have increased and the employer must impose additional employee cost sharing in the form of (a) increased employee contributions, (b) deductibles, or (c) coinsurance, the FSA approach minimizes employee outlay since the FSA converts after-tax employee expenditures to before-tax expenditures.

3. The FSA provides a tax benefit for employees (tax exclusion for various benefits) that is not available through any other plan.

4. Because of administrative costs, FSAs are usually impractical for businesses with only a few employees. Most FSAs involve employers with 25 or more employees, but the plan could be considered for as few as 10 employees.

5. FSA benefits cannot be provided to self-employed persons — partners or sole proprietors.

ADVANTAGES

1. Since it is a type of cafeteria plan, the plan provides employees some degree of choice as to whether to receive compensation in cash or benefits, and what form the benefits will take.

2. The FSA is funded through employee salary reductions, which requires no extra outlay by the employer, except for administrative costs.

3. The plan may result in a reduction in some employment taxes paid by the employer, since taxable payroll is reduced.

4. Salary reductions elected by employees to fund nontaxable benefits under the plan are not subject to federal income taxes.

5. The list of potential nontaxable benefits available from the plan is large and includes many benefits that employers might not otherwise provide to employees — for example, dependent care.

DISADVANTAGES

1. An FSA must meet all of the complex nondiscrimination requirements for cafeteria plans (see Chapter 2). Monitoring compliance with these rules raises administrative costs. Also, particularly in some closely held corporations, there could be a loss of tax benefits to highly compensated employees if the nondiscrimination rules are not met.

2. FSAs require employees to evaluate their personal and family benefit situations and file a timely election form every year. They must estimate — at the end of each year — the amount that will be required for covered expenses in the following year. This is sometimes both confusing and difficult, and some employees may not fully utilize the plan because of the perceived complexity or paperwork involved. Others may not want to risk the forfeiture required of any funds left in the account at the end of the year (see number 6 in the discussion below).

3. The plan could result in "adverse selection" that would ultimately raise benefit costs. For example, dental plan options might be selected primarily by employees who know that they will soon undergo a regime of expensive dental procedures. This will tend to raise the cost of dental insurance made available by the employer to fund dental benefits.

4. Administrative costs are greater than in a fixed benefit plan.

Tools and Techniques

HOW IT WORKS — AND AN EXAMPLE

These are the basic features of an FSA plan:

1. The employer decides what benefits are to be provided in the FSA and adopts written plans to provide these benefits, if the plans are not already in place. (The design of these individual plans is generally covered in separate chapters of this book.) For example, the employer might decide that the FSA will allow employee salary reductions to be applied to

- the employee's share of health insurance premiums

- medical expenses not covered under the health insurance plan (this requires the employer to adopt a medical reimbursement plan)

- expenses of dependent care (the employer must adopt a dependent care assistance plan)

2. The employer advises employees to review their benefit needs toward the end of each year and estimate their next year's expenses for items covered in the plan.

3. Before the end of the calendar year, employees file with the employer a written election to reduce salary by the amount they choose (the amount they estimate they will spend on covered benefits) and allocate it among the benefits in the plan. The chosen salary reduction goes into a "benefit account." The benefit account is a book account — it is not actually funded by the employer in most cases.

4. Each employee keeps a record of expenses in each benefit category and makes a claim on the plan for reimbursement. Claims are usually made on a quarterly basis for administrative convenience. (The employee does not have to make a written claim for expenses that would otherwise be a payroll deduction, such as the employee share of health insurance. Such claims are handled automatically by the plan.)

5. The employer issues checks to employees for reimbursement. These reimbursements are free of income tax.

6. At the end of the year, if anything is left in the employee's benefit account, it is forfeited. It cannot be carried over to the next year. This feature requires careful planning by the employee.

As an example, suppose employee Patella earns $40,000 per year and is covered under an FSA having the features noted in this discussion. On December 31, 1989, having reviewed his probable benefit needs for 1990, he files an FSA election with his employer to reduce his 1990 salary by $2,000. The $2,000 will go into his FSA benefit account and he elects to allocate it as follows:

- $600 ($50 per month) to cover his share of health insurance premiums

- $1,000 for medical expenses covered under the medical reimbursement plan but not the health insurance (Patella anticipates orthodontic expenses during 1990 for his daughter Rubella)

- $400 for expenses under the dependent care plan (Patella plans to send his daughter, age 11, to summer day camp costing about $400)

If Patella's expenses run as expected, the FSA will have turned $2,000 of nondeductible after-tax expenditures into before-tax payments, saving Patella the federal income tax on $2,000, and saving the employer the employment taxes on $2,000 of compensation paid.

If Patella's covered expenses are higher, he will simply lose the tax benefits that would have been available if he had made a larger salary reduction election.

However, if Patella's expenses are less than predicted, he will actually forfeit the amount remaining in his FSA benefit account at the end of the year. The amount forfeited in effect reverts to the employer, since it represents compensation that will not have to be paid.

DESIGN FEATURES

1. An FSA is a cafeteria plan under Code section 125, and it must meet all the complex rules prohibiting discrimination in favor of highly compensated employees. These rules are discussed in detail in Chapter 2, Cafeteria Plan.

    In general, these rules will be satisfied if all employees are allowed to participate and if benefits, as a percentage of compensation, are approximately equal for all employees. If the employer wants more selective coverage and benefits compliance with the nondiscrimination rules must be carefully analyzed.

    The cost of noncompliance with the rules is not disqualification of the plan as a whole. What happens is that tax benefits for highly compensated employees — only — are lost.

2. What benefits can be provided in the plan? These are the same as for cafeteria plans in general. Thus, employers can include the following types of benefits in an FSA arrangement:

    - Health insurance (the FSA can be used to cover the employee-paid portion or even the entire cost of the insurance).

    - Medical reimbursement, including anything not covered in the health insurance plan — dental care, eyeglasses, hearing aids, etc. The potentially wide range of this option is discussed further in Chapter 22 of this book.

• Group term life insurance on the employee's or dependent's life. Insurance on the employee's life up to $50,000 is a tax-free option; additional insurance on the employee or dependent life insurance is a taxable option.

• Disability insurance premiums under an employer group arrangement (disability *benefits* under such a plan are taxable — see Chapter 21).

• Legal services provided under a group legal services plan

• Contributions to a Section 401(k) plan

• Extra vacation days (but unused days cannot be cashed out or carried over to a subsequent year).

Some benefits are specifically prohibited by the Code for an FSA or other cafeteria plan. These are —

— deferred compensation, other than under a Section 401(k) plan

— educational benefits, including scholarships and fellowships

— employee discounts (for department store employees, for example)

— van pooling, commuter transportation, or employee parking

3. On the practical side, the critical design feature is *adequate employee communication* so that employees use the plan and the employer's efforts in instituting the plan pay off in employee appreciation.

TAX IMPLICATIONS

1. Employee salary reductions applied to nontaxable benefits are not subject to income tax. Highly compensated employees may be taxed on these benefits if the plan is discriminatory.

   Salary reductions, to be effective for tax purposes, must be made before the compensation is earned. IRS regulations require FSA elections to be made annually before the beginning of the calendar year for which the salary reduction is to be effective.

2. Code section 89(k) states that all employees, not just those who are highly compensated, must include the value of the benefits received in income if the following requirements are not met:

   — employees must be notified of plan benefits

   — the plan must be intended as a permanent plan

   — there must be a written plan for the exclusive benefit of employees

— the plan must provide legally enforceable rights for employees

3. The employer gets a tax deduction for the amounts it pays to reimburse employees for covered expenditures.

4. The employer's payroll subject to payroll taxes is reduced by the amount of any employee salary reductions under an FSA. Payroll taxes include:

   (a) FICA (social security),

   (b) FUTA (federal unemployment tax),

   (c) state unemployment taxes, and

   (d) workers' compensation.

   State laws relating to unemployment taxes and workers' compensation may vary and should be checked. One exception to the above rules is that FICA and FUTA may be payable on amounts that are contributed to a Section 401(k) plan as part of an FSA arrangement.

ERISA REQUIREMENTS

The ERISA requirements are those applicable to the various individual plans — health insurance, dependent care, etc. — that are part of the FSA arrangement. Generally, these plans are exempt from any requirement of advance funding and follow the rules applicable to welfare benefit plans under ERISA (Appendix D). Written plans, a summary plan description, and a formal claims procedure are required under ERISA; these requirements may overlap with the Section 89(k) requirements listed earlier.

HOW TO INSTALL A PLAN

Suppose an FSA plan is to be effective January 1, 1990. The essential step before this date is to obtain effective employee salary reduction elections. Thus, the plan must be designed, communicated to employees, and the salary reduction forms must be designed and furnished to employees before January 1, 1990.

Formal plan documents for the FSA and for each plan included in the FSA — medical reimbursement, dependent care, etc. must be drafted and adopted by the employer. (All these can be incorporated in a single document but separate documents are often convenient.) To be effective January 1, 1990, a corporation would have to formally adopt these documents, with a written resolution of the board of directors, before the end of the corporation's taxable year in which the effective date — January 1, 1990 — falls. For example, a calendar-year corporation would have to formally adopt these plans no later than December 31, 1990.

WHERE CAN I FIND OUT MORE ABOUT IT?

Fundamentals of Employee Benefit Programs, 3rd ed. Washington, DC: Employee Benefit Research Institute, 1987.

QUESTIONS AND ANSWERS

Question — Is an employee "locked-in" for a full year to his or her FSA salary reduction amount and benefit allocation, or can it be changed during the year?

Answer — Changes are not generally allowed unless there are major life events that affect benefit needs. The regulations list marriage, divorce, death of a spouse or child, birth of a child or addition of a dependent, and loss of a spouse's job as qualifying events.

Question — Since FSA salary reductions eliminate social security taxes on the salary reduction, are social security benefits also affected?

Answer — If an FSA salary reduction reduces an employee's wages below the taxable wage base for the year ($48,000 for 1989), then social security benefit credit for that year will also be reduced. This probably will not reduce an employee's ultimate social security retirement benefit by very much, but it may deter FSA participation by lower-paid employees. It is advisable for employers to investigate exactly how much effect this will have and communicate it to employees to allay any unreasonable fears they may have. Also, for a relatively low cost, employers can provide an insurance or annuity benefit to compensate employees for this loss.

Question — Are FSA salary reductions recognized for state or local income tax purposes?

Answer — If state or local income taxes are based on federal taxable income — as most are — then salary reductions are generally effective for state tax purposes. However, state and local laws vary. For example, as of 1988 the state income tax laws of Alabama, Arkansas, New Jersey, and Pennsylvania do not recognize salary reduction elections.

Question — Is there a dollar limit on annual salary reductions in an FSA plan?

Answer — There is no dollar limit applicable to FSA salary reductions as such. However, the separate employee benefit plans that are part of an FSA program may have their own dollar limits. For example, there is a $5,000 annual limit for dependent care plans (see Chapter 7). Also, employers often limit salary reductions to a relatively small amount in order to meet the nondiscrimination rules of Section 125. If the plan permits large salary reductions, highly compensated employees are likely to use the plan disproportionately.

Question — If an employee uses up his or her benefit account allocated to one form of benefit, can amounts allocated to another form of benefit be reallocated?

Answer — The IRS takes the position that there can be no such "crossover" of benefit allocations during the year. This emphasizes the importance (and difficulty) of careful employee planning in making the annual salary reduction election and allocation of the benefit account.

Chapter 11

GOVERNMENTAL EMPLOYER DEFERRED COMPENSATION (SECTION 457) PLAN

WHAT IS IT?

Section 457 of the Code provides rules governing all non-qualified deferred compensation plans of governmental units, governmental agencies, and also non-church controlled tax-exempt organizations. A plan designed to comply with these rules is referred to as a Section 457 plan.

WHEN IS IT INDICATED?

If the employer is an effected organization, Section 457 is mandatory. Any nonqualified deferred compensation plan adopted by such an employer must comply with the rules discussed here.

DESIGN FEATURES

What Employers Are Covered by Section 457?

Section 457 applies to nonqualified deferred compensation plans of:

(a) a state, a political subdivision of a state (such as a city, township, etc.), and any agency or instrumentality of a state or political subdivision of a state (for example, a school district or a sewage authority), and

(b) any organization exempt from federal income tax, except for a church or synagogue or an organization controlled by a church or synagogue.

Limit on Amount Deferred

The amount deferred annually by an employee under a plan covered by Section 457 cannot exceed the lesser of $7,500 or one-third of the employee's compensation currently includable in gross income.

The $7,500 limit is applied on a per-individual not a per-plan basis. For example, if an individual is employed by two different governmental employers, the individual's total annual deferral from both employers cannot exceed $7,500.

The $7,500 limit is not indexed for inflation. By comparison, various limits for qualified plans (such as the $7,000 limit for salary reductions under Section 401(k) plans) are subject to indexing.

If an employee is covered under a Section 403(b) tax deferred annuity plan or a simplified employee pension (SEP), then any 403(b) or SEP salary reductions will reduce

the $7,500 limit. Deferrals to certain cash or deferred arrangements adopted generally before 1986 may also reduce the $7,500 limit. For example, if an individual employed by a tax-exempt college elects a salary reduction of $7,500 for 1989 under the college's 403(b) plan, then that individual cannot contribute anything for 1989 to a nonqualified deferred compensation arrangement governed by Section 457.

For employees nearing retirement there is a "catch-up" provision. The $7,500 ceiling can be increased in each of the last three years before normal retirement age to the lesser of

(a) $15,000 or

(b) the regular limit of the lesser of $7,500 or one-third of taxable compensation plus the total amount of deferral not used in prior years.

Catch-up Example:

Lew Sludge begins working at age 60 as a part-time engineer for the Effluent City, PA, Sewage Authority. His compensation is $30,000 annually. The authority has a Section 457 plan with a normal retirement age of 65. Lew makes contributions of $5,000 annually to the plan until his last year of service, for which he wants to make the maximum contribution. This maximum is $15,000, as shown by the following table:

Year	Max Deferral	Actual Deferral	Difference
1	$ 7,500	$ 5,000	$ 2,500
2	7,500	5,000	2,500
3	12,500	5,000	7,500
4	15,000	5,000	10,000
5	15,000	15,000	

Year 3 is the beginning of the last 3 years prior to retirement. The maximum deferral amount in Year 3 is the lesser of $15,000 or the regular ceiling of $7,500 plus the potential deferral of $2,500 not used in Year 1 and the $2,500 not used in Year 2 — a total of $5,000. Thus the maximum deferral in Year 3 is $7,500 plus $5,000 or $12,500. The maximums for Years 4 and 5 are computed in the same manner. In Year 4 Lew can contribute $15,000. This consists of the $7,500 he could have contributed (but did not) in year 3, plus the $7,500 regular limit. In Year 5, his last year, Lew's regular limit of

$7,500 plus his unused Year 4 amount totals $17,500, but the $15,000 maximum holds his contribution to $15,000 for that year.

Timing of Salary Reduction Elections

Employee elections to defer compensation monthly under Section 457 must be made under an agreement entered into before the beginning of the month.

Distribution Requirements

Plan distributions cannot be made before:

(a) the calendar year in which the participant attains age 70½ or

(b) separation from service or

(c) an "unforeseeable emergency" as defined in regulations. The definition of unforeseeable emergency is discussed in the "Questions and Answers," below.

Distributions must begin no later than April 1 of the calendar year after the year in which the plan participant attains age 70½. Minimum distributions must be made under the rules of Code section 401(a)(9). This Code section applies to qualified plans as well, and the minimum distribution rules are discussed in detail in Appendix B.

There are three special rules governing death or survivorship benefits under Section 457 plans.

1. If a plan distribution begins before the death of the participant the amount payable with respect to the participant must be paid at times not later than those determined under Section 401(a)(9)(G) relating to incidental death benefits.

2. Any amount distributed to the beneficiary after the participant's death must be distributed at least as rapidly as it would have been if the participant survived.

3. If the plan distribution begins after the participant's death, the entire amount must be paid out over no more than 15 years (or if a surviving spouse is the beneficiary over the life expectancy of the spouse).

Coverage and Eligibility

There are no specific coverage requirements for Section 457 plans. For a governmental organization, the plan can be offered to all employees, or to any group of employees, even a single employee.

However, most private non-church related tax-exempt organizations, unlike governmental organizations, are subject to ERISA. Therefore, the ERISA eligibility rules may apply to the Section 457 plan of the tax-exempt organization. The eligibility requirements would be the same as those applicable to a nonqualified deferred compensation plan for a taxable employer, as discussed in Chapter 24. Such plans can avoid the ERISA rules only if they are unfunded and

cover only a select group of management and highly compensated employees — the "top-hat" group.

Funding

A Section 457 plan may not be funded. However, "financing" the plan with insurance or annuity contracts is allowed and is almost always appropriate, as discussed in the "Questions and Answers."

For a tax-exempt organization, the no funding requirement of Section 457 may conflict directly with the ERISA funding requirements if the plan covers more than the "top-hat" group; this issue has not yet been resolved.

TAX IMPLICATIONS

1. Since the employer in a Section 457 plan does not pay federal income taxes, deductibility is not an issue.

2. Employees or their beneficiaries include Section 457 plan distributions in income when they are actually paid or otherwise made available.

   However, if a nonqualified deferred compensation plan of a governmental or tax-exempt employer does not comply with Section 457 compensation deferred is included in the employee's income in the first taxable year in which there is no substantial risk of forfeiture of the rights to the compensation. Any distributions from an ineligible plan are treated in the same manner as annuity distributions under Section 72. The implications of this are discussed in the "Questions and Answers."

3. Section 457 plan distributions are not eligible for the favorable lump sum 5-year averaging treatment available for qualified plans.

4. Section 457 plan distributions are not eligible for tax-free rollover to an individual retirement account or annuity plan (IRA). However, they can be rolled over tax-free to another Section 457 plan.

ERISA REQUIREMENTS

Governmental employers are not subject to ERISA. However, tax-exempt private employers will encounter the ERISA compliance problems discussed above.

ALTERNATIVES

Tax-exempt employers can adopt qualified pension and profit-sharing plans for employees. In addition, tax-exempts can adopt Section 403(b) plans that provide as good or better benefits for employees as a Section 457 plan.

Governmental employers can also adopt governmental pension plans similar to qualified private plans. However, since the 403(b) type of plan is not available to governmental employers such employers are more likely to use Section 457 plans to supplement a pension plan.

The problems in designing nonqualified deferred compensation plans for top management employees of governmental and tax-exempt employers are discussed in the "Questions and Answers."

HOW TO INSTALL A PLAN

A written plan containing the provisions described above should be adopted. Also, forms must be furnished to employees to carry out the required monthly salary reduction elections. For tax-exempt private employers subject to ERISA, the same ERISA requirements applicable to nonqualified deferred compensation will apply. These are discussed in Chapter 24.

WHERE CAN I FIND OUT MORE ABOUT IT?

1. *Fundamentals of Employee Benefit Programs*, 3rd ed. Washington, DC: Employee Benefit Research Institute, 1987.

2. *Tax Facts 1*, Cincinnati, OH: The National Underwriter Company, (revised annually).

QUESTIONS AND ANSWERS

Question — Can a governmental or tax-exempt organization have a nonqualified deferred compensation plan other than one following the rules of Section 457 — in particular, a plan allowing more than $7,500 of annual deferral?

Answer — There are some limited "loopholes" that might allow some flexibility or deferral above $7,500.

First, under the Technical and Miscellaneous Revenue Act of 1988 Section 457 does not apply to bona fide vacation leave, sick leave, compensatory time, severance pay, disability pay, and death benefit plans.

Second, the 1988 Act added a "grandfather" provision that may preserve some existing executive deferred compensation plans. Under that provision, Section 457 does not apply to "nonelective" deferred compensation that was deferred either before or after that date under a written agreement covering the individual in question that was in effect on July 14, 1988 and provided for deferral of a fixed amount or deferral under a fixed formula. A nonelective plan is one that does not provide for salary reductions- essentially the type of plan that would be provided for top management employees who negotiate individual employment contracts.

Third, the 1988 Act provides that nonelective deferred compensation plans for nonemployees- for example, doctors working for hospitals as independent contractors- are not subject to Section 457. However, for this exception to apply all such nonemployees must be treated the same under the plan, with no individual variations.

Another final factor permitting some flexibility is that if an employee defers more than the $7,500 limit, the deferral is not taxed immediately, but rather is taxed in the first taxable year in which there is no substantial risk of forfeiture. Thus, if the deferred compensation plan has forfeiture provisions, any amount can be deferred at least until the forfeiture provision lapses. Although not every executive would be satisfied with forfeitable deferred compensation, it may be useful in some cases.

Question — What constitutes an "unforeseeable emergency" that permits distributions from a Section 457 plan?

Answer — The current regulations under Section 457 define unforeseeable emergency as severe financial hardship to the participant resulting from a sudden and unexpected illness or accident of the participant or a dependent, a loss of property due to casualty, or other similar extraordinary and unforeseeable circumstances arising as a result of events beyond the control of the participant.

The regulations specifically mention that the purchase of a residence or college education of children is not considered an unforeseeable emergency. Any amount distributed from the plan as the result of an emergency cannot exceed the amount reasonably needed to satisfy the emergency.

Question — How is a Section 457 plan informally funded or "financed" through the purchase of insurance or annuities?

Answer — Although a Section 457 plan cannot be funded in the same sense as a qualified plan, that is with an irrevocable trust fund for the exclusive benefit of employees, the employer can, and in most cases should, finance its obligations under the plan by setting aside assets in advance of the time when payments will be made. Life insurance or annuity contracts are often used for this purpose.

If the employer purchases life insurance contracts to finance the plan, there is no current life insurance cost to employees as long as the employer retains all incidents of ownership in the policies, is the sole beneficiary under the policies, and is under no obligation to transfer the policies or pass through the proceeds of the policies.

Chapter 12

GROUP-TERM LIFE INSURANCE

WHAT IS IT?

A group-term life insurance plan provides insurance for a group of employees under a group insurance contract held by the employer. If the plan qualifies under Code section 79, the cost of the first $50,000 of insurance is tax-free to employees.

WHEN IS IT INDICATED?

Since virtually all employees have at least some basic need for life insurance, and since there are few other ways to obtain tax-free life insurance, most employers would find it difficult to find reasons not to provide a group-term plan, at least at levels up to the $50,000 tax-free limit.

At levels above $50,000, group-term plans are still a cost effective way to provide a life insurance benefit, both for employer and employee.

DESIGN FEATURES

Requirements of Section 79 Regulations

The regulations under Code section 79 require group-term insurance to have the following characteristics in order to obtain the $50,000 exclusion:

1. It must provide a *general death benefit*. Accident and health insurance, including double indemnity riders, or travel accident insurance are not considered part of the Section 79 plan. Also, life insurance as an incidental benefit in a qualified pension or profit-sharing plan is not considered part of the Section 79 plan.

2. It must be provided to a *group of employees* as compensation for services. The group can be all employees or a group defined in terms of employment-related factors — union membership, duties performed, etc. — or a group restricted solely on the basis of age or marital status. (Nondiscriminatory coverage requirements also apply, as discussed below.) The plan cannot cover company shareholders who are not employees, or a group consisting only of shareholder-employees.

3. The insurance policy must be *carried directly or indirectly by the employer*. This requirement is met if the employer pays any part of the cost of the plan.

4. Insurance amounts for employees must be determined under a *formula that precludes individual selection*. The formula must be based on factors such as age, years of service, compensation, or position in the company.

The plan can, however, provide a given level of coverage to persons in a position defined such that only a few (but at least more than one) highly compensated employees are in that category. (However, note the nondiscrimination rules discussed below.)

Section 89 Nondiscrimination Rules

Highly compensated employees may lose the benefit of the $50,000 exclusion in a group-term plan unless the nondiscrimination requirements of Code section 89 are satisfied. In summary, these are:

1. *Highly compensated* is defined as it is for qualified plans under Code section 414(q) — Appendix A discusses the complete definition, which is both precise and complicated.

2. The plan's eligibility provisions must meet three requirements —

— at least 90% of all nonhighly compensated employees are eligible and have available an employer-provided benefit that is at least 50% of the largest employer-provided benefit under the plan.

— at least 50% of employees eligible for the plan are not highly compensated. This requirement is deemed met if the percentage of highly compensated eligible employees is no greater than the percentage of nonhighly compensated eligible employees.

— the plan must contain no provision relating to eligibility that discriminates in favor of highly compensated employees.

3. For any plan year, the plan's benefit provisions are nondiscriminatory if the average employer-provided benefit received by nonhighly compensated employees is at least 75% of that received by highly compensated employees. The value of the benefit received by employees for this purpose is the Table I cost for a forty year old employee, that is, $.17 per $1,000 per month. (see below).

4. There is an alternate test that, if met, will satisfy both the eligibility and benefit nondiscrimination requirements of Section 89. This test is met if the plan covers 80% of the nonhighly compensated employees and does not contain any provision that would allow eligibility discrimination in favor of the highly compensated employees.

Tools and Techniques

5. Under the Technical and Miscellaneous Revenue Act of 1988, compliance with Section 89 can be demonstrated on the basis of a statistically valid sample. This will greatly simplify compliance for large companies. Testing for compliance is done on the basis of the facts as of a "testing day" designated in the plan.

TAX IMPLICATIONS

1. The cost of the first $50,000 of insurance provided for each employee is tax-free to the employee. Highly compensated employees may lose this benefit if the plan does not meet the Section 89 nondiscrimination rules discussed above. The cost of any discriminatory coverage (including any coverage over $50,000) is included in the highly compensated employee's income at the greater of the Table I rates (see below) or the actual cost.

2. For the cost of nondiscriminatory coverage above $50,000, the amount taxable to the employee is determined on a monthly basis. The amount of coverage in excess of $50,000 is multiplied by the "Table I" rates (see below). The annual taxable amount is the sum of the monthly amounts, less any premiums paid by the employee.

"TABLE I" RATES FOR GROUP TERM INSURANCE

5-year age bracket	Cost per $1,000 of insurance for 1-month period
Under 30	$ .08
30 to 34	.09
35 to 39	.11
40 to 44	.17
45 to 49	.29
50 to 54	.48
55 to 59	.75
60 to 64	1.17

NOTES

1. Age of the employee is attained age on the last day of the employee's taxable year.

2. If the employee is older than 64: before 1989, he or she is treated as if in the 60 to 64 age bracket; for tax years beginning after 1988, Treasury is authorized to prescribe brackets for ages over 64.

For example, suppose an employee age 32 was covered under a group-term plan providing insurance of $100,000 for all twelve months of the year, and the employee paid $30 for this coverage for the year. The amount of coverage in excess of the $50,000 tax-free level is $50,000 ($100,000 - $50,000). Using Table I, 50 times $0.09 equals $4.50 of monthly cost, which multiplied by 12 (for 12 months) equals $54. The employee paid $30, and the difference between $54 and $30, $24, is taxable income for the year.

3. The death benefit from the insurance is tax-free to the beneficiary, just as if the insurance was personally-owned (except as noted in the following paragraph).

4. Under Code section 89(k), the following qualification requirements must be met or the tax exemption for the death benefit is lost. Regulations will coordinate the inclusion of the death benefit with inclusion of any discriminatory excess. The includable death benefit is taxable to the beneficiary instead of the employee. The qualification requirements are as follows:

— employees must be notified of plan benefits

— the plan must be intended as a permanent plan

— there must be a written plan for the exclusive benefit of employees

— the plan must provide legally enforceable rights for employees

5. Premiums paid by the employer for group-term life insurance of employees are deductible business expenses.

6. The employer must pay employment taxes on the extra compensation that each employee includes in income as a result of plan coverage with insurance amounts over $50,000 or any coverage or benefits included by reason of Section 89. Employment taxes include FICA (social security) and FUTA (federal unemployment tax). State unemployment and workers' compensation taxes may apply in some states — state law varies and should be checked in each case.

ERISA AND OTHER REQUIREMENTS

A group-term plan is a "welfare benefit plan" subject to the ERISA requirements discussed in Appendix D. In addition, Code section 6039D requires filing an information return with the IRS.

ALTERNATIVES

1. Life insurance in a qualified plan

2. Split dollar life insurance

3. Death benefit only (employer death benefit)

4. Personally-owned insurance

HOW TO INSTALL A PLAN

A written plan meeting both the Section 79 and the Section 89(k) requirements listed above must be adopted, and employees must be notified of the plan benefits.

WHERE CAN I FIND OUT MORE ABOUT IT?

1. *Tax Facts 1*, Cincinnati, OH: The National Underwriter Co., (revised annually).

2. *Fundamentals of Employee Benefit Programs*, 3rd ed. Washington, DC: Employee Benefit Research Institute, 1987.

QUESTIONS AND ANSWERS

Question — Can group-term insurance be provided for self-employed persons or S corporation shareholders?

Answer — The exclusion from taxable income of the cost of the first $50,000 of group-term insurance under Code section 79 is not available to self-employed persons — partners or proprietors — or to shareholders of S corporations who own more than 2% of the corporation. (These more-than-2% shareholders are treated as partners for employee benefit purposes).

However, self-employed persons and more than 2% shareholders of S corporations can be included in the insured group for purposes of determining group coverage and premiums. The full cost of such insurance is taxable to the individual covered.

Question — How small a group can be covered under group-term insurance and are there any special rules for small groups?

Answer — Under the Section 79 Regulations, group insurance for fewer than 10 employees qualifies for the tax exclusion under Section 79 if

— it is provided for all full-time employees, and

— the amount of protection is computed either as a uniform percentage of compensation, or on the basis of coverage brackets established by the insurer under which no bracket exceeds 2½ times the next lower bracket and the lowest bracket is at least 10 percent of the highest bracket.

For example, a plan dividing employees into four classes with insurance amounts according to the following brackets would meet the test in the regulations:

Class A:	$ 10,000
Class B:	25,000
Class C:	50,000
Class D:	100,000

Eligibility and amount of coverage may be based on evidence of insurability but this must be determined solely on the basis of a medical questionnaire completed by the employee and not by requiring a physical examination.

Meeting the under-10 employee regulations described in this answer is no guarantee that the plan will also be deemed nondiscriminatory. An under-10 employee plan must also meet the Section 89 nondiscrimination requirements.

Question — Can insurance providing a permanent benefit be used in a group-term life insurance plan?

Answer — Yes, under certain conditions. A policy is considered to provide a permanent benefit if it provides an economic value extending beyond one policy year. For example, a policy with a cash surrender value would be considered to provide a permanent benefit.

A policy with a permanent benefit may be treated as part of a group-term plan if

— the amount of death benefit considered part of the group-term plan is specified in writing, and

— the group-term portion of the death benefit each year complies with a formula in the regulations.

If permanent insurance is used in a group-term plan, the cost of the permanent benefit, less any amount contributed by the employee towards that permanent benefit, is included in the employee's taxable income for the year. The regulations contain a formula for computing the annual cost of permanent benefits.

Question — Can "group universal life insurance programs" (sometimes referred to as "GULP") be used in a Section 79 group-term plan?

Answer — Group universal life programs are universal life insurance arrangements for a group of employees. These programs provide covered employees with (a) the advantages of universal life coverage — variation in the timing and amount of premiums, and cash values with attractive rates of investment return — as well as (b) the advantages of group underwriting — convenience for employees, reduced costs, and coverage without evidence of insurability, within limits.

Group universal life contracts can be used as part of a plan of group-term insurance meeting the requirements of Section 79 and the regulations. However, application of this Code section to a GULP plan does not produce a good tax result due to the rules for taxing "permanent" insurance benefits contained in Section 79. Thus, most GULP plans are designed specifically to *avoid* the application of Section 79. This can be done by using an employee-pay-all arrangement and structuring coverage through a third party (such as a trustee) so that the policy is not deemed to be "carried directly or indirectly by the employer" as required under Section 79. Planning requires close adherence to technical requirements and must be done with the advice of an expert.

It is possible to provide Section 79 group-term insurance up to the tax-free level, and also provide the GULP benefit as a (non-Section 79) supplement to the Section 79 plan, if adequate coverage for group underwriting can be obtained.

41

Chapter 13

HEALTH INSURANCE

WHAT IS IT?

Health insurance is the most widespread employee benefit, covering more than 75 million employees in the United States. It is widespread as an employee benefit not only because it meets a critical employee need, but also because it receives almost unique tax benefits: the entire cost is deductible to employers, but nothing is includable in employees' taxable income as a result of plan coverage or payment of plan benefits, if the plan meets the rules discussed below. Thus health insurance is a completely tax-free form of employee compensation.

There are two main types of health insurance plans:

- prepaid plans, in which health care providers are paid in advance of providing services

- postpaid plans, which pay health care providers for services rendered, or reimburse employees for payments to providers.

The principal form of prepaid plans is the Health Maintenance Organization, or HMO. HMOs are discussed separately in Chapter 14. This chapter will focus primarily on postpaid plans, which are the traditional form of health insurance.

PLAN DESIGN

Health insurance plans provided by employers are usually complicated and may even be "customized" to some degree, particularly for larger employers. However, three fundamental types of plan design are usually identified — the "basic" plan, the "major medical" plan, and the "comprehensive" plan.

Basic Plan. A basic plan primarily provides health care services that are connected with hospitalization. The types of benefits provided in a basic plan are

(1) Inpatient hospital charges, such as room and board, nursing care, supplies, and other hospital expenses.

(2) In-hospital visits by physicians. Home or office visits are not covered in a basic plan.

(3) Surgical fees, including surgeons' fees as well as anesthesiologists' and other surgical assistants' fees. These plans often cover fees for surgical procedures performed in an doctor's office or at an out-patient facility — not just those performed on patients admitted to a hospital.

Major Medical Plan. A major medical plan covers medical services excluded from basic plans. For this reason it is sometimes referred to as a "supplemental major medical plan." Although the objective of the plan is to fill gaps in basic coverage, few plans cover all medical expenses. Routine doctors' office visits are usually excluded. Also, most plans do not cover dental, vision, and hearing care, although employers often provide these through separate plans.

Comprehensive Plan. The comprehensive type of plan combines the coverage of basic and major medical plans into one single plan. This is currently the dominant type of plan. Many employers have replaced basic/major medical plans with comprehensive plans.

BENEFIT STRUCTURE

Many health plans do not pay the full cost of covered benefits. Major medical and comprehensive plans in particular, but also some basic plans, use "deductibles" and "coinsurance" to reduce plan costs by requiring employees to share benefit costs. The plan also usually has a per-individual maximum coverage limit on covered expenses.

Deductibles. A deductible is an amount of initial expense specified in the plan that is paid by the employee toward covered benefits. For example, if the plan has a $200 deductible, the participant pays the first $200 of covered expenses and the plan covers the rest up to a specified limit. Deductibles generally range from $100 to $500.

Deductibles are usually computed annually. For example, if the deductible is $500 and a covered individual incurs $400 of doctors' bills covered under the plan between January and November, the plan does not pay anything. However, if the same individual incurs an additional covered medical expense of $200 in December, the $500 deductible will have been satisfied and the plan will pay the $100 in excess of the deductible. Some plans have carryover provisions to avoid an unfair impact of the deductible. For example, with a three-month carryover provision, medical bills incurred during the last three months of the year can be used toward the next year's deductible. Thus, if an individual has a serious illness in December and incurs a $1,000 medical expense, subsequent bills in January and thereafter will not be subject to another deductible.

Tools and Techniques

Most deductibles are *all-causes* deductibles — that is, the deductible is cumulative over the year or other period even though the medical bills may reflect many different illnesses or medical conditions. However, some plans have *per-cause* deductibles. Under a per-cause deductible, the deductible amount must be satisfied for each separate illness or other medical condition.

Most employee plans use a *per-family* deductible as well as individual deductibles to minimize the payment burden for families. For example, the plan may have a $200 per individual deductible, but also a provision under which the plan pays for all covered expenses in full when total expenses for all family members exceed $500.

Coinsurance. Under a coinsurance provision, the plan participant is responsible for a specified percentage, usually 20 percent, of covered expenses. For example, if a plan has a $100 deductible, and a participant incurs expenses of $1100 during the year, the plan pays $800 of these and the participant pays the rest (the $100 deductible plus 20% of the remaining $1,000 of expenses).

The participant's 20% share can become burdensome quickly in the event of a major illness, so good plan design requires an upper dollar limit on the participant's share. The participant's costs are usually limited to several thousand dollars on an annual basis.

Maximum Coverage Limits. To limit the plan's ultimate liability, there is usually an upper "lifetime limit" on the amount the plan will pay for any one individual's medical expenses. This limit should be high enough so that only the rarest of medical events will cause it to be exceeded. Limits of $500,000 to $1 million are commonly used. If the limit is too low, the plan violates the basic principle of insurance, which is to share catastrophic losses that no one individual can bear. Also, extending the upper limit substantially is usually not expensive because of the rarity of medical catastrophes. It is best to obtain coverage of $1 million, or unlimited coverage, whenever possible.

PLAN FUNDING

Employers fund postpaid-type health plans in one or a combination of three ways:

(a) commercial insurance company contracts

(b) Blue Cross/Blue Shield contracts

(c) "self-funding" or self insurance (without an insurance contract)

Commercial Insurers. A health insurance contract from a commercial insurance company usually provides reimbursement to employees for their expenses for covered medical procedures. Some insurers may pay health care providers directly, however. Reimbursement is usually limited to the "usual, customary, and reasonable" (UCR) charges for a given procedure in the employee's geographical area. Thus, an employee may not receive full reimbursement for a medical claim if the insurer's claims department considers the amount charged to be greater than the UCR amount.

Premiums for commercial health insurance contracts reflect six elements:

(a) expected benefit payments

(b) administrative expenses

(c) commissions

(d) state premium taxes

(e) risk charges; and

(f) return on the insurer's capital allocated to the contract (profit).

For groups of 50 employees or more, premiums are usually "experience rated." That is, the insurer keeps separate records for the employer group and adjusts charges to reflect above or below-average benefit utilization by the group itself.

Blue Cross/Blue Shield. Blue Cross and Blue Shield plans were originally designed by organizations of hospitals and physicians in order to facilitate the payment of hospital and doctor bills. Blue Cross and Blue Shield plans generally provide direct payment in full to "participating" hospitals and doctors for medical benefits provided to covered employees. A participating hospital or doctor is one that agrees to preestablished rates and billing schedules with Blue Cross or Blue Shield. If an employee is admitted to a hospital or uses a doctor that is not participating, the Blue Cross or Blue Shield plan pays or reimburses on a UCR basis.

Blue Cross and Blue Shield plans can be obtained by individuals as well as by employers. A basic principle of the "Blues" is to offer coverage to any individual who requests it and to provide terminating employees under an employer plan the ability to convert to an individual product.

Blue Cross (for hospital bills) and Blue Shield (for doctors' bills) are nonprofit organizations operating within a given geographical area. However, they must meet standards prescribed by their national associations. Recently, federal tax law was changed to provide income taxation of these organizations on a basis similar to insurance companies.

Self-Funding. With self-funding (self insurance), the employer pays claims and other costs directly, either on a pay-as-you-go basis (that is, the employer pays claims out of current operating revenues as they are incurred by covered employees), or out of a reserve fund accumulated in advance. (However, as indicated below, the employer can accelerate its tax deductions for health and accident plans only to a limited extent even if a fund is accumulated in advance.)

Self-funding can be combined with an insurance contract that provides "administrative services only" (an ASO contract). Also, the employer can obtain a "stop-loss" insurance contract under which plan claims above a stated level are assumed by the insurer. This protects the employer against large unanticipated losses.

A self-funded plan can be referred to as a "medical reimbursement" plan. However, the term medical expense reimbursement plan (MERP) is usually reserved for a plan designed to supplement existing insured health plans and to provide special tax benefits. These plans are discussed in Chapter 22.

ELIGIBILITY AND COVERAGE

Employer health insurance plans generally cover all employees. Employees are usually covered immediately upon being hired, or after a brief waiting period for coverage such as three months. Some employers maintain separate plans for collective bargaining unit employees or some other identifiable group.

If any health insurance plan of the employer does not meet the nondiscrimination rules of section 89 of the Code, the discriminatory portion of benefits under that plan is taxable to highly compensated employees.

Section 89 Nondiscrimination Rules

Section 89 provides detailed rules to prevent health plans from discriminating in favor of highly compensated employees, either in terms of plan coverage or benefits. In summary, these are:

1. *Highly compensated* is defined as it is for qualified plans under Code section 414(q) — Appendix A discusses the complete definition of this term, which is both precise and complicated.

2. The plan's *eligibility* provisions must meet three requirements in any testing year —

   — at least 90% of all nonhighly compensated employees are eligible and have available a benefit that is at least 50% of the largest employer-provided benefit available to any highly compensated employee under all health plans of the employer,

   — at least 50% of employees eligible for the plan are not highly compensated. This requirement is deemed met if the percentage of highly compensated eligible employees is no greater than the per-centage of nonhighly compensated eligible employees, and

   — the plan must contain no provision relating to eligibility that discriminates in favor of highly compensated employees.

3. For any testing year, the plan's *benefit* provisions are nondiscriminatory if the average employer-provided benefit received by nonhighly compensated employees is at least 75% of that received by highly compensated employees.

4. As an alternative to the tests listed in 2 and 3 above, a health plan is deemed nondiscriminatory for a testing year if at least 80 percent of the employer's nonhighly compensated employees are covered, and the plan does not contain participation requirements that discriminate in favor of highly compensated employees.

5. Under the Technical and Miscellaneous Revenue Act of 1988, compliance with Section 89 can be demonstrated on the basis of a statistically valid sample. This will simplify compliance for larger companies. Testing of benefits is to be done with respect to a "testing year" and on the basis of facts as of the "testing day" designated in the plan.

For a further discussion of Section 89, see Appendix F.

Continuation of Coverage

Many employers have plans that continue health insurance coverage for employees and their dependents for a period of time after termination of employment. Some methods of funding continued coverage after retirement are discussed in the "Questions and Answers," below.

Employer flexibility in this area is significantly limited since passage of the Consolidated Omnibus Budget Reconciliation Act of 1985 (COBRA). The COBRA continuation provisions apply for a given year if the employer had 20 or more employees on a typical business day in the preceding year. (Government and church plans are exempt.) COBRA *requires* continuation of coverage for former employees and their dependents in several situations.

In general, under COBRA the employer must provide the option to continue an employee's existing health plan coverage (including dependent coverage) for 36 months after the following events:

(a) death of the employee

(b) divorce or legal separation of the covered employee (coverage continues for the former spouse and dependents)

(c) the employee's entitlement to Medicare benefits

(d) filing by the employer for Chapter 11 bankruptcy

(e) a child ceasing to be a dependent for plan purposes

Health plan coverage must be continued for 18 months after termination of employment or reduction in hours of employment.

Continuation coverage can be terminated before the 36 (or 18) month period if

- the employer terminates its health plan for all employees

- the employee or beneficiary fails to pay his or her share of the premium

- the employee or beneficiary becomes covered under another group health plan.

The employer can require the former employee or beneficiary to pay part of the cost of continuation coverage. However, this former employee or beneficiary share can't be more than 102% of the cost to the plan of coverage for similarly situated beneficiaries with respect to whom a qualifying event has not occurred (whether the cost is paid by the employer or employee).

The requirement to provide for continuation of coverage became effective for plan years which began after July 1, 1986. Originally, the penalty for noncompliance with these requirements was disallowance of the employer's deduction. However, for tax years beginning after December 31, 1988, the penalty is, generally, a tax of $100 a day during the period any failure with respect to a qualified beneficiary continues.

TAX IMPLICATIONS

1. The employer may deduct the cost of health insurance premiums in an insured plan or benefits paid in an uninsured plan. Plan administrative expenses are also deductible.

2. Deductions for prefunding medical benefits (that is, setting funds aside and deducting amounts for medical benefits to be paid in future years) are limited under rules set out in Code sections 419 and 419A. Generally, for a given year an employer can deduct expenditures for medical benefits up to a limit equal to the total of (a) the direct costs of the plan for the year — claims paid plus administrative costs, plus (b) contributions to an asset account up to 35 percent of the preceding year's direct costs.

3. The employee does not have taxable income when (a) the employer pays insurance premiums, (b) when benefits are paid, or (c) when the plan reimburses the employee for covered expenses. However, highly compensated employees may have to pay taxes on these items to the extent they are discriminatory under the rules described above.

4. The employee is eligible for an itemized medical expense deduction under Code section 213 for (a) any portion of health insurance premiums paid by the employee, (b) unreimbursed out-of-pocket costs resulting from deductibles or coinsurance, and (c) any other medical expenses eligible for a Section 213 deduction. The Section 213 deduction is available only if the taxpayer itemizes deductions on the tax return. The deduction is limited to the amount by which the total of all eligible medical expenses exceeds 7.5% of the taxpayer's adjusted gross income.

5. If the following requirements of Section 89(k) are not met, all employees, not just the highly compensated employees, must include in income the value of the employer provided-benefits under the health plan (in this case, the reimbursements paid and services provided instead of the value of coverage):

- the plan must be in writing

- the plan must provide legally enforceable rights for employees

- employees must be notified of plan benefits

- the plan must be maintained for the exclusive benefit of employees

- the plan must be intended as a permanent plan

ERISA AND OTHER REQUIREMENTS

An employer's health and accident plan is a "welfare benefit plan" subject to the ERISA requirements discussed in Appendix D.

WHERE CAN I FIND OUT MORE ABOUT IT?

1. Beam, Burton T., Jr. and John J. McFadden, *Employee Benefits*, 2nd ed. Homewood, IL: Richard D. Irwin, 1988.

2. *Tax Facts 1*, Cincinnati, OH: The National Underwriter Co., (revised annually).

QUESTIONS AND ANSWERS

Question — How do employer health and accident benefits fit into a cafeteria or FSA plan?

Answer — Since employees have varying needs for health benefits (some may prefer lower deductibles, others may want broader coverage such as dental expense coverage, etc.), the plan can be made attractive to employees by offering a number of optional plans under a "cafeteria" arrangement. Cafeteria plans are discussed further in Chapter 2. One thing to note about multiple health plan options: each option is considered a separate "plan" for Section 89 nondiscrimination purposes. The availability of numerous optional health plans can make it more difficult to satisfy the Section 89 rules.

The flexible spending account (FSA) or salary reduction type of cafeteria plan offers another attractive possibility in the health care area. An FSA makes possible the conversion of after-tax employee expenditures in a health plan to nontaxable expenditures. Such expenditures include the employee share of health insurance, deductibles, coinsurance payments, and medical expenses not covered by the plan. These expenditures are technically deductible as itemized medical deductions under Code section 213, but because of the 7.5% of adjusted gross income floor, few employees will be able to deduct them. The FSA approach in effect allows these items to be excluded from taxable income without any floor limit. FSA plans are discussed in detail in Chapter 10.

Question — How can an employer fund or finance the continuation of health plan benefits for retirees?

Answer — The mandatory COBRA continuation provisions discussed earlier require continuation of health plan benefits in many situations where the employer probably would not do so voluntarily. Often, employers want to continue benefits for retirees and have done so for many years.

The main problem in providing postretirement benefits is cost. These benefits can be very expensive. Funding on a pay-as-you-go basis can present cash flow problems. Many employers prefer to fund these benefits in advance of the employee's retirement.

Three methods of providing postretirement health insurance benefits are commonly used; each has advantages and disadvantages.

(a) Require employees to pay for the continuation coverage, but increase qualified pension benefits accordingly. For example, assume the continuation plan could charge each employee $100 per month. The pension plan is amended to increase benefits by $100 per month, and this increased pension benefit can be funded in advance under the pension plan funding rules (see Appendix A). The main disadvantage of this is that the employee must pay taxes on the pension benefit, so the potentially tax-free nature of the health benefit is lost.

(b) Provide continued health insurance coverage as an "incidental" benefit under the qualified pension or profit-sharing plan. This allows the health coverage to be funded directly as part of the qualified plan cost. However, incidental benefits in a qualified plan cannot cost more than 25% of the aggregate plan cost (see Chapter 20). This potentially limits the amount of health coverage that can be funded in this manner.

(c) Fund continuation coverage through a separate trust fund. This fund can be designed as a "VEBA" or Code section 501(c)(9) organization. VEBAs are tax-exempt trusts used to fund employee benefits. There are two problems in using VEBAs in this situation.

First, investment earnings on the plan fund are considered taxable income, unlike earnings in a qualified plan fund. This raises the cost of using a VEBA for funding.

Second, advance funding of health benefits is limited under Code sections 419 and 419A. Although these provisions do allow a tax deduction for contributions to the VEBA used to fund future health benefits to retirees, compliance with these rules adds a level of complexity to the plan.

Due to recent tax law changes, many employers find that their qualified pension plans have become "overfunded." Planners have raised the possibility of using the surplus funding to pay for health benefits for retirees. This may be possible by amending the plan to add the health coverage as an incidental benefit. It is probably not possible to transfer the excess funds directly to a VEBA or other trust fund to finance continuation health coverage; the IRS position is that such a transfer constitutes a transfer or "reversion" of the funds to the employer, which is taxable at ordinary income rates to the employer and in addition carries a 15% penalty.

Question — Can a self-employed person (sole proprietor or partner in an unincorporated business) be covered under his business's health insurance plan and obtain any tax advantage?

Answer — A self-employed person can be covered under a business's health insurance plan. This may provide a more economical means of obtaining health benefits than individual insurance because of the group underwriting of an insured employer plan.

The cost of health insurance for a self-employed individual would ordinarily not be a deductible expense to the business because the self-employed individual is not considered an employee. However, a special Code provision, section 162(l), permits a limited special deduction in order to partially equalize the treatment of incorporated and unincorporated businesses in this regard. Under Section 162(l), a self-employed individual is entitled to a business expense deduction equal to 25 percent of the amount paid for health insurance under a health insurance plan meeting the requirements of Section 89 for the self-employed individual and his spouse and dependents. The deduction cannot exceed the self-employed individual's earned income for the year from the trade or business with respect to which the plan is established. The deduction cannot be used to reduce self-employment income subject to self-employment tax. Rules are provided to prevent duplication of deductions for other medical insurance covering the taxpayer or itemized medical expense deductions. This special deduction provision is scheduled to expire for taxable years beginning after 1989.

Question — What are the tax consequences of an employer plan that provides annual physical examinations to selected executives only?

Answer — A physical examination benefit is considered a health plan and is subject to the Section 89 nondiscrimination rules. Thus the value of annual physical examinations would be taxable to covered executives in a discriminatory plan.

Chapter 14

HEALTH MAINTENANCE ORGANIZATION (HMO)

WHAT IS IT?

A Health Maintenance Organization, or HMO, is an organization of physicians or other health care providers that provides a broad and nearly complete range of health care services on a prepaid basis. An HMO is an alternative to traditional health insurance.

WHEN IS IT INDICATED?

1. As an alternative to traditional health insurance, HMOs are attractive to younger employees and employees with many dependents because the HMO typically covers all medical expenses without significant deductibles or co-pay provisions. Where such employees are predominant in an employer's work force, the employer may get the most perceived value for its benefit dollar by offering an HMO, or choice of HMOs, as its health benefit plan.

2. In certain circumstances, employers *must* offer HMO coverage to employees as an alternative; see the discussion below.

ADVANTAGES

1. HMOs typically cover more health care services than traditional health insurance, with fewer deductibles. Typically there is no co-payment provision.

2. HMOs are said to emphasize preventive medicine, and thus control overall costs better than plans that pay only when employees are hospitalized or sick.

DISADVANTAGES

1. An HMO subscriber generally must receive care from a doctor or other service provider who is part of the HMO. Except for certain emergencies, the HMO will not pay for services of non-HMO providers.

2. The cost advantage, if any, of HMOs may be due to the fact that they enroll younger and healthier participants than traditional health insurance plans, which emphasize coverage for major medical procedures. In time, therefore, the cost advantage of HMOs will diminish.

HMO BENEFIT STRUCTURE

Conventional health insurance reimburses employees for expenses or pays providers for health care as required by covered employees. By contrast, an HMO either employs the providers or contracts directly with providers (see the discussion below on types of HMO). The providers agree to provide medical services to HMO subscribers when required, in return for an annual payment determined *in advance*. Each subscriber to the HMO (or employer who sponsors the plan) pays a fee based on the HMO's projected annual cost.

As a result of this arrangement, the HMO assumes the risk that services required will cost more than the annual payment. In other words, the HMO has an incentive to hold down the costs of health care to subscribers. In theory, these reduced costs will be passed along in the form of reduced costs to the HMO subscribers or to employers who pay for the plan.

HMO subscribers generally must use physicians and other health care providers who are part of the HMO contractual arrangement. Exceptions are usually allowed for emergency services out of the HMO's geographic area, and for medical specialties not available within the HMO, if referred by the primary HMO physician. In return for this reduction in freedom of choice, HMO plans provide for almost all health care services, including routine physician visits. (The HMO must provide broad coverage in order to become *federally qualified* as discussed below.) Usually there are no deductibles. There may be a small copayment fee for some services. For example, subscribers may be required to pay $2 for each visit to a doctor's office and $2.50 for each prescription.

A comparison of one employer's insured health plan with two alternative HMOs is included at the end of this chapter to give some idea of the benefits provided under typical HMO plans and how they differ from insured plans. See Figure 14.1 at the end of this chapter.

TYPES OF HMOs

HMOs are organized in one of three ways:

(1) the *staff model* HMO is an HMO organization that directly employs doctors and other health care providers who provide the HMO's services to subscribers.

(2) the *group practice* or medical group model involves contracts between the HMO and a medical group or groups that provide services to subscribers. The individual doctors and other providers are not directly employed by the HMO as an entity.

Both staff model and group practice HMOs are sometimes referred to as *closed panel* plans, because subscribers must use doctors and other providers who are employed by the HMO or under contract to the HMO.

(3) the *individual practice association* or IPA plan, under which the HMO is an association of individual doctors or medical groups that practice in their own offices. Most see non-HMO as well as HMO patients. These plans are often referred to as *open panel* plans, since HMO subscribers can choose any doctor who is part of the IPA. In some areas, many doctors participate in these plans, giving HMO subscribers a wide range of choice.

The structure of an HMO is relevant to an employer's benefit planning in that different types of HMOs may have varying attractiveness to employees. Many employees may be reluctant to give up their own doctors in order to sign up with an unfamiliar closed-panel type of HMO. On the other hand, the choice of doctors in a large IPA plan may be appealing. The IPA may even include some employees' own doctors already. So, an HMO affiliation may effectively change nothing from some employees' viewpoints except to drastically lower the cost of their doctor bills.

The appeal of HMOs in a given geographical area depends in large part on the local medical community's support of the HMO concept. If local doctors and hospitals, particularly the most prestigious ones, are in favor of HMOs, then many local health care providers will join HMOs. HMO subscribers will then have almost the same amount of choice as they would in a conventional insured plan.

FEDERAL HMO ACT REQUIREMENTS

Congress enacted the Health Maintenance Organization Act of 1973 to encourage HMOs as a way of keeping down health care costs. Under this Act, an employer may be required to offer HMO coverage to employees as an alternative to Blue Cross/Blue Shield coverage or conventional insurance. This is referred to as the "dual choice" option. (Under current legislation, the dual choice option is scheduled to expire in 1995.) The dual choice option is required if all of the following conditions exist:

(a) The employer is subject to the minimum wage requirements of the Fair Labor Standards Act.

(b) The employer has 25 or more employees, counting both full and part time employees.

(c) The employer has a health care plan for which the employer pays part or all.

(d) The employer has received a request from an HMO to make coverage available to its employees. The HMO must be *federally qualified* and at least 25 of the employer's employees must reside in the HMO's geographically defined operating area.

An HMO must meet various requirements of the HMO Act and accompanying federal regulations in order to be federally qualified. In addition, the employer may not financially discriminate against employees who elect the HMO.

The most important of the requirements for a federally qualified HMO lists the minimum basic benefits the HMO must provide to subscribers in return for the prepaid annual fee. These services must be provided at no additional cost or for a nominal copayment fee. The required services are:

- Physicians' services, including specialist consultant and referral services

- Inpatient and outpatient hospital services

- Emergency health services

- Outpatient mental health services up to 20 visits

- Medical care for alcohol or drug addiction

- Laboratory and radiologic (x-ray) diagnostic services

- Home health services

- Preventive services (immunizations, physical examinations, family planning, well-baby care)

- Medical social services (education in health or medical care)

Many HMOs provide services in addition to those required for federal qualification; for example dental or vision care services, prescription drugs (usually for a small copayment), additional mental health services, or nursing and rehabilitation facilities.

TAX IMPLICATIONS

The tax treatment of payments to HMOs and benefits received is the same as that for health insurance, described in Chapter 13.

WHERE CAN I FIND OUT MORE ABOUT IT?

1. Beam, Burton T., Jr. and John J. McFadden, *Employee Benefits*, 2nd ed. Homewood, IL: Richard D. Irwin, 1988.

QUESTIONS AND ANSWERS

Question — If a federally qualified HMO makes a request for coverage to an employer, is the employer obligated to offer that particular HMO to employees?

Answer — The dual choice provision requires only that the employer make an HMO available to employees in the particular geographical region where the requesting HMO operates. The HMO made available does not have to be the one making the request. The employer may choose which HMOs to make available.

Figure 14.1

	EMPLOYER, INC. Comparison of Health Care Benefits		
	Insured Plan	Health Maintenance Organization A	Health Maintenance Organization B
TYPE OF PLAN	Health insurance plan covering, full, or partial, cost of medical services after they are provided	Prepaid Individual Practice Association — HMO A contracts with private physicians' offices located in the community.	Prepaid Group Practice Plan — a team of physicians and medical professionals practice together to provide members preventive, comprehensive care for a fixed, advanced payment
CHOICE OF PHYSICIAN	Member may select any licensed physician or surgeon.	Member selects a physician from one of the 230 primary medical offices. All types of specialists are available by referral.	Member selects a personal physician from the Health America medical group who coordinates and directs all health care needs including referrals to specialists.
WHERE PRIMARY AND SPECIALITY CARE IS AVAILABLE	Care provided in physician's office or outpatient facility.	Care provided in HMO-A participating private physician's offices (see brochure for locations).	Care provided at 5 multi-specialty centers (see brochure for locations).
CHOICE OF HOSPITALS	Member may select any accredited hospital. Choice depends on where physician has admitting privileges.	Member goes to hospital where physician has admitting privileges.	Selection among HMO-B participating hospitals (see brochure for locations).
DEDUCTIBLE AND COINSURANCE	Annual deductible; $200 individual, $500 Family. 10% or 50% coinsurance on covered charges after satisfying deductible. Selected procedures/care covered in full, no deductible. No coinsurance on covered services after $4,000, individual $10,000 Family annual expense incurred.	No deductible. No coinsurance (except small co-payments for office visits, home visits, prescriptions and out-patient mental health and other deductibles as noted in the comparison).	No deductible. No coinsurance except small co-payments for outpatient mental health.
MAXIMUM BENEFIT	No lifetime maximum.	No overall maximum limit.	No overall maximum limit.

Tools and Techniques

Figure 14.1 (cont.)

PREVENTIVE CARE			
Routine Physicians	Not covered.	Covered in full.	Covered in full.
Well Baby Care	Covered at 90%.	Covered in full.	Covered in full.
Pap Smears	Routine Exams not covered.	Covered in full.	Covered in full; care provided by Gynecologist.
Immunizations	Not covered.	Covered in full.	Covered in full.
Eye Exam	Not covered.	Covered in full and $35 allowance for eyeglasses or contact lenses.	Covered in full including written prescriptions for lenses.
Hearing Exam	Not covered.	Covered in full.	Covered in full.
Health Education	Available through some physicians' offices.	Weight watchers programs, YMCA physical fitness program, other programs offered periodically.	Periodic classes held on diet, prenatal care and physical fitness, smoking cessation, stress management, etc. Discount programs at many Nautilus clubs and health spas.

PHYSICIAN CARE			
Surgery	Outpatient—covered at 100% no deductible. (Charges for hospital, surgicenter or miscellaneous physician's expense connected to outpatient surgery covered at 90% after deductible.) Inpatient-covered at 90% after deductible. Specified elective procedures require 2nd opinion to ensure unreduced benefits.	Covered in full.	Covered in full.
Inpatient Visits	Covered at 90% after satisfying deductible.	Covered in full.	Covered in full.
Office and Home	Covered at 90% after satisfying deductible.	Office visits covered with $2 co-pay at primary office. Physician home visits covered with $5 co-pay. No co-pay for specialist visits.	Office visits covered in full. Home visits covered in full.
X-rays and Lab	Pre-Admission status— covered at 100% with no deductible. Other instances covered at 90% after satisfying deductible when deemed medically necessary.	Covered in full.	Covered in full.

Figure 14.1 (cont.)

HOSPITAL SERVICES			
Room and Board	Covered at 90% for unlimited days after satisfying deductible.	Covered in full for unlimited days in semiprivate room (Private room covered in full when medically necessary.)	Covered in full for unlimited days in semiprivate room. (Private room covered in full when medically necessary.)
Supplies, Tests, Medication, etc.	Covered at 90% after satisfying deductible. In hospital charges in connection with a scheduled surgical procedure incurred more than 24 hours prior are not covered.	Covered in full.	Covered in full.
Private Duty Nurse	Covered at 90% after satisfying deductible up to a maximum of $1,000 a year.	Covered in full when medically necessary.	Covered in full when medically necessary.
EMERGENCY CARE	Covered at 100% with no deductible if rendered in physician's office or an emergency care center within 48 hours of accidental injury. Hospital emergency room service covered at 90% after the deductible.	Covered with $15 Co-pay at hospital and $5 Co-pay at doctor's office.	Covered in full for around-the-clock emergency care by HMO-B physicians and in participating hospitals. Emergency care by non-HMO-B physicians or hospitals also covered when obtaining HMO-B care is not reasonable because of distance and urgency.
Ambulance Service	Covered at 90% for local transportation after satisfying deductible when medically necessary.	Covered in full when medically necessary.	Covered in full.
MATERNITY CARE			
Hospital	Co-pays and deductibles apply. See Hospital Services.	Covered in full.	Covered in full.
Physician	Co-pay and deductibles apply. See Physician Care.	Covered in full.	Covered in full.
Waiting Period	No waiting period — limitation of pre-existing conditions apply.	No waiting period.	No waiting period.

Tools and Techniques

Figure 14.1 (cont.)

MENTAL HEALTH CARE			
Hospital	Co-pays and deductibles apply. See Hospital Services.	Covered in full for 35 days per year.	Covered in full for 45 days per 12 months.
Inpatient physician	Co-pays and deductibles apply. See Physician Care.	Covered in full 35 days per year.	Covered in full for 45 days per 12 months.
Outpatient physician	Covered at 50% up to $40 per visit and $1,000 per year.	Covered for 20 visits per year. First 2 visits covered in full. Next 8 visits you pay $10 per visit. Next 10 visits, you pay $25 per visit. Member charge never exceeds 50% of fee.	Covered for 30 visits per 12 months. First 3 visits covered in full. Next 27 visits you pay $10 per visit.
Alcohol and Drug Addiction	Covered as other mental health services.	Covered in full for acute phase of alcohol or drug abuse.	No special limits. Covered as other medical and mental health services. Detoxification covered for acute phase only.
DENTAL CARE			
Hospital	Separate Dental option offered to all employees — Contact Personnel for details.	Covered for: hospital costs when confinement is necessary for dental care due to covered medical problem; treatment of accidental injury to natural teeth occurring while insured; impacted wisdom teeth, partially, or totally covered by bone.	Covered for: hospital costs when confinement is necessary for dental care; and treatment of accidental injury to natural teeth occurring while insured; and certain oral surgical procedures, e.g., impacted wisdom teeth partially or totally covered by bone.
Office visits	Separate Dental option offered to all employees.	Oral hygiene exams for children under 12, including cleaning and scaling to teeth, instruction and fluoride treatment.	Covered for: 2 checkups and 1 cleaning per year, 20% discount on other dental services including speciality areas and orthodontia at participating dental offices.
OUTPATIENT MEDICATION			
Prescription Drug	Covered at 90% after deductible.	Covered w/$2.50 Co-pay.	Covered w/$2 Co-pay.
Injections	Covered at 90% after deductible.	Covered in full.	Covered in full.

Figure 14.1 (cont.)

PRESCRIBED HOME HEALTH SERVICES	Home Health Extension Services paid at 100% with no deductible if recommended by discharging hospital.	Covered in full except for travel.	Covered in full.
ALLERGY CARE	Covered at 90% after deductible.	Covered in full.	Covered in full.
ELIGIBILITY	Spouse; and unmarried dependent children to age 19 or age 23 if a full time student.	Spouse; and unmarried dependent children to age 19 or age 23 if a full time student.	Spouse; and unmarried dependent children to age 19 or age 23 if a full time student.
MEDICARE	Regular plan coverage continued coordinated with Medicare.	Medicare plan available.	Medicare coordinated benefit available.
CONVERSION	Conversion to individual coverage available.	Conversion to HMO-PA Non-Group coverage available. RX is not available for conversion.	Conversion to HSP Non-Group coverage available.

NOTE: This comparison is not a contract. It is intended to highlight some of the principal differences between the plans. For a more detailed description of benefits, refer to the benefits brochures of each plan.

Chapter 15

HR 10 (KEOGH) PLAN

WHAT IS IT?

A Keogh plan, sometimes referred to as an HR 10 plan, is a qualified retirement plan that covers one or more self-employed individuals. A self-employed individual is a sole proprietor or partner who works in his or her unincorporated business. Like all qualified plans, a Keogh plan enables those covered under the plan to accumulate a private retirement fund that will supplement their other pension and Social Security benefits.

A Keogh plan works much like any qualified plan; the details of the various types of qualified plans such as defined benefit, money purchase, or profit-sharing plans are discussed in separate chapters of this book. This chapter focuses on the special features of a qualified plan that covers self-employed individuals.

WHEN IS IT INDICATED?

1. When long-term capital accumulation, particularly for retirement purposes, is an important objective of a self-employed business owner.

2. When an owner of an unincorporated business wishes to adopt a plan providing retirement benefits for regular employees as an incentive and employee benefit, as well as retirement savings for the business owner.

3. When a self-employed person has a need to shelter some current earnings from federal income tax.

4. When an employee has self-employment income as well as income from employment, and wishes to invest as much as possible of the self-employment income and defer taxes on it.

ADVANTAGES

1. Keogh contributions are deducted from taxable income and the tax is deferred until funds are withdrawn from the plan at a later date.

2. Income generated by the investments in a Keogh plan is also free of income taxes until it is withdrawn from the plan. This reinvestment of income and build-up of tax deferred earnings is one of the main features that make Keogh plans attractive.

    For example, the following table shows the results of investing $7,500 annually in a Keogh plan where the rate of return is 8 percent, compounded daily:

Number of Years	Total Contribution	Tax Deferred Interest	Total Value
5	$ 37,500	$ 10,645	$ 48,145
10	75,000	45,365	120,365
15	112,500	116,201	228,701
20	150,000	241,213	391,213
25	187,500	447,490	634,990

As can be seen, the tax-deferred earnings portion of the program will eventually exceed the amount of personal annual contributions. This is a strong incentive to start early and continue to make the largest possible contribution to such a plan.

3. Certain lump sum distributions from Keogh plans may be eligible for favorable 5-year (or 10-year) averaging income tax treatment.

4. The limits on Keogh plan contributions are more liberal than those applied to IRAs (individual retirement accounts). IRAs have an annual contribution limit of $2,000 ($2,250 for spousal IRAs) as compared with the maximum contribution of $30,000 permitted under a Keogh plan. Thus, a self-employed person may contribute up to 15 times as much to a Keogh plan as a person may contribute to an IRA. In addition, deductions for IRA contributions may be limited if the individual (or his spouse) is an active participant in a qualified retirement plan (see Chapter 17).

5. From the viewpoint of an employee of an unincorporated business, Keogh plans are advantageous because employees of the business must participate in the plan (within the limits of the coverage requirements for qualified plans described in Appendix A).

DISADVANTAGES

1. Keogh plans involve all the costs and complexity associated with qualified plans. However, for a small plan, particularly one covering only one self-employed individual, it is relatively easy to minimize these factors by using prototype plans offered by insurance companies, mutual funds, banks, and other financial institutions.

2. If a self-employed person has a significant number of employees, the qualified plan coverage requirements, which require nondiscriminatory plan coverage (see Appendix A), may increase the cost of the plan substantially.

Tools and Techniques

3. As with all qualified plans, there is a 10% penalty, in addition to regular federal income tax, for withdrawal of plan funds generally before age 59½, death, or disability (see Appendix B).

4. Again as with regular qualified plans, benefit payments from the plan generally must begin by April 1 of the year after the plan participant attains age 70½, even if the participant is not retired. There is a penalty for noncompliance (see Appendix B). Thus, Keogh plans, like all qualified plans, can not be viewed as a means of avoiding income tax and passing assets to succeeding generations tax free.

5. Loans from the plan to a plan participant who is an owner-employee (a self-employed person owning more than 10% of the business) are "prohibited transactions" subject to penalty. Thus, owner-employees cannot make use of plan loans which are permitted (up to $50,000 or half the vested benefit) for regular employees. (However, a loan to an owner-employee is permitted if the Department of Labor grants an administrative exemption from the prohibited transaction rules with respect to such a loan.)

6. Life insurance in a qualified plan for a self-employed person, described below, is treated somewhat less favorably than for regular employees.

TYPES OF KEOGH PLANS

In general any type of qualified plan can be designed to cover self-employed persons. However, the typical Keogh plan covering one self-employed person, and possibly the spouse of the self-employed person, as well as a few employees, is usually designed as either (a) a profit-sharing plan or (b) a money purchase plan.

In a *profit-sharing plan* the annual contribution can be any amount up to 15% of the total payroll of plan participants. Plan contributions can be omitted entirely in a bad year. However, the IRS requires "substantial and recurring" contributions or the plan may be deemed terminated. This contribution flexibility is very advantageous for a small business whose income typically may fluctuate substantially from year to year.

For a self-employed person with earned income of $200,000 or more — not unusual for a successful professional — the 15% profit-sharing limit permits the maximum possible plan contribution available under any kind of defined contribution plan. Under Code section 415, annual contributions to a defined contribution plan can never be more than $30,000 annually (as indexed for inflation — see Appendix A). Fifteen percent of $200,000 of earned income produces the maximum annual contribution of $30,000 for this successful professional, so there is no reason to adopt any defined contribution plan other than a profit-sharing

plan. (See below for a discussion of the special definition of "earned income" of self-employed persons.)

A *money purchase plan* permits annual contributions for each self-employed person of 25% of earned income (25% of compensation for any regular employees covered under the plan) up to the $30,000 dollar limit. However, a money purchase plan is subject to the Code's minimum funding requirements (see Appendix A). These require the employer to make contributions to each employee's and self-employed person's account each year equal to a percentage of compensation stated in the plan. For plan years after 1988, these contributions must be made on at least a quarterly basis. And, such contributions must be made regardless of good or bad business results for the year.

A self-employed person can adopt other types of qualified plans as well. A defined benefit plan (see Chapter 6) is attractive to the older self-employed person who is just starting a plan, because the actuarial funding approach allows a greater relative contribution for older plan participants. Often considerably more can be contributed annually to a defined benefit plan than the $30,000 maximum for defined contribution plans.

A target plan (see Chapter 33) permits funding based on age like a defined benefit plan, but with annual funding limited to the lesser of $30,000 or 25% of earned income or compensation. The target plan is attractive because of its simplicity, and the 25%/$30,000 limit permits adequate contribution levels for self-employed persons earning relatively lower amounts.

HOW ARE KEOGHS DIFFERENT FROM OTHER QUALIFIED PLANS?

The unique feature of a Keogh plan, as compared with qualified plans adopted by corporations, is that the Keogh plan covers self-employed individuals, who are not technically considered "employees." This leads to some significant special rules for self-employed individuals covered under the plan.

Earned Income

The most important special rule is the definition of earned income. For a self-employed individual, "earned income" takes the place of "compensation" in applying the qualified plan rules. Earned income is defined as the self-employed individual's net income from the business after all deductions *including the deduction for Keogh plan contributions*.

Example: Dot Matrix is a self-employed computer consultant with no regular employees. She earned $100,000 of net income in 1989, after all deductions (not counting Keogh plan deductions). She adopts a money purchase Keogh plan for 1989. (This must be done by the end of 1989, as with any qualified plan — see Appendix C. A simplified employee pension plan is an alternative for "late" adoption — see Chapter 30). How much can Dot put into the plan for 1989?

A money purchase plan permits an annual contribution of up to 25% of compensation or earned income, with a maximum of $30,000. Dot's earned income is determined by subtracting her Keogh contribution from $100,000. This requires an algebraic computation. If Dot contributes $20,000 to the plan, her earned income will be $80,000. The $20,000 contribution is just 25% of the $80,000 earned income figure. Thus, $20,000 is Dot's maximum Keogh contribution for 1989.

In the example above, 25% of earned income turned out to be 20% of net income without considering the Keogh contribution. Since many self-employed individuals are in a situation similar to Dot's, (a sole practitioner with no employees) it is useful to develop a table to show the relationship between various percentages of earned income and the equivalent percentage of net income.

The algebraic formula for this is not too complicated. Suppose you want to contribute x percent of earned income to a Keogh plan. If net income is, say $100,000, multiply $100,000 by $x / (100 + x)$. The table below works out the value of $x / (100 + x)$ for various percentages.

This percentage of earned income	is equivalent to	this percentage of net income
5		4.76
6		5.66
7		6.54
8		7.41
9		8.26
10		9.09
11		9.91
12		10.71
13		11.50
14		12.28
15		13.04
16		13.79
17		14.53
18		15.25
19		15.97
20		16.67
21		17.36
22		18.03
23		18.70
24		19.35
25		20.00

Example: Frank Slick is a lawyer and sole practitioner with no employees. He has a Keogh profit-sharing plan and earns $100,000 of net income in 1989. He wants to make the maximum contribution which, for a profit-sharing plan, is 15% of covered payroll (earned income or compensation). From the table, 15% of earned income is equivalent to 13.04% of net income. Therefore, Frank can contribute $13,040 to the plan in 1989.

Life Insurance

Life insurance can be used as an incidental benefit in a plan covering self-employed individuals, but the tax treatment for the self-employed individuals is different from that applicable to regular employees in a qualified plan.

The entire cost of life insurance for regular employees is deductible as a plan contribution. Employees then pick up the value of the pure life insurance element as extra taxable compensation valued under the "P.S. 58" table (see Chapter 20).

By contrast, for a self-employed individual, the pure life insurance element of an insurance premium is *not* deductible. Only the portion of the premium that exceeds the pure protection value of the insurance is deductible. The pure protection value of the insurance is determined using the P.S. 58 table. Since all income and deductions flow automatically to the owners in an unincorporated business, the nondeductible life insurance element in effect becomes additional taxable income to the self-employed individual.

Example: Leo, a self-employed individual, has a Keogh plan providing incidental insurance through a cash value life insurance contract. The 1989 premium is $3,000, of which $1,200 is for pure life insurance protection and the remainder is used to increase the cash value. Leo can deduct $1,800 of the premium as a plan contribution. The remaining $1,200 is nondeductible. Leo therefore must pay tax on the $1,200 used for pure life insurance protection.

Another difference in the treatment of life insurance comes when benefits are paid from the plan. Regular employees have a "cost basis" (a nontaxable recovery element) in a plan equal to any P.S. 58 costs they have included in income in the past, so long as the plan distribution is made from the same life insurance contract on which P.S. 58 costs were paid (see Chapter 20). For a self-employed individual, however, the P.S. 58 costs, although effectively included in income since they were nondeductible, are not includable in cost basis.

Loans

Qualified plans can make loans to regular employees, within a $50,000 maximum and certain other limits (see Appendix B). However, loans to an "owner-employee" are prohibited transactions under the Internal Revenue Code. An owner-employee is a self-employed person who is either a sole proprietor or a partner owning more than 10% of the business.

A prohibited transaction does not cause a plan to become disqualified and lose all tax benefits. However, there is a two-level penalty tax on prohibited transactions. The initial tax is five percent of the amount involved, with an additional tax of 100% of the amount involved if the transaction is not rescinded.

Because this rule arbitrarily penalizes owner-employees, as compared with business owners who incorporate their businesses, Congress recently changed the law to permit a plan to make a loan to an owner-employee if the Department of Labor grants an administrative exemption from the prohibited transaction rules with respect to such a loan.

TAX AND ERISA IMPLICATIONS

Except for the differences described just above, Keogh plans have the same tax and ERISA implications as regular qualified plans. For example, see Chapter 25 for the tax treatment of Keogh profit-sharing plans, etc.

The annual reporting requirement for qualified plans has been simplified for many Keogh plans and other small plans. If a plan covers only the business owner or partners, or the owner or partners and their spouses, the reporting requirement is satisfied by filing Form 5500EZ instead of the longer form 5500C. A sample Form 5500EZ is included at the end of this chapter.

ALTERNATIVES

1. The disadvantages, if any, of Keogh status of any qualified plan can be eliminated if the business owner incorporates the business and adopts a corporate plan. The owner is then a shareholder and employee of the corporation. Generally under current law it is not advantageous to incorporate a business simply to obtain corporate treatment for qualified plans. Incorporation may result in higher taxes overall and the advantages of corporate plans over Keogh plans are minimal in most cases.

2. A simplified employee pension (SEP) may be even simpler to adopt than a Keogh plan, particularly if only one self-employed individual is covered. In addition, SEPs can be adopted as late as the individual's tax return filing date, when it is too late to adopt a new Keogh plan. SEP contributions, however, are limited to 15% of earned income. See Chapter 20 for more discussion of SEPs.

3. Tax deductible IRAs are available up to $2,000 annually, if the individual (or his spouse) is not an active participant in a qualified plan. The $2,000 deduction is subject to cutbacks based on adjusted gross income if the individual (or his spouse) is an active participant in a qualified plan (see Chapter 17). Because of these limitations, a Keogh plan often permits much greater levels of tax-deferred savings.

HOW TO INSTALL A PLAN

A Keogh plan follows the installation procedure for qualified plans described in Appendix C. However, in adopting a Keogh plan it is customary to use a "prototype" plan designed by a bank, insurance company, mutual fund, or other financial institution. With a prototype, the sponsoring institution does most of the paperwork involved in installing the plan, at low or nominal cost to the self-employed individual. In return, the self-employed individual must keep most or all of the plan funds invested with that institution.

WHERE CAN I FIND OUT MORE ABOUT IT?

1. Banks, insurance companies, and other financial institutions actively market Keogh plans and will usually provide extensive information about their services.

2. IRS Publication 560, *Self-Employed Retirement Plans*, covers Keogh plans in detail. It is revised annually and available free from the IRS.

3. *Tax Facts 1*, Cincinnati, OH, The National Underwriter Co. (revised annually).

QUESTIONS AND ANSWERS

Question — Who can establish a Keogh retirement plan?

Answer — Any sole proprietor or partnership, whether or not the business has employees — for example, doctors, lawyers, accountants, writers, etc. Generally, employees of the business must be included as participants in the plan on the same general basis as the key employees.

Question — Can I collect benefits if I become disabled?

Answer — In the event that any participant in the plan becomes so disabled as to render him or her unable to engage in any substantial gainful activity, all contributed amounts plus earnings may be paid immediately without being subject to a premature distribution penalty.

Question — What happens to my plan if I die?

Answer — In the event that any participant dies, all contributed amounts plus earnings may be immediately paid to the participant's designated beneficiary or estate.

Question — May I set up a Keogh plan in addition to an Individual Retirement Account?

Answer — Yes. If you are eligible to set up a Keogh plan you may also create an IRA as well. Remember, though, that the general limit on IRA contributions is $2,000 ($2,250 for an individual and spousal IRA). Also, because you are an active participant in the Keogh plan, IRA contributions will not be tax deductible if your income is above certain limits (see Chapter 17).

Question — Can a Keogh plan be established if the self-employed person is covered under a corporate retirement plan of an employer?

Answer — Yes. An individual who works for a regular employer, and is covered under that employer's qualified plan, can establish a separate Keogh plan for an additional business carried on separately as a self-employed individual. For example, an engineering professor at a university may have additional income earned as a consulting engineer for outside clients. A Keogh plan will shelter some of that income from taxation and provide increased retirement savings on a tax-favored basis. The deduction limits for Keogh contributions are not affected unless the individual also controls or owns the regular employer.

For example, suppose the engineer earns $60,000 this year from his university position and is covered under the university's qualified pension plan. The engineer earns an additional $40,000 in consulting fees from outside clients. If he adopts a Keogh money purchase plan for this year, he can contribute and deduct up to $8,000 (25% of earned income or 20% of net income) to the Keogh plan.

Form **5500EZ**

Department of the Treasury
Internal Revenue Service

Please type or
machine print

Annual Return of One-Participant (Owners and Their Spouses) Pension Benefit Plan

For the calendar year 1988 or fiscal plan year beginning [   ] , 19 [   ] ,
and ending [   ] , 19 [   ]

5588   ▶ **For Paperwork Reduction Act Notice, see page 1 of the instructions.**

OMB No. 1545-0956

1988

This Form Is Open to Public Inspection

This return is: *(i)* ☐ the first return filed *(ii)* ☐ an amended return *(iii)* ☐ the final return *(iv)* ☐ filed for identification purposes

Use IRS label. Otherwise, please type or machine print.

1a Name of employer

Address (number and street)

City or town, state, and ZIP code

1b Employer identification number

1c Telephone number of employer

1d If plan year has changed since last return, check here . . . . . ▶ ☐

2a *(i)* Name of plan ▶ _____

_____

(ii) ☐   Check if name of plan has changed since last return

2b Date plan first became effective

Month   Day   Year

2c Enter three-digit plan number . . ▶ ☐ ☐ ☐

		Month	Year	Yes	No
3a	Enter the date the most recent plan amendment was adopted				
b	Enter the date of the most recent IRS determination letter				
c	Is a determination letter request pending with IRS?				

4 Enter the number of other qualified pension benefit plans maintained by the employer . . . ▶ _____

5 Type of plan: *a* ☐ Defined benefit pension plan (attach Schedule B (Form 5500)) *b* ☐ Money purchase plan
c ☐ Profit-sharing plan   *d* ☐ Stock bonus or ESOP plan

6 Were there any noncash contributions made to the plan during the plan year? . . . .

7 Enter the number of participants in each category listed below:

		Number
a	Less than age 59½ at the end of the plan year	**7a**
b	Age 59½ or more at the end of the plan year, but less than age 70½ at the beginning of the plan year . . .	**b**
c	Age 70½ or more at the beginning of the plan year.	**c**

8a A fully insured plan with no trust and which is funded entirely by allocated insurance contracts that fully guarantee the amount of benefit payments should check the box at the right and not complete 8b through 10d . . . . ☐

b	Contributions received for this plan year	**8b**
c	Net plan income other than from contributions	**c**
d	Plan distributions	**d**
e	Plan expenses other than distributions	**e**

Note: *Do not complete 9 through 12 if this plan completed items 8 through 12 as applicable on the 1986 or 1987 Form 5500EZ.*

9a	Total plan assets at the end of the year	**9a**
b	Total plan liabilities at the end of the year	**b**

10 During the plan year, if any of the following transactions took place between the plan and a party-in-interest (see instructions), check "Yes" and enter amount. Otherwise, check "No."

			Yes	Amount	No
a	Sale, exchange, or lease of property	**10a**			
b	Loan or extension of credit	**b**			
c	Acquisition or holding of employer securities	**c**			
d	Payment by the plan for services	**d**			

		Yes	No
11a	Does your business have any employees other than you and your spouse (and your partners and their spouses)? If "No," do NOT complete the rest of this question; go to question 12.		
b	Total number of employees (including you and your spouse and your partners and their spouses) ▶ _____		
c	Does this plan meet the percentage tests of Code section 410(b)(1)(A)? . . . . See the specific instructions for line 11c.		

12 Answer this question only if there was a benefit payment, loan, or distribution of an annuity contract made during the plan year and the plan is subject to the spousal consent requirements (see instructions).

a Was there consent of the participant's spouse to any benefit payment or loan within the 90-day period prior to such payment or loan? .

b If "No," check the reason for no consent: *(i)* ☐ the participant was not married
(ii) ☐ the benefit payment made was part of a qualified joint and survivor annuity *(iii)* ☐ other
c Were any annuity contracts purchased by the plan and distributed to the participants? . . . .

Under penalties of perjury and other penalties set forth in the instructions, I declare that I have examined this return, including accompanying schedules and statements, and to the best of my knowledge and belief, it is true, correct, and complete.

Date ▶ _____   Signature of employer/plan sponsor ▶ _____

For IRS Use Only

| 1 | 1 | 1 | 1 | 1 | 1 | 2 | 2 | 2 | 2 | 2 | 2 | 2 | 3 | 4 | 4 | 4 | 4 | 5 | 6 | 7 | 8 | |

★ U.S.GPO:1988-0-205-304

Chapter 16

INCENTIVE STOCK OPTION (ISO)

WHAT IS IT?

An incentive stock option (ISO) plan is a tax-favored plan for compensating executives by granting options to buy company stock. Unlike regular stock options, ISOs generally do not result in taxable income to executives either at time of the grant or the time of the exercise of the option. If the ISO meets the requirements of Internal Revenue Code section 422A, the executive is taxed only when stock purchased under the ISO is sold. (Regular or "nonstatutory" stock options are discussed in Chapter 32. Also, see Appendix E for a comprehensive outline of stock option and similar plans used for compensating executives, particularly in large corporations.)

WHEN IS IT INDICATED?

ISOs are primarily used by larger corporations to compensate executives. ISOs are generally not suitable for closely held corporations because (a) ISOs are valuable to executives only when stock can be sold, and there is usually no ready market for closely held stock, and (b) shareholders of closely held corporations often do not want unrelated outsiders to become shareholders of the company.

ADVANTAGES

1. The ISO provides greater deferral of taxes to the executive than a nonstatutory stock option (see Chapter 32).

2. The ISO is a form of compensation with little or no out-of-pocket cost to the company. The real cost of stock options is that the company forgoes the opportunity to sell the same stock on the market and realize its proceeds for company purposes.

DISADVANTAGES

1. The corporation granting an ISO option does not ordinarily receive a tax deduction for it at any time.

2. The plan must meet complex technical requirements of Code section 422A and related provisions.

3. The exercise price of ISO options must be at least equal to the fair market value of the stock when the option is granted. There is no similar restriction on nonstatutory options.

4. There is no preferential capital gain tax rate at this time. Therefore, the taxation of the ISO is relatively less beneficial than in the past. The value of an ISO's tax deferral is accordingly reduced.

5. An executive may incur an alternative minimum tax (AMT) liability when an ISO option is granted or exercised.

TAX IMPLICATIONS

1. The executive is not subject to federal income tax on an ISO either at the time he is granted the option or at the time he exercises the option (i.e., when he buys the stock). Tax consequences are deferred until the time of disposition of the stock.

2. In order to obtain this tax treatment for incentive stock options, Section 422A prescribes the following rules:

   • the options must be granted under a written plan specifying the number of shares to be issued and the class of employees covered under the plan. There are no nondiscrimination rules; the plan can cover key executives only.

   • only the first $100,000 worth of ISO stock granted any one employee, which becomes exercisable for the first time during any one year, is entitled to the favorable ISO treatment; to the extent that the value of the stock exceeds $100,000, this amount is treated as a non-statutory (regular) stock option.

   • no option, by its terms, may be exercisable more than ten years from the date of grant.

   • the person receiving the option must be employed by the company granting the option at all times between the grant of the option and three months before the date of exercise (twelve months in the case of disability, and no limit in the event of death).

   • stock acquired by an employee under the ISO must be held for at least two years after the grant of the option and one year from the date stock is transferred to the employee.

   • no options may be issued more than ten years from the date the ISO plan is adopted.

   • corporate stockholders must approve the ISO plan within twelve months of the time it is adopted by the company's board of directors.

   • the exercise price of the option must be at least equal to the fair market value of the stock on the date the option is granted.

Tools and Techniques

- ISOs may not be granted to any employee who owns, directly or indirectly, more than 10% of the corporation unless the term of the option is limited to not more than five years and the exercise price is at least 110% of the fair market value of the stock on the date of the grant.

3. Although there is no regular income tax to the executive when an ISO option is exercised, the alternative minimum tax (AMT) may have an impact. The difference between the stock's fair market value and the option price at the time of exercise may increase alternative minimum taxable income, which is subject to the tax.

4. If the executive holds the stock for the periods specified above, (two years after grant or one year after exercise) the gain on any sale is taxed at long term capital gain rates. Currently there is no preferential rate for capital gains, but conceivably the preferential rate may be reestablished by Congress in the future.

5. If the stock is sold before the two year/one year holding period specified above, the difference between the fair market value of the shares at the time of exercise and the exercise price is treated as compensation income to the executive in the year the stock is sold. However, in the absence of a preferential rate for capital gains, this "penalty" has no substantial effect on the executive's taxes.

Example: Executive Flo Through is covered under her company's ISO plan. Under the plan, Flo is granted an option in 1990 to purchase company stock for $100 per share. In January, 1992, Flo exercises this option and purchases 100 shares for a total of $10,000. The fair market value of the 100 shares in January, 1992, is $14,000. In October, 1992, Flo sells the 100 shares for $16,000. Flo's taxable gain is $6,000 ($16,000 amount realized less $10,000 cost). Of this amount, $4,000 (fair market value of $14,000 less $10,000 exercise price) is treated as compensation income for the year 1992. The remaining $2,000 is capital gain.

6. The corporation does not get a tax deduction for granting an ISO option. Nor does it get a deduction when an executive exercises an option or sells stock acquired under an ISO plan. However, the corporation *does* get a deduction for the compensation income element that an executive must recognize if stock is sold before the two year/one year holding period, as described in paragraph 4 above.

WHERE CAN I FIND OUT MORE ABOUT IT?

Graduate Course: Executive Compensation (GS 842), The American College, Bryn Mawr, PA.

Chapter 17

INDIVIDUAL RETIREMENT ACCOUNT (IRA)

WHAT IS IT?

An IRA (which stands for either individual retirement account or individual retirement annuity) is a type of retirement savings arrangement under which IRA contributions, up to certain limits, and investment earnings are tax-deferred. That is, interest earned and gains received inside the IRA are free of federal income tax until withdrawn from the IRA.

IRAs are primarily plans of individual savings, rather than employee benefits. However, their features should be understood since they fit into an employee's plan of retirement savings and therefore they influence the form of employer retirement plans to some degree.

Employers can sponsor IRAs for employees, as a limited alternative to an employer-sponsored qualified retirement plan. Employer-sponsored IRAs are discussed in the "Questions and Answers" at the end of this chapter. An arrangement similar to the employer-sponsored IRA which allows greater annual employer contributions is the SEP (simplified employee pension) discussed in Chapter 30.

WHEN IS IT INDICATED?

1. When there is a need to shelter current compensation or earned income from taxation.

2. When it is desirable to defer taxes on investment income.

3. When long-term accumulation, especially for retirement purposes, is an important objective.

4. When a supplement or alternative to a qualified pension or profit-sharing plan is needed.

ADVANTAGES

1. Eligible individuals may contribute up to $2,000 to an IRA ($2,250 if a spousal IRA is available) and deduct this amount from their current taxable income.

2. Investment income earned on the assets held in an IRA is not taxed until it is withdrawn from the account. This deferral applies no matter what the nature of the investment income. It may be in the form of interest, dividends, rents, capital gain, or any other form of income. Such income will be taxed only when it is withdrawn from the account and received as ordinary income.

DISADVANTAGES

1. The IRA deduction is limited to $2,000 maximum each year ($2,250 if a spousal IRA is available), with even more stringent limits, or a complete unavailability of the deduction, if the individual (or his spouse) is an active participant in a tax-favored employer retirement plan, as discussed below.

2. IRA withdrawals are subject to the 10% penalty on premature withdrawals applicable to all tax-favored retirement plans.

3. IRA withdrawals are not eligible for the 5-year (or 10-year) averaging tax computation that applies to certain lump sum distributions from qualified plans.

4. IRAs cannot be established once an individual reaches age 70½ and withdrawals from the account are required by April 1 of the year after the year in which the individual reaches age 70½. For additional information on required distributions, see the section on "Tax Implications" below.

TAX IMPLICATIONS

1. The maximum deductible IRA contribution for an individual is the lesser of (a) $2,000 or (b) 100% of the individual's earned income — that is, income from employment or self-employment; investment income cannot be counted. If the individual has a spouse with no earned income (or one who elects to be treated as having no earned income), then a spousal IRA can be set up and the maximum contribution for both spouses is $2,250.

   If both spouses have earned income, each can have an IRA. The deduction limit for each spouse with earned income is the $2,000/100% limit.

2. The 1986 Tax Reform Act imposed income limitations on the deductibility of IRA contributions for those persons who are "active participants" in a an employer retirement plan that is tax-favored — a qualified retirement plan, simplified employee pension (SEP), or Section 403(b) tax deferred annuity plan.

   Single individuals who are active participants may make a deductible contribution up to the full $2,000 if their adjusted gross income (AGI) is less than $25,000.

   • Single active participants can make a partial deductible contribution (less than $2,000) if their income is between $25,000 and $35,000.

- Single active participants cannot make any deductible contribution if their AGI exceeds $35,000.

A similar structure exists for married couples where *either spouse*, or both spouses, are active participants in a qualified plan. The income limitations are higher than for single individuals, as follows:

- Married couples, where one or both are active participants can each make up to a $2,000 deductible contribution if their combined AGI is less than $40,000.

- Partial contributions are allowed if their combined AGI is between $40,000 and $50,000.

- No deductible contributions can be made if their combined AGI exceeds $50,000.

Both single and married persons can make nondeductible contributions up to $2,000 even though their incomes exceed the $35,000 or $50,000 maximums (see number 3, below).

A reduction formula determines the amount of any IRA contribution which will not be tax deductible if AGI falls into the $25,000-$35,000 range for singles or $40,000-$50,000 for married couples. This formula reduces the deductible contribution by the percentage of ''excess'' AGI, or the amount of AGI over the figures of $25,000 and $40,000, respectively.

The ''nondeduction'' formula is

$$\$2,000 \times \frac{\text{Excess AGI}}{\$10,000} = \text{Nondeductible Amount}$$

Example: A single person with AGI of $30,000 who is an active participant in a qualified retirement plan can contribute $2,000 to his or her IRA but only $1,000 of the contribution can be taken as a current tax deduction. The reduction amount is [$2,000 × ($5,000/$10,000)].

There is a $200 ''floor'' under the reduction formula. As long as the taxpayer is below the AGI level where deductions cut off entirely, at least $200 can be contributed and deducted. For example, if married taxpayers have AGI of $49,900, they can contribute and deduct $200, even though the reduction formula would produce a lesser deduction.

3. An individual or married couple can also make *nondeductible* IRA contributions, within limits. The limit is the same regardless of income level; it is the difference between (a) the overall contribution limit ($2,000, or $2,250 for SPIRAs) *and* (b) the amount of deductible contributions made for the year. If the individual or couple make no deductible contributions, they can therefore contribute up to $2,000/$2,250 on a nonde-

ductible basis. Nondeductible contributions will be free of tax when they are distributed, but income earned on such contributions will be taxed. If nondeductible contributions are made to an IRA, amounts withdrawn will be treated as partly tax free and partly taxable.

4. Eligible persons may establish an IRA account and claim the appropriate tax deduction any time prior to the due date of their tax return, *without* extensions, even if the taxpayer actually receives an extension of the filing date. For most individuals or married couples the contribution cutoff date is April 15th. However, since earnings on an IRA account accumulate tax-free, taxpayers may want to make contributions as early as possible in the tax year. The advantage of making an IRA contribution at the beginning of the year can be seen in the following table which assumes $2,000 annual contributions and a rate of return of eight percent.

YEARS OF GROWTH	BEGINNING OF YEAR JANUARY 1	END OF YEAR DECEMBER 31	ADVANTAGE OF EARLY CONTRIBUTIONS
5	$ 12,572	$ 11,733	$ 939
10	31,291	28,973	2,318
15	58,649	54,304	4,344
20	98,846	91,524	7,322
25	157,909	146,212	11,697
30	244,692	226,566	18,125
35	372,204	344,634	27,571
40	559,562	518,113	41,449
45	834,852	773,011	61,841

5. In addition to offering tax incentives for contributions, the government penalizes certain early withdrawals from IRAs. The premature distribution penalty is 10 percent of the taxable amount withdrawn from the IRA. Therefore, IRA contributions should be made from funds that can be left in the account until one of the ''non-penalty'' events listed below occurs.

The premature distribution penalty (discussed further in Appendix B) does *not* apply to IRA distributions

- made on or after attainment of age 59½

- made to the IRA participant's beneficiary or estate on or after the participant's death

- attributable to the participant's disability

- that are part of a series of substantially equal periodic payments made at least annually over the life or life expectancy of the participant, or the participant and a designated beneficiary

This last exception — the periodic payment exception — provides some flexibility and can be very favorable in some cases. For example, suppose Ira Participant decides at age 52 to take some money out of his IRA. Ira can do so without penalty, as long as the amount taken

Figure 17.1

IRA WITHDRAWAL — REQUIRED MINIMUM

INPUT: INDIVIDUAL'S CURRENT AGE 71   Years
         (Ages 71 and over)

         REMAINING LIFE EXPECTANCY .... 15.3   Years
         (Males and Females)

INPUT: Remaining IRA Balance $500,000

         Required Withdrawal in Current Year .... $ 32,680

Reprinted with permission from *Financial Planning TOOLKIT*, Financial Data Corporation, P.O. Box 1332, Bryn Mawr, PA 19010.

---

out annually is substantially what the annual payment would be under a life annuity (or joint life annuity) purchased with his IRA account balance. No actual annuity purchase is required. Then, when Ira reaches age 59¹/₂, he can withdraw all the rest of the money in his IRA account. Ira doesn't have to continue the annuity payments since he is now relying on a different penalty exception, the exception for payments after age 59¹/₂.

However, if the series of payments is changed before the participant reaches age 59¹/₂ or, if after age 59¹/₂, within five years of the date of the first payment, the tax which would have been imposed, but for the periodic exception, is imposed with interest in the year the change occurs. In the example above, if Ira Participant had begun receiving payments under the periodic payment exception when he was 57, he would have to continue the annuity payments for at least five years to avoid the penalty.

6. Distributions must begin by April 1 of the year after the year in which age 70¹/₂ is reached. The IRA owner can receive the entire IRA balance in a lump sum or, if preferred, choose some other payment option. Typical permissible payment options include (a) periodic payments over the IRA owner's life and the life of a designated beneficiary, (b) periodic payments over a fixed period not longer than the IRA owner's life expectancy, or a fixed period not longer than the life expectancy of the owner and a designated beneficiary. Life expectancy for this purpose is determined from tables provided in IRS regulations.

The Financial Planning TOOLKIT illustration (see below) indicates that a person age 71, with an IRA account of $500,000, would have to begin making withdrawals of at least $32,680, based on his remaining life expectancy of 15.3 years.

If, after distributions are required to begin, sufficient amounts are not withdrawn from an IRA in a tax year,

there is a 50 percent excise tax on the under-distribution. An under-distribution is the difference between the minimum payout required for the tax year and the amount actually paid.

7. Beginning in 1987, an additional penalty tax of 15% will be imposed if aggregate "retirement" distributions to an individual in a calendar year exceed the greater of (1) $150,000, or (2) $112,500 as adjusted for inflation ($117,529 in 1988). This tax is in addition to any regular income taxes due and applies only to the excess portion of the distribution. All qualified plans and individual retirement plans are aggregated for this additional tax.

8. An IRA can be used to receive a "rollover" of certain distributions of benefits from employer-sponsored retirement plans. The distribution must be transferred to the rollover IRA within 60 days after it is received. It is advisable to create a special IRA for a rollover and not make further contributions to it; the right to roll these amounts back into a qualified plan (which is often a possibility) is lost if the funds in the special IRA are mixed with funds from other sources.

IRA rollovers are usually straightforward, but there are some complicated rules in special situations. These are discussed further in Appendix B.

9. When an IRA owner dies, a somewhat complex pattern of tax rules applies. Planners need to understand the tax treatment of this common situation in order to prevent unnecessary tax penalties for their clients. These rules are generally designed to prevent IRA distributions from being "stretched out" unduly to increase tax deferral.

(1) If the owner dies after payments under the IRA have begun, payments must continue to the beneficiary or heir to the IRA at least as rapidly as under the method of distribution in effect during the owner's life. The

Tools and Techniques

only exception to this is if the beneficiary or heir is the owner's spouse (see 3 below).

(2) If the owner had *not* begun receiving payments and the heir or beneficiary is not the owner's spouse, there are two possible options for distribution:

(a) the entire amount must be distributed within five years, or

(b) the benefit can be paid (annuitized) over the life expectancy of that beneficiary; distributions under this option must begin within one year of the decedent's death.

(3) If the heir or beneficiary is the owner's spouse, the recipient spouse can elect to treat the inherited IRA as his or her own. This means that distributions don't have to begin until April 1 of the year following the year in which the *recipient spouse* reaches age 70^1/$_2$. This election is permitted whether or not the decedent had begun receiving distributions from the IRA prior to death. As an alternative to making this election, the recipient spouse can roll the decedent's IRA over to the recipient spouse's own IRA, which accomplishes the same result.

WHERE CAN I FIND OUT MORE ABOUT IT?

1. Most banks, savings and loans, insurance companies, and brokerage firms actively market IRAs, and can provide brochures describing their IRA plans. These firms will indicate the types of investments available as well as any charges that may be applied to such accounts.

2. IRS Publication 590, *Individual Retirement Arrangements (IRAs)*, is available without charge from the IRS or the U.S. Government Printing Office.

QUESTIONS AND ANSWERS

Question — If neither an individual nor his or her spouse is covered by a tax-favored retirement plan, are there any limitations on the deductibility of IRA contributions?

Answer — No. If neither the individual or spouse is covered by a qualified retirement plan, simplified employee pension (SEP), or Section 403(b) annuity plan, they may contribute up to the full deduction limit (the lesser of $2,000 or 100 percent of earned income for each spouse with earned income, or a total of $2,250 if only one spouse has earned income) and deduct the full amount of the contribution regardless of the level of AGI.

Examples:

1. Minnie and Bill, a married couple, each earn $75,000 annually. Neither is an active participant in any qualified plan, SEP or Section 403(b) plan.

Minnie and Bill can each contribute and deduct up to $2,000 to their own IRA plan (a total of $4,000 for both).

2. Mabel earns $75,000 annually. Her husband, Alf, has no earned income (although he has investment income over $100,000 annually). Neither spouse is an active participant in a tax-favored plan. Mabel can contribute and deduct a total of $2,250 to an IRA for herself and an IRA for her spouse.

3. Stan earns $75,000 annually, and his wife Fran has earned income of $1,200. Neither is an active participant in a tax-favored retirement plan. Stan can contribute and deduct up to $2,000 to his IRA, and Fran can contribute and deduct up to $1,200 to her IRA (she is limited by 100 percent of her earned income).

Question — What does it mean to be an "active" participant in a qualified plan, SEP, or TDA plan?

Answer — A person is an active participant in an employer's retirement plan only if the participant actually receives an employer contribution for that year or accrues a benefit under an employer's defined benefit plan.

For example, in a qualified profit-sharing plan it is possible for an employer to omit making a plan contribution in a given year. For such a year, an employee is *not* considered an active plan participant even though covered under the plan, so long as there was no contribution made to the employee's account under the plan.

Note, however, that an employee is considered an active participant if a contribution is made for him by the employer but the employee is not vested in the amount in his account. If the employee stays long enough to become vested, he will acquire full rights to that amount, so he is considered an active participant for the year in which the contribution was made.

Question — If only one spouse is an active participant, can the other spouse receive a full IRA deduction by filing a separate return?

Answer — The reduced deduction limit can be avoided by the non-active participant spouse only if a separate return is filed *and* the spouses lived apart at all times during the taxable year.

Question — Is there any minimum contribution required each year?

Answer — No, there is no required minimum contribution to an IRA. An individual can put aside relatively small amounts each year and still see them grow into a considerable sum for retirement. Also, a contribution does not have to be made every year. It is possible to skip a year or any number of years without jeopardizing the tax-deferred status of the account. However, failure to make contributions reduces the value of the account for tax-shelter purposes and limits the amount of earnings that will build up on a tax-free basis.

Question — What kind of income is eligible to be contributed to an IRA account?

Answer — The income must be produced from personal services which would include wages, salaries, professional fees, sales commissions, tips, and bonuses.

Unearned income such as dividends, interest, or rent cannot be used in determining the amount of the IRA contribution.

Question — Do married couples with two incomes contribute to one or two regular IRAs?

Answer — Two. Each should establish a separate IRA account. Contributions are based on each separate income and each contribution is a separate tax deduction. This is true even though a couple may live in a community property state.

Question — How are IRA benefits paid?

Answer — Benefits must be paid in one of two ways (a) a single lump-sum payment, or (b) payments over a period which is not longer than a period equal to the life expectancy of the contributor or the joint life expectancies of the contributor and his designated beneficiary. Special rules apply if the spouse is the beneficiary.

Payments to a beneficiary must only be "incidental" under IRS regulations. These regulations in general require a payment schedule under which more of the expected benefit will be paid to the original IRA owner than is paid to the beneficiary.

Question — Are IRA contributions locked into any one particular investment?

Answer — No. First, the IRA participant may select more than one organization which sponsors IRA programs, as long as the total of all deductible investments made each year is within the contribution limit. For example, part of the contribution could be placed in a savings account and the remainder in a mutual fund plan. Second, at any time the IRA participant may request an IRA sponsor to transfer IRA assets directly from one sponsoring organization to another; not all IRA sponsors will agree to do this, however. Alternatively, assets may be taken out of an IRA and reinvested with another IRA sponsor within 60 days without any tax consequences. However, the IRA participant is allowed to make this type of transaction — a "rollover" — only once every 12 months.

Question — If an IRA participant becomes disabled, can an early withdrawal be made from the IRA account?

Answer — Yes. In order to avoid the 10 percent early distribution penalty, a person under age $59\frac{1}{2}$ must have a total and permanent physical or mental disability which prevents gainful employment and which is determined by a physician to be terminal or expected to continue for at least one year.

Question — When are taxes paid on IRA plans?

Answer — If IRA funds are taken out in a lump sum, the entire account, including principal and earnings is ordinary income in the year of receipt. However, if nondeductible contributions have been made to the account, they are recovered tax-free. If money is withdrawn periodically in installments or an annuity, only the amount received each year is taxable. If nondeductible contributions have been made, a portion of each payment is received tax-free.

Question — What happens if too much is contributed to an IRA account in any one year?

Answer — If more than the maximum allowable amount is contributed in any year, a 6 percent excise tax will be imposed on the excess contribution. However, the 6 percent tax can be avoided by withdrawing the excess contribution and earnings prior to the filing date for the federal income tax return (normally April 15). If the excess contribution plus earnings is not withdrawn by the tax return filing date, the 6 percent excise tax will be imposed in each succeeding year until the excess is eliminated.

Question — How can an employer sponsor IRAs for employees?

Answer — An employer (or a labor union) can sponsor IRAs for its employees as an alternative to a pension plan. There is no requirement of nondiscrimination in coverage. The IRAs can be made available to any employee or a discriminatory group of employees.

Contributions to the IRA can be made either as additional compensation from the employer or as a salary reduction elected by the employee. If the employer contributes extra compensation, it is taxable to the employee, but the employee is eligible for the IRA deduction.

The deduction limit for an employer-sponsored IRA is the same as for regular individual IRAs (the lesser of $2,000 or 100 percent of compensation).

An arrangement similar to the employer-sponsored IRA is the SEP (simplified employee pension) discussed in Chapter 30. SEPs allow greater annual employer contributions — up to a limit of 15% of compensation,

Tools and Techniques

or $30,000 (as indexed for inflation), whichever is greater. However, SEPs require nondiscriminatory coverage of employees.

Question — In what types of assets can IRA funds be invested?

Answer — IRA funds can be invested in any type of asset, with one specific limitation under the Internal Revenue Code. An IRA cannot be invested in a "collectible" as defined in Code section 408(m). A collectible is any work of art, rug, antique, metal or gem, stamp, coin, alcoholic beverage, or any other item designated as a collectible by the IRS. The IRA can, however, invest in U.S. gold or silver coins. After November 10, 1988, an IRA can also invest in any coin issued under the law of a state.

Another limitation should be kept in mind. Since IRAs cannot make loans to an IRA participant, the participant's note is in effect another type of property the IRA cannot invest in.

Chapter 18
KEY EMPLOYEE LIFE INSURANCE

WHAT IS IT?

Key employee life insurance is insurance on a key employee's life owned by the employer, with the death benefit payable to the employer. Technically, key employee insurance is designed to compensate the employer for the loss of a key employee and is not an employee benefit for the key employee. However, in closely held corporations, key employee insurance can be used to indirectly benefit shareholder-employees by providing a source of liquid assets in the corporation. Key employee policies make assets available from policy cash values during the employee's lifetime and from the policy proceeds on the death of the employee. These assets can be used to finance the employer's obligation under one or more employee benefit plans.

WHEN IS IT INDICATED?

1. When a corporation will incur an obligation to pay a specified beneficiary or class of beneficiaries at an employee's death under a death benefit only (DBO) plan — see Chapter 5.

2. When an employer has a nonqualified deferred compensation arrangement with one or more key executives or other employees and needs a way to finance its obligation upon the death of the employee. For example, such a plan might provide a benefit of $50,000 a year for 10 years if the employee lives to retirement or $50,000 a year for 10 years to a designated beneficiary if the employee dies either before or after retirement- See Chapter 24.

3. When a closely held corporation anticipates a need for liquid assets upon the death of a key employee to stabilize the corporation financially and enable it to continue contributing to employee benefit plans for surviving employees.

4. When a shareholder-employee expects the corporation to buy stock from his or her estate as part of an estate plan and the corporation needs additional liquid assets to carry out such a purchase.

TAX IMPLICATIONS

To the Employee

1. There is no income tax to a key employee or the key employee's estate when the corporation owns the policy, pays the premiums, and receives death proceeds from key employee life insurance.

2. Corporate-owned key employee life insurance may have some effect on the federal estate tax payable by the deceased key employee's estate.

    *   The value of corporate stock held by a decedent at death is included in the decedent's gross estate for federal estate tax purposes. If the corporation held life insurance on the decedent's life, the insurance proceeds increase the value of the corporation, and therefore can be included in the value of the stock held by the decedent. The general rule for key employee life insurance, where the corporation is the beneficiary, is that the insurance proceeds are taken into account in valuing the decedent's stock, but not necessarily included in the decedent's estate dollar for dollar. However, in many situations the IRS attempts to increase the value of the stock as much as possible where the corporation held key employee life insurance.

    *   If the insured key employee was a majority shareholder (more than 50%), the tax law provides that policy proceeds, to the extent payable to or for the benefit of a party other than the corporation or its creditors, will be taxed in the insured key employee's estate as life insurance. For this reason, policy proceeds of corporate-owned life insurance should generally be payable only to the corporation or its creditors.

To the Corporation

1. Corporate-paid premiums on life insurance on the life of a key employee, where the corporation is the owner and beneficiary of the life insurance contract, are not deductible for federal income tax purposes.

2. The death proceeds of key employee life insurance are tax-free when paid to the corporation, except for the potential application of the alternative minimum tax (AMT) discussed below.

3. If the corporation has accumulated earnings of more than $250,000 ($150,000 for a personal service corporation) then the accumulation of further income to pay life insurance premiums for key employee insurance potentially exposes the corporation to the accumulated

Tools and Techniques

earnings tax. There are, however, many exceptions to the application of this tax. The purchase of life insurance to cover the potential loss of a bona fide key employee should not result in a significant risk of accumulated earnings tax exposure in most cases.

4. Key employee life insurance involves some potential corporate exposure to the corporate alternative minimum tax (AMT). The purpose of the AMT is to require corporations to pay a minimum level of income tax on actual economic income, even if taxable income has been reduced by significant amounts of tax-exempt or tax-preferred income. The AMT is a tax computed on a base of reported income plus certain "tax preferences." Generally, a corporation must pay the larger of its regular tax or the AMT.

One AMT tax preference that is significant here is defined as 50% of business untaxed reported profits or BURP. BURP is the difference between a corporation's adjusted book income and its alternative minimum taxable income. (After 1989 BURP is defined by reference to "adjusted current earnings" rather than adjusted book income.)

Corporations must maintain a separate set of records in order to keep track of book income. Book income currently has no specific tax definition, but generally it refers to the income reported to creditors or stockholders in financial statements or annual reports, as opposed to the income reported on federal income tax returns. Book income contains items normally not reported as taxable income including:

(a) dividends received that are excluded from taxable income

(b) tax-free interest on municipal bonds

(c) the net inside buildup (cash value increase less premiums paid) of corporate-owned life insurance

(d) net death proceeds received (proceeds less aggregate premiums paid) from corporate-owned life insurance.

A simple example will illustrate the impact of the AMT on corporate-owned life insurance.

Example: Professional Services, Inc. (PSI) has book income in 1989 of $500,000 which includes $300,000 of net death proceeds from corporate-owned life insurance. PSI's taxable income is $200,000. Its regular income tax is 34% of $200,000 or $68,000. The AMT is computed as follows:

Adjusted Net Book Income	$500,000
Less Pre-book Alternative Minimum Taxable Income	- $200,000
BURP	$300,000
	× 50%
BURP Preference	$150,000
Plus Pre-book Alternative Minimum Taxable Income	+$200,000
Alternative Taxable Income	$350,000
× AMT Tax Rate	× 20%
AMT	$70,000
Less Regular Tax	- $68,000
Additional Tax	$2,000

This example shows an additional tax of $2,000, which is less than 1% of the insurance proceeds of $300,000. In general, the maximum tax that can be imposed on net death proceeds is 10%. That is, 20% of 50% of BURP, or 10% of BURP. (This will increase to 15% after 1989.)

Although the AMT is unfavorable to corporate-owned life insurance, its maximum impact is not extreme. Furthermore, the best way to avoid the impact of the AMT is to purchase additional life insurance, to insure that the corporation receives the full amount expected, after AMT.

ALTERNATIVES

Personally-owned insurance can provide estate liquidity and funds to meet the needs of beneficiaries. Corporate funds can be used indirectly by paying extra compensation to the employee as discussed in Chapter 1. This extra compensation is deductible so long as it meets the reasonableness test discussed in Chapter 4. In a situation where the corporation's marginal income tax bracket is higher than the employee's, personally-owned insurance may provide a better tax result.

WHERE CAN I FIND OUT MORE ABOUT IT?

1. Leimberg, Stephan R., et al., *The Tools and Techniques of Estate Planning*, 7th ed. Cincinnati, OH: The National Underwriter Co., 1988.

2. Stoeber, Edward A., *Tax Planning Techniques for the Closely Held Corporation*, 3rd ed. Cincinnati, OH: The National Underwriter Co., 1987.

3. CLU/ChFC Course: Planning for Business Owners and Professionals (HS 331), The American College, Bryn Mawr, PA.

4. Graduate Courses: Business Tax Planning (GS 845) and Advanced Estate Planning (GS 815 and 816), The American College, Bryn Mawr, PA.

Chapter 19
LEGAL SERVICES PLAN

WHAT IS IT?

A legal services plan (sometimes referred to as a "prepaid legal services plan") is an employer-funded plan that makes legal services available to employees when needed. If the plan meets qualification rules under Code section 120, as described below, the expenses of the plan are deductible to the employer and neither the employer's payments to cover costs of the plan nor the legal services provided are taxable income to employees. Code section 120 was extended through the end of 1988 by the Technical and Miscellaneous Revenue Act of 1988.

WHEN IS IT INDICATED?

In theory, any group of employees can benefit from the advantages of these plans. However, in practice they are used primarily by larger employers for employees in collective bargaining units. Such plans are usually funded through multiemployer trusteeships sponsored by labor unions. Group insurance for funding these plans is also available but is not yet widely used.

ADVANTAGES

1. A legal services plan that meets the standards of Code section 120 provides a tax-free form of compensation income for employees.

2. Many employees, particularly middle and lower income employees, are not well-served by the traditional fee-for-service system of delivering legal services and, as a result, often do without a lawyer when they really need one. For example, many middle income people do not have adequate legal advice in tax and domestic matters. A legal services plan provides these services without additional employee expenditure.

3. Legal expenses such as the cost of criminal trial can be the kind of catastrophic expense that is best provided through an insurance-type or group benefit program such as a legal services plan.

DISADVANTAGES

1. Since most employees rarely need a lawyer, or rarely perceive the need for one, a legal services plan may not be fully appreciated by employees compared with other forms of employee compensation.

2. Funding and administering a legal services plan is difficult in light of the limited availability of group legal insurance or multiemployer arrangements.

3. Some employers fear that a legal services plan will make it more likely that employees will sue the employer in the event of a dispute. However, legal services for actions by employees against the employer can be (and usually are) excluded from the plan.

4. If the standards of Code section 120 are not met by a legal services plan, either employer expenditures for the plan or the value of legal services provided will be taxable income to covered employees.

DESIGN FEATURES

1. Eligibility must be nondiscriminatory in order to meet the Code section 120 standards discussed below. If this is not a factor, any group of employees can be covered.

2. Benefits are usually provided on either a *scheduled* or a *comprehensive* basis.

   With a scheduled plan only those benefits listed in the plan are provided. Most plans provide at least the following benefits:

   • legal consultations and advice on any matter

   • preparation of wills, deeds, powers-of-attorney and other routine legal documents

   • personal bankruptcy

   • adoption proceedings

   • defense of civil and criminal matters

   • juvenile proceedings

   • divorce, separation, child custody, and other domestic matters.

   A plan that provides comprehensive benefits pays for all legal services, with specified exclusions. The most common exclusions include:

   • audits by the IRS

- actions against the employer, the plan, or a labor union sponsoring the plan

- contingent fee cases or class action suits

- actions arising out of the employee's separate business transactions

3. Some plans provide benefits on an indemnity basis, that is, by reimbursing the employee for covered expenditures. In that case, benefits are usually limited to a flat amount for a given legal service or a maximum hourly rate. There may also be a maximum annual benefit such as $1,000.

Prepayment-type plans are more common than indemnity plans. In a prepayment plan there is no direct expenditure by employees. In a *closed-panel* prepayment plan, the most common type, employees must obtain covered services from specified groups of lawyers who are either employed by or under contract with the plan (similar to an HMO; see Chapter 14). In an *open-panel* prepayment plan employees can choose their own lawyer or choose a lawyer from an approved list. The lawyer must agree in advance to a fee schedule set by the legal services plan. A plan can combine both the closed panel and open panel approaches, allowing occasional use of top legal specialists for serious matters, while routine matters are handled by the closed panel.

TAX IMPLICATIONS

1. Costs of a legal services plan, whether or not it meets the standards of Code section 120, are deductible to the employer, with certain limitations:

   (a) as with all deductions for employee compensation, the overall compensation of each employee must meet the "reasonableness" test discussed in Chapter 4;

   (b) if the plan is funded in advance the amount of deductible advance funding is limited to approximately the benefits provided during the taxable year plus administrative expenses under Code section 419.

2. If the plan does not meet the requirements of Code section 120:

   (a) if the plan is prefunded by the employer — for example, if the employer pays a group legal insurance premium to an insurance company — the employee is taxed on his or her share of the premium at the time the employer pays it, if the employee is fully vested in the benefit (legally entitled at that time to receive benefits under the plan).

   (b) if the employer pays for benefits out of current revenues as employees receive benefits the employee is taxed on the value of benefits as they are received.

3. If the plan meets the requirements of Code section 120, neither employer payments for funding the plan nor benefits received from the plan are taxable income to the employee. Code section 120 has been allowed to expire several times and subsequently been revived by Congress. Currently, it is in effect through the end of 1988. Section 120 imposes the following requirements:

- contributions or benefits must not discriminate in favor of "highly compensated" employees. For the definition of highly compensated, see Appendix A.

- eligibility must be nondiscriminatory. Certain employees may be excluded (those described in Section 89(h) such as part-timers, employees in collective bargaining units that have bargained separately on legal services benefits, and similar exclusions).

- not more than 25 percent of the amounts contributed under the plan can be for employees who own more than 5 percent of the employer.

- the IRS must be notified in accordance with regulations that the employer has adopted a qualified legal services plan.

- employer contributions for the plan can be paid only to an insurance company, a special type of tax-exempt trust set up under Code section 501(c)(20) to fund legal services plans, a nonprofit organization such as a labor union or state bar organization that funds prepaid legal services plans, or providers of legal services, as prepayments. Any combination of these four methods of funding may be used.

- coverage above a $70 annual premium value is taxable to the employee.

- the following requirements of Code section 89(k) must be met

  — the plan must be in writing

  — employees' rights must be legally enforceable

— employees must be notified of benefits

— the plan must be for the exclusive benefit of employees

— the employer must intend initially that the plan be permanent.

A Section 120 plan can provide benefits to employees and also to their spouses or dependents. Section 120 does not restrict the types of legal benefits that can be provided or require any specific legal benefits to be included.

HOW TO INSTALL A PLAN

For a plan intended to qualify under Section 120, the formal requirements listed above must be complied with, including the Section 89(k) requirements, and notice given to the IRS. For a non-Section 120 plan, the procedure can be more informal, but a written document is advisable in any case.

WHERE CAN I FIND OUT MORE ABOUT IT?

Beam, Burton T., Jr. and John J. McFadden, *Employee Benefits*, 2nd ed. Homewood, IL: Richard D. Irwin, 1988.

Chapter 20

LIFE INSURANCE IN A QUALIFIED PLAN

WHAT IS IT?

Life insurance for employees covered under a qualified plan can often be provided favorably by having the insurance purchased and owned by the plan, using deductible employer contributions to the plan as a source of funds. This chapter deals with the advantages and methods of doing this, as well as the limitations.

WHEN IS IT INDICATED?

1. When a substantial number of employees covered under a qualified plan have an otherwise unmet life insurance need, either for family protection or estate liquidity.

2. When there are gaps and limitations in other company plans providing death benefits, such as Section 79 group-term life insurance plans, nonqualified deferred compensation plans, and split dollar plans. Planners should consider using life insurance in a qualified plan to fill those gaps or supplement those plans.

3. When highly compensated plan participants are potentially subject to the 15% excess accumulation tax on plan death benefits or substantial estate taxes on death benefits.

   • Life insurance in the plan can reduce the exposure to the excess accumulation tax since, as discussed below, pure life insurance is not subject to the tax.

   • Insured plan death benefits can (potentially) be structured to avoid estate taxes.

   • Life insurance in a plan can provide funds to pay estate taxes and excess accumulation taxes, if any, thereby enhancing the ability of plan proceeds to provide financial security for the participant's survivors.

4. When life insurance would be attractive to plan participants as an additional option for investing their plan accounts. This technique is most often used in a profit-sharing or 401(k) plan, but can be used in other types of defined contribution plans as well.

5. When an employer wants an extremely secure funding vehicle for a plan, with the best available guarantees as to future plan costs and benefits.

ADVANTAGES

1. The tax treatment of life insurance in a qualified plan, as discussed below, usually provides an overall cost advantage, as compared with individual life policies provided by the employer outside the qualified plan or those personally-owned by plan participants. Recent tax changes have reduced this advantage but have not (in most cases) eliminated it.

2. Life insurance provides one of the safest available investments for a qualified plan.

3. Using appropriate life insurance products for funding a qualified plan can provide extremely predictable plan costs for the employer.

4. Life insurance products in a qualified plan can provide employees with retirement benefits guaranteed by an insurance company as well as by the employer.

5. The ''pure insurance'' portion of a qualified plan death benefit (basically, the death proceeds less any policy cash values) is not subject either to regular income tax or to the 15% tax on excess accumulations. This makes it, dollar for dollar, a more effective means of transferring wealth than any other type of plan asset.

6. Some authorities believe that insured plan death benefits can be structured to keep them out of the plan participant's estate for federal estate tax purposes. (See ''Questions and Answers,'' below.)

7. A fully insured plan (one holding only life insurance policies or annuity contracts) is exempt from the minimum funding standards and the actuarial certification requirement of Code section 412. This can reduce the administrative cost and complexity of a defined benefit plan.

8. Some life insurance companies provide low cost installation and administrative services for plans using their investment products. This also reduces the employer's cost for the plan.

DISADVANTAGES

1. Some life insurance policies may provide a rate of return on their cash values which, as compared with alternative plan investments, may be relatively low. However, rates of return should be compared on investments of similar risk.

2. Policy expenses and commissions on life insurance products may be greater than for comparable investments.

77

Tools and Techniques

HOW IS IT USED?

Insurance Coverage

Insurance coverage should be based on a nondiscriminatory formula related to the retirement benefit or plan contribution formula. For example, the amount of insurance for each employee might be specified as 100 times the expected monthly pension under the plan.

Insurance coverage can be conditioned on taking a medical exam if this does not result in discrimination in favor of highly compensated employees. For employees who do not "pass" the medical exam, insurance is typically limited to the amount, if any, that can be purchased for them using the amount of premium dollars that would be available if they were insurable. For example, if the plan's insurance formula provides insurance of 100 times the monthly benefit for standard risks (employees who pass the medical exam), the insurance provided for a medically "rated" employee might be only 50 times the monthly benefit, since a 50 times benefit for that employee would cost as much to provide as a 100 times benefit for a standard risk.

Turnover costs involved in buying cash value insurance policies can be minimized by having a longer waiting period for insurance than the plan's waiting period for entry. In the interim period, the death benefit for participants not covered by cash value policies can be provided by term insurance. In the past, many plans did not provide insurance for employees who were beyond a specified cutoff age. Under current age discrimination law, this probably is no longer allowed.

How Much Insurance — The "Incidental" Test

Life insurance can be used to provide an "incidental" death benefit to participants in a qualified retirement plan, either a defined contribution or defined benefit plan. The IRS considers any nonretirement benefit in a qualified plan to be incidental so long as the cost of that benefit is less than 25% of the total cost of the plan. Since this standard by itself is difficult to apply, the IRS has developed two practical tests for life insurance in a qualified plan. If the amount of insurance meets either of the following tests, it is considered incidental:

1. The participant's insured death benefit must be no more than 100 times the expected monthly benefit, or

2. The aggregate premiums paid (premiums paid over the entire life of the plan) for a participant's insured death benefit are at all times less than the following percentages of the plan cost for that participant:

"ordinary life" insurance	50%
term insurance	25%
universal life	25%

Traditionally, defined contribution plans such as profit-sharing plans have used the "percentage limits" in determining how much insurance to provide. Defined benefit plans have typically used the "100 times" limit. However, any type of plan can use either limit. It is becoming more common for defined benefit plans to use the percentage limits since the necessary calculations are easily computerized.

Life Insurance in Defined Benefit Plans

Life insurance is particularly advantageous in defined benefit plans because it *adds to* the limit on deductible contributions. This add-on feature allows greater tax-deferred funding of the plan. That is, a defined benefit plan can be funded to provide the maximum tax-deductible contribution for retirement benefits for each participant. The cost for life insurance can then be added to this amount and deducted.

By comparison, in a defined contribution plan, the costs of the life insurance must be part of the contributions to each participant's account. Using life insurance does not increase the Section 415 annual additions limit for participants' accounts in defined contribution plans. That limit is the lesser of (a) 25% of compensation or (b) the greater of $30,000 or ¼ of the dollar limitation for defined benefit plans (see Appendix A), whether or not life insurance is provided.

Life insurance can be used in defined benefit plans in many ways. Two of the most common approaches will be discussed here: the "combination plan" and the "envelope funding" approach.

Combination Plan

In a combination plan, retirement benefits are funded with a combination of (1) whole life policies and (2) assets in a separate trust fund called the "side fund" or "conversion fund." At each participant's retirement, the policies for that participant are cashed in. The participant's retirement benefit is then funded through a combination of the policy cash values and an amount withdrawn from the side fund. (Since whole life policies have a relatively slow cash value buildup, the cash values alone are not usually adequate at age 65 to fund the retirement benefit; this is the reason for the side fund.)

This type of funding combines the advantages of (1) an insured death benefit and the investment security of policy cash values, together with (2) an opportunity to invest more aggressively using side fund assets.

Combination plans are very appropriate for funding smaller pension plans — fewer than about 25 employees — but can be administratively costly for larger plans due to the number of insurance policies necessary for funding.

The amount of death benefit provided for each employee is usually determined using the 100-to-1 test. The annual cost for the plan each year then consists of the insurance premiums required, plus an amount deposited in the side fund that is determined on an actuarial basis. Actuarial methods and assumptions for the side fund can be varied within reasonable limits, providing some flexibility in funding.

The following example shows how a combination plan works and how it differs from an uninsured plan providing the same retirement benefit:

Example: Dr. X, a sole practitioner physician, adopts a pension plan at age 45. His annual compensation is $200,000.

	Insured Plan	Uninsured Plan
Monthly pension at age 65	$ 7,500	$ 7,500
Insured death benefit	750,000	0
Amount required at age 65	900,000	900,000
Less: cash value at age 65	258,750	0
Side fund at 65	641,250	900,000
Level annual deposit at 6% from age 45 to age 65	16,446	23,082
Life insurance premium (not considering dividends)	16,343	0
Total annual contribution	32,789	23,082

Note: Future dividends on the life insurance contract can be applied to reduce the annual premium, and typically will reduce it substantially after a number of years.

Envelope Funding

At the opposite pole from the combination plan, where the entire plan is structured around the insurance policies, is the envelope funding approach, where insurance policies are simply considered as plan assets like any other asset. In funding, the actuary determines total annual contributions (that must be paid in quarterly or more frequent installments) to the plan to provide both retirement and death benefits provided under the plan. The employer makes the contributions as determined by the actuary. Assets, including insurance policies, are purchased by the plan trustee to fund the costs of both the death benefits and the retirement benefits.

The amount of insured death benefit in this approach is kept within the incidental limits either by providing a death benefit of no more than 100 times each participant's projected monthly pension, or by keeping the amount of insurance premiums within the appropriate percentage limits (50 percent of aggregate costs for whole life insurance, 25% for term insurance, and so on).

The envelope funding approach tends to require lower initial contributions to the plan than a combination plan approach, since the actuary's assumptions are usually less conservative than the assumptions used to determine life insurance premiums. Long-term costs, however, will depend on actual investment results, policy dividends, and benefit and administrative costs of the plan.

Life Insurance in Defined Contribution Plans

In defined contribution plans, a part of each participant's account is used to purchase insurance on the participant's life. This plan can provide (a) that insurance purchases are voluntary by participants (using a *directed account* or *earmarking* provision), or (b) the insurance is provided automatically as a plan benefit, or (c) that insurance is provided at the plan administrator's option (on a nondiscriminatory basis).

The amount of insurance must be kept within the incidental limits already discussed. Usually, defined contribution plans rely on the percentage limits applicable to the type of insurance purchased. For example, if whole life insurance is purchased, aggregate premiums paid from each participant's account must be kept below 50% of aggregate contributions to that account.

If a plan has been in existence for a number of years, it may be possible to purchase a considerable amount of insurance in a later year, because the tests are computed in the aggregate.

For example, suppose a money purchase pension plan has existed for ten years and the employer has contributed $10,000 annually to employee Clyde's account. In the eleventh year, suppose the employer contributes another $10,000 to Clyde's account in the plan. In that eleventh year, an insurance premium amounting to just under $55,000 (50% of aggregate contributions of $110,000) can be paid out of Clyde's account to purchase whole life insurance. In some cases, such large purchases of insurance may be justified for planning purposes. For example, Clyde may be facing a potential excess accumulation tax on plan benefits in his estate that can be reduced by providing a large insured plan death benefit, as discussed below. The planner must be sure, however, that application of the percentage limits in the future will not prevent the deductible payment of required periodic premiums under the policy.

Profit-sharing plans have an additional feature that may allow large insurance purchases. Since profit-sharing plans potentially allow in-service cash distributions prior to termination of employment (see Chapter 25), the amount available for an in-service distribution can be used without limit to purchase life insurance. Based on IRS rulings, this means that any employer contribution that has been in the profit-sharing plan for at least two years can be used up to 100% for insurance purchases of any type as long as the plan specifies that the insurance will be purchased only with such funds.

TAX IMPLICATIONS

1. Employer contributions to the plan, including those used to purchase life insurance, are deductible if the amount of life insurance is within the incidental limits discussed earlier.

2. The economic value of pure life insurance coverage on a participant's life is taxed annually to the participant at the lower of the IRS "P.S. 58" table (see below) or the life insurance company's actual term rates for standard risks. Any amount actually contributed to the plan by the participant is subtracted from this amount. (If the participant is an owner-employee in a "Keogh" plan, the taxation is slightly different, as discussed in Chapter 15.)

   Example: Participant Lemm, aged 45, is covered under a defined benefit plan that provides an insured death benefit in addition to retirement benefits. The death benefit is provided under a whole life policy with a face amount of $100,000. At the end of 1988 the policy's cash value is $40,000. The plan is noncontributory (that is, Lemm does not contribute to the plan).

   For 1988 Lemm must report an additional $378 of taxable income on his tax returns (60 times the P.S. 58 rate of $6.30 per thousand for a participant aged 45, to reflect the amount of pure insurance coverage in 1988). The employer is required to report the insurance coverage on Lemm's Form W-2 for the year.

   This computation is shown in more detail in the NumberCruncher software which is illustrated in Figure 20.1.

3. Taxation of an insured death benefit received by a beneficiary can be summarized in the following points:

   • The pure insurance element of an insured plan death benefit (the death benefit less any cash value) is income tax free to a participant's beneficiary.

   • An additional $5,000 may qualify for the employer death benefit exclusion of Code section 101(b).

   • The total of all P.S. 58 costs paid by the participant can be recovered tax free from the plan death benefit (if it is paid from the same insurance contracts that gave rise to the P.S. 58 costs).

   • The remainder of the distribution is taxed as a qualified plan distribution. This taxable portion of the distribution may be eligible for 5 or 10-year averaging if the plan participant was over 59½ at death. If the decedent participated in the plan before 1987, there are also some favorable "grandfather" tax provisions that may apply.

Appendix B contains a detailed discussion of the tax treatment and planning options available for an insured death benefit from a qualified plan.

4. As compared with the tax treatment of life insurance personally owned or provided by the employer outside the plan, there is usually an economic advantage to insurance in the plan, all other things being equal. Insurance outside the plan is paid for entirely with after-tax dollars, so there is no tax deferral. The death benefit of non-plan insurance may be entirely instead of partially tax-free; however, the deferral of tax with plan-provided insurance potentially results in a measurable net tax benefit.

   Recent tax law changes have reduced the potential value of this deferral of taxes. Current personal tax rates have been reduced (though on a broader tax base) and there is an expectation that future tax rates may be higher. On the other hand, the relative increase in corporate tax rates has increased the value of any employee benefit that can be paid for with deductible corporate dollars. Some alternatives to plan-provided life insurance (split-dollar plans, for example — see Chapter 31) involve nondeductible corporate premium payments.

5. The pure insurance amount of a qualified plan death benefit is not subject to the 15% excess accumulation tax of Code section 4980A. Also, P.S. 58 costs can be recovered free of the excess accumulation tax.

6. Qualified plan death benefits are, in general, included in a decedent's estate for federal estate tax purposes. However, it may be possible to exclude the insured portion of the death benefit if the decedent had no "incidents of ownership" in the policy. This planning technique is discussed further in the "Questions and Answers," below.

ALTERNATIVES

1. Personally-owned life insurance

2. Group-term life insurance

3. Life insurance financing in a nonqualified deferred compensation plan

4. Split-dollar life insurance

QUESTIONS AND ANSWERS

Question — Can life insurance be used in a Keogh (HR 10) plan?

Answer — A Keogh plan is a qualified plan covering a proprietor or one or more partners of an unincorporated business. Life insurance can be used to provide a death benefit for regular employees covered under the plan, and the rules discussed in this chapter apply. Life insur-

Figure 20.1

P.S. 58 COMPUTATION

(INSERT CO'S STANDARD INDIVIDUAL 1 YR TERM RATES AT B1 IF LOWER)

PART A

INPUT:	EMPLOYEE'S AGE	45
INPUT:	FACE AMOUNT OF DEATH BENEFIT	$100,000
INPUT:	CASH VALUE TO EMPLOYER	-$40,000
	NET AMOUNT AT RISK	$60,000
	P.S. 58 CHARGE	$6.30
	GROSS AMOUNT INCLUDIBLE	$378.00
INPUT:	EMPLOYEE'S CONTRIBUTION	$.00

PART B

INPUT:	AMOUNT OF DIVIDEND PAID IN CASH TO EMPLOYEE	$.00
INPUT:	AMT OF DIV USED TO REDUCE EE'S PREM CONTRIBUTION	$.00
INPUT:	AMOUNT OF DIVIDEND HELD AT INTEREST FOR EMPLOYEE	$.00
INPUT:	AMOUNT OF DIVIDEND — IF CASH VALUE & DEATH BENEFIT OF PAID UP ADDITIONS ARE CONTROLLED BY EMPLOYEE	$.00
INPUT:	AMOUNT OF DIVIDEND — IF DIVIDENDS WERE USED TO BUY ONE YEAR TERM INSURANCE FOR THE EMPLOYEE	$.00
INPUT:	P.S. 58 COST OR, IF LOWER, PUBLISHED YEARLY RENEWABLE TERM COST — IF EMPLOYER GETS CASH VALUE OF PAID UP ADDITIONAL INSURANCE AND EMPLOYEE'S BENEFICIARY RECEIVES ANY BALANCE	$.00
	REPORTABLE P.S. 58 COST	$378.00

Illustration Courtesy of NumberCruncher Software, Financial Data Corporation, P.O. Box 1332, Bryn Mawr, PA 19010.

ance can also be provided under the plan for a proprietor or partners. However, slightly less favorable rules apply; these are discussed in detail in Chapter 15.

Question — Can life insurance be used in a Section 403(b) tax deferred annuity plan?

Answer — Life insurance can be provided as an incidental benefit under a tax deferred annuity plan. It is provided on much the same basis as in a qualified profit-sharing plan. Covered employees will have P.S. 58 costs to report as taxable income, as in a regular qualified plan.

Question — Can universal life insurance be used to provide an insured death benefit under a qualified plan?

Answer — Universal life and similar products may be used. However, even though universal life has an investment element like that in a whole life policy, the IRS has taken the view that the "incidental" limits applicable to universal life premiums are the same as those that apply to term insurance. So, if the percentage test is used, aggregate universal life premiums must be less than 25% of aggregate plan contributions. This appears to be an overly conservative rule, and may eventually be subject to a court challenge.

Question — What kind of plan qualifies as a "fully insured" plan that is exempt from the minimum funding requirements of the Code and the actuarial certification requirement?

Answer — In order to qualify for the fully insured exception to the minimum funding rules, the plan must have no assets fund except insurance and annuity contracts. Unallocated insurance-company group funding instruments such as deposit administration and IPG contracts, which are like trust funds, do not qualify.

Fully insured plans have not been common in the past, because the high cash value contracts used in these plans tend to have relatively low rates of investment return, and the employer's cost for the plan is relatively high. However, the new restrictive actuarial and minimum funding rules of the Omnibus Budget Reconciliation Act of 1987 reduces funding flexibility and increases the annual costs for actuarially servicing regular noninsured defined benefit plans. This reduces the relative disadvantages of some fully insured plans and makes them more competitive.

Question — Is it possible for an insured death benefit to be excluded from the decedent participant's estate for federal estate tax purposes?

Tools and Techniques

Answer — Although there have not yet been any decisive court cases or IRS rulings on the issue, some planners believe that an insured death benefit in a qualified plan is governed by the estate tax rules relating to insurance policies, and therefore can be kept out of a participant's estate by avoiding "incidents of ownership" in the policies.

For insurance in a qualified plan, this probably requires at least the following steps: (1) having life insurance policies owned by separate "subtrusts" under the plan; (2) appointing the subtrustee and successors (who should be independent parties such as a bank) irrevocably; (3) having all incidents of ownership exercised by the subtrustee, including owning the policy, receiving the proceeds, and selecting the beneficiary; and (4) designing plan provisions so that the participant has no lifetime right to receive policy cash values (policy cash values can be assigned to fund the required spousal survivor annuity).

Question — If a plan participant is uninsurable but already owns insurance policies, can these policies be sold to the plan to fund the plan death benefit?

Answer — Yes. Although the sale of property from a participant to a qualified plan would ordinarily be a prohibited transaction, the Department of Labor has issued an exemption, PTE 77-8, that allows such sales for this purpose. The opportunity to sell personally-owned insurance to the plan must be offered to all participants on a nondiscriminatory basis in order to use this exemption.

Question — How can insurance coverage be continued by a qualified plan after a plan participant has retired or accrued the maximum benefit under the plan?

Answer — If a plan participant's full retirement benefit has accrued, the employer can no longer make deductible contributions to the plan. Several alternatives are available for continuing insurance coverage: (1) the policy can be put on a reduced, paid-up basis; (2) the policy can be sold to the participant for its cash surrender value (possibly financed using a policy loan); (3) the participant can continue to pay premiums (they are nondeductible); or (4) the plan trustee can continue to pay premiums out of fund earnings (P.S. 58 costs to the participant continue under this alternative).

Chapter 21

LONG TERM DISABILITY INSURANCE

WHAT IS IT?

Long term disability insurance is an employer-sponsored program to provide disability income to employees who are disabled (unable to work) beyond a period specified in the plan, usually six months. Such plans are designed to supplement the social security disability coverage available to almost all employees. Disability income under an employer plan usually continues for the duration of the disability, or until death. The plan is usually funded through an insurance contract, particularly for smaller employers.

WHEN IS IT INDICATED?

1. When employees have a need for income to provide for themselves and their families in the event of long term disability.

   Unfortunately, disability is a common event. It is more likely that an employee will become disabled before age 65 than that he or she will die before 65. Social security disability benefits are available only for severe disabilities. Social security benefit levels are not adequate for highly paid employees to maintain their standard of living. Disability income plans are very common as employee benefits because of the great perceived need for them. They would be even more common, or more generous, if it were not for their high cost to employers. The question employers face is not so much whether there is a need for these programs, but rather how they can be financed.

2. When an employer wants to provide a special benefit for executives, if the company has no regular long term disability program for all employees, or if the regular program provides limited benefits. Under current law, employers can provide disability plans on a discriminatory basis — that is, special plans can be provided for selected executives only. The employer is free to choose (1) who will be covered, (2) the amounts of coverage provided (amounts can vary from employee to employee) and (3) the terms and conditions of coverage.

DESIGN FEATURES

Eligibility

Long term disability plans provided by employers are not subject to the nondiscrimination rules of Code section 89 (which applies to most other employee benefit plans).

Therefore, the employer has great flexibility in deciding who is covered under the plan.

Many plans cover only full-time salaried employees, or only a select group of executive employees. This reduces plan costs not only because fewer employees are covered, but also because experience in many firms indicates that disability claims are more frequent among non-salaried employees. Some plans simply use the approach of covering only employees above a specified salary level. Exclusions like these in an employer plan are not necessarily grossly inequitable to lower paid employees because social security disability benefit levels — income replacement ratios — are relatively satisfactory for lower paid employees.

Most long term disability plans require a waiting period of three months to a year before an eligible employee becomes covered.

Definition of Disability

The plan's definition of disability is very important in establishing its cost to the employer. The definition can be strict or liberal, or somewhere in between. Three common definitions will illustrate the range of options:

- the "social security" or "total and permanent" definition — disability is defined as a condition under which the individual "is unable to engage in any substantial gainful activity by reason of any medically determinable physical or mental impairment which can be expected to result in death or which has lasted or can be expected to last for a continuous period of not less than 12 months." This is the strictest (i.e., least favorable to the employee) definition that is commonly used.

- the "qualified for" definition — disability is defined as "the total and continuous inability of the employee to engage in any and every gainful occupation for which he or she is qualified or shall reasonably become qualified by reason of training, education, or experience." This definition is more liberal than the social security definition since it does not require the disabled employee to be incapable of any gainful employment, only employment for which the employee is qualified. This definition, or some variation of it, is commonly used in employer long term disability plans.

- the "regular occupation" or "own occupation" definition — disability is defined as the "total and

83   **Tools and Techniques**

continuous inability of the employee to perform any and every duty of his or her regular occupation.'' Although this definition is often used in short term disability plans (see Chapter 29), it is generally too liberal for an employer's long term plan. However, if the plan is designed purely as an extra benefit for a selected group of executives, a liberal definition might be used. Most individual disability policies also use a liberal definition since individuals, for themselves, tend to define disability in terms of inability to do their current job.

As these definitions indicate, most long term disability plans require total disability in order to receive benefits. However, some plans provide payments for partial disabilities, particularly if the partial disability is preceded by a total disability. This may encourage rehabilitation and return to gainful employment, which is desirable for both employer and employee.

Disability plans usually contain specific exclusions under which benefits will not be paid even if the definition of disability is otherwise met. Common exclusions are (1) disabilities during periods when the employee is not under a physician's care; (2) disabilities caused by an intentionally self-inflicted injury; and (3) disabilities beginning before the employee became eligible for plan coverage.

Benefit Formulas

Long term plans generally do not provide 100 percent of pre-disability income. The principal reason for this, from the employer's viewpoint, is to avoid disincentives to return to work. Insurers generally do not underwrite plans providing too high a replacement ratio. Disability income amounts of 50 to 70 percent of pre-disability income are typical.

Benefits are usually ''integrated'' with disability benefits from other plans. For example, a plan's benefit formula might provide that the disability benefit from the employer is 70 percent of the employee's pre-disability compensation, less disability benefits from specified other sources. This provides the employee with the desired 70 percent disability income level but the employer only pays whatever additional amount is required after other sources are taken into account. Typical sources of disability benefits, other than the disability plan itself, include (1) social security; (2) workers' compensation; (3) qualified or nonqualified retirement plans; (4) other insurance; or (5) earnings from other employment.

Integration with other plans can use either a full (dollar for dollar) offset of the disability benefit by the other income sources, or an integration formula of some kind can be used under which benefits from the employer plan are reduced by something less than a dollar for each dollar of other disability benefits. There are no federal tax law restrictions on integration similar to those applicable to qualified retirement plans. This means that the employer is free to design any kind of integration formula that meets its cost limits and other objectives for the plan.

TAX IMPLICATIONS

1. Employer contributions to disability income plans, either insurance premium payments or direct benefit payments under an uninsured plan, are deductible as employee compensation. Like all compensation deductions, they are subject to the ''reasonableness'' requirement described in Chapter 4.

2. In some plans, employees pay part of the cost of the plan, usually through payroll deductions. These payments are not deductible by the employee.

3. Employer payments of premiums under an insured disability plan do not result in taxable income to the employee.

4. Benefit payments under an employer plan are fully taxable to the employee (subject to the credit described below) if the plan was fully paid for by the employer. If the employer paid part of the cost, only a corresponding part of the benefit is taxable, again subject to credit. For example, if the employer paid 75 percent of the disability insurance premiums and the employee paid the remaining 25 percent, only 75 percent of the disability benefit received by the employee is taxable.

   IRS regulations specify the time over which the employer and employee percentages are to be measured for this purpose. For group disability insurance, generally, payments over the three year period prior to the disability are taken into account in determining the percentages paid by employer and employee.

5. If an employee receiving benefits meets the ''total and permanent'' disability definition described earlier, a limited tax credit reduces the tax impact of disability payments for lower-income recipients.

   Generally, the disability credit is calculated by taking the maximum amount subject to the credit (see below) and subtracting $1/2$ of the amount by which the taxpayer's adjusted gross income exceeds the AGI limits (see below). The credit is equal to 15 percent of this amount. Thus, the maximum annual tax credit is $1,125 for a joint return, as indicated below. The chart below shows the maximum amounts eligible for the credit, the maximum credit that may be obtained, and the limitations to adjusted gross income (AGI):

   MAXIMUM AMOUNT SUBJECT TO CREDIT

Single Person	$5,000
Joint Return (where one spouse is a qualified individual)	$5,000
Joint Return (where both spouses are qualified individuals)	$7,500
Married Filing Separately	$3,750

MAXIMUM CREDIT

Single Person	$750
Joint Return (where one spouse is a qualified individual)	$750
Joint Return (where both spouses are qualified individuals)	$1,125
Married Filing Separately	$562.50

ADJUSTED GROSS INCOME LIMITS

Single Person	$7,500
Married Filing Jointly	$10,000
Married Filing Separately	$5,000

For example, if a disabled employee has adjusted gross income (from all sources, including taxable disability income) of $14,000, and is married, filing jointly, the amount on which his disability tax credit is calculated would be $5,000 (the maximum amount for a joint return where only one spouse receives disability income payments) less $2,000 ($\frac{1}{2}$ of the amount by which the taxpayer's AGI exceeds $10,000). In short, this is $5,000 - $2,000, or $3,000. The taxpayer's credit is equal to 15 percent of $3,000, or $450. Accordingly, the employee's income tax bill for the year is reduced by $450. Note that to receive this credit the employee must meet the social security total and permanent definition of disability. An employee might receive benefits under some employer plans without meeting this strict definition of disability, as discussed above.

This tax credit is even further reduced by 15 percent of any tax-free income received by the employee from a pension, annuity, or disability benefit, including social security. Since most disability plans are integrated with social security benefits, this further reduction makes the credit even less valuable.

In view of all the reductions applicable to this credit, and the extremely low AGI limits on full availability, the credit has become a minor factor in the design of disability benefits.

6. Disability insurance premiums paid by the employer under the plan are not considered wages subject to employment taxes (FICA - social security - and FUTA - federal unemployment). Generally disability insurance premiums are not subject to state employment taxes either, but individual state laws should be consulted.

7. Disability benefits are subject to federal income tax withholding if paid directly by the employer. If paid by a third party such as an insurance company, withholding is required only if the employee requests it.

8. Disability benefits attributable to employer contributions are subject to social security taxes for a limited period at the beginning of a disability. Thereafter, they are not considered wages subject to social security tax.

ERISA REQUIREMENTS

A disability income plan is considered a welfare benefit plan under ERISA. Such plans require a written document, the naming of a plan administrator, and a formal written claims procedure by which employees can make benefit claims and appeal denials. The plan is not subject to the eligibility, vesting, or funding requirements of ERISA. The plan administrator must provide plan participants with a summary plan description (SPD).

WHERE CAN I FIND OUT MORE ABOUT IT?

1. Beam, Burton T., Jr. and John J. McFadden, *Employee Benefits,* 2nd ed. Homewood, IL: Richard D. Irwin, 1988.

2. *Tax Facts 1*, Cincinnati, OH: The National Underwriter Company. Revised annually.

QUESTIONS AND ANSWERS

Question — What are the alternatives to the classic employer-paid long term disability plan?

Answer — When an employer considers providing a disability income to an executive or group of executives, the advantages and disadvantages of an employer-paid plan versus individual disability insurance must be weighed.

The employer plan results in no current taxable income to the employee, and thus provides deferral of taxes. Disability benefits are, however, fully taxable, except for a credit which benefits only low-income employees. This raises some planning issues. First, the amount of disability benefit for a particular employee may be, and in fact usually is, much more than what the employer paid for it. Thus, the total tax bill to the employee is usually larger if the employee does in fact become disabled. Second, many authorities believe that current tax rates are lower than they will be in the future. So, each dollar of taxable disability income may be subject to more tax in the future than the value of a dollar's worth of current tax exclusion (ignoring the time value of money).

These factors may make individual disability income policies, or a group policy paid for totally by the employee, more attractive to some executives than an employer-paid long term disability plan. An employee-paid policy results in no current tax deduction, but benefits are free of tax. The cost of the policy to the executive can be minimized or eliminated if the employer pays additional compensation or an annual bonus in the amount of the employee's cost for the coverage, plus the income tax on the bonus itself — a so-called ''double bonus'' plan.

Tools and Techniques

Question — Is there any type of disability plan that provides *both* employer payment of premiums and non-taxation of benefits to the employee?

Answer — Under section 105(c) of the Code, disability benefits are tax-free if the amount of benefit is (a) based on permanent loss of use of a member or function of the body and (b) is computed by reference to the nature of the injury and not to the period the employee is absent from work. This Code provision is intended primarily to cover plans such as accidental death and dismemberment (AD&D) plans that pay a lump sum for loss of a leg, eye, etc. However, some planners have made use of this exclusion as a substitute for traditional disability insurance. This is done by designing a plan that pays a stated amount for a heart attack, for arthritis, or for other specified conditions, with benefits based on a schedule in the plan and not specifically on the employee's compensation. These benefits can be paid by the employer directly, or in some cases can be paid out of a qualified pension or profit-sharing plan. However, where the employer pays directly for coverage which provides a tax-free benefit, the coverage must be provided on a nondiscriminatory basis.

Another approach — one with less validity — that is sometimes used in order to get the best of both worlds is to design a plan under which the decision as to whether the employer or the employee pays premiums is postponed to the last possible time each year. This permits an employee to opt for employee payment if he or she becomes disabled during the year. However, if all the facts about such a plan were known to the IRS, it would probably be viewed as a sham — that is, treated as an employer-paid plan if an employee becomes disabled.

Chapter 22

MEDICAL EXPENSE REIMBURSEMENT PLAN (MERP)

WHAT IS IT?

Under a medical expense reimbursement plan, or MERP, an employer reimburses covered employees for specified medical (health and accident) expenses. These reimbursements come directly from corporate funds rather than from a third party insurer.

A MERP is used (1) as a substitute for health insurance (see Chapter 13), or (2) as a supplement to provide payments for medical expenses not covered under the company's health insurance plan (such as dental expenses or cosmetic surgery), or (3) to pay for medical expenses in excess of the limits in the company's health insurance plan. The tax objective of the plan is to provide tax-free benefits to the covered employees and obtain a corresponding employer tax deduction for the benefits paid.

MERPs were often used in the past to provide extra benefits for selected groups of executives. However, current tax law denies tax benefits to highly compensated employees if the plan does not meet the nondiscrimination tests of Code section 89, as described below.

WHEN IS IT INDICATED?

1. Where a corporation is closely held and shareholders and their family members are the primary or only employees.

2. In a professional corporation where the only employee is a professional in a high income tax bracket or where there are few other employees.

3. Where an employer would like to provide employees with medical benefits beyond those provided by the basic medical coverage already in force.

DESIGN FEATURES

Basically, a MERP is simple. The company adopts a plan by corporate resolution specifying (a) the group of employees covered and (b) the types of medical expenses that will be reimbursed, and (c) any limits or conditions on payment by the company. When an employee incurs medical expenses subject to reimbursement the employee submits a claim to the employer. The employer reimburses the employee if the claim is covered under the plan.

The plan's objective is to provide tax-free benefits to employees. Benefits will be tax free if (a) they qualify as medical expenses under the Code, and (b) (for a highly compensated employee) the plan is nondiscriminatory under

Code section 89, as discussed below under "Tax Implications."

A broad range of expenses can qualify as medical expenses under a MERP. This is one of the advantages of these plans — the plan can cover expenses not often available under health insurance plans. For example, a MERP can cover cosmetic surgery, full dental expenses including orthodontia, and even items such as swimming pools prescribed by a physician for treatment of a condition such as arthritis. Any expense that could be deducted by an individual as an itemized medical expense under Code section 213 is eligible for tax free reimbursement under a MERP. See Figure 22.1 at the end of this chapter for a partial list of items that have been approved for deduction under Section 213 and, thus, are eligible for tax free reimbursement under a MERP.

The plan can be fully funded and administered by the employer or the employer can obtain an insurance contract to provide one or more features. Insurance contracts can help to make plans more workable by providing (a) administrative services, (b) claims evaluation, or (c) insurance against large claims — known as "stop loss" coverage.

Stop loss coverage is generally very important if the employer is small and the MERP could become potentially liable for a large medical expense. For example, suppose Mullions, P.C., an architectural firm, has a MERP for its sole shareholder-employee Ornate Mullions and its two employees. The reimbursement plan supplements the company's health insurance. In some years there have been no claims at all against the plan. However, in 1990 suppose an employee has cosmetic surgery that results in complications and $90,000 in hospital and doctors' bills. Such a payment could bankrupt a small company.

An insurance stop loss contract could be obtained that would prevent this disaster by limiting the company's exposure in any one year to some specified amount that the company considers within its means. The premiums for stop loss coverage are usually relatively low because medical catastrophes are rare events.

TAX IMPLICATIONS

1. The employer may deduct 100 percent of the cost of benefits paid to employees under the plan. Plan administrative expenses, and the cost of any insured stop loss coverage, are also fully deductible.

Tools and Techniques

2. Deductions for prefunding medical benefits (that is, setting funds aside and deducting amounts for medical benefits to be paid in future years) are limited under rules set out in Code sections 419 and 419A. Generally, for a given year an employer can deduct expenditures for medical benefits up to a limit equal to the total of (a) the direct costs of the plan for the year — claims paid plus administrative costs, plus (b) contributions to an asset account up to 35% of the preceding year's direct costs. The employer may be subject to an excise tax if such a fund is used in connection with a plan that is discriminatory under Section 89.

3. The employee does not have taxable income when benefits are paid. Benefits are tax free when medical expenses are paid directly to doctors or hospitals or when the plan reimburses the employee for covered expenses, unless the plan does not meet the Section 89(k) requirements discussed below. Highly compensated employees may have to pay taxes on the value of plan coverage to the extent the plan is discriminatory under the Section 89 rules described below. See the "Questions and Answers" for further discussion.

4. The employee is eligible for an itemized medical expense deduction under Code Section 213 for any medical expenses not covered by the MERP or an employer health insurance plan. The Section 213 deduction is available only if the taxpayer itemizes deductions on the tax return. The deduction is limited to the amount by which the total of all eligible medical expenses exceeds 7.5% of the taxpayer's adjusted gross income.

Section 89 Nondiscrimination Rules

Section 89 provides detailed rules to prevent health plans from discriminating in favor of highly compensated employees, either in terms of plan coverage or benefits. If a plan does not meet these rules, plan coverage for highly compensated employees loses (entirely or in part) its tax-free status. Highly compensated employees must pay taxes on "excess benefits," i.e., the value of plan coverage provided to highly compensated employees that exceeds the value which would be considered nondiscriminatory under the Section 89 rules. The implications of this are discussed further in the "Questions and Answers."

In summary, the Section 89 rules are:

A. *Highly compensated* is defined as it is for qualified plans under Code section 414(q) — Appendix A discusses the complete definition of the term, which is both precise and complicated.

B. The plan's *eligibility* provisions must meet three requirements —

(1) at least 90% of all nonhighly compensated employees must be eligible and have available a benefit that is at least 50% of the largest employer-provided benefit under the plan,

(2) at least 50% of employees eligible for the plan must not be among the highly compensated group. This requirement is deemed met if the percentage of highly compensated eligible employees is no greater than the percentage of nonhighly compensated eligible employees, and

(3) the plan must contain no provision relating to eligibility that discriminates in favor of highly compensated employees.

C. *Benefits* must be "nondiscriminatory." For any testing year, the plan's benefit provisions are considered nondiscriminatory if the average employer-provided benefit received by nonhighly compensated employees is at least 75% of that received by highly compensated employees.

D. As an alternative to the tests listed in B and C above, a health plan is deemed nondiscriminatory for a testing year if at least 80 percent of the employer's nonhighly compensated employees are covered, and the plan does not contain participation requirements that discriminate in favor of highly compensated employees.

E. The nondiscrimination tests are applied to the benefits available and provided during a 12 month "testing year" designated in the plan and are made on the basis of the facts as of the "testing day" designated in the plan.

For a further discussion of Section 89, see Appendix F.

Section 89 Qualification Requirements

Unless the following requirements of Section 89(k) are satisfied, all covered employees, not just highly compensated employees, must include in income the value of employer-provided benefits under the health plan (benefits for this purpose are the services of providers and expense reimbursements, not the value of coverage):

- the plan must be in writing

- the plan must provide legally enforceable rights for employees

- employees must be notified of plan benefits

- the plan must be maintained for the exclusive benefit of employees

- the plan must be intended as a permanent plan

Continuation of Coverage

An employer's adoption of any kind of health plan for employees results in an additional and typically unexpected cost due to the passage of the Consolidated Omnibus Budget Reconciliation Act of 1985 (COBRA). COBRA added Code provisions under which the employer is subject to penalties unless the plan makes available continuation of health plan benefits for certain employees and their dependents after termination of employment and certain other qualifying events. There is an exemption for small employers — the COBRA continuation provisions apply for a given year only if the employer had 20 or more employees on a typical business day in the preceding year. Government and church plans are also exempt.

In general, under COBRA the employer must provide the option to continue an employee's existing health plan coverage (including dependent coverage) for 36 months after the following events:

(a) death of the employee

(b) divorce or legal separation of the covered employee (coverage continues for the former spouse and dependents)

(c) the employee's entitlement to Medicare benefits

(d) filing by the employer for Chapter 11 bankruptcy

(e) a child ceasing to be a dependent for plan purposes

Health plan coverage must be continued for 18 months after termination of employment or reduction in hours of employment.

Continuation coverage can be terminated before the 36 (or 18) month period if

- the employer terminates its health plan for all employees

- the beneficiary fails to pay his or her share of the premium

- the beneficiary becomes covered under another group health plan.

The employer can require the former employee or beneficiary to pay part of the cost of continuation coverage. However, this former employee or beneficiary share can't be more than 102% of the cost to the plan of coverage for similarly situated beneficiaries with respect to whom a qualifying event has not occurred (whether the cost is paid by the employer or employee).

The requirement to provide for continuation of coverage became effective for plan years which began after July 1, 1986. Originally, the penalty for noncompliance with these requirements was disallowance of the employer's deduction. However, for tax years beginning after December 31, 1988, the penalty is, generally, a tax of $100 a day during the period any failure with respect to a qualified beneficiary continues.

ERISA AND OTHER REQUIREMENTS

An employer's MERP is a "welfare benefit plan" subject to the ERISA requirements discussed in Appendix D.

WHERE CAN I FIND OUT MORE ABOUT IT?

1. Beam, Burton T., Jr. and John J. McFadden, *Employee Benefits,* 2nd ed. Homewood, IL: Richard D. Irwin, 1988.

2. *Tax Facts 1*, Cincinnati, OH: The National Underwriter Co. (revised annually).

3. Leimberg, Stephan R., et al., *The Tools and Techniques of Estate Planning,* 7th ed. Cincinnati, OH: The National Underwriter Co., 1988.

QUESTIONS AND ANSWERS

Question — Is it possible to design a MERP that excludes rank and file employees by funding the MERP with a health insurance contract?

Answer — No. Under pre-1989 law insured MERPs were exempt from nondiscrimination requirements. However, under the current Section 89 all health plans, insured and noninsured, are required to meet nondiscrimination requirements.

Question — Is there ever any advantage in designing a MERP that discriminates by covering only specific executives?

Answer — The consequence of not meeting the Section 89 nondiscrimination requirements is only that

(a) part or all of the value of plan coverage (the excess benefit, as computed under the complex Section 89 rules) is taxable to highly compensated employees;

(b) the excess benefit is taxable to the employee in the employee's tax year in which the testing year ends (in certain cases, the employer may elect the following year); and

(c) taxable excess benefits must (subject to penalty) be reported by the employer on the employee's Form W-2.

The employer does not lose any part of its deduction for a discriminatory plan.

Note that it is the *value of discriminatory plan coverage* and not the amount of benefits paid that is taxable to highly compensated employees in a discriminatory plan. In other words, in a given year highly compensated employees could have taxable income as a result of a discriminatory MERP even if they had no medical expenses and received no plan payments during that year. This in itself may make the use of discriminatory MERPs unattractive to many executives.

However, if there is a case where these consequences are not objectionable, a discriminatory plan may be useful. The consequences of a discriminatory plan can be alleviated by paying bonuses to highly compensated employees — taxable to employees and deductible to the employer — to cover the amount of tax generated by ''excess benefits'' taxed to the employee. Such a plan may still provide some tax advantage, if the employer's outlay exceeds the employee's tax cost. And the cost may be substantially less than providing the benefit on a nondiscriminatory basis.

Question — What employees can an employer exclude from a MERP or other employer health plan and still meet the Section 89 coverage tests?

Answer — Before the eligibility and benefit tests of Section 89 are applied, there is a long list of employees who do not have to be considered in applying the test and who therefore can be excluded from the plan. These are

- employees who have not completed at least one year of service (6 months for core health benefits)

- employees who work fewer than 17½ hours per week or less than 6 months during any year (or shorter hours/months if specified in the plan)

- employees who have not attained age 21 (or lower eligibility age if specified in the plan)

- employees covered under a collective-bargaining agreement if there is evidence that health benefits have been a subject of good faith bargaining

- nonresident aliens who receive no U.S. source income.

- certain students employed by the educational institution in which they are enrolled.

After these employees have been excluded, the plan can then further exclude any other employees, so long as the required tests are met.

Question — Can a MERP be adopted if all the employees in the business are related to the owners of the business?

Answer — The Internal Revenue Code definition of ''highly compensated employee'' provides that family members of 5-percent owners, and family members of the 10 highest paid employees will not be deemed to be separate employees for benefit plan purposes. A family member for this purpose means the highly compensated employee's spouse, lineal descendants and ascendants, and the descendants' and ascendants' spouses.

The result is that in benefit plans for many family companies, all of the participants will be deemed highly compensated. However, the Technical and Miscellaneous Revenue Act of 1988 provides that the eligibility and benefit nondiscrimination requirements of Section 89 do not apply to a plan for any year in which the only employees are highly compensated. Thus, it appears that a MERP under these circumstances would not violate the Section 89 nondiscrimination rules.

Figure 22.1
(pg. 1)

The following is a partial list of items which the IRS or the courts have held to constitute deductible medical expenses. Items traditionally covered under health insurance plans are not included.

- **Professional Services of**
  - Christian Science Practitioner
  - Oculist
  - Unlicensed practitioner if the type and quality of his services are not illegal

- **Equipment and Supplies**
  - Abdominal supports
  - Air conditioner where necessary for relief from an allergy or for relieving difficulty in breathing
  - Arches
  - Autoette (auto device for handicapped person), but not if used to travel to job or business
  - Back supports
  - Contact lenses
  - Cost of installing stair-seat elevator for person with heart condition
  - Elastic hosiery
  - Eyeglasses
  - Fluoridation unit in home

- **Medical Treatments**
  - Acupuncture
  - Cosmetic Surgery
  - Diatheray
  - Healing services
  - Hydrotherapy (water treatments)

- **Medicines**
  - Drugs
  - Patent medicines

- **Miscellaneous**
  - Birth control pills or other birth control
  - Braille books — excess cost of braille books over cost of regular editions
  - Clarinet lessons advised by dentist for treatment of tooth defects
  - Convalescent home — for medical treatment only
  - Face lifting operation, even if not recommended by doctor
  - Fees paid to health institute where the exercises, rubdowns, etc., taken there are prescribed by a physician as treatments necessary to alleviate a physical or mental defect or illness

  - Hair transplant operation
  - Practical or other non-professional nurse for medical services only; not for care of a healthy person or a small child who is not ill.
  - Costs for medical care of elderly person, unable to get about, or person subject to spells
  - Hearing aide
  - Heating devices
  - Invalid chair
  - Orthopedic shoes
  - Reclining chair if prescribed by doctor
  - Repair of special telephone equipment for the deaf
  - Sacroiliec belt
  - Special mattress and plywood bed boards for relief of arthritis of spine
  - Trues
  - Wig advised by doctor as essential to mental health of person who lost all hair from disease
  - Navajo healing ceremonies ("sings")
  - Sterilization
  - Vasectomy
  - Whirlpool baths
  - Vitamins, tonics, etc., prescribed by doctor — but not if taken as food supplement or to preserve your general health
  - Kidney donor's or possible kidney donor's expenses
  - Legal fees for guardianship of mentally ill spouse where commitment was necessary for medical treatment
  - Nurse's board and wages, including social security taxes you pay on wages
  - Remedial reading for child suffering from dyslexia
  - Sanitarium and similar institutions
  - "Seeing-eye" dog and its maintenance
  - Special school costs for physically and mentally handicapped children
  - Wages of guide for a blind person
  - Telephone-teletype costs and television adapter for closed caption service for deaf person

Figure 22.1
(pg.2)

The following is a list of expenses which have been held *not* deductible.

- Antiseptic diaper service
- Athletic club expenses to keep physically fit
- Babysitting fees to enable you to make doctor's visits
- Boarding school fees paid for healthy child while parent is recuperating from illness. It makes no difference that this was done on a doctor's advice
- Bottled water bought to avoid drinking fluoridated city water
- Cost of divorce recommended by psychiatrist
- Cost of hotel room suggested for sex therapy
- Cost of trips for a "change of environment" to boost morale of ailing person. That doctor prescribed the trip is immaterial
- Dance lessons advised by doctors as physical and mental therapy or for the alleviation of varicose veins or arthritis; however, the cost of a clarinet and lessons for the instrument were allowed as deduction when advised as therapy for a tooth defect.
- Deductions from your wages for a sickness insurance under state law
- Domestic help — even if recommended by doctor because of spouse's illness. But part of cost attributed to any nursing duties performed by the domestic is deductible
- Funeral, cremation or burial, cemetery plot, monument, mausoleum
- Health programs offered by resort hotels, health clubs and gyms
- Illegal operation and drugs

- Marriage counseling fees
- Maternity clothes
- Premiums, in connection with life insurance policies, paid for disability, double indemnity or for waiver of premium in event of total and permanent disability or policies providing for reimbursement of loss of earnings or a guarantee of a specific amount in the event of hospitalization
- Scientology fees
- Special food or beverage substitutes — but excess cost of chemically uncontaminated foods over what would have ordinarily been spent on normal food was deductible for allergy patients
- Toothpaste
- Transportation costs of a disabled person to and from work
- Traveling costs to look for a new place to live on doctor's advice
- Travel costs to favorable climate when you can live there permanently
- Tuition and travel expenses to send a problem child to a particular school for a beneficial change in environment
- Veterinary fees for pet; pet is not a dependent
- Weight reduction or stop smoking programs undertaken for general health, not for specific ailments
- Your divorced spouse's medical bills. You may be able to deduct them as alimony

Chapter 23

MONEY PURCHASE PENSION PLAN

WHAT IS IT?

A money purchase plan is a qualified employer retirement plan that is, in many ways, the simplest of all qualified plans:

- Each employee has an individual account in the plan. The employer makes annual contributions to each employee's account under a nondiscriminatory contribution formula. Usually the formula requires a contribution of a specified percentage (up to 25%) of each employee's annual compensation. Annual employer contributions can't be more than $30,000 or, if greater, $1/4$ of the dollar limitation for defined benefit plans. (The dollar limitation for defined benefit plans is $94,023 for 1988.)

- Plan benefits consist of the amount accumulated in each participant's account at retirement or termination of employment. This is the total of employer contributions, interest or other investment return on plan assets, and capital gains realized by the plan on sales of assets in the employee's account.

- The plan may provide that the employee's account balance is payable in one or more forms of annuity equivalent in value to the account balance.

WHEN IS IT INDICATED?

1. When an employer wants to install a qualified retirement plan that is simple to administer and explain to employees.

2. When employees are relatively young and have substantial time to accumulate retirement savings.

3. When employees are willing to accept a degree of investment risk in their plan accounts, in return for the potential benefits of good investment results.

4. When some degree of retirement income security in the plan is desired. (While accounts are not guaranteed, annual employer contributions are required. This provides a degree of retirement security that is intermediate between a defined benefit plan and a profit-sharing plan.)

5. When an employer seeks to reward long-term employee relationships.

ADVANTAGES

1. As with all qualified plans, a money purchase plan provides a tax-deferred retirement savings medium for employees.

2. The plan is relatively simple and inexpensive to design, administer, and explain to employees.

3. The plan formula can provide a deductible annual employer contribution of up to 25% of each employee's compensation, as compared with the 15% of payroll limit on deductible contributions to profit-sharing plans.

4. Plan distributions may be eligible for the special 5-year (or 10-year) averaging tax computation available for qualified plans.

5. Individual participant accounts allow participants to benefit from good investment results in the plan fund.

DISADVANTAGES

1. Retirement benefits may be inadequate for employees who enter the plan at older ages. For example, if an employer contributes 10% of compensation annually to each employee's account, the accumulation at age 65 for employees with varying entry ages will be as follows, assuming the plan fund earns 9% interest on the average (a very good return by current standards):

Age at plan entry	Annual compensation	Account balance at age 65
25	$35,000	$1,289,022
30	35,000	822,937
40	35,000	323,134
50	35,000	112,012
55	35,000	57,961
60	35,000	22,832
60	70,000	45,663

This illustration shows that the "time factor" works faster to increase account balances than increased compensation with less time for accumulation. If a closely held corporation that has been in business for many years adopts a money purchase plan, key employees often will be among the older plan entrants. The money purchase plan's failure to provide adequately for such employees, even with their high compensation levels, can be a serious disadvantage.

2. The annual addition to each employee's account in a money purchase plan is limited to the lesser of (a) 25% of compensation or (b) the greater of $30,000 or $1/4$ of

Tools and Techniques

the defined benefit dollar limitation. (The dollar limitation for defined benefit plans is $94,023 for 1988.) This limits the relative amount of funding available for highly compensated employees. For example, if an employee earns $200,000, no more than $30,000 annually can be contributed for that employee; but that $30,000 is only 15% of the employee's compensation. So for this employee, the money purchase plan offers no advantage over a profit-sharing plan.

3. Employees bear investment risk under the plan. The ultimate amount that can be accumulated under a money purchase plan is very sensitive to investment return, even for an employee who entered the plan at an early age. Figure 23-1 shows this by comparing the ultimate account balance resulting from $1,000 of annual contribution at two different return rates.

   While bearing investment risk is a potential disadvantage to employees, it does tend to reduce employer costs as compared with a defined benefit plan.

4. The plan is subject to the Code's minimum funding requirements. Employers are obligated to make the plan contribution each year or be subject to minimum funding penalties.

DESIGN FEATURES

Most money purchase plans use a benefit formula requiring an employer contribution that is a flat percentage of each employee's compensation. Percentages up to 25 percent may be used. Only the first $200,000 of each employee's compensation can be taken into account in the plan formula. This $200,000 limit is indexed for inflation beginning in 1989.

Some money purchase formulas also use a factor related to the employee's service. However, service-related factors generally favor highly compensated employees. In small, closely held businesses or professional corporations, the IRS might consider a service-related factor to result in prohibited discrimination in favor of highly compensated employees. Plan designers generally avoid service-related contribution formulas in these situations.

A plan benefit formula can be "integrated" with social security. This avoids duplicating social security benefits already provided to the employee and reduces employer costs for the plan. An integrated formula defines a level of compensation known as the "integration level." The plan then provides a higher rate of employer contributions for compensation above that integration level than the rate for compensation below that integration level.

Example: A money purchase plan specifies an integration level of $20,000 and provides for employer contributions of 15% of compensation above the $20,000 integration level and 10% below the $20,000 integra-

tion level. Employee Art Rambo earns $30,000 this year. The employer contribution to Art's account this year totals $3,500 — 15% of $10,000 (Art's compensation in excess of the $20,000 integration level) plus 10% of the first $20,000 of Art's compensation.

The Internal Revenue Code and proposed regulations specify the degree of integration permitted in a plan. Generally, the integration level must equal the social security taxable wage base in effect at the beginning of the plan year ($48,000 for plan years beginning in 1989). The difference in the allocation percentages above and below the integration level can be no more than the lesser of the

(1) the percentage contribution below the integration level or

(2) the greater of 5.7% or the old age portion of the social security tax rate for the year.

Thus, for a plan year beginning in 1989, an integrated plan must have an integration level of $48,000. If the plan allocated employer contributions plus forfeitures at the rate of 15.7% for compensation above the integration level, then it would have to provide at least a 10% allocation for compensation below the integration level (making the difference 5.7%).

Any of the Code's permitted vesting provisions can be used in a money purchase plan. Since money purchase plans tend to be oriented toward longer service employees, the five year "cliff vesting" provision (no vesting until 5 years of service, then 100% vesting) is often used.

If an employee leaves before becoming fully vested in his or her account balance, an unvested amount referred to as a "forfeiture" is left behind in the plan. Forfeitures can be used either to reduce future employer contributions under the plan or they can be added to remaining participants' account balances. Adding forfeitures to participants' account balances tends to be favorable to key employees, since they are likely to participate in the plan over a long time period. For this reason, the IRS requires forfeitures to be allocated in a nondiscriminatory manner. This usually requires forfeiture allocation in proportion to participants' compensation, rather than in proportion to their existing account balances.

Benefits in a money purchase plan are usually payable at termination of employment or at the plan's stated normal retirement age. Money purchase plans traditionally provide that the participant's account balance is converted to an equivalent annuity at retirement, based on annuity rates provided in the plan. This is the origin of the term "money purchase." It is becoming more common to provide for a lump sum or installment payment from the plan as an alternative to an annuity. However, a money purchase plan, as a condition of qualification, must provide a joint and survivor annuity as the automatic form of benefit. The participant, with the con-

Figure 23.1

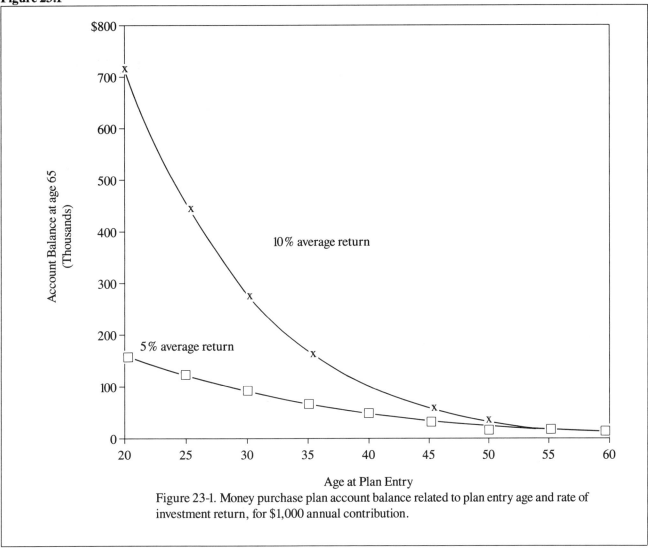

Figure 23-1. Money purchase plan account balance related to plan entry age and rate of investment return, for $1,000 annual contribution.

sent of the spouse, may elect a different benefit option. This is discussed further in Appendix B.

The IRS generally does not allow money purchase plans to provide for "in-service distributions" — that is, benefits payable before termination of employment. However, plan loan provisions are allowable, although relatively uncommon.

Money purchase plan funds are generally invested in a pooled account managed (through a trustee or insurance company) by the employer or a fund manager designated by the employer. Either a trust fund or group or individual insurance contracts can be used. Chapter 20 discusses how life insurance can be used in the plan.

TAX IMPLICATIONS

1. Employer contributions to the plan are deductible when made, so long as the plan remains "qualified." A plan is qualified if it meets eligibility, vesting, funding and other requirements discussed in Appendix A. In addition, the plan must designate that it is a money purchase pension plan.

2. Assuming the plan remains qualified, taxation of the employee on plan contributions is deferred. Both employer contributions and earnings on plan assets are nontaxable to plan participants until withdrawn.

3. Under Code section 415, annual additions to each participant's account are limited to the lesser of (a) 25% of the participant's compensation or (b) the greater of $30,000 or 1/4 of the defined benefit limit. (The dollar limitation for defined benefit plans is $94,023 for 1988.) Annual additions include (1) employer contributions to the participant's account; (2) forfeitures from other participants' accounts; and (3) employee contributions to the account.

4. Distributions from the plan must follow the rules for qualified plan distributions. Certain premature or excessive distributions are subject to penalties. The distribution rules are discussed in Appendix B.

5. Lump sum distributions made after age 59½ are subject to a limited election to use a special 5-year averaging tax calculation. Certain older participants may also be eligible for a 10-year averaging tax calculation for lump sum distributions. Not all distributions are eligible for these special tax calculations. Appendix B covers these rules, including IRS forms.

6. The plan is subject to the minimum funding rules of section 412 of the Code. This requires minimum periodic contributions, subject to a penalty imposed on the employer if less than the minimum amount is contributed. For a money purchase plan, the minimum contribution is generally the amount required under the plan's contribution formula. For example, if the plan formula requires a contribution of 20% of each participant's compensation, this is generally the amount required to meet the minimum funding rules. The employer must make plan contributions on at least a quarterly basis (although this requirement will not be fully phased in until 1992). Appendix A discusses these rules further.

7. The plan is subject to the ERISA reporting and disclosure rules outlined in Appendix D.

ALTERNATIVES

1. Target benefit plans are much like money purchase plans, but the employer contribution percentage can be based on age at plan entry — higher for older entrants. Such a plan may be more favorable where the employer wants to provide adequate benefits for older employees.

2. Profit-sharing plans provide more employer flexibility in contributions, but deductible contributions are limited to 15% of payroll.

3. Defined benefit plans provide more security of retirement benefits and proportionately greater contributions for older plan entrants, but are much more complex to design and administer.

4. Nonqualified deferred compensation plans can be provided exclusively for selected executives, but the employer's tax deduction is generally deferred until benefit payments are made. This can be as much as 20 or 30 years after the employer's contribution is made.

5. Individual retirement savings is available as an alternative or supplement to an employer plan, but except for an IRA there is no tax deferral.

HOW TO INSTALL A PLAN

Installation of a money purchase plan follows the qualified plan installation procedure described in Appendix C.

WHERE CAN I FIND OUT MORE ABOUT IT?

1. McFadden, John J., *Retirement Plans for Employees*, Homewood, IL: Richard D. Irwin, 1988.

2. Gee, Judith Boyers, *Pensions in Perspective*, 2nd ed. Cincinnati, OH: The National Underwriter Co., 1987.

3. Graduate Course: Advanced Pension and Retirement Planning I (GS 814), The American College, Bryn Mawr, PA.

QUESTIONS AND ANSWERS

Question — Can a self-employed person adopt a money purchase plan?

Answer — A self-employed person can adopt a money purchase plan covering not only his or her regular employees, if any, but also covering the self-employed person(s). Such plans are sometimes referred to as "Keogh" or "HR 10" plans. The self-employed person is treated much the same as the regular employees covered, but there are some special rules and planning considerations that are covered in Chapter 15 of this book.

Question — What special issues are involved in money purchase plans covering shareholder-employees in an S corporation?

Answer — S corporations can have money purchase plans that cover shareholder-employees as well as regular employees. However, the plan contribution formula generally can't provide an employer contribution for all of the shareholder-employee's income from the corporation. The employer contribution formula can be based only on the shareholder's compensation for services rendered to the corporation. Any portion of the shareholder's income that represents dividends must be excluded from the plan formula.

A shareholder-employee who holds more than 5 percent of the S corporation's stock is subject to the same restriction on plan loans that applies to an owner-employee of an unincorporated business; this is discussed in Chapter 15 of this book.

Question — Can an employer fund a money purchase plan using employee salary reductions?

Answer — Salary reductions by employees allowing employee contributions on a before-tax basis are allowed only in (1) a profit-sharing (Section 401(k) type) plan, (2) a salary reduction SEP (simplified employee pension) or (3) a Section 403(b) tax deferred annuity plan (tax-exempt employers only). Thus, this kind of funding for a money purchase plan is not available.

However, money purchase plans can allow after-tax contributions by employees to increase account balances (permitting greater tax-sheltered investment accumulation) and ultimate retirement benefits. Such after-tax contribution provisions must meet the administratively complex nondiscrimination rules of Code section 401(m). (These are discussed in Chapter 27.) As a result of these rules, after-tax contribution provisions in money purchase plans are less common than in the past.

Tools and Techniques

Chapter 24
NONQUALIFIED DEFERRED COMPENSATION

WHAT IS IT?

A nonqualified deferred compensation plan is any employer retirement, savings, or deferred compensation plan for employees that does not meet the tax and labor law (ERISA) requirements applicable to qualified pension and profit-sharing plans.

Nonqualified plans are usually used to provide retirement benefits to a select group of executives or to provide such a select group with supplemental benefits beyond those provided in the company's qualified retirement plans.

Nonqualified plans do not provide the same type of tax benefit as qualified plans because in the nonqualified plan the employer's income tax deduction cannot be taken "up front." The employer must wait until the year in which the employee reports income from the deferred compensation plan to take its deduction. However, a nonqualified plan can provide tax deferral for the employee, as well as meet employer and employee compensation and financial planning objectives. Informal financing of the plan through life insurance or some other type of employer-held asset reserve can increase the security of the plan to the employee almost to the level of a qualified plan.

WHEN IS IT INDICATED?

1. When an employer wants to provide a deferred compensation benefit to an executive or group of executives but the cost of a qualified plan would be prohibitive because of the large number of non-executive employees who would have to be covered. A nonqualified plan is ideal for many companies that do not have or cannot afford qualified plans but want to provide key employees with retirement income.

2. When an employer wants to provide additional deferred compensation benefits to an executive who is already receiving the maximum benefits or contributions under the company's qualified retirement plan.

3. When the business wants to provide certain key employees with tax deferred compensation under terms or conditions different from those applicable to other employees.

4. When an executive or key employee wants to use the employer to, in essence, create a forced, automatic, and relatively painless investment program that uses the employer's tax savings to "leverage" the future benefits. Since amounts paid by the employer in the future

will be tax deductible, the after-tax cost of the deferred compensation will be favorable. For example, if the employer is in a combined federal and state tax bracket of 40 percent, it can pay $50,000 to a retired executive at a net after-tax cost of only $30,000 because of its tax deduction which saves it $20,000 (40% of $50,000).

5. Nonqualified plans can help a corporation solve the "3R" (recruit, retain, or retire) problem. These plans are a fundamental tool in designing executive compensation plans to meet these issues.

6. Closely held corporations can use nonqualified deferred compensation to attract and hold non-shareholder employees. For such employees, an attractive deferred compensation package can be a substitute for the equity-based compensation packages — company stock and stock options — that these employees would expect to receive if they were employed by a publicly held company.

ADVANTAGES

1. The design of nonqualified plans is much more flexible than that of qualified plans. A nonqualified plan:

   - allows coverage of any group of employees or even a single employee, without any nondiscrimination requirements;

   - can provide an unlimited benefit to any one employee (subject to the "reasonable compensation" requirement for deductibility);

   - allows the employer to provide different benefit amounts for different employees, on different terms and conditions.

2. A nonqualified plan involves minimal IRS, ERISA, and other governmental regulatory requirements such as reporting and disclosure, fiduciary, funding requirements, etc.

3. A nonqualified plan can provide deferral of taxes to employees (but the employer's deduction is also deferred). The advantage of deferral as such is currently being debated since current income tax rates are low and there is some expectation of higher rates in the future. However, if dollars otherwise paid currently in taxes can be put to work over the period of deferral, planners can show advantages in nonqualified plans even if future tax rates are higher.

Tools and Techniques

4. A nonqualified plan can be used by an employer as a form of ''golden handcuffs'' that help to tie the employee to the company. Since the qualified plan vesting rules do not apply if the plan is properly designed (as discussed below), the plan can provide forfeiture of benefits according to almost any vesting schedule the employer desires and for almost any contingency such as terminating employment before retirement or misconduct such as going to work for a competitor.

5. Although the plan generally involves only the employer's unsecured promise to pay benefits, security to the executive can be provided through informal financing arrangements such as corporate-owned life insurance or a ''rabbi trust'' (defined below).

DISADVANTAGES

1. The company's tax deduction is not available for the year in which compensation is earned but must be deferred until the year in which income is taxable to the employee. This can be a substantial period of time — ten, twenty or even thirty or more years in the future.

2. From the executive's point of view, the principal problem is lack of security as a result of depending only on the company's unsecured promise to pay. In addition, most of the protections of federal tax and labor law (ERISA) that apply to qualified plans — for example the vesting, fiduciary, and funding requirements — are not applicable to the typical nonqualified plan.

3. While accounting treatment is not entirely clear (see below), some disclosure of executive nonqualified plans on financial statements may be required. This would reduce the confidentiality of the arrangement which could be considered undesirable by both employer and employee.

4. Not all employers can take advantage of nonqualified plans. The employer organization must meet two minimum requirements:

   • It must be a regular or ''C'' corporation — not an S corporation or unincorporated organization. (A *nonprofit* corporation or governmental organization can have a nonqualified plan but there are special problems which are discussed in Chapter 11.)

   • The corporation must be one that is likely to last long enough to make the payments promised under the plan. Although funds can be set aside to secure payment even if the corporation disappears, the full tax benefits of the plan cannot be provided unless the corporation exists at the time of payment so it can take its tax deduction. Many closely held businesses, family businesses, and professional corporations do not meet this criterion.

OBJECTIVES IN PLAN DESIGN

Through its considerable flexibility, a nonqualified deferred compensation plan can help both the employer and the employee achieve their planning objectives. The plan should be designed to achieve these objectives to the maximum extent possible.

Employer Objectives

Employers usually adopt nonqualified deferred compensation plans to provide an incentive to hire key employees, to keep key employees, and to provide performance incentives — in other words, the typical employer compensation policy objectives that apply to other forms of compensation planning.

Plans reflecting employer objectives will typically consider the following types of design:

• Eligibility will be confined to key executives or technical employees that the employer wants to recruit and keep.

• Plan eligibility can be part of a predetermined company policy or the plan can simply be adopted for specific individuals as the need arises.

• Performance incentive features will be included. The features include benefits or contributions based on salary, increases if specific profits or sales goals are achieved, or benefits related to the value of the employer's stock.

• Termination of employment will typically cause loss or forfeiture of benefits particularly for terminations resulting in undesirable conduct such as competing with the employer.

• The plan often will not provide immediate vesting of benefits but vesting will occur over a period of time to help retain employees.

• It is generally not in the employer's interest to fund the plan in advance or set aside funds for the plan prior to the commencement of benefit payments.

Employee Objectives

An employee's personal financial planning objective is primarily to obtain additional forms of compensation for which income tax is deferred as long as possible, preferably until the money is actually received. Usually it is only highly compensated employees who wish to (or can afford to) defer compensation to a substantial extent, since only they have enough discretionary income to support substantial saving. From the employee's point of view, the tax deferral, and therefore the compounding of dollars that otherwise would be paid currently in taxes, is a major benefit of the plan. In addition, it is possible that plan benefits may be paid when the employee is in a lower marginal tax bracket. (However, due to frequent changes in the tax laws this factor is difficult to predict.)

An employee who has enough bargaining power to influence the design of a nonqualified deferred compensation plan will favor the following types of provisions:

- Benefit certainty is usually more important than incentive provisions; employees rarely seek contingent features unless the company is definitely growing and the employee wants a benefit based on company growth.

- Employees will want a benefit that is immediately 100 percent vested without forfeiture provisions for cause or otherwise.

- Concern for benefit security is significant and employees will want to explore some of the financing (informal funding) arrangements described later, such as corporate-owned life insurance, the rabbi trust, or a surety bond.

Types of Benefit and Contribution Formulas

Nonqualified deferred compensation plans generally use either a "*salary continuation*" or "*salary reduction*" approach.

- The salary continuation approach provides a specified deferred amount payable in the future without any stated reduction of current salary. The benefit is in the form of a continuation of salary at a specified level at retirement, disability, or other termination of employment.

- The salary reduction design provides for the deferral of a specified amount of the compensation of the employee otherwise payable. Salary reduction plans are sometimes simply called "deferred compensation," but this term will not be used here to avoid confusion. The employer contribution (or deemed contribution) to this type of plan can also be in the form of a "bonus" without actual reduction of salary.

Economically, both the salary continuation and the salary reduction approach amount to the same thing, but represent significantly different underlying compensation philosophies. Employer-instituted plans often use the salary continuation approach rather than salary reduction, but this is not universal.

A salary continuation plan generally uses a defined-benefit type of formula to calculate the benefit amount. The salary reduction approach typically resembles a defined-contribution plan, with individual "accounts" that usually have an investment element for each participant.

Salary Continuation (Defined Benefit) Formulas. The salary continuation or defined-benefit approach usually speci-

fies plan benefits as a percentage of compensation. Compensation for this purpose is typically measured over a three to five year period of the employee's highest earnings, as in a qualified defined-benefit plan. The benefit payable can also be dependent on the employee's years of service.

The salary continuation benefit can be integrated with social security, usually using a 100 percent offset. For example, the nonqualified plan might provide an annual retirement benefit of 60 percent of the employee's final average (or highest three year average) compensation less the actual social security benefit paid to the employee. The complex social security integration rules applicable to qualified plans do not apply so any suitable type of integration formula can be used. An offset for other types of benefits can also be used in the formula; for example, the nonqualified salary continuation payments could be offset by any other retirement or disability payable to the employee under qualified or other plans.

Two common types of salary continuation plan formulas are the "supplemental executive retirement plan" (SERP) and the "excess benefit plan."

A SERP is a plan similar to a qualified defined benefit plan in that it focuses on providing adequate retirement income to executives. Benefit formulas and other provisions are similar to those for qualified defined benefit plans. The term SERP is usually used to refer to a plan covering a relatively broad group of executives. A company may also refer to its entire collection of special retirement benefits for executives as a "SERP."

An excess benefit plan is one that focuses on supplementing the benefits of a qualified plan by providing benefits to executives whose qualified plan benefits are limited under Code section 415. Section 415 limits an employee's annual pension to no more than $90,000, as indexed ($94,023 in 1988).

For example, suppose Blarp Corporation provides a qualified defined benefit plan with an annual retirement benefit equal to 50% of final average compensation. Executive Frank Blarp retires in 1988 with final three year average compensation of $300,000. The qualified plan benefit can provide him with a pension of only $94,023 (less than ⅓ of his preretirement income) because of the Section 415 limit, even though the 50% benefit formula applied to other employees provides an annual pension equal to ⅓ of their preretirement income. If Blarp Corporation has a nonqualified excess benefit plan the excess benefit plan can "make up the difference" by providing additional retirement benefits so that Frank receives a full $150,000 annually.

Salary Reduction (Defined Contribution) Formula. With a defined contribution approach, a specified amount (the salary reduction or employer "bonus") is periodically added to a participant's "account," which can be either a real accumulation of funds or simply a bookkeeping account. The benefit payable at retirement or termination of service represents the accumulation in the participant's account. This is similar to the money purchase approach for qualified plans. Nonqualified plans of this type are sometimes referred to as money purchase plans.

Contributions typically are a specified percentage of the employee's current compensation each year. However, the contribution level can also be an amount determined as the annual funding required to meet a "target" benefit level at retirement. (Chapter 33 discusses the "target" type of benefit formula.)

If the employee's account is only a bookkeeping account, in order for the employee to avoid losing the benefit of investment earnings on the deferred compensation, the employer can guarantee a specified minimum interest rate on the bookkeeping account. Alternatively, the employer can make an annual allocation to the account based on an interest formula or index specified in the plan (usually an index beyond the employer's control such as Moody's Bond Index). Sometimes the rate of return that is guaranteed is tied to the value of the company's stock.

Form of Benefits. Nonqualified deferred compensation plans usually provide payments at retirement in a lump sum or a series of annual payments. Life annuities or joint and survivor annuities for the participant and spouse can also be provided. Since the elaborate restrictions on qualified plan payouts do not apply, considerable design flexibility is available.

Payout options must avoid the triggering of the constructive receipt doctrine — that is, the taxation of benefits before they are actually received by the employee. Constructive receipt problems are discussed further in "Tax Implications," below.

Termination of Employment

If the plan emphasizes employer objectives termination provisions will be designed to maximize incentive features and noncompetition and similar provisions. At the extreme, an employer-instituted plan may even provide a complete forfeiture of nonqualified benefits if the employee terminates employment before retirement. Most employer-instituted plans will at least have a vesting schedule under which benefits do not become vested until a specified number of years of service has been attained. Graduated vesting can also be used. As discussed below, if the plan is unfunded the ERISA vesting provisions do not apply and any type of vesting schedule can be used.

If an executive's termination of employment results from disability, special benefits may be provided, particularly if the employee has some bargaining power in designing the plan. An employee will generally want benefits paid immediately upon disability. For this purpose, the employee will also want to use a definition of disability that is somewhat less than the "total and permanent" disability required for social security disability benefits. A typical disability provision based on employee objectives would provide for disability payments if the employee is no longer able to continue working in his specific profession or executive position. Disability determinations can be shifted to a third party such as an insurer, or a physician chosen by the employer and employee, in order to minimize possible disputes.

Funded versus Unfunded Plans

In the employee benefit area, the term *funded plan* has a very specialized meaning. In the tax and ERISA sense, a plan is formally funded if the employer has set aside money or property to the employee's account in an irrevocable trust, or through some other means that restricts access to the fund by the employer and the employer's creditors.

Assets to informally fund or "finance" the employer's obligation under a nonqualified plan can (and almost always should) be set aside, but if this fund is accessible to the employer and its creditors, providing no explicit security to the employee ahead of other employer creditors, the plan is deemed to be unfunded for tax and ERISA purposes.

Most nonqualified deferred compensation plans are unfunded because of significant tax and ERISA considerations:

- In a funded plan, amounts in the fund are taxable to the employee at the time the employee's rights to the fund become "substantially vested." As discussed in Chapter 26, under the rules of Code section 83 substantial vesting can occur before funds are actually received by the employee.

- Funded plans are subject to the ERISA vesting and fiduciary requirements which create design inflexibility. Under the ERISA vesting rules, the plan must have a vesting schedule that is at least as fast as either the five year schedule (no vesting up to five years of service, 100 percent vesting after five years) or the three to seven year schedule:

Years of Service	Vested Percentage
3	20%
4	40%
5	60%
6	80%
7 or more	100%

The vesting and fiduciary rules for funded nonqualified plans are the same as those for qualified plans, as discussed in Appendix A.

Financing Approaches

Since almost all nonqualified deferred compensation plans are unfunded in the formal sense, employees initiating deferred compensation arrangements are likely to seek ways to increase benefit security. The following approaches are commonly used.

- *Reserve account maintained by employer*. The employer maintains an actual account invested in securities of various types. There is no trust. Funds are fully accessible to the employer and its creditors. The plan is considered unfunded for tax and ERISA purposes.

- *Employer reserve account with employee investment direction*. With this variation, the employee obtains greater security by having the right to "direct" (select) investments in the account. This right must be limited to a choice of broad types of investment (equity, bonds, family of mutual funds, etc.); the ability to choose specific investments may lead to constructive receipt by the employee.

- *Corporate-owned life insurance*. Life insurance policies on the employee's life, owned by and payable to the employer corporation, can provide financing for the employer's obligation under nonqualified deferred compensation plans. With life insurance financing, the plan can provide a substantial death benefit even in the early years of the plan. This is of significant value to younger employees.

- *Rabbi trust*. A rabbi trust is a trust set up to hold property used for financing a deferred compensation plan, where the funds set aside are subject to the employer's creditors. The IRS has ruled that trusts designed this way do not constitute formal funding in the tax sense. These trusts are referred to as rabbi trusts because an early IRS letter ruling involved an arrangement between a rabbi and the employing congregation. The design of rabbi trusts is discussed in the "Questions and Answers," below.

- *Third-party guarantees*. In these arrangements, the employer obtains a guarantee from a third party to pay the employee if the employer defaults. The guarantor may be a shareholder, a related corporation, or a "letter of credit" from a bank. Employer involvement raises the possibility that the guarantee will cause the plan to be deemed formally funded for tax purposes. However, it appears that if the employee, independently of the employer, obtains a third-party guarantee, the IRS will not necessarily view the plan as formally funded.

TAX IMPLICATIONS

Constructive Receipt

Under the constructive receipt doctrine (Code section 451), an amount is treated as received for income tax purposes, even if it is not actually received, if it is "credited to the employee's account, set aside, or otherwise made available."

Constructive receipt does not occur if the employee's control over the receipt is subject to a "substantial limitation or restriction." A requirement of a passage of time until money can be received by the employee is usually considered a substantial limitation or restriction. In a typical deferred compensation plan, for example, if the plan provides that an amount is not payable for five years or not payable until the employee terminates employment or retires, it will not be constructively received before that time.

If a nonqualified plan uses salary reductions to fund the plan the employee's election to reduce salary must be made before rendering the services for which the compensation is paid. In order to defer compensation *after* services have already been performed, the IRS view is that the plan must have a substantial risk of forfeiture of the benefits.

Plan distribution provisions must also be designed to avoid constructive receipt. For example, if the plan provides for distribution in ten equal annual installments, if the employee can elect at any time to accelerate payments, under the constructive receipt doctrine the employee would have to include in income each year any amount that the employee could have elected to receive. As another example, if the plan provides for a payout in ten annual installments with an election at any time to spread payments out further, the constructive receipt doctrine would require taxation under the original ten payment schedule, regardless of any election to further defer payments, unless the election to further defer also involved a substantial risk of forfeiture. A typical forfeiture provision found in nonqualified plan distribution provisions of this type is a requirement that the employee be available for consulting and refrain from competing with the employer. As discussed in Chapter 26 the question of whether this constitutes a substantial risk of forfeiture depends on the specific facts and circumstances of the situation.

Economic Benefit

A compensation arrangement that provides a current "economic benefit" to an employee can result in current taxation to the employee even though the employee has no current right to receive cash or property. For example, suppose that an employee is covered under a funded nonqualified deferred compensation plan that has an irrevocable trust for the benefit of the employee. Under the economic benefit doctrine, the employee will be taxed as soon as the employee is vested in contributions made to the fund, even though the employee does not at that time have a right to withdraw cash. This factor makes funded plans extremely unattractive.

The economic benefit doctrine does not generally affect unfunded plans, and as discussed earlier, almost all nonqualified deferred compensation plans are unfunded. It is possible that some incidental benefits in the plan could create an economic benefit. This issue has sometimes been raised where the plan includes an insured death benefit. However, currently the IRS does not claim that there is an economic benefit resulting from the insured death benefit in a properly designed nonqualified plan.

Payments under a deferred compensation plan, like other forms of compensation, are not deductible unless the amounts meet the reasonableness test discussed in Chapter 4. The same issues can arise with deferred compensation as with regular cash compensation or bonus arrangements.

The reasonableness issue is raised by the IRS in the year in which an employer attempts to take a deduction. For nonqualified deferred compensation, this is generally the year in which the employee includes the amount in income — that is, a year that is later than the year in which the services were rendered. Compensation can be deemed reasonable on the basis of prior service; however, it is possible that a combination of deferred compensation and current compensation received in a given year could raise reasonableness issues, particularly if the deferred amount is very large.

Income Taxation of Benefits and Contributions

Employees must pay ordinary income tax on benefits from unfunded nonqualified deferred compensation plans in the first year in which the benefit is actually or constructively received. The 5-year (or 10-year) averaging provisions available for qualified plan lump sum distributions do not apply to payments from nonqualified plans.

Death benefits from nonqualified plans that are payable to a beneficiary are taxable as ordinary income to the recipient. However, up to $5,000 can be excluded as an employee death benefit under Code section 101(b) if the employee did not have vested rights to the benefit immediately before death.

Social Security (FICA) and Federal Unemployment (FUTA) Taxes

Nonqualified deferred compensation payments are not subject to social security taxes until the year in which the employee no longer has any substantial risk of forfeiture of the amount. In other words, as soon as the covered executive cannot lose his interest in the plan, he will be subject to social security taxes. Conceivably, this could be earlier than the year of actual receipt.

For example, social security tax liability would occur when the employee becomes vested in a funded plan. In an unfunded plan, (which almost all plans are), there is usually no substantial vesting until the amounts are constructively or actually received, because in the absence of a formal fund the employee bears the risk of employer insolvency.

If for the year in question the employee's wages for social security purposes are already above the social security taxable wage base ($48,000 in 1989) there is no further tax as a result of including deferred compensation. Few executives covered under deferred compensation plans will have annual earnings below the taxable wage base. In some cases, however, a retired executive's wages (which do not include qualified plan benefits) might be below the social security wage base and nonqualified deferred compensation benefits would then effectively be subject to social security taxes. Also, in some cases deferred compensation is provided to a lower-earning spouse of an executive who earns a large income because the couple can afford to defer a large portion of the spouse's salary.

Federal Estate Tax Treatment

The amount of any death benefit payable to a beneficiary under a nonqualified deferred compensation plan is generally included in the deceased employee's estate for federal estate tax purposes, at its then present value. In other words, the commuted value of payments made to the employee's beneficiary will be included in the employee's gross estate. But such payments will be considered "income in respect of a decedent" (Code section 691 income) and an income tax deduction will be allocated to the recipient of that income for the additional estate tax the inclusion generated. To the extent payments are made to the employee's spouse in a qualifying manner, the unlimited marital deduction will eliminate any federal estate tax.

A plan can be designed so that the decedent did not have a right to receive the benefit prior to death. A plan designed to provide only death benefits is referred to as a death benefit only (DBO) plan. For employees potentially liable for substantial federal estate taxes, the DBO plan may be an appropriate design. DBO plans are covered in Chapter 5.

Taxation of the Employer

For a nonqualified deferred compensation plan the employer does not receive a tax deduction until its tax year which includes the year in which the employee includes the compensation in taxable income. If the plan is unfunded the year of inclusion is the year in which the compensation is actually or constructively received. For a formally funded plan, compensation is included in income in the year in which it becomes substantially vested, as discussed earlier.

If assets are set aside in a reserve used to finance the employer's obligation under the plan income on these assets is currently taxable to the employer. Consequently, the use of assets providing a deferral of taxation can be advantageous. Life insurance policies are often used because their cash value build-up from year to year is not currently taxed. Death proceeds from the policy are also free of tax, except for a possible alternative minimum tax (AMT) liability (see Chapter 18 for discussion).

If assets to finance the plan are held in a rabbi trust, the employer's tax consequences are much the same as if assets were held directly by the employer. For tax purposes, the rabbi trust is a "grantor trust." A grantor trust's income, deductions, and tax credits are attributed to the grantor (the employer corporation) for tax purposes.

ERISA REQUIREMENTS

Two types of nonqualified deferred compensation plans are eligible for at least partial exemptions from the ERISA requirements. The first exemption is for an unfunded excess benefit plan. This type of nonqualified deferred compensation plan, designed to supplement the qualified retirement benefits limited in amount by Code section 415, is not subject to any ERISA requirements. The second exemption deals with a type of plan often referred to as a "top-hat" plan. Under ERISA, if a nonqualified plan is unfunded and maintained by an employer primarily for the purpose of providing deferred compensation for a "select group of management or highly compensated employees," the plan is exempt from all provisions of ERISA except for a simple reporting requirement of notifying the Department of Labor concerning some basic plan data. Figure 24.1 is an example of such a notice.

The term "highly compensated" for this purpose is not clearly defined as it is for qualified and other plans (see Appendix A). The Department of Labor is responsible for interpreting this provision of ERISA and it has not yet issued clear guidelines. However, a plan that covers only a few highly paid executives probably will meet this ERISA exemption.

If a plan does not meet this ERISA exemption, it must comply with most of the ERISA provisions applicable to qualified pension plans, including the vesting, fiduciary, minimum funding, and reporting and disclosure provisions.

As a result of these ERISA aspects, almost all nonqualified deferred compensation plans are limited to management or highly compensated employees and are formally unfunded, even though they may utilize some informal financing methods as discussed earlier.

WHERE CAN I FIND OUT MORE ABOUT IT?

1. Graduate Course: Executive Compensation (GS 842), The American College, Bryn Mawr, PA.

2. Leimberg et al., *Tools and Techniques of Estate Planning*, 7th ed. Cincinnati, OH: The National Underwriter Co., 1988.

QUESTIONS AND ANSWERS

Question — How is life insurance used to finance an employer's obligation under a nonqualified deferred compensation plan?

Answer — Life insurance can be used in many ways, much like any other asset set aside to finance the plan. Life insurance has several advantages such as its tax-free build-up of cash values and the availability of substantial death benefits even in early years of the plan.

Because of the particular advantages of life insurance, many deferred compensation plans are designed specifically to make use of life insurance financing.

For example, suppose Crood Petroleum Corporation enters into a deferred compensation agreement with its executive Frank Furness under which Frank agrees to defer an anticipated $10,000 annual salary increase in return for the following specified benefits: (a) If Frank dies before retirement, $10,000 a year will be paid to his widow for a period equal to the number of years he was covered under the plan; (b) If Frank remains employed by Crood until retirement at age 65, he will receive $20,000 per year for ten years, in addition to other company retirement benefits.

Frank's deferred $10,000 per year of compensation would have had an after-tax cost of $6,600 to the corporation if paid currently (assuming a 34 percent marginal corporate tax bracket). The corporation can use this $6,600 instead to finance Frank's benefits by purchasing a life insurance policy on Frank's life. If Frank is age 45, about $150,000 of cash value insurance (paid up at 65) can be purchased with this $6,600 annually. The corporation would be the policyowner, the policy beneficiary, and would pay the premiums, which would be nondeductible. (The tax implications of corporate-owned insurance are discussed in detail in Chapter 18.)

If Frank died at age 50, the corporation would receive $150,000 of tax free policy proceeds (in addition to policy dividends and perhaps interest, but reduced by any corporate AMT liability). It would have paid about $33,000 in premiums over the past five years. It is obligated to pay a total of $50,000 ($10,000 a year for five years) to Frank's widow, but since these payments are deductible their after-tax cost is only $33,000 (66% of $50,000). This results in a net gain to the corporation of approximately $84,000 ($150,000 insurance proceeds less $33,000 of premiums and less $33,000 of after-tax cost of benefit payments). (This example does not take into account the time value of money, but to do so does not change the result significantly since the corporation's loss of the use of five annual premium payments is balanced by being reimbursed in advance for the five years of benefit payments due Frank's widow.)

Question — What provisions should (or should not) be included in a "rabbi trust" agreement?

Answer — The IRS has issued numerous private letter rulings involving variations on the rabbi trust approach. Planners of rabbi trust arrangements attempt to follow these rulings as closely as possible. If the arrangement involves any deviation from provisions that have been clearly approved by the IRS, the corporation should apply to the IRS for a private letter ruling on its own rabbi trust arrangement.

On the basis of favorable letter rulings issued to date, a rabbi trust arrangement should have the following provisions:

(a) Assets of the rabbi trust must be available to all general creditors of the employer if the employer becomes bankrupt or insolvent. The executive cannot have greater rights to these assets than creditors would have under applicable state law.

(b) The rabbi trust arrangement must include a requirement for the employer to notify the trustee if the employer becomes insolvent or subject to bankruptcy proceedings. The IRS defines insolvency for this purpose as the employer's inability to satisfy current liabilities. On receiving this notice, the trustee must suspend all payments to the executive and hold all assets for the benefit of creditors. Under the trust, assets must not then be distributed to the executive until allowed by a bankruptcy court.

It appears that a rabbi trust may not have an "insolvency trigger" provision. An insolvency trigger is a provision which triggers immediate payments to the executive from the rabbi trust if the employer becomes insolvent or experiences a drop in net worth below a specified level. The IRS view is that such a provision gives the executive greater rights to the assets than other creditors of the corporation.

Question — Can a corporation provide a nonqualified deferred compensation plan to an executive who is a controlling shareholder (more than 50%) in the corporation?

Answer — In principle, a deferred compensation arrangement can be provided for a controlling shareholder under the rules discussed in this chapter. However, the IRS generally will not issue an advance private letter ruling on the tax effect of such a plan. The IRS will carefully scrutinize such an arrangement because of the controlling shareholder's legal right to require corporate distributions at any time.

Figure 24.2 provides a sample design worksheet for nonqualified deferred compensation plans.

Question — How can an executive determine whether it is better to defer compensation and pay the taxes later or to receive the compensation currently and pay taxes at relatively low income tax rates?

Answer — Because of the uncertainty of future tax rates and investment return, there can never be a certain answer to this question. However, some simple computations can provide a "handle" on the question. Figure 24.3 shows the "break-even" point or the number of years of deferral required to make deferral pay, given a higher estimated rate of tax in future years.

As an example of the use of Figure 24.3, suppose an executive is currently in the 28 percent marginal income tax bracket. If the marginal tax rate is assumed to be 40 percent in future years, and investments can earn 9 percent before taxes, then it will take 4.14 years of deferral for deferred compensation to be better than current taxable compensation. Figure 24.3 indicates that deferred compensation is generally still a good idea for a relatively wide range of assumptions and reasonably short periods of deferral.

Question — What is a "secular trust?"

Answer — The secular trust (so named to contrast it with a rabbi trust) is an arrangement that meets two current employee objections to deferred compensation plans: the fear that tax savings will disappear because future tax rates will be very high, and the lack of security to the employee in relying on a formally unfunded plan.

A secular trust is an irrevocable trust for the benefit of the employee, with funds placed beyond the reach of the employer's creditors. This is generally thought to result in taxation to the employee in the year in which assets are placed in the trust, with a corresponding deduction to the employer in that year. The amounts already taxed can be distributed tax free to the employee at retirement, even if tax rates have gone up considerably.

The secular trust arrangement provides considerable security of benefits to the employee, as well as the ability to take advantage of currently low income tax rates. In addition, since corporate tax rates are higher than individual rates in some cases, the acceleration of the employer's tax deduction may provide more tax benefit than is lost by the employee in paying tax currently instead of deferring.

Secular trusts do have some problems. First, the employee has currently taxable income even though actual receipt of the compensation is deferred. Thus, the employer may need to provide additional compensation to the employee for paying the current tax. Second, the plan may be deemed "funded" for tax and ERISA pur- poses, and therefore be subject to some of the ERISA provisions discussed in the text. In many cases, how- ever, compliance may not be so difficult as to wipe out the benefits of the plan.

Figure 24.1

ALTERNATIVE REPORTING AND DISCLOSURE STATEMENT
FOR UNFUNDED NONQUALIFIED DEFERRED COMPENSATION PLANS
FOR CERTAIN SELECTED EMPLOYEES

To: Top Hat Plan Exemption
Pension and Welfare Benefits Administration
Room N-5644
U.S. Department of Labor
200 Constitution Avenue, N.W.
Washington, D.C. 20210

In compliance with the requirements of the alternative method of reporting and disclosure under Part 1 of Title I of the Employee Retirement Income Security Act of 1974 for unfunded or insured pension plans for a select group of management or highly compensated employees, specified in Department of Labor Regulations, 29 C.F.R. Sec. 2520.104-23, the following information is provided by the undersigned employer.

Name and Address of Employer: _____

_____

_____

Employer Identification Number:_____

(Name of employer) maintains a plan (or plans) primarily for the purpose of providing deferred compensation for a select group of management or highly compensated employees.

Number of Plans and Participants in Each Plan:

_____ Plan covering _____ employees (or)

_____ Plans covering _____, _____, and

_____ employees; respectively)

Dated _____, 19_____

(Name of Employer)

By _____

Plan Administrator

Figure 24.2
(pg. 1)

NONQUALIFIED DEFERRED COMPENSATION

Design Worksheet

A. EMPLOYER AND EMPLOYEE DATA

Employer _____

Employer's address _____

_____

_____ Zip _____

Telephone No. ( ) _____

Employer I.D. No. _____

S corporation election? Yes _____ No _____

Date of S election _____

Accounting year _____

Company contact (name and title) _____

Telephone No. ( ) _____

Employee _____

Title _____

Employee address _____

_____ Zip _____

Telephone No. ( ) _____

Social Security No. _____

Percent ownership of employer _____

Effective date of deferred compensation arrangement _____

B. PLAN FORMULA

Formula type (check)

_____ Salary reduction

_____ Salary continuation

_____ Other _____

Figure 24.2
(pg. 2)

Salary reduction formula (if applicable)

Reduction amount _____

Per (month, year, other) _____

Date of initial election _____

Annual election date thereafter _____

Other election date (specify) _____

Company contribution, if any _____

Conditions on company contribution _____

Company guarantee of interest on account balance (check one)

_____ fixed rate of _____ percent

_____ rate based on

_____ adjusted (how often)_____

Salary continuation formula (if applicable)

Benefits payable at (check)

_____ age 65

_____ other specified age _____

Benefit formula

_____ percent of compensation monthly
(times years of service) (up to _____ years)

Compensation means

_____ Annual compensation over highest _____ years

_____ Other (specify) _____

_____

Offset for other benefits

_____ percent of social security benefits actually received

_____ percent of qualified retirement plan benefits

Other (describe — e.g., workers compensation, disability)

_____

_____

Benefit payable at termination of employment prior to retirement

_____ No benefit

_____ Account balance (not applicable to salary continuation plan)

_____ Vested accrued benefit determined as follows _____

_____

_____

Figure 24.2
(pg. 3)

C. VESTING

Vesting Schedule

_____ Immediate 100 percent vesting

_____ Graduated schedule (specify) _____

_____

Forfeiture provisions

_____ None

_____ Forfeiture for _____

_____

D. DISABILITY BENEFIT

_____ Disability treated like other termination of employment
or
_____ Special disability provisions

_____ Full vesting

_____ Special benefit computation (specify) _____

_____

_____ Service continues to accrue for purposes of this plan

Definition of disability _____

_____

E. BENEFIT PAYMENT

Options

_____ Lump sum (actuarially equivalent to _____)

_____ Periodic payment options (specify) _____

_____

Optional forms must be elected before _____

_____

After benefits commence, payment option (cannot be changed) (can be changed or modified) (annually)
(other _____) by election prior to _____.

After benefits commence, future benefits are forfeited if _____

_____

Figure 24.2
(pg. 4)

F. DEATH BENEFITS

_____ Benefits forfeited at death

_____ Death benefit payable to named beneficiary or estate if no named beneficiary

_____ Other _____

_____

Amount of Benefit

_____ Amount that would have been paid to employee at termination of employment

_____ Face amount of insurance contracts (describe contracts)_____

_____

_____ Other _____

_____

_____

Payment Form

_____ Lump sum only

_____ Beneficiary has same options employee would have had if terminated employment on date of death. Describe how beneficiary makes elections _____

_____

_____ Other _____

_____

G. FINANCING

_____ Formal funding (specify) _____

_____

_____ Informal financing

_____ Insurance contracts (specify)_____

_____

_____ Rabbi trust (describe) _____

_____

_____ Third party guarantees, surety bonds, etc.

(describe) _____

_____

_____

_____ No financing arrangement

Figure 24.3

YEARS UNTIL BREAK EVEN FOR DEFERRED COMPENSATION ASSUMING TAX RATES WILL INCREASE AND CURRENT RATE IS 33 PERCENT

Current Tax Rate		33%	33%	33%	33%	33%
Projected Tax Rate		35%	40%	45%	50%	55%
		Number of Years to Break Even*				
	3%	1.99	6.51	10.49	14.06	17.28
	4%	1.50	4.90	7.91	10.59	13.02
	5%	1.21	3.94	6.36	8.52	10.47
	6%	1.01	3.30	5.32	7.13	8.77
Before-tax	7%	0.87	2.84	4.58	6.14	7.55
Return on Plan	8%	0.76	2.50	4.03	5.40	6.64
Investments	9%	0.68	2.23	3.60	4.82	5.93
	10%	0.62	2.02	3.25	4.36	5.36
	11%	0.56	1.84	2.97	3.98	4.89
	12%	0.52	1.70	2.74	3.67	4.51
	13%	0.48	1.57	2.54	3.40	4.18

YEARS UNTIL BREAK EVEN FOR DEFERRED COMPENSATION ASSUMING TAX RATES WILL INCREASE AND CURRENT RATE IS 28 PERCENT

Current Tax Rate		28%	28%	28%	28%	28%
Projected Tax Rate		35%	40%	45%	50%	55%
		Number of Years to Break Even				
	3%	7.55	12.07	16.05	19.62	22.84
	4%	5.69	9.09	12.10	14.78	17.21
	5%	4.57	7.31	9.72	11.88	13.84
	6%	3.83	6.12	8.14	9.95	11.59
Before-tax	7%	3.30	5.27	7.01	8.57	9.98
Return on Plan	8%	2.90	4.63	6.16	7.53	8.77
Investments	9%	2.59	4.14	5.51	6.73	7.83
	10%	2.34	3.74	4.98	6.08	7.08
	11%	2.14	3.42	4.55	5.56	6.47
	12%	1.97	3.15	4.19	5.12	5.96
	13%	1.83	2.92	3.88	4.74	5.52

$$*\text{number of years} = \frac{\text{natural log of (new tax rate/current tax rate)}}{\text{natural log of } (1 + \text{interest rate})}$$

Source: *Financial Services Professional's Guide to the State of the Art 1989,* The American College, Bryn Mawr, PA 19010, 1-800-841-8000, ext. 19.

Chapter 25
PROFIT-SHARING PLAN

WHAT IS IT?

A profit-sharing plan is a qualified, defined contribution plan featuring a flexible employer contribution provision. The major characteristics are:

- The employer's contribution to the plan each year can be either a purely discretionary amount (or nothing at all, if the employer wishes) or can be based on some type of formula, usually relating to the employer's annual profits.

- Each participant has an individual account in the plan. The employer's contribution is allocated to the individual participant accounts on the basis of a nondiscriminatory formula. The formula usually allocates employer contributions in proportion to each employee's compensation for the year.

- Plan benefits consist of the amount accumulated in each participant's account at retirement or termination of employment. This is the total of (a) employer contributions, (b) forfeitures from other employees' accounts (discussed below), and (c) the interest, capital gains, and other investment return realized over the years on plan assets.

- The plan usually provides payment of the employee's account balance in a lump sum at termination of employment, although other forms of payout may be available or, in the case of certain plans, may be required.

WHEN IS IT INDICATED?

1. When an employer's profits, or financial ability to contribute to the plan, varies from year to year. A profit-sharing plan is particularly useful as an alternative to a qualified pension plan where the employer anticipates that there may be years in which no contribution can be made.

2. When the employer wants to adopt a qualified plan with an incentive feature by which employee accounts increase with the employer's profits.

3. When the employee group has the following characteristics:

- many employees are relatively young and have substantial time to accumulate retirement savings

- employees can and are willing to accept a degree of investment risk in their accounts, in return for the potential benefits of good investment results.

4. When the employer wants to supplement an existing defined benefit plan. The advantages of a profit-sharing plan tend to provide exactly what is missing in a defined benefit plan — and vice versa — so that the two together provide an ideal balanced tax-deferred savings and retirement program.

ADVANTAGES

1. A profit-sharing plan provides the maximum contribution flexibility from the employer's viewpoint.

2. Contributions can be made even if there are no current or accumulated profits. Even a nonprofit organization can have a qualified profit-sharing plan.

3. As with all qualified plans, a profit-sharing plan provides a tax-deferred retirement savings medium for employees.

4. The plan is relatively simple and inexpensive to design, administer, and explain to employees.

5. Plan distributions may be eligible for the special 5-year or (10-year) averaging tax computation available for qualified plans.

6. Individual participant accounts allow participants to benefit from good investment results in the plan fund.

DISADVANTAGES

1. Deductible annual contributions to a profit-sharing plan are limited to 15 percent of total payroll of covered employees; other types of qualified plans permit higher annual contributions. For example, a money purchase plan allows an employer contribution of up to 25 percent of each employee's compensation.

2. Retirement benefits may be inadequate for employees who enter the plan at older ages. This is discussed, with some illustrations, in Chapter 23 relating to money purchase plans. The problem of adequate benefits is even worse in a profit-sharing plan than in a money purchase plan because a profit-sharing plan does not involve any required minimum annual contribution by the employer. Thus, ultimate retirement benefits in a profit-sharing plan are quite speculative. Some planners argue that a profit-sharing plan should be considered

primarily as a supplemental form of incentive based deferred compensation and not as a retirement plan.

3. The annual addition to each employee's account in a profit-sharing plan is limited to the *lesser of* (a) 25 percent of compensation or (b) the greater of $30,000 or ¼ of the defined benefit dollar limitation. (The defined benefit dollar limitation is $94,023 in 1988.) This limits the relative amount of plan funding available for highly compensated employees. For highly paid employees (those earning more than $120,000 annually), the "$30,000" limit represents a smaller percentage of their compensation than can be contributed for lower-paid employees.

4. Employees bear investment risk under the plan. While bearing investment risk is a potential disadvantage to employees, from the employer's viewpoint it is an advantage compared with a defined benefit plan. The employer's risk and costs tend to be lower for a profit-sharing plan.

5. From the employee's standpoint, profit-sharing plans are disadvantageous because there is no predictable level of employer funding under the plan. However, employees have a right to expect that employer contributions will be "substantial and recurring," as discussed below.

DESIGN FEATURES

Employer Contribution Arrangements

Employer contribution provisions in a profit-sharing plan can be either (a) discretionary or (b) formula type.

Under a *discretionary* provision, the employer can determine each year the amount to be contributed. A contribution can be made to a profit-sharing plan even if there are no current or accumulated profits. If the employer desires to make a contribution, any amount up to the maximum deductible limit can be contributed.

An employer can omit a contribution under a discretionary provision, but IRS regulations require "substantial and recurring" contributions. There are no clear guidelines from the IRS as to how often contributions can be omitted. If too many years go by without contributions, the IRS will likely claim that the plan has been terminated. When a qualified plan is terminated, all nonvested amounts in participants' accounts become 100 percent vested. This is usually an undesirable result from the employer's viewpoint.

Under a *formula* provision, a specified amount must be contributed to the plan whenever the employer has profits. For example, a formula might provide that the employer will contribute 10 percent of all company profits in excess of $100,000 (but not to exceed the deduction limit discussed below under "Tax Implications"). The IRS does not dictate

how to define profits for this purpose, so the employer can specify any appropriate formula. The most common approach is to define profits as determined on a before-tax basis under generally accepted accounting principles. As mentioned earlier, even a nonprofit corporation can adopt a profit-sharing plan with contributions based on some appropriately defined surplus account.

Once a formula approach has been adopted, the employer is legally obligated to contribute the amount determined under the formula. However, formulas can be drafted that allow an omitted contribution if certain adverse financial contingencies occur. A suitable "fail-safe" provision of this type will avoid the necessity of amending the plan in the future if financial difficulties arise.

Allocation to Participant Accounts

All profit-sharing plans, regardless of how the total amount of employer contributions are determined, must have a formula under which the employer's contribution is allocated to employee accounts. This allocation formula must not discriminate in favor of highly compensated employees.

Most formulas make allocation to participants on the basis of their compensation as compared with the compensation of all participants.

Example: Participant Fred earns $50,000 in 1989. Total payroll for all plan participants in 1989 is $500,000. For 1989, the employer contributes $100,000 to the plan and the amount allocated to Fred's account is determined as follows:

$$\text{Total employer contribution} \times \frac{\text{Fred's Compensation}}{\text{Compensation of All Participants}}$$

$$\$100,000 \times \frac{\$50,000}{\$500,000} = \$10,000$$

Allocation to Fred's account equals 1/10 of $100,000, or $10,000.

The plan must define the term "compensation" in a nondiscriminatory way. For example, if compensation is defined to include bonuses, and only highly compensated employees receive bonuses, the IRS might deem the formula discriminatory.

It is important for planners to note that only the first $200,000 (as indexed for inflation beginning in 1989) of each employee's compensation can be taken into account in the allocation formula, as well as for the 15% deduction limit discussed below under "Tax Implications."

Some profit-sharing allocation formulas also take into account the years of service of each employee. However, the longest service employees are usually among the "highly compensated" group, so in a given situation the IRS may deem a service-related formula to be discriminatory.

The allocation formula can be "integrated" with social security. This helps the employer avoid duplicating social security benefits that are already provided to the employee. It also reduces the employer's cost for the plan.

An integrated formula defines a level of compensation known as the "integration level." The plan then provides a higher rate of allocation of the employer contribution for compensation above that integration level than the rate for compensation below that integration level.

> Example: For the year 1989, a profit-sharing plan has two participants with compensation as shown below. For 1989, the employer contributes $10,000 to the plan. The plan's integration level is $20,000. Under the plan's allocation formula, each participant's account is to receive the maximum permitted percent allocation for compensation above $20,000. (As discussed below, this is 5.7% for 1989.) The remaining amount of the employer contribution is allocated in proportion to total compensation. Plan allocations would then be as follows:

Employee	1989 Compensation	Compensation above $20,000	5.7% of Excess	Allocation of Remainder	Total Allocation
Al	$30,000	$10,000	$570	$6,287	$ 6,857
Betty	15,000	0	0	3,143	3,143
					$10,000

The amount in column 4 is arrived at by (a) taking the difference between the excess allocations (total of column 3) and the $10,000 employer contribution; this is $9,430; (b) for each participant, this difference ($9,430) is then multiplied by a fraction, the numerator of which is the participant's total compensation and the denominator of which is the total payroll of $48,000. This allocation meets the integration limits discussed in the next paragraph.

The Internal Revenue Code and proposed regulations specify the degree of integration permitted in a plan. Generally, the integration level must (unless revised in future regulations) equal the social security taxable wage base in effect at the beginning of the plan year ($48,000 for plan years beginning in 1989). The difference in the allocation percentages above and below the integration level can be no more than the *lesser of*

(1) the percentage contribution below the integration level, or

(2) the *greater of* (a) 5.7 percent or (b) the old age portion of the social security tax rate.

Thus, for a plan year beginning in 1989, an integrated plan generally must have an integration level of $48,000. If the plan allocated employer contributions plus forfeitures at the rate of 15.7 percent of compensation above the integration level, then it would have to provide at least a 10 percent allocation for compensation below the integration level (making the difference 5.7 percent).

Vesting

Any vesting (nonforfeiture) provision permitted by the Code can be used in a profit-sharing plan. Vesting tends to be relatively generous in a profit-sharing plan since it is designed as an employee incentive.

Usually the graded "3 to 7"-year vesting provision is used. This provides 20 percent vesting after 3 years of service. Vesting increases by 20 percent for each subsequent year of service and reaches 100 percent after 7 years of service. (See Appendix A).

If an employee leaves before becoming fully vested in his or her account balance, the nonvested amount, referred to as a "forfeiture," is left behind in the plan. In profit-sharing plans, forfeitures are usually added to remaining participants' account balances. Adding forfeitures to participants' account balances tends to favor key employees, since they are more likely to participate in the plan over a long time period. For this reason, the IRS requires forfeitures to be allocated in a nondiscriminatory manner. This usually requires forfeiture allocation in proportion to participants' compensation rather than in proportion to their existing account balances. In profit-sharing plans, the formula for allocating forfeitures is usually the same as the formula for allocating employer contributions to participants' accounts.

Benefits from a profit-sharing plan are usually payable at termination of employment or at the plan's stated normal retirement age. Profit-sharing plans usually provide payment in the form of either a lump sum or a series of installment payments. The minimum installment payment must meet the minimum distribution rules discussed in Appendix B. Some profit-sharing plans also offer annuity options with a life contingency, but this is relatively uncommon. (Note, however, that certain plans are subject to the joint and survivor annuity requirements discussed in Appendix B.)

Profit-sharing plans typically allow "in service distributions" — that is, benefits payable before termination of employment. Many plans allow such distributions only in the event of "hardship" as specified in the plan. Typical hardship situations might include medical emergencies, home repair, or educational expenses. Employers traditionally administer such hardship provisions fairly liberally for the benefit of employees. The strict hardship definition applicable to Section 401(k) plans (see the "Questions and Answers" in Chapter 28) does not apply to profit-sharing plans.

The amount that a participant can withdraw before retirement or termination of employment cannot exceed the participant's vested account balance. In addition, the IRS has generally required that employer contributions cannot be withdrawn from the plan before termination of employment unless they have been in the plan for at least a 2-year period. In some cases, the 2-year period can be waived if the participant has a minimum specified number of years of service, such as 5. In order to control and limit withdrawals to prevent depletion of plan funds, many plans impose a "plan penalty" for withdrawals, such as suspending an employee from the plan for a period of 6 months after a withdrawal. No plan penalty, however, can take away any of the participant's vested benefits.

In addition to any plan penalties that may apply, there is a 10 percent early distribution penalty for many distributions to participants before age 59½. This penalty is discussed further in Appendix B.

Because of the impact of the 10 percent early distribution penalty, it is very much in plan participants' interests to have a loan provision in a profit-sharing plan. Loan provisions allow participants access to plan funds for emergencies and other financial needs without incurring the tax penalty of an early withdrawal. Plan loans are discussed further in Appendix B.

Profit-sharing plan funds are generally invested in a pooled account managed (through a trustee or insurance company) by the employer or a fund manager designated by the employer. Either a trust fund, or group or individual insurance contract, can be used. Chapter 20 discusses how life insurance can be used in the plan.

In a profit-sharing plan, it is common to use "participant investment direction" or "earmarking" of participants' accounts. Earmarked accounts can be invested at the participant's direction. Usually, the plan limits the number of possible investments to reduce administrative costs. If the participant-directed account provision meets Department of Labor regulations, the plan trustee is relieved from any fiduciary responsibility for the success or failure of an investment chosen by the participant. Typically, the plan will offer the participant a choice of investments from a family of mutual funds. Under Department of Labor regulations, at least four such choices must be permitted. One of the options must be either federally insured bank deposits or a pooled fund invested in securities issued by the U.S. government or guaranteed by the U.S. government or one of its agencies.

TAX IMPLICATIONS

1. Employer contributions to the plan are deductible when made, so long as the plan remains "qualified." A plan is qualified if it meets eligibility, vesting, funding, and other requirements discussed in Appendix A. In addition, the plan must designate that it is a profit-sharing plan.

    The maximum total employer contribution to the plan cannot exceed 15 percent of the payroll of all employees covered under the plan. Any excess over this amount is not only nondeductible, but is also subject to a 10 percent penalty. Only the first $200,000 (as indexed for inflation beginning in 1989) of each employee's compensation can be taken into account for purposes of this limit.

    If, in addition to the profit-sharing plan, an employer maintains a defined benefit plan covering some of same employees, the total contribution for both plans is limited to 25 percent of compensation of the covered employees (or, if greater, the amount necessary to meet the minimum funding standard for the defined benefit plan; in which case the contribution to the profit-sharing plan is not deductible).

2. Assuming the plan remains qualified, taxation of the employee is deferred. That is, (1) employer contributions, (2) forfeitures added to the participant's account, (3) investment earnings on the account and (4) capital gains realized in the account, are all nontaxable to a plan participant until withdrawn.

3. Under Code section 415, annual additions to each participant's account are limited to the *lesser of* (a) 25 percent of the participant's compensation or (b) the greater of $30,000 or ¼ of the defined benefit dollar limitation. (The defined benefit dollar limitation is $94,023 in 1988.) Annual additions include (1) employer contributions to the participant's account; (2) forfeitures from other participants' accounts; and (3) employee contributions to the account.

4. Distributions from a plan must follow the rules for qualified plan distributions. These distribution rules are discussed in Appendix B.

5. Lump sum distributions made after age 59½ are subject to a limited election to use a special 5-year averaging tax calculation. Certain older participants may also be eligible for a 10-year averaging tax calculation for lump sum distributions. Not all distributions are eligible for these special tax calculations. Appendix B covers the applicable rules and includes the appropriate IRS forms for making the calculation.

6. The plan is subject to the ERISA reporting and disclosure rules outlined in Appendix D.

ALTERNATIVES

1. Money purchase plans are defined contribution plans similar to profit-sharing plans except that the employer contribution percentage can be up to 25 percent of each participant's compensation. However, unlike a profit-sharing plan, the employer is required to make a contribution to a money purchase plan each year. (See Chapter 23.)

2. Target benefit plans are a defined contribution alternative similar to money purchase plans. With a target plan, the employer contribution percentage can be based on age at plan entry — higher for older entrants. A target plan may be favorable where the employer wants to provide adequate benefits for older (often key) employees. (See Chapter 33.)

3. Defined benefit plans provide more security of retirement benefits and proportionately greater contributions for older plan entrants, but are much more complex to design and administer. (See Chapter 6.)

4. Nonqualified deferred-compensation plans can be provided exclusively for selected executives. But the employer's tax deduction when a nonqualified plan is used is generally deferred until benefit payments are made. This can be as much as 20 or 30 years after the employer's contribution is made. (See Chapter 24.)

5. Individual retirement savings is an alternative or a supplement to an employer plan. But there is generally no tax deduction and tax deferral available except for the limited IRA provisions.

HOW TO INSTALL A PLAN

Installation of a profit-sharing plan follows the qualified plan installation procedure described in Appendix C.

WHERE CAN I FIND OUT MORE ABOUT IT?

1. McFadden, John J., *Retirement Plans for Employees*. Homewood, IL: Richard D. Irwin, 1988.

2. Gee, Judith Boyers, *Pensions in Perspective*, 2nd ed. Cincinnati, OH: The National Underwriter Co., 1987.

3. Graduate Course: Advanced Pension and Retirement Planning I (GS 814), The American College, Bryn Mawr, PA.

QUESTIONS AND ANSWERS

Question — Can a self-employed person adopt a profit-sharing plan?

Answer — A self-employed person (sole proprietor or partner in a partnership) can adopt a profit-sharing plan covering not only his or her regular employees, if any, but also covering the self-employed person(s). Such a plan is one type of "Keogh" or "HR 10" plan dis-

cussed in Chapter 15. Generally the self-employed person is treated the same as regular employees in a profit-sharing plan, but there are some special rules that apply.

Question — Can employees make contributions to a profit-sharing plan?

Answer — Employees can contribute to the plan only on an after-tax basis. If employees want to contribute on a before-tax (salary reduction) basis, the plan must meet the additional requirements of Section 401(k); these are discussed in Chapter 28. Furthermore, if the plan allows employee after-tax contributions, an additional set of nondiscrimination requirements must be met, the "Section 401(m)" rules. These are discussed in Chapter 27.

Question — How can an employer decide when a profit-sharing plan should be integrated with social security, and what are the factors involved in choosing the integration level?

Answer — A "stand alone" profit-sharing plan — where the employer has no qualified defined benefit or other plan — is almost always integrated with social security because (1) employer costs are reduced and (2) the employer contribution in an integrated plan is disproportionately allocated to higher paid key employees.

If an employer has two or more qualified plans covering even one employee in common, IRS integration rules do not allow both plans to be fully integrated; the degree of integration in one or all plans must be cut back under complex guidelines. Planners generally find that if an employer has both a defined benefit plan and a profit-sharing plan covering a common group of employees, it is most favorable to the employer and key employees to maximize the integration in the defined benefit plan and not to integrate the profit-sharing plan at all.

Prior to 1989, the most favorable integration level in an integrated profit-sharing plan was not necessarily the maximum level allowed by law. A lower level generally provided greater relative contributions for key employees. As a general guideline, the best integration level for maximizing contributions for key employees was a level just above the maximum compensation level of rank and file employees. Proposed regulations issued by the IRS currently require that the integration level equal the taxable wage base; however, future nondiscrimination regulations may allow, under limited conditions, an integration level below the wage base.

Chapter 26

RESTRICTED STOCK PLAN

WHAT IS IT?

A restricted stock plan is an arrangement to compensate executives by giving them shares of stock subject to certain restrictions or limitations. Usually the stock used in such plans is stock of the employer corporation or its subsidiary.

Company stock is attractive to executives as an element of compensation because it allows sharing in company growth. To the employer, the use of stock is attractive as a "double incentive" plan for executives, because the terms of the plan can be based on executive performance and, in addition, increases in the value of the stock may reflect to some extent the executive's performance.

Employers often adopt stock plans with restrictions designed to help retain employees or discourage conduct the employer deems undesirable, such as going to work for a competitor. These restrictions can also serve the employee's interest by postponing taxability of compensation to the employee.

For an outline of some advanced types of stock and other plans used for compensating executives, particularly in large corporations, see Appendix E.

WHEN IS IT INDICATED?

1. When the employer is willing to create new shareholders of the company. Shareholders of a closely held corporation often do not want to share company stock and potential control of the business outside of the existing group of shareholders.

2. When a corporation wants to provide an executive with an incentive-based form of compensation. In restricted stock plans, the ultimate amount the executive receives generally depends on the value of the stock. If the plan is well designed, the value of company stock will reflect the executive's performance at least to some extent.

3. When an employer wants to use a compensation arrangement as a way of discouraging certain specified conduct such as leaving employment within a short time or going to work for a competitor.

4. When an executive wants an "equity-based" form of compensation — that is, compensation based on the value of the company's stock. Equity-based compensation allows an executive to share in the upside potential of a company's growth. This type of compensation is particularly useful in the startup phase of a high technology company where growth can be very significant.

ADVANTAGES

1. Restricted stock plans can allow deferral of taxation to the employee until the year in which the restricted stock becomes "substantially vested." Essentially this means nonforfeitable, as discussed below under "Tax Implications."

2. A stock plan allows employees an interest in the increase in value of a company's stock. This type of payment, especially when coupled with deferral of taxation, can be much more valuable than straight compensation.

3. A restricted stock plan allows an employer to grant an executive an equity interest in the company but withdraw it if the executive leaves prematurely or goes to work for a competitor.

4. For non-tax purposes, an executive has all the advantages of stock ownership, such as voting rights, dividends, and appreciation potential, but is not taxed on receipt of the stock to the extent it is not substantially vested.

DISADVANTAGES

1. The employer does not receive a tax deduction for a restricted stock plan until the year in which the property becomes substantially vested and therefore taxable to the executive (unless the executive elects to be taxed earlier under Section 83(b), as discussed under "Tax Implications").

2. The possibility of a Section 83(b) election by the executive means that the employer may not have control of the amount or timing of its tax deduction.

3. Issuing new shares of restricted stock tends to dilute ownership of the corporation. This may be particularly undesirable for closely held corporations. Shareholders of these corporations seldom want to share control or profits, or share company assets on sale or liquidation of the business.

4. If the change (up or down) in value of the stock is not consistent with the executive's performance, this can be disadvantageous to both employer and executive. If the stock goes up with little or no effort by the executive, other shareholders will be resentful. If the stock drops in value in spite of excellent executive performance, the incentive element of the plan is lost or diminished.

Tools and Techniques

WHAT CAN BE ACCOMPLISHED WITH RESTRICTIONS ON STOCK

The types of restrictions used in restricted stock plans can be tailored to meet employer and employee objectives.

Employee Retention

Employers often use stock plans to tie key employees to the company. With this type of objective, stock might for example be transferred to an employee subject to a restriction that it can't be sold or otherwise transferred by the employee during a specified period — for instance, 5 years. If the employee quits before this time, the stock must be returned to the company. This simple form of restriction can also be used as a way of keeping retirees tied to the company and providing them with some useful deferral of income. The stock can be transferred to an executive retiree subject to a provision that the retiree remain available for consulting services to the employer during a specified time, such as 5 years.

Discouraging Bad Conduct

Restrictions can also be associated with specific employee conduct that the company wants to discourage. For example, a restricted stock plan might provide that stock must be returned to the employer if during a period of 5 years the employee is discharged by the company for cause, or discharged for some specific reason such as embezzlement or disclosure of trade or marketing information. In certain industries, typically high technology industries, stock in restricted stock plans is forfeitable if the employee engages in competition with the employer — for example, starts a competitive business or goes to work for a competitor.

From a non-tax legal point of view, restrictions involving noncompetition agreements may be unenforceable in the courts if they go beyond reasonable limits. However, the courts generally will enforce a noncompetition provision if it is *reasonable* as to (a) the geographic area to which it applies, and (b) the period of time for which it applies.

For example, suppose Apex Industries operates a plumbing fixture business only on the east coast and has no plans to expand geographically. Apex's restricted stock agreement with employee Hank, aged 35, provides a forfeiture of stock if Hank works in a competing business anywhere in the country. Hank quits and starts a plumbing fixture business in California. If Apex tries to enforce the noncompetition provision, the courts are likely to deem it unreasonable and unenforceable because it goes beyond a reasonably broad geographic area. The same result would probably apply if the plan restricted Hank from competing in the immediate geographic area "for the rest of his life."

Incentives

Restricted stock plans can be designed as incentive plans similar to bonus plans. For example, a restricted stock plan might give an executive 1,000 shares of company stock subject to a forfeiture if gross sales in the executive's division do not increase by at least 20 percent within 5 years. When sales reach the targeted level, the forfeitability restrictions would end. The stock would then belong to the executive without restriction. The advantage of this arrangement over a cash bonus is simply that it increases the security of the benefit to the employee compared with the mere promise by the company to pay a cash bonus. However, there are some risks from the employee's point of view compared with the stated contingent bonus amount, since the value of the stock could very well go down even though the employee works effectively and meets or exceeds the designated target sales level.

TAX IMPLICATIONS

1. Under Section 83 of the Internal Revenue Code, an employee is not subject to tax on the value of restricted property received as compensation from the employer until the year in which the property becomes "substantially vested" (unless the employee makes a "Section 83(b) election" to include it in income in the year received, as discussed in section 2 below).

   The definition of substantial vesting in Code section 83 and the regulations thereunder is of great significance in designing restricted stock plans. These plans are obviously much less attractive to employees if they are not carefully designed to provide tax deferral within the rules of Section 83.

   For example, if an employee receives restricted stock in 1989 that is deemed (for tax purposes) to be substantially vested in 1989, the employee will pay tax in that year even if under state law the employee doesn't completely own the stock (and the corporation will get a corresponding deduction; see below). In spite of the taxability to the employee, the restrictions on the stock received may still be legally effective under state property law so that the employee can't sell the stock in 1989 and realize any cash at that time.

   Substantial vesting. Under Section 83, property is not considered substantially vested so long as it is subject to a "substantial risk of forfeiture" and is not transferable by an employee to a third party free of this risk of forfeiture.

   The question whether a substantial risk of forfeiture exists depends on the facts and circumstances in each case. The regulations under Section 83 contain various examples and guidelines.

   - Generally, a substantial risk of forfeiture is considered to exist if the employee must return the property unless a specified period of service for the employer is completed.

• A forfeiture only as a result of some event that is relatively unlikely generally would not constitute a substantial risk of forfeiture. For example, the plan might provide that an employee must return the stock if he commits embezzlement within a specified period of time. This unlikely event, which furthermore is within the control of the employee, probably would not constitute a substantial risk of forfeiture. (The executive would therefore be taxed immediately upon receipt of the stock.)

• A forfeiture as a result of failing to meet certain incentive targets, such as a certain level of sales, generally is a substantial risk of forfeiture.

• A forfeiture resulting from going to work for a competitor constitutes a substantial risk if the employee has scarce skills in an active job market.

Where an employee is an owner or major shareholder in a company, forfeiture provisions of almost any type are likely to be challenged by the IRS as being insubstantial, because the employee's control or influence over the company can render them relatively ineffective.

As indicated above, property will not be considered subject to a substantial risk of forfeiture if it can be transferred by the employee to another person or entity who takes the stock free of the risk of forfeiture. When employer stock is used in a restricted property plan, this requirement is usually met by a "legend" or statement imprinted on share certificates indicating that transfer and ownership of the shares are subject to a restricted property plan. This notifies any perspective buyer or other recipient that the employee is not free to sell, give away, or otherwise transfer the shares without restrictions.

2. Under Code section 83(b), an executive can elect to recognize income as of the date of receipt of the restricted property, rather than waiting until it becomes substantially vested. This election must be made within thirty days of receiving the property and must comply with requirements in the IRS Regulations.

The amount included in income under this Section 83(b) election is the excess, if any, of the fair market value of the property at the time of transfer (determined without regard to any restrictions other than "non-lapse" restrictions — see below) over any amount the executive paid for the property. For example, if the stock is worth $60 per share at the time of receipt and the executive pays nothing for it, under a Section 83(b) election the executive would report ordinary income of $60 per share in the year of receipt.

Why would an executive make a Section 83(b) election? If a Section 83(b) election is made, any subsequent appreciation in value of the property is treated as capital gain. That gain is not subject to tax until the stock is sold. When capital gain rates were significantly lower than ordinary income rates, this was a major consideration in deciding whether to make a Section 83(b) election. Under current law, Section 83(b) elections may be advantageous only in special situations; for example, where the executive wants to maximize taxable income in a particular year in order to offset deductible losses. If the differential tax rate for capital gains is restored in the future, the Section 83(b) election may become more meaningful.

When an executive includes an amount in income under a Section 83(b) election, the employer gets a tax deduction at that time for the same amount. The employer gets no further tax deduction if the property subsequently increases in value in the hands of the executive, whether or not the executive sells the property. Another disadvantage of the Section 83(b) election is that if the stock is forfeited for any reason, no deduction is allowed to the executive for the loss.

The executive making a Section 83(b) election is therefore gambling (1) that the stock will increase substantially in value from the date of the election, (2) that there will be a meaningful tax break for capital gains at the time the stock is actually sold, and (3) that the stock will not be forfeited before the executive is able to sell or dispose of it without restriction.

3. Sometimes the stock received does not have a forfeiture provision as such but rather a restriction that reduces the value of the stock to the employee. In that case, the value of the stock is includable in income when received. But the amount includable is less than the full market value.

For example, a plan may provide an employee with a fully vested interest in the stock, but with a provision that the employee cannot resell the stock without first offering it back to the company at a specified price. In that case, because of the "first offer" provision, the value of the stock in the hands of the executive would not be its unfettered market value, but rather a reduced value reflecting the restriction.

A restriction will be taken into account for this purpose only if it is a "non-lapse restriction" — a restriction that by its terms will never lapse. The first offer requirement of the type described in the above example would probably qualify as a non-lapse restriction. The issue whether a restriction constitutes a non-lapse restriction is one of facts and circumstances. The IRS takes a restrictive view in its regulations and rulings, so non-lapse restrictions are difficult to design.

4. When an employee has become substantially vested in restricted property, its value is taxed in that year as compensation income. Gain on any subsequent sale of the property is generally taxed as capital gain, as in the case of similar property acquired by any other means. When capital gain rates were lower than ordinary income rates, this rate provided an additional benefit from restricted stock plans. The benefit of a special capital gain rate could appear again in the future, as there is always an on-going possibility that the tax laws will be changed to provide favorable treatment for some capital gains.

5. The employer's tax deduction for compensation income to the executive under a restricted stock plan is deferred until the year in which the employee is substantially vested and includes the amount in income. Technically, the employer's tax deduction occurs in the employer's taxable year in which, or with which, ends the taxable year of the employee in which the amount is includable in the employee's income. This is the usual rule for the timing of an employer's deduction for deferred compensation payments as discussed in Chapter 4. As with other types of compensation, the employer is required to withhold and pay tax. Withholding is particularly important here because the employer's deduction is, under the regulations, conditioned on the employer's actually withholding and paying tax.

WHERE CAN I FIND OUT MORE ABOUT IT?

1. Leimberg, Stephan R. et al., *The Federal Income Tax Law*. Warren, Gorham, and Lamont, 1989.

2. Graduate Course: Executive Compensation (GS 842), The American College, Bryn Mawr, PA.

QUESTIONS AND ANSWERS

Question — How does a restricted stock plan affect an employer's accounting statements?

Answer — If stock is issued with restrictions based only on continued employment, the excess of the stock's fair market value when issued over the amount paid for it by the executive is a compensation expense for accounting purposes and is charged to earnings on a systematic basis over the related period of employment — the period during which the restrictions are in effect. If restrictions are based on contingent factors such as executive or company performance, the charge to expense can be delayed until the result is known for certain. These rules are set out in the currently effective official accounting statement, APB 25. The accounting profession is currently reconsidering the treatment of many executive compensation arrangements and some changes may appear in the future.

Question — Do federal securities laws apply to restricted stock, and what is their effect?

Answer — Federal securities registration is not generally required if stock is issued without cost, since no "sale" is deemed to occur for securities law purposes. However, the SEC (Securities Exchange Commission) views stock issued to executives as compensation to have been bargained for and thus sold, so the securities laws may apply. Most restricted stock arrangements qualify for one or more of the exemptions from securities registration, typically the "private placement" exemption whereby registration is not required where securities are issued to a limited number of persons.

Planners must also determine whether executives are restricted under the federal securities laws from reselling stock acquired under the plan. SEC Rule 144 includes conditions under which such stock can be resold freely. Executives holding stock in a restricted stock plan may also be subject to the anti-fraud provisions of the securities law such as the insider trading restrictions.

Chapter 27

SAVINGS PLAN

WHAT IS IT?

A savings plan (or "thrift plan") is a qualified defined contribution plan that is similar to a profit-sharing plan, with features that provide for and encourage after-tax employee contributions to the plan.

A typical savings plan provides after-tax employee contributions with matching employer contributions. Each employee elects to contribute a certain percentage of his or her compensation, and these employee contributions are matched — either dollar for dollar or under some other formula — by employer contributions to the plan. Employee contributions are not deductible — the employee pays tax on the money before contributing it to the plan.

In recent years, "pure" savings plans featuring only after-tax employee contributions have generally been replaced by the 401(k) type of plan described in Chapter 28. However, a savings plan with after-tax employee contributions is often added to a Section 401(k) plan.

WHEN IS IT INDICATED?

1. As an add-on feature to a Section 401(k) plan to allow employees to increase contributions beyond the $7,000 annual limit on salary reductions under Section 401(k) plans. (The $7,000 limit is indexed for inflation and is $7,313 in 1988.) However, after-tax contributions are subject to their own complex limitations as discussed under "Tax Implications," below.

2. When the employee group has the following characteristics:

   • Many employees are relatively young and have substantial time to accumulate retirement savings.

   • Many employees are willing to accept a degree of investment risk in their plan accounts in return for the potential benefits of good investment results.

   • There is a wide variation among employees in the need or desire for retirement savings.

3. When the employer wants to supplement the company's defined benefit pension plan with a plan that features individual participant accounts and the opportunity for participants to save on a tax-deferred basis. The use of a combination of plans provides a balanced retirement program. The defined benefit plan appeals to older employees with a desire for secure retirement benefits, while the savings plan (or other defined contribution plan such as a profit-sharing or Section 401(k) plan) generally appeals to younger employees who prefer to see their savings build up year-by-year rather than anticipating a projected benefit when they retire.

ADVANTAGES

1. As with all qualified plans, a savings plan provides a tax-deferred retirement savings medium for employees. The tax on the after-tax employee contribution itself is not deferred. However, subsequent investment earnings on after-tax employee contributions are generally not subject to tax until distributions are made to employees from the plan.

2. The plan allows employees to control the amount of their savings. Employees have the option of taking all their compensation in cash and not contributing to the plan. (However, if they do so, they generally lose any employer matching contributions under the plan.)

3. Plan distributions may be eligible for the special 5-year (or 10-year) averaging tax computation available for qualified plans.

4. Individual participant accounts allow participants to benefit from good results in the plan fund.

DISADVANTAGES

1. The plan cannot be counted on by employees to provide an adequate benefit. First, benefits will not be significant unless employees make substantial contributions to the plan on a regular basis. Furthermore, employees who enter the plan at older ages may not be able to make sufficient contributions to the plan, even if they wish to do so, because of (a) the limits on annual contributions discussed under "Tax Implications," below, and (b) the limited number of years remaining for plan contributions prior to retirement.

2. Employees bear investment risk under the plan. Bearing the investment risk is a potential disadvantage to employees, but from the employer's perspective the shift of risk is a positive feature. Employer costs are lower for a defined contribution plan such as a savings plan, as compared with a defined benefit plan.

3. Since employee accounts and matching amounts must be individually accounted for in the plan, the administrative costs for a savings plan are greater than those for

125

a money purchase or simple profit-sharing plan without employee contributions.

4. The annual addition to each employee's account in a savings plan is limited to the *lesser of* (a) 25 percent of compensation or (b) the greater of $30,000 or ¼ of the defined benefit dollar limitation. (The defined benefit dollar limitation is $94,023 in 1988.) This limits the relative tax advantage available to highly compensated employees under a savings plan or any other defined contribution plan.

DESIGN FEATURES

Typical savings plans provide after-tax employee contributions with employer matching contributions. Participation in the plan is voluntary; each employee elects to contribute a chosen percentage of compensation up to a maximum percentage specified in the plan. The employee receives no tax deduction for this contribution and the contribution is fully subject to income tax as if it were in the employee's hands.

The employer makes a matching contribution to the savings plan. The employer match can be dollar-for-dollar, or the employer may put in some percentage of the employee contribution. A typical plan might permit an employee to contribute annually any whole percentage of compensation from one to six percent, with the employer contributing at the rate of half the chosen employee percentage. In this example then, if the employee elected to contribute 4 percent of compensation, the employer would be obligated to contribute an additional 2 percent.

In general, higher paid employees are in a position to contribute considerably more to this type of plan than lower paid employees. To prevent discrimination in savings plans, there is a numerical limit on the contributions by highly compensated employees (Code section 401(m) discussed under "Tax Implications," below). One of the principal administrative burdens in a savings plan is a need to monitor employee contribution levels to be sure the Section 401(m) tests are met.

Apart from the employee contribution features, savings plans have features similar to profit-sharing plans. Emphasis is usually put on the "savings account-like" features of the plan. Usually there are generous provisions for employee withdrawal of funds and for plan loans. Savings plans often feature participant investment direction or earmarking. Earmarking is usually provided by allowing employees a choice among several specified pooled investment funds (such as mutual funds). However, it is possible, although administratively burdensome, to allow participants to direct virtually any type of investment for their account. The use of a participant-directed investment provision relieves the plan trustee and the employer from fiduciary liability for investments chosen by the participant. However, where mutual funds are the only option available, there must be at least 4 different

funds available to the employee, one of which must be invested in federally guaranteed money market funds or federal securities. Life insurance can be used in the plan, as discussed in Chapter 20.

Although savings plans with only after-tax employee contributions and employer matching contributions were very popular in the past, the after-tax employee contribution approach is currently used primarily as an add-on to a Section 401(k) plan. Employers often adopt a plan that combines all the features of a regular profit-sharing plan, a savings plan, and Section 401(k) salary reductions. These combined plans can have one or more of the following features:

- employee after-tax contributions
- employer matching of employee after-tax contributions
- employee (before-tax) salary reductions (Section 401(k) amounts)
- employer matching of Section 401(k) amounts
- employer contribution based on a formula
- discretionary employer contribution

These are discussed further in Chapter 28.

TAX IMPLICATIONS

1. Employer contributions to the plan are deductible when made so long as the plan remains "qualified" and separate accounts are maintained for all participants in the plan. A plan is qualified if it meets eligibility, vesting, funding and other requirements discussed in Appendix A.

2. Employee contributions to the plan, whether or not matched, are not tax deductible. (Before-tax employee salary reductions must meet the rules of Section 401(k) discussed in Chapter 28.)

3. Assuming a plan remains qualified, taxation of the employee is deferred with respect to (a) employer contributions to the plan and (b) investment earnings on both employer and employee contributions. These amounts are nontaxable to plan participants until a distribution is made from the plan.

4. In order to prevent discrimination in favor of highly compensated employees, the plan must meet a special test under Code section 401(m). Under Section 401(m), the plan is not deemed discriminatory for a plan year if, for highly compensated employees, the average ratio (expressed as a percentage) *of* employee contributions (both matched and non-matched) plus employer matching contributions *to* compensation, does not exceed the greater of

- 125 percent of the contribution percentage (i.e., ratio) for all other eligible employees, or

- the lesser of (a) 200 percent of the contribution percentage for all other eligible employees, or (b) such percentage plus 2 percentage points.

For example, if employee contributions and employer matching contributions for nonhighly compensated employees are 6 percent of compensation, those for highly compensated employees can be up to 8 percent (6 percent plus 2 percent).

Administratively, the employer must monitor the level of contributions made by nonhighly compensated employees, and then make sure that highly compensated employees do not exceed this level in order for the plan to remain qualified.

Under the Code and proposed regulations, in meeting this test the employer may take into account certain 401(k) salary reduction contributions and certain employer plan contributions may be considered. The definition of highly compensated employee is the same as that applicable to all benefit plans (and is discussed in detail in Appendix A).

5. Distributions from the plan must follow the rules for qualified plan distributions. Certain premature or excessive distributions are subject to penalties. The distribution rules are discussed in Appendix B.

6. Lump sum distributions made after age 59½ are subject to a limited election to use a special 5-year averaging tax calculation. Certain older participants may also be eligible for a 10-year averaging tax calculation for lump sum distributions. Not all distributions are eligible for these special tax calculations. The rules are discussed in detail in Appendix B.

7. The plan is subject to the ERISA reporting and disclosure rules outlined in Appendix D.

HOW TO INSTALL A PLAN

Installation of a savings plan follows the qualified plan installation procedures described in Appendix C.

WHERE CAN I FIND OUT MORE ABOUT IT?

1. McFadden, John J., *Retirement Plans for Employees*. Homewood, IL: Richard D. Irwin, 1988.

2. Gee, Judith Boyers, *Pensions in Perspective*, 2nd ed. Cincinnati, OH: The National Underwriter Co., 1987.

Tools and Techniques

Chapter 28

SECTION 401(k) PLAN

WHAT IS IT?

A Section 401(k) plan (also known as a "qualified cash or deferred plan") is a qualified profit-sharing or stock bonus plan under which plan participants have an option to put money in the plan (up to $7,000 annually, as indexed for inflation — $7,313 in 1988) or receive the same amount as taxable cash compensation. Amounts contributed to the plan under this option are not taxable to the participants until withdrawn. Aside from features related to the cash or deferred option, a Section 401(k) plan is much like a regular qualified profit-sharing plan described in Chapter 25.

WHEN IS IT INDICATED?

1. When an employer wants to provide a qualified retirement plan for employees but can afford only minimal extra expense beyond existing salary and benefit costs. A Section 401(k) plan can be funded entirely from employee salary reductions, except for installation and administration costs. In most plans, however, additional direct employer contribution to the plan can enhance its effectiveness.

2. When the employee group has one or more of the following characteristics:

   - Many would like some choice as to the level of savings — that is, a choice between various levels of current cash compensation and tax deferred savings. A younger, more mobile work force often prefers this option.

   - Many employees are relatively young and have substantial time to accumulate retirement savings.

   - Many employees are willing to accept a degree of investment risk in their plan accounts in return for the potential benefits of good investment results.

3. When an employer wants an attractive, "savings-type" supplement to its existing defined benefit or other qualified retirement plan. Such a supplement can make the employer's retirement benefit program attractive to both younger and older employees by providing both security of retirement benefits and the opportunity to increase savings and investment on a tax-deferred basis.

ADVANTAGES

1. As with all qualified plans, a Section 401(k) plan provides a tax-deferred retirement savings medium for employees.

2. A Section 401(k) plan allows employees a degree of choice in the amount they wish to save under the plan.

3. Section 401(k) plans can be funded entirely through salary reductions by employees. As a result, an employer can adopt the plan with no additional cost for employee compensation; the only extra cost is plan installation and administration. The plan may actually result in some savings as a result of lower state or local (but not federal) payroll taxes.

4. Plan distributions may be eligible for the special 5-year (or 10-year) averaging tax computation available for qualified plans.

5. In-service withdrawals by employees for "hardship" are permitted; these are not available in qualified pension plans.

DISADVANTAGES

1. As with all defined contribution plans (except target plans), account balances at retirement age may not provide adequate retirement savings for employees who entered the plan at later ages.

2. The annual employee salary reduction under the plan is limited to $7,000, as indexed for inflation ($7,313 in 1988). However, this amount can be supplemented by direct employer contributions to provide additional tax-deferred savings.

   Furthermore, $7,000 annually is a substantial amount of savings for most employees. A Section 401(k) plan must limit salary reductions to about 15% of compensation in any event, because of the employer deduction limit (see "Tax Implications" below). Thus, the $7,000 limit is not really a limiting factor for employees with compensation below about $50,000 annually.

   Moreover, saving $7,000 annually, adjusted for inflation, provides a substantial amount of retirement savings, especially for those who enter a Section 401(k) plan at earlier ages. For illustration, the ultimate account balances for plan participants who enter the plan in 1988 and who save the maximum amount each year until retirement are as follows, assuming (a) an inflation rate (and corresponding increase in the $7,313 limit) of 3% annually and (b) investment return of 7% annually on the plan account balance:

Tools and Techniques

Age at Plan Entry	Account Balance at age 65	Account Balance at age 65 (1988 dollars)
25	$ 2,291,215	$ 702,388
35	1,014,302	417,879
45	403,682	223,509
55	121,919	90,719

3. Employer deductions for plan contributions (including employee salary reductions as well as direct employer contributions) cannot exceed 15% of the total payroll of employees covered under the plan. This contrasts with a limit of 25% of compensation for a money purchase or target plan — and no percentage limit for a defined benefit plan. These other types of plans can provide greater tax-deferred savings than a Section 401(k) plan. (Many employers combine a Section 401(k) plan with a pension plan to provide maximum benefits for employees.)

4. Because of the "actual deferral percentage" (ADP) nondiscrimination tests described below, a Section 401(k) plan can be relatively costly and complex to administer.

5. Employees bear investment risk under the plan. (However, they can also potentially benefit from good investment results.)

DESIGN FEATURES

Salary Reductions

Virtually all Section 401(k) plans are funded entirely or in part through salary reductions elected by employees. An alternative sometimes used is for the employer to provide all employees with an annual "bonus" that employees can either receive in cash or contribute to the plan. In substance both approaches are the same, but the salary reduction approach is more popular because it uses existing salary scales as a starting point.

Salary reductions must be elected by employees before compensation is earned — that is, before they render the services for which compensation is paid. Salary reductions elected after compensation is earned are ineffective as a result of the tax doctrine of "constructive receipt."

The usual practice is to provide plan participants with a salary reduction election form that they must complete before the end of each calendar year. The election specifies how much will be contributed to the plan from each paycheck received for the forthcoming year. The amount cannot be increased later in the year. But usually the employee can reduce or entirely withdraw the election for pay not yet earned, if circumstances dictate. The plan must restrict each participant's salary reductions to no more than the annual limit of $7,000, as indexed for inflation ($7,313 in 1988).

The participant is always 100% vested in any salary reductions contributed to the plan and any plan earnings on those salary reductions. Even if a participant leaves employment after a short time, his plan account based on salary reductions cannot be forfeited. Usually plan account balances are distributed in a lump sum when a participant terminates employment.

Salary reductions, as well as any other plan contribution if the employee has the option to receive the amount in cash (the tax law refers to these amounts as "elective deferrals"), are subject to an annual limit. The employee must add together each year all elective deferrals from (1) Section 401(k) plans, (2) salary reduction SEPs (see Chapter 30) and (3) Section 403(b) tax deferred annuity plans (see Chapter 34). All elective deferrals from all employer plans that cover the employee must be aggregated. The total must not exceed $7,000, as indexed for inflation ($7,313 in 1988). (As discussed in Chapter 34, a higher $9,500 limit may apply for a Section 403(b) tax deferred annuity plan. Salary reductions under a Section 457 deferred compensation plan (see Chapter 11) maintained by a government employer must also be coordinated with these elective deferrals.) Any excess elective deferrals over this limit are taxable income to the employee.

Employer Contributions

Many Section 401(k) plans provide direct employer contributions in order to encourage employee participation and make the plan more valuable to employees. Plans typically use one or more of the following types of employer contributions:

- Formula matching contributions. The employer matches employee salary reductions, either dollar for dollar or under another formula. For example, the plan might provide that the employer contributes an amount equal to 50% of the amount the employee elects as a salary reduction. So, if an employee elects a salary reduction of $6,000, the employer puts an additional $3,000 into the employee's plan account.

- Discretionary matching contributions. Under this approach, the employer has discretion to make a contribution to the plan each year; the employer contribution is allocated to each participant's plan account in proportion to the amount elected by the participant as a salary reduction during that year. For example, at the end of a year the employer might decide to make a discretionary matching contribution of 40% of each participant's salary reduction for the year. Thus, if a participant had salary reductions of $5,000 for that year, the employer would contribute another $2,000 to that participant's account.

- Pure discretionary or "profit-sharing" contribution. The employer makes a discretionary contribution to the plan that is allocated simply on the basis of each employee's compensation, without regard to the amount of salary reductions elected by that employee. For example, at the end of a year the employer might decide to contribute another $100,000 to the plan. This contribution would be allocated to plan participants' accounts in the same manner as a discretionary profit-sharing contribution, as described in Chapter 25.

- Formula contribution. For example, the plan might provide that the employer will contribute 3 percent of compensation to the plan for employees whose annual compensation is less than $50,000. So, for an employee who earned $30,000, the employer would contribute 3 percent, or $900, to that employee's plan account.

Direct (nonelective) employer contribution provisions in Section 401(k) plans are usually intended to help the plan meet the ADP tests discussed below. The plan designer will use whatever contribution provision is most likely to be helpful for this purpose, given the group of employees covered under the plan. Note that nonelective employer contributions can be used to help meet the ADP tests only if they are immediately 100% vested.

Section 401(k) plans can also include nonelective employer contributions that are not intended to be counted in the ADP tests. The advantage of this is that such employer contributions need not be 100% vested. Graded vesting under the 3-to-7-year provision is usually used (see Appendix A). Graded vesting reduces employer cost for the plan since employees who leave employment before they are fully vested forfeit the nonvested part of their account balances. These "forfeitures" can then be used to reduce future employer contributions or, more commonly, redistributed to remaining participants' accounts in the plan. (Forfeitures cannot be repaid to the employer in cash in any qualified plan.)

Plan Distributions

Distributions from Section 401(k) plans are subject to the qualified plan distribution rules detailed in Appendix B. Most plans provide for distributions in a lump sum at termination of employment.

Section 401(k) plans often allow participants to make in-service withdrawals (withdrawals before termination of employment). However, there are a variety of restrictions that reduce the attractiveness of such provisions to employees. First, there is a special rule that Section 401(k) accounts based on elective deferrals can't be distributed prior to occurrence of one of the following:

- retirement
- death
- disability

- separation from service with the employer
- attainment of age 59½ by the participant
- plan termination (if the employer has no other defined contribution plan other than an ESOP)
- hardship.

"Hardship" is defined more restrictively than many participants may think, as discussed in the "Questions and Answers," below.

Note also that many pre-retirement distributions will be not only taxable, but also subject to the 10% early withdrawal penalty tax discussed in Appendix B. To summarize, a 10% penalty tax applies to the taxable amount (amount subject to regular income tax) of any qualified plan distribution, except for distributions

- after age 59½
- on the employee's death
- upon the employee's disability
- that are part of a joint or life annuity payout following separation from service
- that are paid after separation from service after attaining age 55
- that do not exceed the amount of medical expenses deductible as an itemized deduction for the year.

From this list, it is evident that many "hardship" distributions from a Section 401(k) plan, though permitted by the terms of the plan, will be subject to the 10% penalty tax.

Many Section 401(k) plans have provisions for plan loans to participants. A plan loan provision is extremely valuable to employees because it allows them access to their plan funds without the "hardship" restriction or the 10% penalty tax. Plan loans are discussed in detail in Appendix B.

TAX IMPLICATIONS

1. Employee elective deferrals (including salary reductions) are not currently income taxable to the employee, within the $7,000 ($7,313 in 1988) annual limit discussed earlier. However, elective deferrals are subject to social security tax (both employer and employee). In other words, even though salary has been deferred for income tax purposes, it is treated as received for social security purposes.

2. Nonelective employer contributions to the plan and employee elective deferrals are deductible by the employer for federal income tax purposes up to a limit of 15% of the total taxable payroll of all employees covered under the plan. Elective deferrals, but not nonelective employer contributions, are subject to social security (FICA) and federal unemployment (FUTA)

payroll taxes. The impact of state payroll taxes depends on the particular state's law. Both elective deferrals and nonelective employer contributions may be exempt from state payroll taxes in some states.

3. Elective deferrals must meet a special test for nondiscrimination — the "actual deferral percentage" or ADP test. The plan must meet one of the following two tests in actual operation:

> *Test 1* — The ADP for eligible highly compensated employees must not be more than the ADP of all other eligible employees multiplied by 1.25.

> *Test 2* — The ADP for eligible highly compensated employees must not exceed the ADP for other eligible employees by more than 2 percent *and* the ADP for eligible highly compensated employees must not be more than the ADP of all other eligible employees multiplied by 2.

For example, if the ADP for nonhighly compensated employees is 6 percent, the ADP for highly compensated employees can be as high as 8 percent (6 percent plus 2 percent). This meets Test 2.

"Highly compensated employee" is defined as it is for virtually all employee benefit purposes. In summary (more details are in Appendix A), a highly compensated employee is an employee who

- was at any time, during the current or preceding plan year, a more-than-5 percent owner of the employer,

- received compensation from the employer over $75,000, as indexed for inflation ($78,353 in 1988),

- received compensation over $50,000, as indexed ($52,235 in 1988) and was in the highest-paid 20% of the employer's employees, or

- was an officer and received compensation in excess of 50% of the defined benefit dollar limitation (see Appendix A).

4. Under Code section 415, as with any defined contribution plan, annual additions to each participant's account are limited to the *lesser of* (a) 25 percent of compensation or (b) the greater of $30,000 or $\frac{1}{4}$ of the defined benefit dollar limitation. (The defined benefit dollar limitation is $94,023 in 1988.) Annual additions include the total of (1) nonelective employer contributions to the participant's account, (2) salary reductions or other elective deferrals contributed to the account, (3) forfeitures from other participants' accounts, and (4) after-tax employee contributions to the account.

5. Distributions from the plan to employees are subject to income tax when received. Lump sum distributions made after age 59½ are subject to a limited election to use a special 5-year averaging tax calculation. Certain older participants may also be eligible for a 10-year averaging tax calculation. Not all distributions are eligible for these special tax calculations. The details of taxation of distribution are discussed in Appendix B.

HOW TO INSTALL A PLAN

Installation of a Section 401(k) plan follows the qualified plan installation procedure described in Appendix C.

In addition, elective deferral or salary reduction forms must be completed by plan participants before the plan's effective date so that salary reduction elections will be immediately effective.

The success of a Section 401(k) in meeting the employer's objectives and the ADP tests depends on effective communication with employees. Effective employer-employee communication is always important in employee benefit plans, but it is particularly essential for a Section 401(k) plan because of the active role of employees in the plan.

WHERE CAN I FIND OUT MORE ABOUT IT?

1. McFadden, John J., *Retirement Plans for Employees*. Homewood, IL: Richard D. Irwin, 1988.

2. Gee, Judith Boyers, *Pensions in Perspective*, 2nd ed. Cincinnati, OH: The National Underwriter Co., 1987.

3. Graduate Course: Advanced Pension and Retirement Planning I (GS 814), The American College, Bryn Mawr, PA.

QUESTIONS AND ANSWERS

Question — What kinds of organizations can adopt Section 401(k) plans?

Answer — Any incorporated or unincorporated business can adopt a Section 401(k) plan for its employees. The plan of an unincorporated business can cover partners or a sole proprietor as well as regular employees.

Nonprofit organizations and governmental (federal, state, or local) organizations are generally not eligible to maintain a Section 401(k) plan. (However, such employers who maintained pre-1987 plans that were "grandfathered" under the Tax Reform Act of 1986 and certain rural cooperative organizations are exempt from this prohibition). Nonprofit organizations should investigate adoption of a Section 403(b) tax deferred annuity plan (see Chapter 34) as an alternative. Both nonprofit and governmental organizations can also adopt Section 457 plans (see Chapter 11), which provide some features similar to a Section 401(k) plan.

Question — Can a Section 401(k) plan participant make deductible IRA contributions and well as salary reductions under a Section 401(k) plan?

Answer — Yes, but only within the reduced deductible IRA limits allowed for active qualified plan participants — see Chapter 17. No deduction is allowed for a year in which adjusted gross income on a joint basis is $50,000 or more ($35,000 for a single person), with reduced deductions for adjusted gross income between $40,000 and $50,000 joint ($25,000 to $35,000 single).

Question — What is a "hardship" that permits a Section 401(k) plan participant to make withdrawals?

Answer — The IRS regulations require that a hardship distribution must meet two conditions: (a) The distribution must be necessary in light of immediate and heavy financial needs of the employee, and (2) funds must not be reasonably available from other resources of the employee.

As guidance in interpreting the first requirement, the regulations list the following as meeting the "immediate and heavy" requirement:

• Medical expenses incurred by the participant or the participant's spouse or dependents.

• Purchase of a principal residence for the participant (mortgage payments do not typically constitute a hardship).

• Payment of tuition for post-secondary education for a participant or his spouse, children, or dependents.

• Payments of amounts necessary to prevent the eviction of the participant from his principal residence or from foreclosure on the mortgage.

The second issue — the existence of other resources — is determined on the basis of individual facts and circumstances. To simplify plan administration, there is a "safe harbor" test for this — the requirement will be deemed met if the following circumstances exist:

(1) The distribution does not exceed the amount of the immediate and heavy financial need,

(2) the employee must obtain all distributions other than hardship distributions and all nontaxable loans available under all plans maintained by the employer, and

(3) the plan must provide that the employee's elective deferral contributions and nondeductible contributions will be suspended for 12 months after the distribution and that the maximum contribution in the year following the suspension will be reduced by the amount contributed in the prior year.

Question — What types of investments are appropriate for Section 401(k) plans?

Answer — Generally, investments traditionally used in qualified profit-sharing plans are also used in Section 401(k) plans. Employee accounts in the plan fund are usually pooled for investment purposes. Investment tends toward bonds, money market, and liquid, cash-type media. Smaller plans often use a "family" of mutual funds for plan investments. The level of equity investment (common stocks) in Section 401(k) plans is usually lower than in defined benefit plans.

Many plans use a "directed investment" or "earmarking" provision that allows participants some degree of choice in the investment of their plan accounts. Directed investment provisions increase administrative costs of the plan. But they are attractive to employees and, if the directed investment provision meets the standards of Labor Department regulations, the employer is relieved of fiduciary responsibility for any investment directed by the participant.

Life insurance is often provided in Section 401(k) plans in much the same way as it is used in a regular profit-sharing plan. The use of life insurance in a qualified plan is discussed in Chapter 20.

Chapter 29
SICK PAY (SHORT TERM DISABILITY)

WHAT IS IT?

A sick pay or short term disability plan is a plan that continues employees' salary or wages during periods of illness or other disability for a limited time. Generally, sick pay or short term disability payments do not extend beyond about six months. Programs covering disabilities lasting more than six months are considered long term disability programs and are discussed in Chapter 21.

WHEN IS IT INDICATED?

1. Almost all employers have a broad based program providing some sick pay for short absences from work. This is a "high visibility" benefit that employees count on and appreciate.

2. An employer may want to provide special favorable short term disability programs for selected executives. Under current law, such plans can be provided on a discriminatory basis. That is, the employer can choose (1) who will be covered, (2) the level of benefits, which can vary from employee to employee, and (3) the terms and conditions of coverage.

DESIGN FEATURES

Most planners divide short term coverage into two types of plans: (1) sick pay and (2) short term disability plans. Although there is some overlap in these concepts, *sick pay* generally refers to uninsured continuation of salary or wages (usually 100% replacement) for a short period of time beginning on the first day of illness or disability. A *short term disability plan* is one that goes into effect when the employee's sick pay benefits run out and extends until the six month limit has been reached, when the employer's long term plan (if any) and social security disability go into effect. Short term plans, as defined this way, can be and often are insured.

Sick Pay

Sick pay benefits are usually provided for a broad group of employees. However, an employer can have a plan for selected executives only or a plan with more favorable benefits for executives.

Usually only full-time employees are covered under sick pay plans. The employer can define the term "full-time" for this purpose in any reasonable manner; the 1000 hour "year of service" definition applicable to qualified plans does not apply.

The duration of sick pay benefits is often tied to the length of an employee's service. For example, there may be no benefits until an employee has three months of service, then the plan will provide full benefits. Or, duration of benefits can be graded based on service. For example, employees may be entitled to 20 days of sick pay annually after 10 years of service, with the number of days of sick pay reduced for shorter service. One danger in providing increasingly generous sick pay as a "benefit" is that employees may come to believe that they are expected to take advantage of such sick days and abuse the benefit.

Some sick pay plans allow "carryover" of unused benefits. For example, if an employee is entitled to 10 days of sick pay in 1989 and uses only 5 of them, then the plan could allow the employee to carry over these 5 days to 1990, thus having 15 days of sick pay available in 1990. Plans allowing carryovers usually provide some maximum limit on the sick pay available for any one year. Usually no more than six months of sick pay can be accumulated.

If long periods of sick pay are allowed, benefits are often reduced below 100% of salary after a specified period of time (such as 30 days). This reduces employer costs and helps to "phase in" the long term benefits available, which usually do not provide 100% salary replacement.

Preventing sick pay abuse is a major management problem in many organizations. Some employers require a physician's certificate to obtain sick pay, particularly if the employee's absence is longer than one week. In some organizations management simply accepts the idea that employees will take whatever "sick days" are available and limits them accordingly. Generally speaking, absenteeism is a symptom of management problems that cannot be solved simply by the design of employee benefit programs.

Short Term Disability Plans

A short term disability plan fills the gap between sick pay and the employer's long term disability plan, if any. These plans are often insured, particularly for smaller employers, since the employer's liability to continue a disabled employee's salary for six months or so can be a considerable burden.

The design of short term plans, particularly if they are insured, is similar to the long term plans discussed in Chapter 21. However, there are some significant differences:

Tools and Techniques

- Short term plans often have broader coverage than long term plans. An employer's long term plan may be limited to selected executives.

- Short term plans often require less service for coverage. Long term plans may be reserved for career employees, such as those with five or more years of service.

- The definition of disability is typically more generous (i.e., easier to meet) in a short term plan than in a long term plan. Usually the "regular occupation" definition is used. That is, disability in a short term plan is typically defined as "the total and continuous inability of the employee to perform any and every duty of his or her regular occupation."

Coverage exclusions in insured short term plans are similar to those in long term plans, as discussed in Chapter 21. As with long term plans, the Civil Rights Act of 1964 prohibits exclusion of pregnancy-related disabilities if the employer has 15 or more employees. (State civil rights laws may apply even to smaller employers.)

TAX IMPLICATIONS

1. The employer can deduct payments made directly to employees under a sick pay or short term disability plan, as compensation to employees. The employer can also deduct premium payments made under an insured plan. Like all compensation deductions, these payments are subject to the "reasonableness" requirement described in Chapter 4.

2. In some insured plans, employees pay part of the cost of the plan, usually through payroll deductions. These payments are not tax deductible by the employee.

3. Employer payments of premiums under an insured disability plan do not result in taxable income to the employee.

4. Benefit payments under an employer-paid plan are fully taxable to the employee as received (subject to the credit described below) if the plan was fully paid for by the employer. If the employer paid only part of the cost, only a corresponding part of the benefit is taxable, again subject to credit. For example, if the employer paid 75 percent of the disability insurance premiums and the employee paid the remaining 25 percent, only 75 percent of the disability benefit received by the employee would be taxable.

   IRS regulations specify the time over which the employer and employee percentages are to be measured for this purpose. For group disability insurance, generally, payments over the three year period prior to the disability are taken into account in determining the percentages paid by employer and employee.

5. *Disability credit.* If an employee receiving benefits meets the "total and permanent" disability definition, a limited tax credit reduces the tax impact of disability payments for lower-income recipients. Because of this definition, the credit has little or no impact on most employees receiving sick pay or short term benefits, but it may come into effect for more serious or long term conditions.

   "Total and permanent disability" (the social security definition) means a condition under which the individual "is unable to engage in any substantial gainful activity by reason of any medically determinable physical or mental impairment which can be expected to result in death or which has lasted or can be expected to last for a continuous period of not less than 12 months." This is the strictest disability definition that is commonly used for any purpose.

   Generally, the disability credit is calculated by taking the maximum amount subject to the credit (see below) and subtracting $1/2$ of the amount by which the taxpayer's adjusted gross income exceeds the AGI limits (see below). The credit is equal to 15 percent of this amount. Thus, the maximum annual tax credit is $1,125 for a joint return as indicated below. The chart below shows the maximum amounts eligible for the credit, the maximum credit that may be obtained and the limitations to adjusted gross income (AGI):

MAXIMUM AMOUNT SUBJECT TO CREDIT

Single Person	$5,000
Joint Return (where one spouse is a qualified individual)	$5,000
Joint Return (where both spouses are qualified individuals)	$7,500
Married Filing Separately	$3,750

MAXIMUM CREDIT

Single Person	$750
Joint Return (where one spouse is a qualified individual)	$750
Joint Return (where both spouses are qualified individuals)	$1,125
Married Filing Separately	$562.50

ADJUSTED GROSS INCOME LIMITS

Single Person	$7,500
Married Filing Jointly	$10,000
Married Filing Separately	$5,000

For example, if a disabled employee has adjusted gross income (from all sources, including taxable disability income) of $14,000, and is married, filing jointly, the amount on which his disability tax credit is calculated would be $5,000 (the maximum amount for a joint return where only one spouse receives disability income payments) less $2,000 ($1/2$ of the amount by which the taxpayer's AGI exceeds $10,000). In short, this is $5,000 - $2,000, or $3,000. The taxpayer's credit is equal to 15 percent of $3,000, or $450. Accordingly, the employee's income tax bill for the year is reduced by $450. Note that to receive this credit the employee must meet the social security total and permanent definition of disability. An employee might receive benefits under some employer plans without meeting this strict definition of disability, as discussed above.

This tax credit is even further reduced by 15 percent of any tax-free income received by the employee from a pension, annuity, or disability benefit, including social security. Since most disability plans are integrated with social security benefits, this further reduction makes the credit even less valuable.

In view of all the reductions applicable to this credit, and the extremely low AGI limits on full availability, the credit is a minor factor in the design of disability benefits, and plays practically no part in designing benefits for executives.

6. Disability insurance premiums paid by the employer under the plan are not considered wages subject to employment taxes (FICA - social security - and FUTA - federal unemployment). Generally disability insurance premiums are not subject to state employment taxes either, but individual state laws should be consulted.

7. Disability benefits are subject to federal income tax withholding if paid directly by the employer. If paid by a third party such as an insurance company, withholding is required only if the employee requests it.

8. Disability benefits attributable to employer contributions are subject to social security taxes for a limited period at the beginning of a disability. Thereafter, they are not considered wages subject to social security tax.

ERISA REQUIREMENTS

A sick pay or short term disability income plan is considered a welfare benefit plan under ERISA. Such plans require a written document, the naming of a plan administrator, and a formal written claims procedure by which employees can make benefit claims and appeal denials. The plan is not subject to the eligibility, vesting, or funding requirements of ERISA. The plan administrator must provide plan participants with a summary plan description (SPD).

WHERE CAN I FIND OUT MORE ABOUT IT?

1. Beam, Burton T., Jr. and John J. McFadden, *Employee Benefits*, 2nd ed. Homewood, IL: Richard D. Irwin, 1988.

2. *Tax Facts 1*. Cincinnati, OH: The National Underwriter Company. Revised annually.

Chapter 30

SIMPLIFIED EMPLOYEE PENSION (SEP)

WHAT IS IT?

A simplified employee pension (SEP) is an employer-sponsored retirement/deferred compensation arrangement that is similar to a qualified profit-sharing plan. Congress enacted the SEP provisions of the Code to provide employers with a "simplified" alternative to a qualified plan.

Like a qualified profit-sharing plan, a SEP combines simplicity of design with a high degree of flexibility from the employer's viewpoint. In substance, a SEP is merely an employer agreement to contribute on a nondiscriminatory basis to IRAs maintained by employees. The limits for SEP contributions are much higher than those for individually-owned IRAs, however — up to the lesser of (a) 15 percent of compensation or (b) $30,000 (as indexed for inflation — see Appendix A).

WHEN IS IT INDICATED?

1. When the employer is looking for an alternative to a qualified profit-sharing plan that is easier and less expensive to install and administer. For very small employers, a SEP is probably the simplest type of tax-deferred employee retirement plan available. For larger employers (more than about 10 employees) the cost of installing and administering a regular qualified plan can be spread over enough employees that the advantages of a SEP are less significant.

2. When an employer wants to install a tax-deferred plan and it is too late to adopt a qualified plan for the year in question. (Qualified plans must be adopted before the end of the year in which they are to be effective. SEPs can be adopted as late as the tax return filing date for the year in which they are to be effective.)

ADVANTAGES

1. A SEP can be adopted by completing a simple IRS form (Forms 5305 - SEP or 5305A - SEP, copies of which are at the end of this chapter) rather than by the complex procedure required for qualified plans (described in Appendix C). However, if the employer adopts a master or prototype qualified plan, the installation costs and complexity may not actually be much greater than that for a SEP, even though the documentation is more voluminous.

2. Benefits of a SEP are totally portable by employees since funding consists entirely of IRAs for each employee and employees are always 100 percent vested in their benefits. Employees own and control their SEP-IRA accounts, even after they terminate employment with the original employer.

3. A SEP provides as much flexibility in the amount and timing of contributions as a qualified profit-sharing plan. The employer is free at its discretion to make no contribution to the plan in any given year.

4. Individual IRA accounts allow participants to benefit from good investment results (as well as run the risk of bad results).

5. A SEP can be funded through salary reductions by employees, if conditions described in "Tax Implications," below, are met.

DISADVANTAGES

1. Employees can't rely upon a SEP to provide an adequate retirement benefit. First, benefits are not significant unless the employer makes substantial, regular contributions to the SEP. The employer has no obligation to do this under the plan. Furthermore, employees who enter the plan at older ages have only a limited number of years remaining prior to retirement to build up their SEP accounts.

2. Employees bear investment risk under the plan.

3. The annual contribution to each employee's account in a SEP is limited to the lesser of (a) 15 percent of compensation or (b) the greater of $30,000 or ¼ of the dollar limitation for defined benefit plans. (The dollar limitation for defined benefit plans is $94,023 for 1988.) This limits the relative tax advantage available to highly compensated employees under a SEP.

4. Distributions from SEPs are not eligible for the 5-year (or 10-year) averaging provisions available for certain qualified plan distributions.

TAX IMPLICATIONS

1. An employer may deduct contributions to a SEP, up to the 15%/$30,000 limit, if they are made under a written formula that meets various requirements of the Internal Revenue Code. These requirements are somewhat similar to those for qualified plans. The "qualified plan rules," as such, do not apply to SEPs.

The major SEP requirements are:

Tools and Techniques

• A SEP must cover all employees who are at least 21 years of age and who have worked for the employer during 3 out of the preceding 5 calendar years. Part-time employment counts in determining years of service.

• Contributions need not be made on behalf of employees whose compensation for the calendar year was less than $300, as indexed for inflation ($313 in 1988).

• The plan can exclude employees who are members of collective bargaining units if retirement benefits have been the subject of good-faith bargaining; nonresident aliens can also be excluded.

The employer need not contribute any particular amount to a SEP or make any contribution at all. The employer contribution, if made, must be allocated to plan participants under a written formula that does not discriminate in favor of highly compensated employees. The definition of "highly compensated" is that used for most employee benefit purposes, as discussed in Appendix A.

SEP formulas usually provide allocations as a uniform percentage of total compensation of each employee. In the allocation formula, only the first $200,000 (as indexed — $208,940 in 1988) of each employee's compensation can be taken into account.

SEP allocation formulas can be integrated with social security under the integration rules applicable to qualified defined contribution plans; these are discussed in Appendix A. A salary reduction SEP (see below) may not be integrated.

2. If an employer has 25 or fewer eligible employees during the preceding year, SEPs can be funded through employee salary reductions. With a salary reduction plan, employees have an election to receive cash or have amounts contributed to the SEP. The arrangement works very much like a Section 401(k) salary reduction arrangement described in Chapter 28. The $7,000 limit as indexed ($7,313 in 1988) on elective deferrals applies to the total of salary reduction SEP and 401(k) salary reductions, if any.

An employer cannot use a salary reduction SEP unless 50 percent or more of the employees eligible to participate elect to make SEP contributions. In addition, "average deferral percentage" (ADP) rules similar to the 401(k) rules apply to a salary reduction SEP.

The ADP for each highly compensated eligible employee who participates must be no more than 1.25 times the ADP of nonhighly compensated eligible employees. For example, if nonhighly compensated employees elect salary reductions averaging 6 percent of compensation, no highly compensated employee can elect more than a 7.5 percent salary reduction.

3. If an employer maintains a SEP and also maintains a regular qualified plan, contributions to the SEP reduce the amount that can be deducted for contributions to the regular plan.

4. In a SEP plan, each participating employee maintains an IRA. Employer contributions made directly or employee salary reductions are contributed to the employee's IRA. Employer contributions and employee salary reductions, within the limits discussed above, are not included in the employee's taxable income.

5. Salary reductions, but not direct employer contributions, are subject to social security (FICA) and federal unemployment (FUTA) taxes. The impact of state payroll taxes depends on the particular state's law. Both salary reductions and employer contributions may be exempt from state payroll taxes in some states.

6. Distributions to employees from the plan are treated as distributions from an IRA. All the restrictions on IRA distributions apply and the distributions are taxed the same. The taxation of IRA distributions is discussed in Chapter 17. In particular, note that the 5-year (or 10-year) averaging provisions are not available for either IRA or SEP distributions.

HOW TO INSTALL A PLAN

Installation of a SEP can be very simple. The employer merely completes Form 5305 - SEP. For a salary reduction SEP, Form 5305A - SEP is used. Copies of these forms and instructions are reproduced at the end of this chapter. To adopt the SEP, the relevant form is completed and signed by the employer prior to the tax filing date for the year in which the SEP is to take effect. The form does not have to be sent to the IRS or other government agency.

Note that a SEP adopted by filling out Form 5305 - SEP does not have an integrated contribution formula. An integrated SEP plan must be custom designed. Furthermore, Forms 5305 - SEP and 5305A - SEP can't be used if the employer (1) currently maintains a qualified plan or (2) maintained a qualified defined benefit plan at any time in the past covering one or more of the employees to be covered under the SEP. In such cases, a SEP can be adopted but also must be custom designed. Costs for custom designing and installing a SEP are comparable to those for a qualified profit-sharing plan.

ERISA REQUIREMENTS

The reporting and disclosure requirements for SEPs are simplified if the employer uses the IRS form of SEP contained on Form 5305 - SEP or 5305A - SEP. The annual report form (5500 series) need not be filed if these forms are used. In other cases, reporting and disclosure requirements are similar to those for a qualified profit-sharing plan.

WHERE CAN I FIND OUT MORE ABOUT IT?

1. IRS Publication 334, *Tax Guide for Small Business,* and Publication 535, *Business Expense Deductions*, available free from the IRS; revised annually.

2. Gee, Judith Boyers, *Pensions in Perspective*, 2nd ed. Cincinnati, OH: The National Underwriter Co., 1987.

QUESTIONS AND ANSWERS

Question — How does the "last minute" adoption feature of a SEP operate?

Answer — Suppose an employer reviews financial results shortly after the close of the employer's tax year — say it's a calendar year — and decides that the company should have a qualified plan for the year just ended. It is not possible to adopt a qualified plan after the close of the taxable year, as discussed in Appendix C. However, a SEP can be adopted at any time up to the tax return filing date for the year, including extensions. For example, if an incorporated employer uses the calendar year, the tax return filing date for the year 1989 is March 15, 1990, with extensions possible to September 15, 1990. Therefore a SEP could be adopted for 1989 as late as September 15, 1990.

Question — Can an unincorporated business adopt a SEP covering partners or a sole proprietor?

Answer — Yes. Partners and proprietors can be covered under the SEP of an unincorporated employer, as well as regular employees.

Question — Can an employer make contributions to a SEP for employees who are over age 70$\frac{1}{2}$?

Answer — An individual cannot make contributions to his or her own IRA after attaining age 70$\frac{1}{2}$. However, employers can make contributions to SEPs for employees who are over age 70$\frac{1}{2}$. In fact, the age discrimination law, if applicable, would generally require such contributions to be made.

Question — Can a family business adopt a salary reduction SEP?

Answer — If family members are the only employees of the business, it is possible that all of the employees would be considered "highly compensated" under the Code definition (Appendix A). Technically, the ADP test could not be met. However, the IRS has acknowledged in its final regulations under Section 401(k) that a Section 401(k) plan does not fail to qualify just because all eligible employees are highly compensated. This reasoning should also apply to a SEP.

Question — Can an employee participating in a SEP also make deductible contributions to his or her own IRA?

Answer — For individual IRA purposes, a SEP participant is treated the same as a participant in a regular qualified plan. That is, if the individual is an "active participant" in the plan, individual IRA contributions can be made and deducted, but the $2,000/$2,250 deduction limit is reduced for individuals with adjusted gross income (AGI) of more than $25,000 or married couples with AGI of more than $40,000. If the individual is not an active participant in the plan, the full IRA deduction is available. These rules are discussed in detail in Chapter 17.

An employee covered under a SEP would be considered an active participant in any year in which salary reductions or employer contributions were allocated to his or her SEP account. However, in a year in which no allocation was made to the individual's SEP account, the individual would have a full individual IRA deduction available (up to the $2,000/$2,250 limit). The higher SEP limit is not available for individual IRA contributions, only for employer contributions or salary reductions under a SEP arrangement.

Form **5305-SEP**
(Rev. June 1988)
Department of the Treasury
Internal Revenue Service

Simplified Employee Pension-Individual Retirement Accounts Contribution Agreement
(Under Section 408(k) of the Internal Revenue Code)

OMB No. 1545-0499
Expires 7-31-91

Do NOT File with Internal Revenue Service

_____ makes the following agreement under the terms of section 408(k) of
(Business name—employer)
the Internal Revenue Code and the instructions to this form.

The employer agrees to provide for discretionary contributions in each calendar year to the Individual Retirement Accounts or Individual Retirement Annuities (IRA's) of all eligible employees who are at least _____ years old (not over 21 years old) (see instruction "Who May Participate") and worked in at least _____ years (enter 1, 2, or 3 years) of the immediately preceding 5 years (see instruction "Who May Participate"). This ☐ includes ☐ does not include employees covered under a collective bargaining agreement and ☐ includes ☐ does not include employees whose total compensation during the year is less than $300.

The employer agrees that contributions made on behalf of each eligible employee will:
- Be made only on the first $200,000 of compensation (as adjusted per Code section 408(k)(8)).
- Be made in an amount that is the same percentage of total compensation for every employee.
- Be limited to the smaller of $30,000 (or if greater, ¼ of the dollar limitation in effect under section 415(b)(1)(A)) or 15% of compensation.
- Be paid to the employee's IRA trustee, custodian, or insurance company (for an annuity contract).

_____
Signature of employer

_____
Date

_____
By

Instructions for the Employer
(Section references are to the Internal Revenue Code, unless otherwise noted.)

Paperwork Reduction Act Notice.—The Paperwork Reduction Act of 1980 says we must tell you why we are collecting this information, how it is to be used, and whether you have to give it to us. The information is used to determine if you are entitled to a deduction for contributions made to a SEP. Your completing this form is only required if you want to establish a Model SEP.

Purpose of Form.—Form 5305-SEP (Model SEP) is used by an employer to make an agreement to provide benefits to all employees under a Simplified Employee Pension (SEP) plan described in section 408(k). This form is NOT to be filed with IRS.

What Is a SEP Plan?—A SEP provides an employer with a simplified way to make contributions toward an employee's retirement income. Under a SEP, the employer is permitted to contribute a certain amount (see below) to an employee's Individual Retirement Account or Individual Retirement Annuity (IRA's). The employer makes contributions directly to an IRA set up by an employee with a bank, insurance company, or other qualified financial institution. When using this form to establish a SEP, the IRA must be a model IRA established on an IRS form or a master or prototype IRA for which IRS has issued a favorable opinion letter. Making the agreement on Form 5305-SEP does not establish an employer IRA as described under section 408(c).

This form may not be used by an employer who:
- Currently maintains any other qualified retirement plan.
- Has maintained in the past a defined benefit plan, even if now terminated.
- Has any eligible employees for whom IRA's have not been established.

- Uses the services of leased employees (as described in section 414(n)).
- Is a member of an affiliated service group (as described in section 414(m)), a controlled group of corporations (as described in section 414(b)), or trades or businesses under common control (as described in section 414(c)), UNLESS all eligible employees of all the members of such groups, trades, or businesses, participate under the SEP.
- This form should only be used if the employer will pay the cost of the SEP contributions. This form is not suitable for a SEP that provides for contributions at the election of the employee whether or not made pursuant to a salary reduction agreement.

Who May Participate.—Any employee who is at least 21 years old and has performed "service" for you in at least 3 years of the immediately preceding 5 years must be permitted to participate in the SEP. However, you may establish less restrictive eligibility requirements if you choose. "Service" is any work performed for you for any period of time, however short. Further, if you are a member of an affiliated service group, a controlled group of corporations, or trades or businesses under common control, "service" includes any work performed for any period of time for any other member of such group, trades, or businesses. Generally, to make the agreement, all eligible employees (including all eligible employees, if any, of other members of an affiliated service group, a controlled group of corporations, or trades or businesses under common control) must participate in the plan. However, employees covered under a collective bargaining agreement and certain nonresident aliens may be excluded if section 410(b)(3)(A) or 410(b)(3)(C) applies to them. Employees whose total compensation for the year is less than $300 may be excluded.

Amount of Contributions.—You are not required to make any contributions to an employee's SEP-IRA in a given year. However, if you do make contributions, you must make them to the IRA's of all eligible employees, whether or not they are still employed at the time contributions are made. The contributions made must be the same percentage of each employee's total compensation (up to a maximum compensation base of $200,000 as adjusted per section 408(k)(8) for cost of living changes). The contributions you make in a year for any one employee may not be more than the smaller of $30,000 or 15% of that employee's total compensation (figured without considering the SEP-IRA contributions).

For this purpose, compensation includes:
- Amounts received for personal services actually performed (see section 1.219-1(c) of the Income Tax Regulations); and
- Earned income defined under section 401(c)(2).

In making contributions, you may not discriminate in favor of any employee who is highly compensated.

Under this form you may not integrate your SEP contributions with, or offset them by, contributions made under the Federal Insurance Contributions Act (FICA).

Currently, employers who have established a SEP using this agreement and have provided each participant with a copy of this form, including the questions and answers, are not required to file the annual information returns, Forms 5500, 5500-C, 5500-R, or 5500EZ for the SEP.

Deducting Contributions.—You may deduct all contributions to a SEP subject to the limitations of section 404(h). This SEP is maintained on a calendar year basis and contributions to the SEP are deductible for your taxable year with or within which the calendar year ends. Contributions made for a particular taxable year and contributed by the due date of your income tax return (including extensions) shall be deemed made in that taxable year.

Form **5305-SEP** (Rev. 6-88)

Tools and Techniques

Making the Agreement.— This agreement is considered made when (1) IRA's have been established for all of your eligible employees, (2) you have completed all blanks on the agreement form without modification, and (3) you have given all your eligible employees copies of the agreement form, instructions, and questions and answers.

Keep the agreement form with your records; do not file it with IRS.

Information for the Employee

The information provided explains what a Simplified Employee Pension plan is, how contributions are made, and how to treat your employer's contributions for tax purposes.

Please read the questions and answers carefully. For more specific information, also see the agreement form and instructions to your employer on this form.

Questions and Answers

1. Q. What is a Simplified Employee Pension, or SEP?

A. A SEP is a retirement income arrangement under which your employer may contribute any amount each year up to the smaller of $30,000 or 15% of your compensation into **your own** Individual Retirement Account/Annuity (IRA).

Your employer will provide you with a copy of the agreement containing participation requirements and a description of the basis upon which employer contributions may be made to your IRA.

All amounts contributed to your IRA by your employer belong to you, even after you separate from service with that employer.

The $30,000 limitation referred to above may be increased by ¼ of the dollar limitation in effect under section 415(b)(1)(A).

2. Q. Must my employer contribute to my IRA under the SEP?

A. Whether or not your employer makes a contribution to the SEP is entirely within the employer's discretion. If a contribution is made under the SEP, it must be allocated to all the eligible employees according to the SEP agreement. The Model SEP specifies that the contribution on behalf of each eligible employee will be the same percentage of compensation (excluding compensation higher than $200,000) for all employees.

3. Q. How much may my employer contribute to my SEP-IRA in any year?

A. Under the Model SEP (**Form 5305-SEP**) that your employer has adopted, your employer will determine the amount of contribution to be made to your IRA each year. However, the contribution for any year is limited to the smaller of $30,000 or 15% of your compensation for that year. The compensation used to determine this limit does not include any amount which is contributed by your employer to your IRA under the SEP. The agreement does not require an employer to maintain a particular level of contributions. It is possible that for a given year no employer contribution will be made on an employee's behalf.

Also see Question 5.

4. Q. How do I treat my employer's SEP contributions for my taxes?

A. The amount your employer contributes for years beginning after 1986 is excludable from your gross income subject to certain limitations including the lesser of $30,000 or 15% of compensation mentioned in 1.A. above and is not includible as taxable wages on your Form W-2.

5. Q. May I also contribute to my IRA if I am a participant in a SEP?

A. Yes. You may still contribute the lesser of $2,000 or 100% of your compensation to an IRA. However, the amount which is deductible is subject to various limitations.

Also see Question 11.

6. Q. Are there any restrictions on the IRA I select to deposit my SEP contributions in?

A. Under the Model SEP that is approved by IRS, contributions must be made to either a Model IRA which is executed on an IRS form or a master or prototype IRA for which IRS has issued a favorable opinion letter.

7. Q. What if I don't want a SEP-IRA?

A. Your employer may require that you become a participant in such an arrangement as a condition of employment. However, if the employer does not require all eligible employees to become participants and an eligible employee elects not to participate, all other employees of the same employer may be prohibited from entering into a SEP-IRA arrangement with that employer. If one or more eligible employees do not participate and the employer attempts to establish a SEP-IRA agreement with the remaining employees, the resulting arrangement may result in adverse tax consequences to the participating employees.

8. Q. Can I move funds from my SEP-IRA to another tax-sheltered IRA?

A. Yes, it is permissible for you to withdraw, or receive, funds from your SEP-IRA, and no more than 60 days later, place such funds in another IRA, or SEP-IRA. This is called a "rollover" and may not be done without penalty more frequently than at one-year intervals. However, there are no restrictions on the number of times you may make "transfers" if you arrange to have such funds transferred between the trustees, so that you never have possession.

9. Q. What happens if I withdraw my employer's contribution from my IRA?

A. If you don't want to leave the employer's contribution in your IRA, you may withdraw it at any time, but any amount withdrawn is includible in your income. Also, if withdrawals occur before attainment of age 59 ½, and not on account of death or disability, you may be subject to a penalty tax.

10. Q. May I participate in a SEP even though I'm covered by another plan?

A. An employer may not adopt this IRS Model SEP (**Form 5305-SEP**) if the employer maintains another qualified retirement plan or has ever maintained a qualified defined benefit plan. However, if you work for several employers you may be covered by a SEP of one employer and a different SEP or pension or profit-sharing plan of another employer.

Also see Questions 11 and 12.

11. Q. What happens if too much is contributed to my SEP-IRA in one year?

A. Any contribution that is more than the yearly limitations may be withdrawn without penalty by the due date (plus extensions) for filing your tax return (normally April 15th), but is includible in your gross income. Excess contributions left in your SEP-IRA account after that time may have adverse tax consequences. Withdrawals of those contributions may be taxed as premature withdrawals.

Also see Question 10.

12. Q. Do I need to file any additional forms with IRS because I participate in a SEP?

A. No.

13. Q. Is my employer required to provide me with information about SEP-IRA's and the SEP agreement?

A. Yes, your employer must provide you with a copy of the executed SEP agreement (**Form 5305-SEP**), these Questions and Answers, and provide a statement each year showing any contribution to your IRA.

Also see Question 4.

14. Q. Is the financial institution where I establish my IRA also required to provide me with information?

A. Yes, it must provide you with a disclosure statement which contains the following items of information in plain, nontechnical language:

(1) the statutory requirements which relate to your IRA;

(2) the tax consequences which follow the exercise of various options and what those options are;

(3) participation eligibility rules, and rules on the deductibility and nondeductibility of retirement savings;

(4) the circumstances and procedures under which you may revoke your IRA, including the name, address, and telephone number of the person designated to receive notice of revocation (**this explanation must be prominently displayed at the beginning of the disclosure statement);**

(5) explanations of when penalties may be assessed against you because of specified prohibited or penalized activities concerning your IRA; and

(6) financial disclosure information which:

(a) either projects value growth rates of your IRA under various contribution and retirement schedules, or describes the method of computing and allocating annual earnings and charges which may be assessed;

(b) describes whether, and for what period, the growth projections for the plan are guaranteed, or a statement of the earnings rate and terms on which the projection is based;

(c) states the sales commission to be charged in each year expressed as a percentage of $1,000; and

(d) states the proportional amount of any nondeductible life insurance which may be a feature of your IRA.

See **Publication 590,** Individual Retirement Arrangements (IRA's), available at most IRS offices, for a more complete explanation of the disclosure requirements.

In addition to this disclosure statement, the financial institution is required to provide you with a financial statement each year. It may be necessary to retain and refer to statements for more than one year in order to evaluate the investment performance of the IRA and in order that you will know how to report IRA distributions for tax purposes.

✿ U.S. Government Printing Office: 1988—201-993/60256

Form **5305A-SEP**

(Rev. October 1987)

Department of the Treasury
Internal Revenue Service

**Salary Reduction and Other Elective Simplified
Employee Pension-Individual Retirement Accounts
Contribution Agreement**

(Under Section 408(k) of the Internal Revenue Code)

OMB No. 1545-1012
Expires 9-30-90

**Do NOT File with
Internal Revenue
Service**

Caution: *This form may only be used if the three conditions found at Article III, items E, F, and G are met.*

_____ establishes the following arrangement under the terms of section

(Business name—employer)

408(k) of The Internal Revenue Code and the instructions to this form.

Article I—Eligibility Requirements

Provided the requirements of Article III are met, the employer agrees to permit elective deferrals to be made in each calendar year to the Individual Retirement Accounts or Individual Retirement Annuities (IRA), established by or on behalf of all employees who are at least _____ years old (see instructions) and have performed services for the employer in at least _____ years (see instructions) of the immediately preceding 5 years. This ☐ includes ☐ does not include employees covered under a collective bargaining agreement and ☐ includes ☐ does not include employees whose total compensation during the year is less than $300.

Article II—Elective Deferrals

A. Salary Reduction Option. A participant may elect to have his or her compensation reduced by the following percentage or amount per pay period, as designated in writing to the employer (check appropriate box, or boxes, and fill in the blanks):

  1. ☐ An amount not in excess of _____ % (enter a specified percent of 15% or less) of a participant's compensation.

  2. ☐ An amount not in excess of $ _____ (not to exceed $7,000 per year as adjusted per Code section 415(d)).

B. Cash Bonus Option. A participant may base elective deferrals on bonuses that, at the participant's election, may be contributed to the SEP or received by the participant in cash during the calendar year. Check here ☐ if such elective deferrals may be made to this SEP.

Article III—SEP Requirements

The employer agrees that each employee's elective deferrals to this SEP will:

A. Be based only on the first $200,000 of compensation (as adjusted annually per Code section 408(k)(8)).

B. Be limited annually to the lesser of:

  1. 15% of compensation (see instructions for Article III); **or**

  2. $7,000 (as adjusted annually per Code section 415(d)).

Amounts in excess of these limits will be treated as excess SEP deferrals.

C. Be further reduced, as necessary in accordance with Code section 415, if the employer also maintains a SEP to which non-elective SEP employer contributions are made for a calendar year.

D. Be paid to the employee's IRA trustee, custodian, or insurance company (for an annuity contract) or, if necessary, an IRA established for an employee by an employer.

E. Be made only if at least 50% of the employer's employees eligible to participate elect to have amounts contributed to the SEP.

F. Be made only if the employer had 25 or fewer employees eligible to participate at all times during the prior calendar year.

G. Be adjusted only if deferrals to this SEP for any calendar year do not meet the "ADP" requirements described in the instructions on page 3.

Article IV—Excess SEP Contributions

The employer agrees to notify each employee by March 15 of each year of any excess SEP contributions to the employee's SEP-IRA for the preceding calendar year.

Article V—Top-heavy Requirements

A. Unless paragraph B below is checked, the minimum top-heavy contribution for each year must be allocated to the SEP-IRA of each non-key employee eligible to participate in this SEP in accordance with Code section 416. This allocation may not be less than the smaller of: **(1)** 3% of the non-key employee's compensation; **or (2)** the largest percentage of elective deferrals, as a percentage of the first $200,000 of the key employee's compensation, deferred by any key employee for that year.

B. ☐ The top-heavy requirements of section 416 will be satisfied through contributions to this employer's non-elective SEP-IRA.

_____

Signature of employer

_____

By

_____

Date

Form **5305A-SEP** (Rev. 10-87)

Tools and Techniques

Instructions for the Employer

(Section references are to the Internal Revenue Code, unless otherwise noted.)

Paperwork Reduction Act Notice.—The Paperwork Reduction Act of 1980 says we must tell you why we are collecting this information, how it is to be used, and whether you must give it to us. The information is used to determine if you are entitled to a deduction for contributions made to a SEP. Completion of this form is required only if you want to establish a Model Elective SEP.

Purpose of Form.—Form 5305A-SEP (model elective SEP) is used by an employer to permit employees to make elective deferrals to a Simplified Employee Pension (SEP) described in section 408(k). This form is NOT to be filed with IRS.

What is a SEP?—A SEP is a plan that provides an employer with a simplified way to enhance the employee's retirement income. Under an elective SEP, employees may choose whether or not to make elective deferrals to the SEP. The employer puts the amounts deferred by employees directly into an IRA set up by or on behalf of the employee with a bank, insurance company, or other qualified financial institution. When using this form to establish a SEP, the IRA established by or on behalf of an employee must be a model IRA or a master or prototype IRA for which IRS has issued a favorable opinion letter. Making the agreement on Form 5305A-SEP does not establish an employer IRA as described under section 408(c).

This form may NOT be used by an employer who:

1. Currently maintains any other qualified retirement plan. This does not prevent an employer from also maintaining a Model SEP (Form 5305-SEP) or other SEP to which either elective or non-elective contributions are made.

2. Has maintained in the past a defined benefit plan, even if now terminated.

3. Has any eligible employees by or for whom IRAs have not been established.

4. Has only highly compensated employees.

5. Is a member of one of the groups described in the Specific Instructions for Article III, G, 2 below, UNLESS all eligible employees of all the members of such groups, trades, or businesses are eligible to make elective deferrals to this SEP, and PROVIDED that in the prior calendar year there were never more than 25 employees eligible to participate in this SEP, in total, of all the members of such groups, trades, or businesses.

6. Is a state or local government or a tax-exempt organization.

This form should be used only if the employer intends to permit elective deferrals to a SEP. If the employer wishes to establish a SEP to which non-elective employer contributions may be made, Form 5305-SEP or a non-model SEP should be used instead of, or in addition to, this form.

Making the Agreement.—This agreement is considered made when:

1. IRAs have been established by or for all of your eligible employees;

2. You have completed all blanks on the agreement form without modification; **and**

3. You have given all your eligible employees copies of the agreement form, instructions, and questions and answers.

Keep the agreement form with your records; do NOT file it with IRS.

Currently, employers who have established a SEP using this agreement and have provided each participant with a copy of this form, including the questions and answers, are not required to file the annual information returns, Forms 5500, 5500-C, 5500-R, or 5500EZ for the SEP.

Deducting Contributions.—You may deduct contributions made by the due date of the employer's tax return, and extensions thereof, to a SEP subject to the limitations of section 404(h). This SEP is maintained on a calendar year basis, and contributions to the SEP are deductible for your taxable year with or within which the calendar year ends.

However, please see the Actual Deferral Percentage worksheet on page 6 in this booklet.

Specific Instructions

Article I.—Eligibility Requirements

Any employee who is at least 21 years old and has performed "service" for you in at least 3 years of the immediately preceding 5 years must be permitted to participate in the SEP. However, you may establish less restrictive eligibility requirements if you choose. Service is any work performed for you for any period of time, however short. Further, if you are a member of one of the groups described in Article III, G. 2 below, service includes any work performed for any period of time for any other member of such group, trades, or businesses. Generally, to make the agreement, all eligible employees, including leased employees within the meaning of section 414(n), of the affiliated employer must be permitted to make elective deferrals to the SEP. However, employees covered under a collective bargaining agreement and certain nonresident aliens may be excluded if section 410(b)(3)(A) or 410(b)(3)(C) applies to them. Employees whose total compensation for the year is less than $300 also may be excluded.

Article II.—Elective Deferrals

You may permit your employees to make elective deferrals through salary reduction or on the basis of bonuses that, at the participant's option, may be contributed to the SEP or received by the participant in cash during the calendar year.

You are responsible for telling your employees how they may make, change, or terminate elective deferrals based on either salary reduction or cash bonuses. You must also provide a form on which they may make their deferral elections. (This requirement may be satisfied by use of the model form provided on page 5 of this booklet or by use of a form setting forth, in a manner calculated to be understood by the average plan participant, the information contained in the "Model SEP Deferral Form.") No deferral election may be made with respect to compensation already received.

Article III.—SEP Requirements

A. Elective deferrals may not be based on more than $200,000 of compensation, as adjusted per section 408(k)(8) for cost of living changes. Compensation is the employee's compensation from the employee (figured without including the SEP-IRA contributions) and includes:

● Amounts received for personal services actually performed (see section 1.219-1(c) of the Income Tax Regulations), **and**

● Earned income defined under section 401(c)(2).

Note: *The deferral limit of 15% of compensation (less employer SEP-IRA contributions) is computed using the following formula: (compensation including employer SEP-IRA contribution ÷ 115%) × .15 = 15% of compensation limitation.*

B. The maximum limit on the amount of compensation an employee may elect to defer under a SEP for a calendar year is the lesser of:

● 15% of the employee's compensation; or

● $7,000, adjusted as explained below.

Amounts deferred for a year in excess of $7,000 as adjusted are considered excess deferrals and are subject to the consequences described below.

The $7,000 limit on the amount an employee may elect to defer in each year applies to the total elective deferrals the employee makes for the year under the following arrangements:

1. Elective SEPs under section 408(k)(6);

2. Cash or deferred arrangements under section 401(k); and

3. Salary reduction arrangements under section 403(b).

Thus, the employee may have excess deferrals even if the amount deferred under this SEP does not exceed $7,000.

The $7,000 limit will be indexed according to the cost of living. In addition, the limit may be increased to $9,500 if the employee makes elective deferrals to a salary reduction arrangement under section 403(b).

If an employee who elects to defer compensation under this SEP has made excess deferrals for a year, he or she must withdraw those excess deferrals by April 15 following the year of the deferral. Excess deferrals not withdrawn by April 15 following the year of the deferral may also be subject, when withdrawn, to the 10% tax on early distributions under section 72(t).

C. If you also maintain a Model SEP or any other SEP to which you make non-elective contributions, contributions to the two SEPs together may not exceed the lesser of $30,000 or 15% of compensation for any employee. If these limits are exceeded on behalf of any employee for a particular calendar year, that employee's elective deferrals for that year must be reduced to the extent of the excess.

E. and F. Each of these calculations is made after first excluding employees who do not meet the eligibility requirements of Article I, including employees covered under a collective bargaining agreement and nonresident aliens.

F. New employers who had no employees during the prior calendar year will meet this requirement if they have 25 or fewer employees throughout the first 30 days that the employer is in existence.

G. Actual Deferral Percentage (ADP) Requirements. An excess SEP contribution for the calendar year is the amount of each highly compensated employee's elective deferrals that exceeds the ADP for a calendar year. In order to meet the ADP requirements for a calendar year, the following test must be satisfied. The ADP of any "highly compensated employee" eligible to participate in this SEP may not be more than the product obtained by multiplying the average of the ADPs for that year of all non-highly compensated employees eligible to participate by 1.25. Only elective deferrals count for this test; non-elective SEP contributions may not be included.

For purposes of making this computation, the calculation of a highly compensated employee's ADP is made on the basis of the entire "affiliated employer." The determination of the number and identity of highly compensated employees is also made on the basis of the affiliated employer.

In addition, for purposes of determining the ADP of a highly compensated individual, the elective deferrals and compensation of the employee will also include the elective deferrals and compensation of any "family member." This special rule applies, however, only if the highly compensated employee is a 5% owner and is one of a group of the ten most highly compensated employees. The elective deferrals and compensation of family members used in this special rule do not count in computing the ADP of individuals who do not fall into this group.

The following definitions apply for purposes of this ADP computation:

1. ADP—the ratio of an employee's elective deferrals for a calendar year to the employee's compensation (as defined in III A. above) for that year. The ADP of an employee who is eligible to make an elective deferral, but who does not make a deferral during the year, is zero.

2. Affiliated employer—the employer and any member of an affiliated service group (as described in section 414(m)), a controlled group of corporations (as described in section 414(b)) or trades or businesses as described in section 414(c), or any other entity required to be aggregated with the employer under section 414(o).

3. Family member—an individual who is related to a highly compensated individual as a spouse, or as a lineal ascendant, such as a parent or grandparent, or a descendent such as a child or grandchild, or spouse of either of those.

4. Highly compensated individual—an individual who (as described in section 414(q)) during the current or preceding calendar year:

(i) was a 5% or more owner;

(ii) received compensation in excess of $75,000;

(iii) received compensation in excess of $50,000 and was in the top-paid group (the top 20% of employees, by compensation); **or**

(iv) was an officer and received compensation in excess of 150% of the section 415 dollar limit for defined contribution plans. (No more than 3 employees need be taken into account under this rule. At least one officer, the highest-paid officer if no one else meets this test, however, must be taken into account.)

A worksheet to calculate the ADP test and excess SEP contributions is provided on page 6.

Article IV.—Excess SEP Contributions

A. As stated above, a worksheet to calculate excess SEP contributions is provided on page 6 of this booklet. This worksheet should be used to determine the amount of excess SEP contributions to be reported to employees with respect to a calendar year. The employer is responsible for notifying each employee by March 15 of the amount, if any, of any excess SEP contributions to that employee's SEP-IRA for the preceding calendar year. If you do not notify any of your employees by March 15, you must pay a tax equal to 10% of the excess SEP contributions for the preceding calendar year. If you fail to notify your employees by December 31 of the calendar year following the year of the excess SEP contributions, your SEP no longer will be considered to meet the requirements of section 408(k)(6). This means that the earnings on the SEP are subject to tax immediately, that no more deferrals can be made under the SEP, and that deferrals of all employees in the uncorrected excess are includible in their income in that year.

Your notification to each affected employee of the excess SEP contributions must specifically state in a manner calculated to be understood by the average plan participant: (i) the amount of the excess contributions attributable to that employee's elective deferrals; (ii) the calendar year for which the excess contributions were made; (iii) that the excess contributions are includible in the affected employee's gross income for the specified calendar year; and (iv) that failure to withdraw the excess contributions and income attributable thereto by the due date (plus extensions) for filing the affected employee's tax return for the preceding calendar year may result in significant penalties, with a reference to Question 6 of Form 5305A-SEP for further information concerning possible penalties. If you wish, you may use the model form we have included for this purpose on page 5 following the "Model Elective SEP Deferral Form." If you already have issued W-2s to your employees by the time of the notification of the excess SEP contributions, you must also issue to the affected employees any required forms that reflect the fact that excess SEP contributions must be included in an employee's taxable income.

Example: Employee "A," a highly-compensated employee of employer "X," elects to defer $4,000 for calendar year 1987 to his SEP-IRA. A's compensation for 1987, excluding his SEP contribution, was $60,000. On January 15, 1988, X issues to A a W-2 stating that A's taxable income for 1987 was $60,000.

In February of 1988 X calculates the ADP test for 1987 for the SEP and discovers that A's maximum permissible SEP-IRA contribution for 1987 was $3,500. A is the only employee of X with excess SEP contributions. Therefore, on February 20, 1988, X notifies A that A had an excess SEP contribution of $500 for 1987. In addition, X issues the required form to A on that date that specifies that A's corrected taxable income for 1987 was $60,500. X is not liable for the 10% tax on excess SEP-IRA contributions because he notified A of the excess SEP-IRA contributions by March 15, 1988.

In order to avoid excess SEP contributions with respect to which you must notify employees you may want to institute a mechanism that would monitor elective deferrals on a continuing basis throughout the calendar year to insure that the deferrals comply with the limits as they are paid into each employee's SEP-IRA.

Article V.—Top-heavy Requirements

A. For purposes of determining whether a plan is top-heavy under section 416, elective deferrals are considered employer contributions. Elective deferrals may not be used, however, to satisfy the minimum contribution requirement under section 416. Thus, in any year in which a key employee makes an elective deferral, this Model SEP is deemed top-heavy for purposes of section 416 and the employer is required to make the minimum contribution to the SEP-IRA of each non-key employee eligible to participate in the SEP.

A key employee under section 416(i)(1) is any employee or former employee (and the beneficiaries of these employees) who, at any time during the "determination period," was:

1. an officer of the employer (if the employee's compensation exceeds 150% of the limit under section 415(c)(1)(A));

2. an owner of one of the ten largest interests in the employer (if the employee's compensation exceeds 100% of the limit under section 415(c)(1)(A));

3. a 5% or more owner of the employer; **or**

4. a 1% owner of the employer (if the employee has compensation in excess of $150,000).

The "determination period" is the current calendar year and the four preceding years.

B. The employer may satisfy the minimum contribution requirement of section 416 by making the required contributions through a non-elective SEP.

Information for the Employee

The following information explains what a Simplified Employee Pension plan is, how contributions are made, and how to treat these contributions for tax purposes.

Please read the questions and answers carefully. For more specific information, also see the agreement form and instructions to your employer on this form.

Questions and Answers

1. Q. What is a Simplified Employee Pension, or SEP?

A. A SEP is a retirement income arrangement. In this particular "elective" SEP, you may choose to defer compensation to your own Individual Retirement Account/Annuity (IRA). These elective deferrals may be based either on a salary reduction arrangement or on bonuses that, at your election, may be contributed to your IRA or received by you in cash. This type of elective SEP is available only to an employer with 25 or fewer eligible employees.

Your employer will provide you with a copy of the agreement containing eligibility requirements and a description of the basis upon which contributions may be made to your IRA.

All amounts contributed to your IRA belong to you, even after you separate from service with that employer.

2. Q. Must I make elective deferrals to an IRA?

A. No. However, if more than half of the eligible employees choose not to make elective deferrals in a particular year, then no employee may participate in an elective SEP of that employer for the year.

3. Q. How much may I elect to defer to my SEP-IRA in a particular year?

A. The amount that may be deferred to this SEP for any year is limited to the lesser of:

(1) 15% of compensation; **or**

(2) $7,000 (as adjusted for increases in the cost of living).

These limits may be reduced if your employer also maintains a SEP to which non-elective contributions are made. In that case, total contributions on your behalf to both SEPs may not exceed the lesser of $30,000 or 15% of your compensation. If these limits are exceeded, the amount you may elect to contribute to this SEP for the year will be correspondingly reduced.

The $7,000 is an overall cap on the maximum amount you may defer in each calendar year to all elective SEPs and cash-or-deferred arrangements under section 401(k), regardless of how many employers you may have worked for during the year.

The $7,000 will be indexed according to the cost of living and is increased to $9,500 (more in some cases) if you make salary reduction contributions under a section 403(b) arrangement of another employer.

If you are a highly compensated employee there may be a further limit on the amount you may contribute to a SEP-IRA for a particular year. This limit is calculated by your employer and is based on a special kind of non-discrimination test known as an ADP test. This test is based on a mathematical formula that limits the percentage of pay that highly compensated employees may elect to defer to a SEP-IRA. As discussed below, your employer will notify you if you have exceeded the ADP limits.

4. Q. How do I treat elective deferrals for tax purposes?

A. The amount you elect to defer to your SEP-IRA is excludible from your gross income, subject to the limitations discussed above, and is not includible as taxable wages on your Form W-2. These amounts are treated as amounts subject to FICA taxes.

5. Q. How will I know if too much is contributed to my SEP-IRA in one year?

A. There are two different ways in which you may contribute too much to your SEP-IRA. One way is to make "excess elective deferrals," i.e., exceed the $7,000 limitation described above. The second way is to make "excess SEP contributions," i.e., violate the "ADP" test, as discussed above. You are responsible for calculating whether or not you have exceeded the $7,000 limitation. Your employer is responsible for determining whether you have made any excess SEP contributions.

Your employer is required to notify you by March 15 if you have made any excess SEP contributions for the preceding calendar year. Your employer will notify you of an excess SEP contribution by providing you with any required form for the preceding calendar year.

6. Q. What must I do about excess deferrals to avoid adverse tax consequences?

A. Excess deferrals are includible in your gross income in the year of the deferral. You should withdraw excess deferrals under this SEP and any income allocable to the excess deferrals from your SEP-IRA by April 15. These amounts cannot be transferred or rolled over to another SEP-IRA.

If you fail to withdraw your excess deferrals and any income allocable thereto by April 15 of the following year, your excess deferrals will be subject to a 6% excise tax for each year they remain in the SEP-IRA.

If you have both excess deferrals and excess SEP contributions (as described in 6a below), the amount of excess deferrals you withdraw by April 15 will reduce your excess SEP contributions.

6a. Q: What must I do about excess SEP contributions to avoid adverse tax consequences?

A. Excess SEP contributions are includible in your gross income in the year of the deferral. You should withdraw excess SEP contributions for a calendar year and any income allocable to the excess SEP contributions by the due date (including extensions) for filing your income tax return for the year. These amounts cannot be transferred or rolled over to another SEP-IRA.

If you fail to withdraw your excess SEP contributions and income allocable thereto by the due date (including extensions) for filing your income tax return, your excess SEP contributions will be subject to a 6% excise tax for each year they remain in the SEP-IRA.

7. Q. Can I reduce excess elective deferrals or excess SEP contributions by rolling over or transferring amounts from my SEP-IRA to another IRA?

A. No. Excess elective deferrals or excess SEP contributions may be reduced only by a distribution to you. Excess amounts rolled over or transferred to another IRA will be includible in income and subject to the penalties discussed above.

8. Q. How do I know how much income is allocable to my excess elective deferrals or any excess SEP contributions?

A. The rules for determining and allocating income to excess elective deferrals or SEP contributions are the same as those governing regular IRA contributions. The trustee or custodian of your SEP-IRA may be able to inform you of the amount of income allocable to your excess amounts.

9. Q. May I also contribute to my IRA if I am a participant in a SEP?

A. Yes. You may still contribute the lesser of $2,000 or 100% of compensation to an IRA. However, the amount that is deductible is subject to various limitations. See Publication 590 for more specific information.

10. Q. Are there any restrictions on the IRA I select to deposit my SEP contributions in?

A. Under the Model Elective SEP that is approved by IRS, contributions must be made either to a Model IRA that is executed on an IRS form or a master or prototype IRA for which IRS has issued a favorable opinion letter.

11. Q. Can I move funds from my SEP-IRA to another tax-sheltered IRA?

A. Yes. It is permissible for you to withdraw, or receive, funds from your SEP-IRA, and no more than 60 days later, place such funds in another IRA or SEP-IRA. This is called a "rollover" and may not be done without penalty more frequently than at one-year intervals. However, there are no restrictions on the number of times you may make "transfers" if you arrange to have such funds transferred between the trustees, so that you never have possession.

12. Q. What happens if I withdraw my elective deferrals to my SEP-IRA?

A. If you don't want to leave the money in the IRA, you may withdraw it at any time, but any amount withdrawn is includible in your income. Also, if withdrawals occur before you are 59½, and not on account of death or disability, you may be subject to a 10% penalty tax. (As discussed above, different rules apply to the removal of excess amounts contributed to your SEP-IRA.)

13. Q. May I participate in a SEP even though I'm covered by another plan?

A. An employer may adopt this IRS Model Elective SEP (Form 5305A-SEP) and at the same time maintain an IRS Model SEP (Form 5305-SEP) or other non-elective SEP. However, an employer may not adopt this IRS Model Elective SEP if the employer maintains any qualified retirement plan or has ever maintained a qualified defined benefit plan. If you work for several employers, however, you may be covered by a SEP of one employer and a different SEP or pension or profit-sharing plan of another employer.

Simplified Employee Pension (SEP)

You should remember, however, as discussed in Question 3 above, that your elective deferrals to all plans or arrangements, even if maintained by unrelated employers, are subject to a $7,000 limit (more if one is a section 403(b) annuity). If you participate in two arrangements that permit elective deferrals, you should take care that this limit is not exceeded for any calendar year.

14. Q. Do I need to file any additional forms with IRS because I participate in a SEP?

A. No.

15. Q. Is my employer required to provide me with information about SEP-IRAs and the SEP agreement?

A. Yes. Your employer must provide you with a copy of the executed SEP agreement (Form 5305A-SEP), these Questions and Answers, the form used by the employee to defer amounts to the SEP, the notice of excess SEP contributions, if applicable, and a statement each year showing any contribution to your SEP-IRA.

16. Q. Is the financial institution where my IRA is established also required to provide me with information?

A. Yes. It must provide you with a disclosure statement that contains the following items of information in plain, nontechnical language:

(1) the statutory requirements that relate to your IRA;

(2) the tax consequences that follow the exercise of various options and what those options are;

(3) participation eligibility rules, and rules on the deductibility and nondeductibility of retirement savings;

(4) the circumstances and procedures under which you may revoke your IRA, including the name, address, and telephone number of the person designated to receive notice of revocation (this explanation must be prominently displayed at the beginning of the disclosure statement);

(5) explanations of when penalties may be assessed against you because of specified prohibited or penalized activities concerning your IRA; and

(6) financial disclosure information which:

(a) either projects value growth rates of your IRA under various contribution and retirement schedules, or describes the method of computing and allocating annual earnings and charges which may be assessed;

(b) describes whether, and for what period, the growth projections for the plan are guaranteed, or a statement of earnings rate and terms on which these projections are based; and

(c) states the sales commission to be charged in each year expressed as a percentage of $1,000.

See Publication 590, Individual Retirement Arrangements (IRAs), available at most IRS offices, for a more complete explanation of the disclosure requirements.

In addition to this disclosure statement, the financial institution is required to provide you with a financial statement each year. It may be necessary to retain and refer to statements for more than one year in order to evaluate the investment performance of the IRA and in order that you will know how to report IRA distributions for tax purposes.

Model Elective SEP Deferral Form

I. Salary reduction deferral

Subject to the requirements of the Model Elective SEP of _____ , I authorize the following amount or percentage of my
(insert name of employer)

compensation to be withheld from each of my paychecks and contributed to my SEP-IRA:

(a) _____ percent of my salary (not in excess of 15%); or **(b)** _____ dollar amount.

This salary reduction authorization shall remain in effect until I give a written modification or termination of its terms to my employer.

II. Cash bonus deferral

Subject to the requirements of the Model Elective SEP of _____ , I authorize the following amount to be contributed to my
(insert name of employer)

SEP-IRA rather than being paid to me in cash: _____ dollar amount.

III. Amount of deferral

I understand that the total amount I defer in any calendar year to this SEP may not exceed the lesser of: **(a)** 15% of my compensation; or **(b)** $7,000 (as adjusted per Code section 415(d)).

IV. Commencement of deferral

The deferral election specified in either I. or II. above shall not become effective before: _____
(Month, Day, Year)

(Specify a date no earlier than the next payday beginning after this authorization.)

Signature ▶ _____   Date ▶ _____

Notification of Excess SEP Contributions

To: _____
(Name of employee)

Our calculations indicate that the elective deferrals you made to your SEP-IRA for calendar year _____ exceed the maximum permissible limits under section 408(k)(6) of the Internal Revenue Code. You made excess SEP contributions of $_____ for that year.

These excess SEP contributions are includible in your gross income for the calendar year specified above.

These excess SEP contributions must be distributed from your IRA by the due date (plus extensions) for filing your tax return for the preceding calendar year (normally April 15th) in order to avoid significant penalties. Income allocable to the excess amounts must be withdrawn at the same time and is includible in income along with the excess contributions. Excess contributions left in your SEP-IRA account after that time are subject to a 6% excise tax.

Signature ▶ _____   Date ▶ _____

Simplified Employee Pension (SEP)

Elective SEP Actual Deferred Percentage Worksheet

a Employee Name	**b** Status H = Highly compensated F = Family 0 = Other	**c** Compensation (Including compensation from related employers and compensation of family.)	**d** Deferrals (Add all SEP deferrals; add deferrals of family to HCE*)	**e** Ratio (if family member enter N.A. - otherwise d ÷ c)	**f** Permitted ratio (for HCE* only from below)	**g** Permitted amount (for HCE* only) c X f	**h** Excess (for HCE* only) d minus g
1.							
2.							
3.							
4.							
5.							
6.							
7.							
8.							
9.							
10.							
11.							
12.							
13.							
14.							
15.							
16.							
17.							
18.							
19.							
20.							
21.							
22.							
23.							
24.							
25.							

Permitted Ratio Computation for column f:

A. Enter the total of all the ratios of the employees marked as "-0-" in column b _____

B. Divide line A by the number of employees marked as "-0-" in column b _____

C. Permitted ratio—Multiply line B by 1.25 and enter the permitted ratio here _____

* Highly compensated employee

☆ U.S. Government Printing Office: 1987—201-993/60118

Chapter 31
SPLIT DOLLAR LIFE INSURANCE

WHAT IS IT?

Split dollar life insurance is an arrangement, typically between an employer and an employee, in which there is a sharing of the costs and benefits of the life insurance policy. (Split dollar plans can also be adopted for purposes other than providing an employee benefit — for example between parent corporation and subsidiary, or between a parent and a child or in-law.) Usually split dollar plans involve a splitting of premiums, death benefits, and/or cash values, but they may also involve the splitting of dividends or ownership.

Under the classic approach, the employer corporation pays that part of the annual premium which equals the current year's increase in the cash surrender value of the policy. The employee pays the balance, if any, of the premium. In the long run this provides a low outlay protection incentive for selected employees to stay with the employer. If the insured employee dies, the corporation recovers its outlay (an amount equal to the cumulative cash value) and the balance of the policy proceeds is paid to the beneficiary chosen by the employee.

There are an almost infinite number of variations on the "splitting of dollars" theme, limited only by the needs and premium paying abilities of the parties and the creativity of the planner.

WHEN IS IT INDICATED?

1. When an employer wishes to provide an executive with a life insurance benefit at low cost and low outlay to the executive. Split dollar plans are best suited for executives in their 30's, 40's, and early 50's since the plan requires a reasonable duration in order to build up adequate policy cash values and the cost to the executive (the P.S. 58 cost — see below) can be excessive at later ages.

2. When a preretirement death benefit for an employee is a major objective, split dollar can be used as an alternative to an insurance-financed nonqualified deferred compensation plan.

3. When an employer is seeking a totally selective executive fringe benefit; an employer can reward or provide incentives for employees on a "pick and choose" basis. Neither the coverage, amounts, nor the terms of the split dollar arrangement need to meet nondiscrimination rules that add cost and complexity to many other benefit plans.

4. When an employer wants to make it easier for shareholder-employees to finance a buy out of stock under a cross purchase buy-sell agreement or make it possible for non-stockholding employees to effect a one way stock purchase at an existing shareholder's death. This helps establish a market for what otherwise might be unmarketable stock while providing an incentive for bright, creative, productive employees to remain with the company and increase profits.

ADVANTAGES

1. A split dollar plan allows an executive to receive a benefit of current value (life insurance coverage) using employer funds, with minimal or no tax cost to the executive.

2. In most types of split dollar plans, the employer's outlay is at all times fully secured. At the employee's death or termination of employment, the employer is reimbursed from policy proceeds for its premium outlay. The net cost to the employer for the plan is merely the loss of the net after-tax income the funds could have earned while the plan was in effect.

3. Many types of split dollar design are possible so the plan can be customized to meet employer and employee objectives and premium paying abilities.

DISADVANTAGES

1. The employer receives no tax deduction for its share of premium payments under the split dollar plan.

2. The employee must pay income taxes each year on the current "P.S. 58 cost" (less any premiums paid by the employee) of life insurance protection under the plan.

3. The plan must remain in effect for a reasonably long time — 10 to 20 years — in order for policy cash values to rise to a sufficient level to maximize plan benefits.

4. The plan must generally be terminated at approximately age 65, since the employee's tax cost for the plan, the P.S. 58 cost, rises sharply at later ages.

DESIGN FEATURES

In a split dollar arrangement between employer and employee, at least three aspects of the policy can be subject to different types of "split": (1) the premium cost, (2) the cash value, and (3) the policy ownership. Following is a

151   **Tools and Techniques**

brief discussion of these variations, their advantages and disadvantages, and when they are used.

Premium Cost Split

There are four major categories of premium split:

(a) the classic or *"standard"* split dollar plan under which the employer pays a portion of the premiums equal to the increase in cash surrender value of the policy for the year, or the net premium due, if lower. (See Figure 31.1.) The employee pays the remainder of the premium.

Advantages of this approach are that the employer's risk is minimized (since the cash value is enough to fully reimburse its outlay even if the plan is terminated in the early years) and the plan is (arguably) simple to design and explain.

The principal disadvantages are that the employee's outlay is very high in the initial years of the plan, when cash values increase slowly, and the tax benefits available are not maximized under this option, as discussed in "Tax Implications," below.

(b) the *"level premium"* plan, under which the employee's premium share is leveled over an initial period of years, such as 5 or 10. (See Figure 31.2.) This alleviates the large initial premium share required of the employee under the standard arrangement. If the plan stays in existence long enough the employee and employer ultimately pay nearly the same total amount as under the standard arrangement.

The disadvantage of the level premium plan is that if the plan is terminated in the early years, the policy cash value is not sufficient to fully reimburse the employer for its total premium outlay. This possibility should be considered in drafting the split dollar agreement.

(c) the *"employer pay all"* arrangements, with the employer paying the entire premium and the employee paying nothing. (See Figure 31.3.) This arrangement is used when the employee's funds to pay for the plan are severely limited. The employee's cost in this arrangement is limited to the "P.S. 58" cost of pure insurance coverage that must be reported by the employee as taxable income, as discussed below under "Tax Implications."

As with the level premium plan, if the plan is terminated early, the policy cash value will not fully reimburse the employer outlay; again, the agreement between the employer and employee should address this problem.

(d) the *"P.S. 58 offset"* plan, under which the employee pays an amount equal to the P.S. 58 cost for the coverage (or if less, the net premium due) each year. The employer pays the balance of the premium. (See Figure 31.4.) The purpose of this arrangement is to "zero out" the employee's income tax cost for the plan, as discussed below.

As a further refinement, the employer can reduce the employee's out-of-pocket cost for this arrangement by paying a tax deductible "bonus" to the employee equal to the employee's payment under the split dollar plan. The employer might want to go a step further and pay an additional amount equal to the tax on the first bonus as a "double bonus."

The P.S. 58 offset arrangement is an advantageous one that is commonly used. However, as with most variations on the standard plan, the employer remains exposed to some risk if the plan is terminated early, since the cash value will be less than the employer's outlay in some cases. The split dollar agreement should deal with this issue.

Cash Value and Death Proceeds Split

The purpose of the split of cash value or death proceeds is to reimburse the employer, in whole or in part, for its share of the premium outlay, in the event of the employee's death or termination of the plan.

At the employee's death, any policy proceeds not used to reimburse the employer go to the employee's designated beneficiary. This provides a significant death benefit in the early years of the plan, one of the principal objectives of a split dollar plan.

Most plans are designed to provide cash value growth sufficient to reimburse the employer after a number of years. The excess cash value can also benefit the employee, by allowing the plan to provide an attractive investment element (in a sense, a "deferred compensation" or "pension" element) in addition to the death benefit. Some plans are designed primarily to maximize this element. The "equity" type plan, described below, is one example.

The following are commonly used cash value/death proceeds split arrangements:

(a) the employer's share is the *greater* of (i) the aggregate premiums it has paid or (ii) the policy's cash value;

(b) the employer can recover only up to the amount of its aggregate premiums paid (a feature of the "equity" split dollar plan described below); or

(c) the employer is entitled to the entire cash value.

Figure 31.1

"STANDARD" PLAN

WHOLE LIFE
FACE AMOUNT: $100,000
DIVIDENDS APPLIED TO BUY ONE-YEAR TERM INSURANCE,
REMAINDER TO REDUCE PREMIUM
MALE AGE: 40
FIRST-YEAR PREMIUM = $2,298.00

Year	Guar. Cash Value	Premium Split		Payment on Death	
		Paid By Employer	Paid By Employee	To Employer	To Employee's Beneficiary
1	0	0	2,298	0	100,000
2	1,700	1,700	598	1,700	98,300
3	3,600	1,900	219	3,600	100,000
4	5,500	1,900	189	5,500	100,000
5	7,500	2,000	60	7,500	100,000
6	9,500	2,000	32	9,500	100,000
7	11,500	2,000	0	11,500	100,000
8	13,600	1,974	0	13,474	100,126
9	15,700	1,948	0	15,421	100,279
10	17,800	1,926	0	17,347	100,453
Total		17,347	3,396		
Average		1,735	340		
11	20,000	1,905	0	19,252	100,748
12	22,200	1,888	0	21,141	101,059
13	24,400	1,864	0	23,004	101,396
14	26,700	1,869	0	24,874	101,826
15	29,000	1,866	0	26,740	102,260
Total		26,740	3,396		
Average		1,783	226		
16	31,300	1,870	0	28,609	102,691
17	33,700	1,879	0	30,488	103,212
18	36,000	1,895	0	32,383	103,617
19	38,400	1,926	0	34,309	104,091
20	40,900	1,969	0	36,278	104,622
Total		36,278	3,396		
Average		1,814	170		

Figure 31.2

"LEVEL PREMIUM" PLAN

WHOLE LIFE
FACE AMOUNT: $100,000
DIVIDENDS APPLIED TO BUY ONE-YEAR TERM INSURANCE,
REMAINDER TO REDUCE PREMIUM
MALE AGE: 40
FIRST-YEAR PREMIUM = $2,298.00

		Premium Split		Payment on Death	
	Guar.	Paid	Paid		To
	Cash	By	By	To	Employee's
Year	Value	Employer	Employee	Employer	Beneficiary
1	0	2,004	294	2,004	97,996
2	1,700	2,004	294	4,008	95,993
3	3,600	1,824	294	5,832	97,768
4	5,500	1,795	294	7,626	97,874
5	7,500	1,766	294	9,392	98,108
6	9,500	1,738	294	11,130	98,370
7	11,500	1,706	294	12,836	98,664
8	13,600	1,680	294	14,515	99,085
9	15,700	1,653	294	16,169	99,531
10	17,800	1,631	294	17,800	100,000
Total		17,800	2,943		
Average		1,780	294		
11	20,000	1,905	0	19,705	100,295
12	22,200	1,888	0	21,594	100,606
13	24,400	1,864	0	23,457	100,943
14	26,700	1,869	0	25,327	101,373
15	29,000	1,866	0	27,193	101,870
Total		27,193	2,943		
Average		1,813	196		
16	31,300	1,870	0	29,062	102,238
17	33,700	1,879	0	30,941	102,759
18	36,000	1,895	0	32,836	103,164
19	38,400	1,926	0	34,762	103,638
20	40,900	1,969	0	36,731	104,169
Total		36,731	2,943		
Average		1,837	147		

Figure 31.3

"EMPLOYER PAY ALL" PLAN

WHOLE LIFE
FACE AMOUNT: $100,000
DIVIDENDS APPLIED TO BUY ONE-YEAR TERM INSURANCE,
REMAINDER TO REDUCE PREMIUM
MALE AGE: 40
FIRST-YEAR PREMIUM = $2,298.00

		Premium Split		Payment on Death	
	Guar.	Paid	Paid		To
	Cash	By	By	To	Employee's
Year	Value	Employer	Employee	Employer	Beneficiary
1	0	2,298	0	2,298	97,702
2	1,700	2,298	0	4,596	95,404
3	3,600	2,119	0	6,715	96,885
4	5,500	2,089	0	8,804	96,696
5	7,500	2,060	0	10,864	96,636
6	9,500	2,032	0	12,896	96,604
7	11,500	2,000	0	14,896	96,604
8	13,600	1,974	0	16,870	96,730
9	15,700	1,948	0	18,817	96,883
10	17,800	1,926	0	20,743	97,057
Total		20,743	0		
Average		2,074	0		
11	20,000	1,905	0	22,649	97,351
12	22,200	1,888	0	24,537	97,663
13	24,400	1,864	0	26,400	98,000
14	26,700	1,869	0	28,270	98,430
15	29,000	1,866	0	30,136	98,864
Total		30,136	0		
Average		2,009	0		
16	31,300	1,870	0	32,005	99,295
17	33,700	1,879	0	33,884	99,816
18	36,000	1,895	0	35,779	100,221
19	38,400	1,926	0	37,705	100,695
20	40,900	1,969	0	39,674	101,226
Total		36,674	0		
Average		1,984	0		

Tools and Techniques

Figure 31.4

"PS 58 OFFSET" PLAN

WHOLE LIFE
FACE AMOUNT: $100,000
DIVIDENDS APPLIED TO BUY ONE-YEAR TERM INSURANCE,
REMAINDER TO REDUCE PREMIUM
MALE AGE: 40
FIRST-YEAR PREMIUM = $2,298.00

Year	Guar. Cash Value	Premium Split		Payment on Death	
		Paid By Employer	Paid By Employee	To Employer	To Employee's Beneficiary
1	0	1,864	434	1,864	98,136
2	1,700	1,842	456	3,706	96,294
3	3,600	1,628	490	5,334	98,266
4	5,500	1,565	524	6,899	98,601
5	7,500	1,499	561	8,398	99,102
6	9,500	1,420	612	9,818	99,682
7	11,500	1,344	656	11,500	100,000
8	13,600	1,268	706	13,600	100,100
9	15,700	1,188	760	15,700	100,000
10	17,800	1,106	820	17,800	100,000
Total		14,724	6,019		
Average		1,472	602		
11	20,000	1,022	883	20,000	100,000
12	22,200	936	952	22,200	100,000
13	24,400	848	1,015	24,400	100,000
14	26,700	759	1,110	26,700	100,000
15	29,000	665	1,201	29,000	100,000
Total		18,956	11,180		
Average		1,264	745		
16	31,300	570	1,300	31,300	100,000
17	33,700	470	1,408	33,700	100,000
18	36,000	367	1,527	36,000	100,000
19	38,400	268	1,658	38,400	100,000
20	40,900	167	1,802	40,900	100,000
Total		20,799	18,875		
Average		1,040	943		

If a plan terminates early — usually when the employee terminates employment before the plan has matured — the cash value of the policy may not be sufficient to fully reimburse the employer for the aggregate premium payments it has made. The plan can provide that the employee is personally responsible to reimburse the employer in that event. As a practical matter, however, it may be difficult to enforce such a requirement, particularly if the amount is insufficient to justify the costs of a lawsuit. (A practical suggestion is to make sure that the company's severance pay arrangement, if any, allows recovery of any such amount out of severance pay otherwise due.)

Policy Ownership

There are two methods of arranging policy ownership under a split dollar plan: the ''endorsement method'' and the ''collateral assignment method.''

Under the *endorsement* method, the employer owns the policy and is primarily responsible to the insurance company for paying the entire premium. The beneficiary designation provides for the employer to receive a portion of the death benefit equal to its premium outlay (or some alternative share), with the remainder of the death proceeds going to the employee's designated beneficiary. An endorsement to the policy is filed with the insurance company under which payment to the employee's beneficiary cannot be changed without consent of the employee (or, in some cases, a designated third person where the employee wishes to avoid incidents of ownership for estate tax purposes).

Advantages of the endorsement method are:

(1) greater control by the employer over the policy.

(2) simpler installation and administration; the only documentation required (except for possible ERISA requirements described below) is the policy and endorsement.

(3) avoidance of any formal arrangement that might be deemed to constitute a ''loan'' for purposes of state laws prohibiting corporate loans to officers and directors.

(4) if the company owns an existing key employee policy on the employee, it can be used directly in the split dollar plan without change of ownership. (Using an existing policy may be important if the employee has developed health problems since the policy was issued.)

Under the *collateral assignment* method, the employee (or a third party) is the owner of the policy and is responsible for premium payments. The employer then makes what are in effect (but not for tax law purposes) interest free ''loans'' of the amount of the premium the employer has agreed to pay under the split dollar plan. To secure these ''loans'' the policy is assigned as collateral to the employer. At the employee's death, the employer recovers its aggregate premium payments from the policy proceeds, as collateral assignee. The remainder of the policy proceeds is paid to the employee's designated beneficiary. If the plan terminates before the employee's death, the employer has the right to be reimbursed out of policy cash values; the employee continues as the owner of the policy.

Some advantages of the collateral assignment method are:

(1) it arguably gives more protection to the employee and the employee's beneficiary.

(2) it is easier to implement using existing insurance policies owned by the employee.

Policy Dividends

If the plan uses a participating life insurance policy, policy dividends can be used in various ways; this significantly increases flexibility in plan design. (See the chart under ''Tax Implications,'' below.) A method of applying dividends should be chosen at the plan's inception.

SPLIT DOLLAR PLAN VARIATIONS

In recent years, changes in the tax law have resulted in a need for new kinds of tax planning. Because of the inherent flexibility of the split dollar concept, planners have been able to devise variations on these plans that meet tax and financial objectives for executives in the changing investment and tax climate. Following is a brief description of some of these variations.

Equity Split Dollar

In the equity split dollar arrangement the employer's interest in the policy cash value is limited at all times to the aggregate premiums it has paid. Thus, after the policy cash value reaches the level of the aggregate employer premium payments, the employee begins receiving a gradually-increasing interest in the investment build-up in the policy.

The tax treatment of these plans has not been definitely settled by the courts or the IRS. Consequently, there is a risk to the employee of premature taxation of some of the benefits of the plan. The IRS may argue that the plan constitutes a transfer of property from the corporation to the employee subject to restrictions — a ''restricted property'' plan. As such, it would be taxed under section 83 of the Code. This means that the employee's share of the policy cash value would be taxable to the employee in the earliest year in which there was no substantial risk of forfeiture. In most split dollar arrangements, there is no risk that the employee will forfeit benefits thus any cash value increases belonging to the employee would be taxed immediately if Section 83 applies. The meaning of the ''substantial risk of forfeiture'' test and other aspects of Section 83 are discussed in detail in Chapter 26.

There are a number of arguments as to why Section 83 does not apply to equity split dollar plans. However, planners should be aware of the tax risk involved. It is possible to include provisions in the plan to create a "substantial risk of forfeiture" that would avoid current taxation but for obvious reasons most employees do not favor such provisions.

To avoid an IRS argument that the employer has "transferred" the policy to the employee (and thus Section 83 applies), many planners believe that only the collateral assignment method of policy ownership should be used in an equity split dollar plan. With collateral assignment there is no "transfer" of property from employer to employee — the employee always owns the policy.

Split Dollar Rollout

The "rollout" type of plan was designed to take advantage of pre-1986 tax law that allowed individuals to deduct personal interest. Interest on a policy loan was deductible to the individual so long as premiums on the policy had been paid without borrowed funds in at least four of the first seven years of the policy's existence. In a rollout arrangement, therefore, the employer paid premiums during the seven year period. Then the policy was "rolled out" (sold) to the employee or a third party. The employee's out-of-pocket cost for the policy could be recovered by making a policy loan. Premiums after the rollout were paid by the employee or third party in part or entirely through policy loans, on which interest was deductible.

Since personal interest is no longer deductible (except in limited amounts during a phaseout period), the advantage of rollout plans has diminished considerably. However, the general principle of rolling out a split dollar policy where the employee wants to continue it as personally held insurance is still available, and may be useful in certain planning situations. For example, a rollout may be advantageous where the employee is terminating employment because he has developed a medical condition that makes it impossible for him to obtain insurance at standard rates. The availability of policy loans, even without interest deductibility, helps the employee to pay for the policy and continue paying premiums. With some types of policies such as variable life and universal life, the employee often pays for the policy through a partial surrender rather than through policy loans. Following the Technical and Miscellaneous Revenue Act of 1988, the use of policy loans and partial surrenders for rollout purposes may be less attractive if the policy is classified as a modified endowment contract. Distributions, including loans, from a modified endowment contract are generally taxed less favorably than distributions from other life insurance contracts.

In theory, a rollout is not taxable to the employee since it is merely a purchase by the employee. However, some planners are concerned that the IRS could view the transaction as a transfer of property by the employer to the employee for compensation purposes, resulting in income tax to the employee to the extent the value of the policy exceeds what the employee pays for it. This risk is particularly significant if the employer originally owned the policy under an endorsement type of split dollar plan.

Reverse Split Dollar

A "reverse split dollar" plan is one in which the *employee* has the right to policy cash values up to the aggregate of his or her premium payments. The employer is beneficiary of the death proceeds in excess of the employee's share. In other words, as its name implies, a reverse split dollar plan is the reverse of the usual arrangement. (Figure 31.5 is a simplified illustration of a reverse split dollar plan.)

The purpose of this reversal is to maximize the investment benefit of the plan to the employee. Policy cash values provide a substantial investment return over the years as they build up free of taxes. At retirement or when the plan terminates the cash value is substantial and the policy is generally substantially funded. In the closely held corporation reverse split dollar can be used to fund a stock redemption buy-sell agreement with the employee paying part of the cost with personal funds.

The disadvantage to the employee of a reverse split dollar arrangement is that the death benefit for the employee's beneficiaries is very low in the early years, since the corporation, not the employee, is the beneficiary of the "amount at risk" (pure term life insurance element) of the arrangement.

The premium is split so that the executive pays a share equal to the cash value build-up, while the corporation pays the remainder of the premium. Most tax planners advise that the corporation should include something in income to reflect the economic benefit of the "amount at risk" or insurance coverage that will benefit the corporation if the employee dies. Although the IRS has not ruled on how this is determined, most advisers assume that the corporation's economic benefit is computed the same as the employee's would be under a conventional split dollar plan. That is, the corporation reports as income the P.S. 58 cost of the amount at risk, less the amount contributed to the plan by the corporation.

The reverse split dollar plan raises unresolved questions concerning the employee's being taxed under Section 83, as with the equity split dollar plan discussed earlier. In addition, if the employee is a majority shareholder, there is a risk of federal estate tax inclusion, as discussed below under "Tax Implications."

Leveraged Split Dollar

The Tax Reform Act of 1986 denied corporate deductions for interest paid on indebtedness over $50,000 with respect

Figure 31.5

REVERSE SPLIT DOLLAR PLAN

The following is a simplified illustration of a reverse split-dollar policy of $100,000 on the life of a male executive aged 45, with a $1,650 annual premium.

Year	Corporate Premium	Executive Premium	Corporate Net Death Benefit	Executive Net Death Benefit
1	635	1,015	100,739	227
2	689	961	101,676	545
3	744	906	101,693	2,066
4	801	849	101,528	4,050
5	866	784	101,476	6,206
6	936	714	101,526	8,548
7	1,014	636	101,677	11,087
8	1,100	550	101,930	13,843

[In later years, the premium "vanishes;" the executive makes no further payment, and the employer pays only the PS 58 cost, which "zeros out" its taxable income. In year 20 the corporate net death benefit is $71,584 and the executive's benefit is $37,324.]

to a life insurance policy covering a corporate officer, employee or other financially interested person. (However, certain existing policies were "grandfathered.") This had an adverse impact on split dollar plans based on the corporation borrowing large amounts to pay for the plan.

The "leveraged split dollar plan" is designed specifically to fully exploit the tax benefits that still remain. The basic concept is for the corporation to borrow $50,000 from the insurance company at the inception of the plan and immediately contribute this amount back as an advance deposit of premiums. The initial $50,000 deposit covers the regular or "scheduled" premiums for a number of years. The corporation's only annual payments to the insurance company are interest payments which are fully deductible as paid. Under the insurance contract all interest paid by the corporation is credited to the cash value of the insurance. The plan participant collaterally assigns the insurance to the corporation to secure the total payment made by the corporation.

This arrangement provides two advantages to the employer corporation:

(1) The corporation's contribution to the plan is tax deductible since it consists only of interest on the $50,000 loan;

(2) On the participant's death or termination of employment, the policy cash value is always ade-

quate to reimburse the corporation for its aggregate outlay. The leveraged split dollar plan also has the usual advantages to employer and employee of a regular split dollar plan.

The IRS has not ruled on the tax consequences of leveraged plans; the problem area is whether the loan will be considered a bona fide loan under the circumstances.

TAX IMPLICATIONS

1. The IRS has ruled (in Rev. Rul. 64-328) that the tax consequences of a split dollar plan are the same regardless of whether the collateral assignment or the endorsement arrangement is used. In effect this ruling holds that the transaction will not be treated as an "interest free loan" to the employee. The tax consequences are:

(a) The employee is considered to be in receipt each year of an amount of taxable "economic benefit." This taxable amount for the basic insurance coverage is equal to the "P.S. 58" rate for the insurance protection under the plan less the premium amount paid by the employee. As an alternative, the annual renewable term insurance rates of the company issuing the split dollar policy may be substituted for the P.S. 58 rates in calculating the employee's reportable economic benefit if the term rates are lower than the P.S. 58 rates.

For example, how much is included in the employee's income in the second year of the policy in Figure 31.2? The amount of the death benefit in the second year is $95,993. At age 41, the P.S. 58 rate from Figure 31.6 is $4.73 per thousand, or $454.05 ($4.73 times 95.993) for $95,993 of insurance protection. The employee paid $294 as his premium share in the second year. The taxable income is $454.05 less $294, or $160.05.

The application of policy dividends further affects the employee's income tax consequences. Figure 31.7 shows the available options for dividends and their income tax consequences.

Figure 31.8 is an illustration of how the P.S. 58 computation is made using NumberCruncher software. (Information about NumberCruncher can be obtained by calling 1-800-654-2227.)

(b) The employer cannot deduct any portion of its premium contribution. The IRS does not allow a deduction even for the part of the employer's contribution that results in taxable compensation income to the employee.

(c) If the employee's share of the premium is greater than the P.S. 58 cost of the insurance protection, the employee cannot carry over any of the excess to future years. In effect, this excess goes to waste. This situation generally occurs in the early years of the "conventional" split dollar plan as illustrated in Figure 31.1. This waste of a potential tax benefit is one of the reasons why other types of split dollar plans have been developed. In particular, the "P.S. 58 offset" design of Figure 31.4 is intended to maximize the use of the P.S. 58 cost.

(d) No extra income tax results to an employee who is a "rated" insured. The same P.S. 58 rates that apply to standard risks are used to determine the reportable income of employees with insurance ratings.

2. Death benefits from a split dollar plan — both the employer's share and the employee's beneficiary's share — are generally income tax free.

The tax-free nature of the death proceeds is lost if the policy has been "transferred for value" in certain situations. The transfer for value trap should be carefully avoided in designing split dollar plans.

The following transfers of insurance policies are exempt from the transfer for value rules — in other words, they will not cause the loss of the death proceed's tax-free nature:

(a) a transfer of the policy to the insured;

(b) a transfer to a partner of the insured or to a partnership of which the insured is a partner;

(c) a transfer to a corporation of which the insured is a shareholder or officer; and

(d) a transfer in which the transferee's basis is determined in whole or in part by reference to the transferor's basis (i.e., a "substituted" or "carryover" basis).

Some examples of potential transfer for value situations to be avoided in split dollar plans are:

• Do not initiate the plan by transferring an existing corporate-owned key employee policy to a third party beneficiary;

• Do not start the plan by transferring an employee owned policy to the corporation unless the employee is a shareholder or officer;

• At termination of the plan, do not transfer the corporation's interest in the policy to a third party beneficiary; although there are some arguments that this presents no problem, it is better to make such a transfer to the insured.

3. If the employee had no "incidents of ownership" in the policy, the death benefit is not includable in the employee's estate for federal estate tax purposes unless the policy proceeds are payable to the employee's estate. If an employee is potentially faced with a federal estate tax liability, all incidents of ownership in the policy should therefore be assigned irrevocably to a third party — a beneficiary or a trust. Proceeds generally should be payable to a named personal beneficiary and not to the employee's estate.

If the employee is a controlling shareholder (more than 50 percent) in the employer corporation, the *corporation's* incidents of ownership in the policy will be attributed to the majority shareholder. The current IRS position is that even if the corporation has only the right to make policy loans against its share of the cash value, this is an incident of ownership that will be attributed to the controlling shareholder and cause estate tax inclusion of the policy death proceeds.

For a majority shareholder, the only way to avoid estate tax inclusion is for not only the employee but also the employer to get rid of the incidents of ownership. The corporation can avoid such incidents by retaining no rights of ownership in the policy, including any policy contract provisions or riders relating to the split dollar agreement. One procedure for accomplishing this is for the employee's personal beneficiary to be the original purchaser of the policy, and the beneficiary to enter into the split dollar agreement with the corporation on a collateral assignment basis.

Figure 31.6

"P.S. NO. 58" RATES

The following rates are used in computing the "cost" of pure life insurance protection that is taxable to the employee under qualified pension and profit sharing plans, split-dollar plans, and tax-sheltered annuities. Rev. Rul. 55-747, 1955-2 CB 228; Rev. Rul. 66-110, 1966-1 CB 12.

One Year Term Premiums for $1,000 of Life Insurance Protection

Age	Premium	Age	Premium	Age	Premium
15	$ 1.27	37	$ 3.63	59	$ 19.08
16	1.38	38	3.87	60	20.73
17	1.48	39	4.14	61	22.53
18	1.52	40	4.42	62	24.50
19	1.56	41	4.73	63	26.63
20	1.61	42	5.07	64	28.98
21	1.67	43	5.44	65	31.51
22	1.73	44	5.85	66	34.28
23	1.79	45	6.30	67	37.31
24	1.86	46	6.78	68	40.59
25	1.93	47	7.32	69	44.17
26	2.02	48	7.89	70	48.06
27	2.11	49	8.53	71	52.29
28	2.20	50	9.22	72	56.89
29	2.31	51	9.97	73	61.89
30	2.43	52	10.79	74	67.33
31	2.57	53	11.69	75	73.23
32	2.70	54	12.67	76	79.63
33	2.86	55	13.74	77	86.57
34	3.02	56	14.91	78	94.09
35	3.21	57	16.18	79	102.23
36	3.41	58	17.56	80	111.04
				81	120.57

The rate at insured's attained age is applied to the excess of the amount payable at death over the cash value of the policy at the end of the year.

Figure 31.7

TAX RESULTS OF DIVIDEND OPTIONS

Dividend option	Income tax results to employee	Income tax results to employer
Cash to employee	Dividend is taxable income	No deduction
Cash to employer	None	Not taxable
Reduce employee's premium share	Dividend is taxable income	No deduction
Reduces employer's premium share	None	Not taxable
Deposit at interest for employee	Dividend is taxable income - interest taxable in year earned	No deduction
Deposit at interest for employer	None	Dividend not taxable - interest taxable in year earned
Paid up additions - cash value and death benefit controlled by employee	Dividend is taxable income	No deduction
Paid up additions - cash value controlled by employer and death benefit in excess of cash value controlled by employee	PS 58 cost of insurance protection provided by dividend is taxable income	No deduction
One year term insurance (5th dividend option) with death benefit controlled by employee	Dividend is taxable income	No deduction
One year term insurance (5th dividend option) with death benefit controlled by employer	None	Not taxable

Figure 31.8

P. S. 58 COMPUTATION

(INSERT CO'S. STANDARD INDIVIDUAL 1 YR. TERM RATES AT B1 IF LOWER)
PART A

Input:	Employee's Age	45
Input:	Face Amount of Death Benefit	$100,000
Input:	Cash Value to Employer	- $40,000
	Net Amount at Risk	$60,000
	P.S. 58 Charge	$6.30
	Gross Amount Includible	$378.00
Input:	Employee's Contribution	$.00

PART B

Input:	Amount of Dividend Paid in Cash to Employee	$.00
Input:	Amount of Dividend to Reduce EE's Premium Contribution	$.00
Input:	Amount of Dividend Held at Interest for Employee	$.00
Input:	Amount of Dividend - If Cash Value & Death Benefit of Paid Up Additions are Controlled By Employee	$.00
Input:	Amount of Dividend - If Dividends Were Used to Buy One Year Term Insurance for the Employee	$.00
Input:	P.S. 58 Cost or, If Lower, Published Yearly Renewable Term Cost - If Employer Gets Cash Value of Paid Up Additional Insurance and Employee's Beneficiary Receives Any Balance	$.00
	Reportable P.S. 58 Cost	$378.00

4. There may be federal gift tax consequences if a person other than the employee owns the insurance policy used in a split dollar plan. The transfer of the policy from the employee to another party is a gift subject to tax. In addition, there is a continuing annual gift if the employee pays premiums. There is also a continuing annual gift by the employee if the *employer* pays premiums, because this employer payment represents compensation earned by the employee that is indirectly transferred to the policyowner. Such potentially taxable gifts may avoid taxation if they qualify for the $10,000 annual gift tax exclusion. Gifts made directly to beneficiaries generally qualify, while gifts to insurance trusts may be considered ''future interests'' that do not qualify for the $10,000 exclusion.

ERISA REQUIREMENTS

A split dollar plan is considered an ''employee welfare benefit plan'' and is subject to the ERISA rules applicable to such plans, as discussed in Appendix D.

A welfare plan can escape the ERISA reporting and disclosure requirements if it is an ''insured'' plan maintained for ''a select group of management or highly compensated employees.'' Most split dollar plans qualify for this exception. If the plan covers more than a select group, it must provide Summary Plan Descriptions (SPDs) to participants.

ERISA further requires a written document, a ''named fiduciary,'' and a formal claims procedure for split dollar plans.

WHERE CAN I FIND OUT MORE ABOUT IT?

1. Graduate Course: Executive Compensation (GS 842), The American College, Bryn Mawr, PA.

2. Floridis, Ronald, *Comprehensive Split Dollar*, 2nd ed., Cincinnati, OH, National Underwriter Company, 1988.

QUESTIONS AND ANSWERS

Question — What is the impact of a split dollar plan on corporate earnings for accounting purposes?

Answer — Many corporate managers, particularly in publicly held corporations, are concerned that adoption of various executive compensation plans may cause a charge to corporate earnings for financial reporting purposes. The tendency in the accounting profession is toward requiring charges to earnings for most types of executive compensation, and the official Financial Accounting Standards Board (FASB) is currently considering new accounting rules in this area.

Under the rules currently in effect, however, there would not be a charge to earnings under a ''standard'' split dollar plan such as that in Figure 31.1, because the corporation controls the cash value of the policy and the premium outlay is always balanced by a cash value increase owned by the corporation.

Question — If a corporation wants to provide insurance for an employee what are the alternatives to split dollar plans?

Answer — Corporate insurance planning for executives can involve many complex alternatives but there are basically four alternatives to split dollar plans: (1) insurance provided directly as a ''bonus;'' (2) insurance provided through a qualified plan; (3) insurance financing for a nonqualified deferred compensation plan; and (4) insurance financing for a death benefit only (DBO) plan.

A bonus plan simply involves an agreement by the employer to pay as a bonus some or all of the premiums on an insurance policy owned by the employee. The other alternatives listed above are discussed in detail in Chapters 5, 20 and 24.

Figure 31.9 compares the basic characteristics of these plans such as premium deductibility, taxation of employer and employee on premium payments and death proceeds, and whether the employer is reimbursed for its outlay.

Figure 31.9

PLAN COMPARISON

	Split Dollar	Bonus Insurance	Insurance in Qualified Plan	Insurance Financing of Nonqualified Deferred Compensation Plan	D.B.O.
Tax deduction for employer cost	None	Yes (deductible compensation)	Yes (within "incidental" limits)	Deduction deferred to year paid	Deduction deferred to year paid
Current taxable income to employee	P.S. 58 cost less employee contribution	Bonus amount fully taxable	P.S. 58 cost less employee contribution	None	None
Reimbursement of employer outlay	Yes	No	No	No	No
Amount of death benefit for employee	Amount at risk (standard plan)	Full death proceeds	Full death proceeds	Full death proceeds "leveraged" by employer's tax deduction	Full death proceeds leveraged by employer's tax deduction
Income taxation of death benefit to employee's beneficiary	Tax free	Tax free	Amount at risk is tax free	Fully taxable	Fully taxable

Chapter 32

STOCK OPTION

WHAT IS IT?

A stock option is a formal written offer to sell stock at a specified price within specified time limits. Employers often use stock options for compensating executives. Such options are generally for stock of the employer company or a subsidiary.

Options are typically granted to an employee as additional compensation at a favorable price either below or near the current market value, with an expectation that the value of the stock will rise, making the option price a bargain beneficial to the executive. Options typically remain outstanding for a period of ten years. If the price of the stock goes down, the executive will not purchase the stock, so the executive does not risk any out-of-pocket loss.

The executive is generally not taxed at the grant of an option; taxation is deferred to the time the stock is purchased or later. Thus, stock options are a form of deferred compensation with the amount of compensation based on increases in the value of the company's stock. This "equity" form of compensation is popular with executives because it gives them some of the advantages of business ownership.

There are two main types of stock option plans used for compensating executives: (1) incentive stock option, (or ISO), plans and (2) nonstatutory stock options. ISOs are a form of stock option plan with special tax benefits; these are discussed in chapter 16. Nonstatutory stock options will be discussed here.

For an outline of some advanced types of stock option and other plans used for compensating executives, particularly in large corporations, see Appendix E of this book.

WHEN IS IT INDICATED?

1. When an employer is willing to compensate employees with shares of company stock. Many family corporations or other closely held corporations do not want to share ownership of the business in this manner. Option plans are most often used by corporations whose ownership is relatively broadly held, and are very common in large corporations whose stock is publicly traded.

2. Where an employer wishes to reward executive performance by providing an equity-type of compensation — that is, compensation that increases in value as the employer stock increases in value.

ADVANTAGES

1. Nonstatutory stock option plans can be designed in virtually any manner suitable to an executive or to the employer. There are few tax or other government regulatory constraints. For example, a stock option plan can be provided for any group of executives or even a single executive. Benefits can vary from one executive to another without restriction. There are no nondiscrimination coverage or benefit rules.

2. Stock options are a form of compensation with little or no out-of-pocket cost to the company. The real cost of stock options is that the company forgoes the opportunity to sell the same stock on the market and realize its proceeds for company purposes.

3. Stock options are a form of compensation on which tax to the employee is deferred. As discussed under "Tax Implications," below, tax is generally not payable at the time a stock option is granted to the executive.

DISADVANTAGES

1. The executive bears the market risk of this kind of compensation. If the market value of stock goes below the option price while the option is outstanding, the employee does not have any actual out-of-pocket loss; however, since the executive will not purchase the stock, there is no additional compensation received. And, after an option is "exercised" (i.e., company stock is purchased by the executive), the executive bears the full market risk of holding company stock.

2. The executive must have a source of funds to purchase the stock (and pay taxes due in the year of exercise) in order to benefit from the plan. Executives often borrow money with the anticipation that dividends from the stock purchased, plus immediate resales of some stock, will be sufficient to pay part or all of the interest on the borrowed funds. However, under current law, the deductibility of such investment interest (in excess of investment income) will be phased out, which raises the cost of using borrowed funds to exercise stock options.

3. Fluctuation in the market value of the stock may have little or no relation to executive performance. This factor weakens the value of a stock option plan as a performance incentive.

4. As discussed under "Tax Implications," below, the employer's tax deduction is generally delayed until the

167

executive exercises the option and purchases stock. Furthermore, the employer generally gets no further deduction even if the executive realizes substantial capital gains thereafter.

TAX IMPLICATIONS

1. If an option is "granted" (i.e., transferred to the executive) to purchase employer stock at a market price as of the date of the grant, the option has no immediate value at the time it is granted. Therefore, there is no taxable income to the executive at the date of the grant.

2. The employee has taxable compensation income (ordinary income) in the year when shares are actually purchased under the option. The amount of taxable income to the employee is the "bargain element" — the difference between the fair market value of the shares at the date of purchase and the option price (the amount the executive actually pays for these shares). The employer must withhold and pay federal income tax with respect to this compensation income.

3. The employer does not get a tax deduction at the time an option is granted. The employer receives a tax deduction in the same year in which the employee has taxable income as a result of exercising the option and purchasing shares. The amount of the deduction is the same as the amount of income the employee must include.

An example will illustrate this tax treatment.

Example: Executive Lee is given an option in 1989 to purchase 1,000 shares of Employer Company stock at $100 per share, the current (1989) market price. The option can be exercised by Lee at any time over the next 5 years. In 1991, Lee purchases 400 shares for a total of $40,000. If the fair market value of the shares in 1991 is $60,000, Lee has $20,000 of ordinary income in 1991. Employer Company gets a tax deduction of $20,000 in 1991, the same amount as Lee's compensation income. (Assuming that Lee's total compensation in 1990 meets the reasonableness test.) If Lee resells this stock in a later year, he has capital gain income. Employer Company gets no further tax deduction even though Lee realizes and reports capital gain income from selling the stock.

4. The executive's basis in shares acquired under a stock option plan is equal to the amount paid for the stock, plus the amount of taxable income reported by the executive at the time the option was exercised. In the example in paragraph 3 above, Lee's basis for the 400 shares purchased in 1991 is $60,000 — the $40,000 that Lee paid, plus the $20,000 of ordinary income that he reported in 1991. Therefore if Lee sells the 400 shares in 1995 for $90,000, he must report $30,000 of capital

gain in 1995 (the selling price of $90,000 less his basis of $60,000). Employer Company gets no additional tax deduction in 1995.

5. If an option is priced at the time of grant at a bargain price compared with the then current market value, the option itself has a fair market value at the time of the grant. Under the Code and Regulations, however, options having a fair market value will not be currently taxed in all cases. The value of an option is taxable to an employee as ordinary compensation income at the time of the grant if (a) the option has a value that is determinable as of the time of the grant, *and* (b) the option can be traded on an established market.

If an option meets these rules and is taxed at the time of the grant, the employer receives a corresponding tax deduction at the time of the grant.

If an employee is taxed when an option is granted, the employee has no further taxable compensation income when the option is later exercised.

If the employer stock is expected to increase in value substantially, there is an advantage in designing an option plan so that it is taxed at the time of the grant. However, this approach can be used only where options can be traded on an established market.

WHERE CAN I FIND OUT MORE ABOUT IT?

1. Leimberg, Stephan R. et al., *The Federal Income Tax Law*, Warren, Gorham, and Lamont, 1989.

2. Graduate Course: Executive Compensation (GS 842), The American College, Bryn Mawr, PA.

QUESTIONS AND ANSWERS

Question — What is the effect of federal securities laws on stock option plans?

Answer — From the employer viewpoint, it is necessary to determine if the stock is subject to the registration requirements of federal securities law. Various exemptions from registration may apply to stock provided only to selected executives for compensation purposes, but the existence of such an exemption must be verified. State securities laws may also apply.

Advisers to the executive must determine if any of the resale restrictions of federal securities law apply to the sale of stock acquired under the plan. In addition, the executive may be considered an "insider" and subject to the insider trading restrictions on resale of stock.

Chapter 33
TARGET BENEFIT PENSION PLAN

WHAT IS IT?

A target benefit (or "assumed benefit") plan is a qualified defined contribution pension plan. It is similar to a money purchase pension plan, except that the formula for annual employer contributions to each participant's account is based not only on the participant's compensation but also the participant's *age* on entering the plan.

The age factor permits the employer to make greater plan contributions (as a percentage of compensation) for older plan entrants. These older employees are often the company's key employees, so the target plan typically permits greater relative plan contributions for such key employees.

A target plan is often described as a hybrid between defined benefit and defined contribution plans, because the contribution formula is designed to achieve account balances at retirement that will provide a "target" level of retirement income that is somewhat like a defined benefit formula. For example, the plan might be based on providing an annual target retirement benefit of 50 percent of average compensation for each employee. The contribution formula is based actuarially on this target benefit level, generally using conservative actuarial assumptions.

Unlike a defined benefit plan, however, once the initial contribution formula has been established, it is not changed just because actuarial assumptions are not met. In operation, a target plan is a defined contribution plan, with the participant assuming the investment risk. At retirement, the benefit is the amount in each participant's account. The target level is rarely exactly achieved.

WHEN IS IT INDICATED?

1. When the features of a money purchase plan would be attractive to the employer, except that there are older employees whose retirement benefits would be inadequate because of the relatively few years remaining for participation in the plan. The target benefit type of formula allows proportionately greater employer contributions for these older employees (greater percentages of their compensation).

2. When the employer is looking for an alternative to a defined benefit plan that provides adequate retirement benefits to older employees but has the lower cost and simplicity of a defined contribution plan.

3. When an employer wants to terminate an existing defined benefit plan in order to avoid the increasing cost

and regulatory burdens associated with these plans under recent changes in the law. If a target plan is substituted for the defined benefit plan, in many cases the new plan will provide approximately the same benefits to most employees, and it will be relatively easy to obtain IRS approval for the defined benefit plan termination.

4. When a closely held business or professional corporation has a relatively large number of key employees who are approximately age 50 or older and who generally want to save $30,000 or less annually under the plan. The target plan is generally the ideal qualified plan to adopt in this situation, because its benefit level is just as high as would be available in a defined benefit plan (given the $30,000 annual restriction), but the target plan is much simpler and cheaper to install and administer.

ADVANTAGES

1. Retirement benefits can be made adequate for employees who enter the plan at older ages. The following comparison with a money purchase plan illustrates this. The illustration shows how the annual contribution and retirement benefit vary for three employees, each earning $30,000 annually:

| Employee age at entry | Annual Contribution | | Accumulation at 65 (5½% return) | |
	Money Purchase (14%)	Target	Money Purchase	Target
30	$4,200	$1,655	$444,214	$175,000
40	4,200	3,243	226,657	175,000
50	4,200	7,402	99,292	175,000

2. From the viewpoint of a business owner, particularly in a small closely held business, the feature illustrated in the paragraph above also means that in a target plan, more of the total employer contributions in a target plan will likely be allocated to owners and key employees, as compared with a money purchase or other defined contribution plan. This will be the case if the owners and key employees are older than the average of all employees when the plan is adopted.

3. As with all qualified plans, a target plan provides a tax-deferred retirement savings medium for employees.

4. The target benefit plan is relatively simple and inexpensive to design, administer, and explain to employees. A target plan is especially simple compared to a defined

Tools and Techniques

benefit plan because actuarial valuations and an enrolled actuary's certification are not required. Yet the plan's benefits can be much the same as those from a defined benefit plan.

5. Plan distributions may be eligible for the special 5-year (or 10-year) averaging tax computation available for certain qualified plan distributions.

6. Individual accounts for participants allow participants to benefit from good investment results in the plan fund.

DISADVANTAGES

1. The annual addition to each employee's account in a money purchase plan is limited to the lesser of (a) 25% of compensation or (b) the greater of $30,000 or ¼ of the defined benefit dollar limit. This limits the relative amount of funding for highly compensated employees. For older employees, a defined benefit plan may allow a much higher level of employer contributions to the plan, as discussed further under "Design Features," below.

2. Employees bear investment risk under the plan. While this is a disadvantage to employees, it also tends to reduce employer costs compared to a defined benefit plan. This is because employers bear the investment risk in a defined benefit plan.

3. The plan is subject to the Code's minimum funding requirements. Employers are obligated to make minimum contributions each year under the plan's contribution formula or be subject to minimum funding penalties.

DESIGN FEATURES

Contribution Formula

The formula for employer contributions to a target plan requires the employer to contribute annually to each plan participant's account. The annual contribution is a percentage of each employee's annual compensation, with the percentage varying according to the age of the employee when that employee first entered the plan.

Compensation must be defined in the plan in a manner that does not discriminate in favor of highly compensated employees. Only the first $200,000 (as indexed after 1988) of each employee's compensation can be taken into account.

There are two basic steps in designing the formula that specifies the percentage of each participant's contribution that the employer will contribute annually:

(1) The employer chooses a "target" level of retirement benefits as a percentage of annual compensation. For example, the employer might want the

plan to aim for an annual retirement benefit of 50% of preretirement compensation for all participants.

(2) The plan designer chooses actuarial assumptions to determine how much must be contributed for each participant in order to provide the targeted level of benefit. Actuarial assumptions include (a) rate of investment return on plan assets, (b) cost of an annuity at age 65 (involving postretirement mortality and investment return), and (c) the form of the benefit (straight life annuity, joint and survivor annuity, etc.) These actuarial assumptions are developed into a table of contribution percentages that are incorporated into the target plan.

Contribution percentages derived from the table are then applied to each employee's annual compensation to determine the annual employer contribution. The percentage for each employee is determined when the employee enters the plan and remains the same thereafter; it doesn't increase each year. Also, the percentages remain the same even if investment results are higher or lower than the initial assumptions. Unlike a defined benefit plan, there are no periodic actuarial valuations. The participant gets the benefit of good investment results and bears the risk of poor results.

An illustrative contribution table is set out in Figure 33.1; this is not the only possible table, since different actuarial assumptions can be used. There are some limits on possible actuarial assumptions:

- The table must be a "unisex" table — the same for both males and females. Current law prohibits plan contribution rates based on sex, since this would result in different benefits at retirement for males and females. (Sex-based actuarial assumptions can be used in defined benefit plans because there they do not affect the amount of benefit a participant receives, only the amount of the employer's cost.)

- Actuarial assumptions must be reasonable.

- If the investment return assumption is not between 5 and 6 percent, the employer must show the IRS that the plan will not discriminate in favor of highly compensated employees.

Example: Archer Co. adopts a target plan with a target benefit of 50% of compensation. Using this table, and based on the employee data below, annual employer contributions are as follows. (The contribution percentages for a target of 50% of compensation are just five times those provided in the table for a target of 10% of compensation. Thus the table can be used for any target level by "scaling" the percentages up or down proportionately.)

Figure 33.1

TARGET BENEFIT TABLE

Target benefit: 10 percent of compensation
Normal retirement age: 65
Benefit form: Straight life annuity
Assumed investment return: 5.5%
Postretirement mortality: 1951 group annuity table projected to 1970, scale C, 2-year setback for males and females

Age at plan entry	Annual employer contribution (percentage of compensation)	Age at plan entry	Annual employer contribution (percentage of compensation)
18	.48	41	2.08
19	.51	42	2.24
20	.54	43	2.42
		44	2.61
21	.57	45	2.83
22	.60		
23	.64	46	3.08
24	.68	47	3.35
25	.72	48	3.66
		49	4.01
26	.77	50	4.41
27	.82		
28	.87	51	4.87
29	.92	52	5.40
30	.99	53	6.03
		54	6.77
31	1.05	55	7.67
32	1.12		
33	1.19	56	8.78
34	1.28	57	10.16
35	1.36	58	11.95
		59	14.34
36	1.46	60	17.70
37	1.56	61	22.75
38	1.67	62	31.19
39	1.79	63	48.07
40	1.93	64	98.80

Employee	Age at entry	Compensation	Annual contribution
A	30	$30,000	$ 1,485
B	50	30,000	6,615
C	30	60,000	2,970
D	50	60,000	13,230

For Employee A, the annual contribution percentage is 5 times .99 percent, or 4.95 percent of compensation. This is multiplied by $30,000, A's annual compensation, to arrive at the annual contribution of $1,485. The others are computed the same way.

Section 415 Limit

A very important limitation on target contributions must be kept in mind: the Section 415 "annual additions limit." This limit, which applies to all defined contribution plans, restricts annual additions to each participant's account to the lesser of (a) 25 percent of compensation or (b) the greater of $30,000 or ¼ of the dollar limitation for defined benefit plans. (The dollar limitation for defined benefit plans is $94,023 for 1988.) If the target percentage from the table calls for a larger contribution than this, the contribution must be cut back to the Section 415 limit.

For example, suppose Archer Co. in the example above employs Hood, who enters the plan at age 55 and earns $80,000 annually. The compensation percentage specified from the table for Archer Co.'s 50% target benefit is 38.35% (5 times 7.67%). This would dictate an annual contribution of $30,680. In fact, however, the company can contribute only $20,000 annually to Hood's account; this is the applicable annual additions limit of 25% of Hood's compensation (the lesser of 25% or $30,000 as indexed).

Tools and Techniques

In effect, an employee in a situation like Hood's is "losing" benefits because the plan is a defined contribution plan subject to the annual additions limit. If the plan were a defined benefit plan, it could provide a 50% of compensation retirement benefit that could be fully funded by the employer, because the annual additions limit would not apply (see Chapter 6).

Hood's situation in the example may be typical of owners or key employees in many closely held businesses. This illustrates the major "tradeoff" in adopting a target benefit plan instead of a defined benefit plan. The target plan is simpler and less expensive. But the upper limit available for tax deferred retirement savings is reduced.

Benefit Payments

Although the target in a target plan is a retirement benefit similar to that provided in a defined benefit plan, a target plan actually provides a benefit like other types of defined contribution plans, particularly a money purchase plan. For example, suppose a participant retires from a company having a target plan with a target of 50% of compensation. The purpose of the target was only to determine the level of employer contributions. The benefit this retiree receives actually has no direct relation to his compensation. As with any other defined contribution plan, his benefit is equal to the amount built up in his account as a result of (a) employer contributions, (b) after-tax employee contributions (rare in target plans), (c) forfeitures from other employees' accounts, and (d) interest, capital gains, and other investment returns realized over the years on plan assets.

As a condition of qualification, a target benefit plan must provide for a qualified joint and survivor annuity as its automatic benefit unless waived by the participant, with the consent of his spouse. If the automatic form of benefit is waived, account balances may be paid at retirement in installments over a period of years, in a lump sum, or other annuity options may be provided whereby the retiree can convert the amount in his or her account to an equivalent life or refund (period certain) annuity.

Other Provisions

Vesting and investment features of target plans are similar to those for money purchase plans discussed in Chapter 23. Integration of target plans with social security is discussed in the "Questions and Answers," below.

TAX IMPLICATIONS

1. Employer contributions to a target benefit plan are deductible when made, so long as the plan remains "qualified." A plan is qualified if it meets eligibility, vesting, funding and other requirements discussed in Appendix A.

2. Assuming the plan remains qualified, taxation of the employee on plan contributions is deferred. Both employer contributions and earnings on plan assets are nontaxable to plan participants until withdrawn.

3. Under Code section 415, annual additions to each participant's account are limited to the lesser of (a) 25% of the participant's compensation or (b) the greater of $30,000 or 1/4 of the dollar limitation for defined benefit plans. (The dollar limitation for defined benefit plans is $94,023 for 1988.) Annual additions include (1) employer contributions to participants' accounts; (2) forfeitures from other participants' accounts; and (3) employee contributions to the account.

4. Distributions from the plan must follow the rules for qualified plan distributions. Certain premature or excessive distributions are subject to penalties. The distribution rules are discussed in Appendix B.

5. Lump sum distributions made after age 59 1/2 are subject to a limited election to use a special 5-year averaging tax calculation. Certain older participants may also be eligible for a 10-year averaging tax calculation for lump sum distributions. Not all distributions are eligible for these special tax calculations. Appendix B covers these rules and includes IRS forms.

6. The plan is subject to the minimum funding rules of section 412 of the Code. This requires minimum periodic contributions, subject to a penalty imposed on the employer if less than the minimum amount is contributed. For a target plan, the minimum funding requirement is generally the amount required under the plan's contribution formula. The minimum funding requirements therefore will be satisfied so long as the employer contributes to each participant's account the percentage of compensation required by the plan. The employer must make plan contributions at least quarterly (although this requirement will not be fully phased in until 1992). Appendix A discusses the minimum funding rules further.

7. The plan is subject to the ERISA reporting and disclosure rules outlined in Appendix D.

ALTERNATIVES

1. Defined benefit plans provide more benefit security because of the employer and government guarantee of benefit levels. Defined benefit plans also allow greater tax deductible employer contributions for older plan entrants who are highly compensated because the 25%/$30,000 annual additions limit does not apply. However, defined benefit plans are more complex and costly to design and administer.

2. Money purchase plans offer an alternative similar to target plans, but without the age-related contribution feature.

3. Profit-sharing plans provide more employer flexibility in contributions, but deductible contributions are limited to 15% of payroll annually.

4. Nonqualified deferred compensation plans can be provided exclusively for selected executives. But with those plans the employer's tax deduction is generally deferred until benefit payments are made. This can be as much as 20 or 30 years after the employer's contribution is made.

5. Individual retirement savings is available as an alternative or supplement to an employer plan, but except for the limited provision for deductible IRAs there is no tax deferral.

HOW TO INSTALL THE PLAN

Installation of a target benefit plan follows the qualified plan installation procedure described in Appendix C.

WHERE CAN I FIND OUT MORE ABOUT IT?

1. McFadden, John J., *Retirement Plans for Employees*. Homewood, IL: Richard D. Irwin, 1988.

2. Gee, Judith Boyers, *Pensions in Perspective*, 2nd ed. Cincinnati, OH: The National Underwriter Co., 1987.

3. Graduate Course: Advanced Pension and Retirement Planning I (GS 814), The American College, Bryn Mawr, PA.

QUESTIONS AND ANSWERS

Question — How is the contribution formula in a target benefit plan integrated with social security?

Answer — Target benefit contribution formulas can be integrated with social security. In the past, this was fre-

quently done. The applicable rules were a combination of those applicable to defined benefit and money purchase plans (See Chapters 6 and 23).

After 1988, new integration rules adopted under the Tax Reform Act of 1986 go into effect for all qualified plans. In drafting the 1986 Act, Congress neglected to cover target plans; however, under proposed regulations, target plans generally must meet the requirements applicable to defined benefit excess plans.

Question — Can a self-employed person adopt a target plan?

Answer — Yes. The plan can cover not only regular employees of the business, but also the self-employed person(s) who own the business — the sole proprietor or partners. Plans covering self-employed persons are known as "Keogh" or "HR 10" plans. These plans are basically the same as regular qualified plans, but some of the special rules that apply are covered in Chapter 15 of this book.

For a target plan, the contribution formula applied to self-employed individuals must be based on their "earned income" as contrasted with the "compensation" base for regular employees. The definition of earned income is covered in Chapter 15.

Question — How is a target plan applied where shareholder-employees of an S corporation are covered?

Answer — For an S corporation, the plan contribution formula can't provide an employer contribution for all of the shareholder-employee's income from the corporation. The formula must be based only on the shareholder's compensation for services rendered to the corporation. Any portion of the shareholder's income that represents dividends from the S corporation must be excluded from the plan formula.

Chapter 34

TAX DEFERRED ANNUITY

WHAT IS IT?

A tax deferred annuity plan (also called a "TDA" plan or Section 403(b) plan) is a tax deferred employee retirement plan that can be adopted only by certain tax-exempt private organizations and certain public schools and colleges. Employees have accounts in a TDA plan to which employers contribute (or employees contribute through salary reductions).

The benefits of a TDA plan to employees are similar to those of a qualified profit-sharing plan, particularly the Section 401(k) type of plan (see Chapter 28): (1) the TDA contribution is, within limits, not currently taxable to employees; (2) plan account balances accumulate tax free, and (3) tax on plan contributions and account earnings is deferred until the employee actually withdraws amounts from the plan.

Because of changes included in the Tax Reform Act of 1986, TDA plans have become much more like qualified plans — Section 401(k) plans in particular. In addition to imposing nondiscrimination rules on TDA plans, the Tax Reform Act of 1986 forbade tax-exempt and governmental organizations from adopting Section 401(k) plans. Thus, in effect the TDA plan is now the "Section 401(k) substitute" for a tax-exempt organization or public school.

WHEN IS IT INDICATED?

1. When (and only when) the employer organization is eligible under the TDA provisions of the Code. An organization must be one of the following in order to adopt a TDA plan:

    (a) A tax-exempt employer described in Section 501(c)(3) of the Code. This means that

        (1) The employer must be "organized and operated exclusively for religious, charitable, scientific, testing for public safety, literary, or educational purposes, or to foster national or international amateur sport competition. . .or for the prevention of cruelty to children or animals."

        (2) The organization must benefit the public, rather than a private shareholder or individual.

        (3) The organization further must refrain from political campaigning or propaganda intended to influence legislation. In other words, most familiar nonprofit institutions such as churches, hospitals, private schools and colleges, and charitable institutions are eligible to adopt a TDA.

    (b) An educational organization with (1) a regular faculty and curriculum and (2) a resident student body, that is operated by a state or municipal agency. In other words, most public schools and colleges may adopt a TDA plan.

2. Assuming the employer organization is eligible, the positive indications for a TDA plan are similar to those for a taxable organization that is considering the adoption of a Section 401(k) plan. A TDA plan is indicated:

    (a) When the employer wants to provide a tax deferred retirement plan for employees but can afford only minimal extra expense beyond existing salary and benefit costs. A TDA plan can be funded entirely from employee salary reductions (except for installation and administration costs, which must be paid for by the employer). In most plans, however, some additional employer contribution to the plan can enhance its effectiveness.

    (b) When the employee group has one or more of the following characteristics:

        • many would like some choice as to the level of savings — that is, a choice between various levels of current cash compensation and tax deferred savings. A younger, more mobile work force often prefers this option.

        • many employees are relatively young and have substantial time to accumulate retirement savings.

        • many employees are willing to accept a degree of investment risk in their plan accounts in return for the potential benefits of good investment results.

    (c) When an employer wants an attractive, "savings-type" supplement to its existing defined benefit or other qualified plan. Such a supplement can make the employer's retirement benefit program attractive to both younger and older employees by providing both security of retirement benefits and the opportunity to increase savings and investment on a tax deferred basis.

ADVANTAGES

1. As with qualified plans, a TDA plan provides a tax-deferred retirement savings medium for employees.

Tools and Techniques

2. A salary reduction-type TDA plan allows employees a degree of choice in the amount they wish to save under the plan.

3. TDA plans can be funded entirely through salary reductions by employees. As a result, an employer can adopt the plan with no additional cost for employee compensation; the only extra cost is plan installation and administration. The plan may actually result in some savings as a result of lower state or local (but not federal) payroll taxes.

4. In-service withdrawals by employees are permitted; these are not available in qualified pension plans.

DISADVANTAGES

1. As with qualified defined contribution plans, account balances at retirement age may not provide adequate retirement savings for employees who entered the plan at later ages.

2. For each employee the annual salary reduction under the plan is limited to $9,500. However, this amount can be supplemented by employer contributions to provide additional tax deferred savings.

3. Because of the nondiscrimination tests described below, a TDA plan can be relatively costly and complex to administer.

4. Employees bear investment risk under the plan. However, TDA funds are in large part invested in low risk annuity contracts. Only the mutual fund (custodial account — see below) type of TDA investment (and possibly some variable annuity contracts) involve significant investment risk, and employees usually are given a choice of mutual fund investments so they can control the degree of risk.

DESIGN FEATURES

In the past, employers had great freedom and discretion in designing TDA plans; they could be provided to any group of employees desired, or even a single employee, and employer contributions could vary from employee to employee on a discriminatory basis. However, after 1988 TDA plans are subject to nondiscrimination rules; with respect to plans other than pure salary reduction plans, the nondiscrimination rules are similar to those for qualified plans. For eligible employers, a TDA plan will be subject to essentially the same rules as a Section 401(k) plan.

However, there are some important differences between TDA plans and Section 401(k) plans and this chapter will focus on these differences:

- The annual limit on contributions for a TDA plan is computed in a different and much more complicated way.

- Salary reductions in a TDA plan are currently subject to a higher ($9,500) limit, and there are "catch up" provisions that allow employees with 15 or more years of service to contribute in excess of this limit.

- Distributions from a TDA plan are not eligible for the 5-year or (10-year) averaging provisions for qualified plans.

- Plan investments are limited to annuity contracts or custodial accounts invested in mutual funds; incidental life insurance is also permitted.

Salary Reductions

Most TDA plans are funded entirely or in part through salary reductions elected by employees. To prevent discrimination, there is a requirement that if the plan permits salary reductions of more than $200 by any participant, then all employees must be given the same option (except for employees covered under a Section 401(k) or Section 457 plan, students employed by the school in which they are enrolled, or employees who normally work less than 20 hours per week).

Salary reductions must be elected by employees before compensation is earned — that is, before they render the services for which compensation is paid. Salary reductions elected after compensation is earned are ineffective as a result of the tax doctrine of "constructive receipt."

The usual practice is to provide plan participants with a salary reduction election form that they must complete before the end of each calendar year. The election specifies how much will be contributed to the plan from each paycheck received for the forthcoming year. The amount can't be increased later in the year. But usually the employee can reduce or entirely withdraw the election for pay not yet earned if circumstances dictate.

Salary reductions in TDA plans are subject to an annual limit. The employee must add together each year all of his or her salary reductions from

(1) TDA plans,

(2) Section 401(k) plans, and

(3) salary reduction SEPs.

The total must not exceed $9,500. This $9,500 limit remains unchanged until the $7,000 limit for Section 401(k) plans, as indexed for inflation, reaches $9,500. (The $7,000 limit reached $7,313 as of 1988.) From then on, there is a single indexed limit for all salary reduction plans.

If the employee has completed 15 years of service for the employer, and the employer is (1) an educational organization, (2) a hospital, (3) a home health care agency, (4) a health and welfare service agency, or (5) a church, synagogue or related organization, the $9,500 salary reduction limit is increased by an additional sum equal to the lesser of

- $3,000 per year, up to a total of $15,000, or

- $5,000 times the employee's years of service with the employer, less all prior salary reductions with that employer.

The $9,500 salary reduction limit (as indexed), plus the "salary reduction catch up" provision described in the preceding paragraph, is the *absolute* limit on the amount of annual salary reductions for any employee. Some (usually relatively lower paid) employees may not be able to reduce salary by this much, since the "exclusion allowance" for them may be less than this. The exclusion allowance is discussed below under "Tax Implications." (See also Figure 34.1, "The Five-Step Procedure.")

Vesting

The participant is always 100% vested in all amounts contributed to the TDA plan and in any plan earnings on those amounts. Unlike a regular qualified plan, graded vesting isn't permitted. Even if a participant leaves employment after a short time, his or her plan account can't be forfeited. Often plan account balances are distributed in a single sum when a participant terminates employment.

Employer Contributions

Many TDA plans provide for employer contributions, either in addition to or instead of salary reduction contributions, in order to encourage employee participation and make the plan more valuable to employees. TDA plans most often use a "formula matching contribution." Under this approach the employer matches employee salary reductions, either dollar for dollar or under another formula. For example, the plan might provide that the employer contributes an amount equal to 50% of the amount the employee elects as a salary reduction. So if an employee elects a salary reduction of $6,000, the employer puts an additional $3,000 into the employee's plan account. Other employer contribution approaches can be used similar to those used in Section 401(k) plans, as discussed in Chapter 28.

As with a qualified plan, employer contributions to the plan must not discriminate in favor of highly compensated employees. "Highly compensated" is defined as for qualified plans (see Appendix A). Furthermore, after 1988 only the first $200,000 (as indexed) of each employee's compensation can be taken into account in any contribution formula; this rule is the same as that for qualified plans.

Plan Investments

All plan funds in TDA plans must be invested in either (1) annuity contracts purchased by the employer from an insurance company, or (2) mutual fund (regulated investment company) shares held in custodial accounts. Many plans provide both types of investments and allow participants full discretion to divide their accounts between the two investment media.

Annuities used in TDA plans can be either group or individual contracts, level or flexible premium annuities, or fixed dollar or variable annuities. Face amount certificates providing a fixed maturity value and a schedule of redemptions are also permitted. Annuity contracts can give participants a degree of choice as to investment strategy. For example, the participant can be given a choice of investment mix between equity funds and fixed investment funds. However, investment "earmarking" or a "directed investment" provision as broad as those in qualified plans is not permitted. Under the IRS view, if a participant can choose specific individual investments, the participant will be currently taxed on investment income of the fund.

"Incidental life insurance" protection under annuity contracts is also permitted. The amount of life insurance is limited by the "incidental" tests discussed in Chapter 20 — i.e., the limits are the same as those for qualified plans. As with qualified plans, the value of the life insurance protection is taxed annually to the employee using the P.S. 58 table reproduced in Chapter 20, and the P.S. 58 costs may be recovered tax free on a subsequent plan distribution.

Plan Distributions

Distributions from TDA plans are subject to the qualified plan distribution rules detailed in Appendix B. Many plans provide for distributions in a lump sum at termination of employment. However, plans subject to ERISA must either provide for a qualified joint and survivor annuity as its automatic benefit or provide that if the participant dies, 100% of his nonforfeitable benefit will be paid to his surviving spouse unless the spouse is deceased or has consented to another beneficiary.

TDA plans often allow participants to make in-service withdrawals (i.e., withdrawals before termination of employment). Withdrawals are not permitted from a TDA custodial account (mutual funds) before (1) attainment of age 59½, (2) death, disability or separation from service, or (3) (with respect to amounts attributable to salary reduction contributions) financial hardship. The same restrictions apply to TDAs other than custodial accounts with respect to distributions of amounts attributable to salary reduction, but the restrictions do not apply to amounts held in the account at the close of the last year beginning before January 1, 1989. The Technical and Miscellaneous Revenue Act of 1988 also permits distributions to former spouses under qualified domestic relations orders (QDROs).

All withdrawals are subject to income tax. In addition, many in-service distributions will be subject to the 10% early withdrawal penalty tax discussed in Appendix B, even if the distribution is permitted under the terms of the TDA plan. To summarize, a 10% penalty tax applies to the taxable amount (i.e., amount subject to regular income tax) of any qualified plan or TDA distribution, except for distributions

- after age 59½

- on the employee's death

- upon the employee's disability

- that are part of a joint or life annuity payout following separation from service

- that are paid after separation from service after age 55

- that do not exceed the amount of medical expenses deductible as an itemized deduction for the year.

Many TDA plans have provisions for plan loans to participants. A plan loan provision is extremely valuable to employees because it allows them access to their plan funds without the 10% penalty tax. Plan loans are discussed in detail in Appendix B.

TAX IMPLICATIONS

1. Employees are not taxed currently on either salary reductions or employer contributions under a TDA plan, so long as these in total do not exceed any of three limits. The first limit is the "exclusion allowance" provided under Section 403(b) of the Code.

The formula for the annual exclusion allowance is:

(1) 20 percent of the participant's "includable compensation" from the employer $_____

multiplied by

(2) the participant's total years of service for the employer   _____ (years)

minus

(3) amounts contributed to the plan in prior years that were excluded from the participant's income $_____

equals

(4) annual exclusion allowance $_____
_____

The third item in the formula — prior contributions — must include not only prior TDA contributions but also prior year contributions to regular qualified plans on behalf of the employee.

Example: Doctor Vanderslice has been employed by Staph Hospital for 10 years, including this year. Her includable compensation from the hospital this year is $60,000. Prior TDA contributions by the hospital on her behalf total $110,000.

Her exclusion allowance for this year is (1) 20 percent of taxable income this year — $12,000 — times (2) 10 years of service — $120,000 — minus (3) prior contributions of $110,000 — a result of $10,000. Because this is not a salary reduction contribution, the hospital can contribute $10,000 to Doctor Vanderslice's TDA account this year, unless the limit explained in 2 below is lower.

Where the TDA plan is funded through salary reductions — as most plans are — the computation has another wrinkle to it. The 20% limit is applied to the participant's "includable compensation." This means the compensation that is includable in the participant's taxable income. Since salary reductions are *not* includable in income, the 20% limit must be applied to the amount of compensation *after* the salary reduction is taken into account.

Example: TDA participant Hal earns $30,000 this year and has no prior service (i.e., one year of total service) and no prior TDA contributions. Hal's maximum exclusion allowance for salary reduction contributions is $5,000. This is because Hal's salary *after* the salary reduction is $25,000. Twenty percent of the reduced salary of $25,000 is $5,000.

A general formula for the maximum salary reduction permitted under the exclusion allowance is:

$$\text{Maximum salary reduction} = \frac{(S \times T) - 5B}{T + 5}$$

where

S = unreduced salary

T = total years of service including current year

B = prior years' excludable contributions.

2. A TDA plan is subject to the "annual additions limit" of Code section 415. Annual additions to each participant's account are limited to the lesser of (a) 25% of the participant's includable compensation or (b) the greater of $30,000 or ¼ of the dollar limitation for defined benefit plans. (The dollar limitation for defined benefit plans is $94,023 for 1988 — see Appendix A.) Annual additions include the total of (1) employer contributions to the participant's account; (2) salary reductions or other elective deferrals contributed to the account; and (3) after-tax employee contributions to the account. (If the employee participates in other retirement plans, contributions to those plans may have to be considered in determining how much may be contributed under this limit.)

Section 415 acts as an upper limit on the exclusion allowance described in the preceding section. Annual additions to a participant's account can't exceed the

Section 415 limit even if the exclusion allowance works out to a higher figure.

Example: Doctor Finster is an employee of Staph Hospital with a total of five years of service. His current annual includable compensation is $200,000. The hospital has made prior TDA contributions of $50,000 to Finster's account.

Doctor Finster's exclusion allowance for this year is 20% of $200,000, or $40,000, times 5 years of service ($200,000), minus prior contributions of $50,000 — a net of $150,000. However, the Section 415 annual additions limit for this year is $30,000 (the lesser of 25% of Finster's compensation or $30,000). Thus, the hospital may contribute no more than $30,000 to Doctor Finster's TDA account this year.

3. There is yet a further complication to the TDA limit. The Section 415 limit and exclusion allowance discussed in the preceding two sections can, in the case of TDA plans for certain employers only, be increased under "catch-up alternatives" that are aimed at long service participants in TDA plans.

    These catch up provisions are available only if the employer is (1) an educational organization, (2) a hospital, (3) a home health care agency, (4) a health and welfare service agency, or (5) a church, synagogue or related organization.

    There are three alternative catch up provisions. An employee must affirmatively elect one of these (on his or her income tax return) in order to use it. Only one of these alternatives can ever be elected by an employee and, once made, the election is irrevocable. However, the alternative elected may be used as many times thereafter as the employee chooses (except that the first, or A, alternative may be used only once). The alternatives are:

    (A) the "last year of service" alternative. In the employee's last year of service only, he can elect to use the regular exclusion allowance (using no more than 10 years of service) instead of the 25% limit under Section 415. The $30,000 limit still applies, however. In other words, this alternative allows a contribution of more than 25% of compensation, but not more than $30,000.

    (B) the "any year" alternative. Instead of the 25% of compensation limit under Section 415, the employee can elect to apply a limit equal to the lesser of

    — $4,000 plus 25% of includable compensation for the year;

    — the regular exclusion allowance for the year; or

    — $15,000.

    (C) the "overall" alternative. Instead of the regular exclusion allowance, the participant can elect simply to use the 25%/$30,000 Section 415 limit.

    There are in addition some special rules for employees of churches, synagogues, and related organizations only.

    The effect of all these overlapping limitations is to make it extremely difficult for employees to understand just exactly how much they can put in a TDA plan. In addition, the administrative cost and complexity to the employer can be considerable. Figure 34.1 summarizes the procedure for determining an employee's maximum allowable salary reduction.

4. Salary reductions, but not employer contributions, are subject to social security (FICA) and federal unemployment (FUTA) payroll taxes. The impact of state payroll taxes depends on the particular state's law. Both elective deferrals and employer contributions may be exempt from state payroll taxes in some states.

5. If the plan provides employer matching contributions or employee after-tax contributions, it must meet the nondiscrimination tests of Code section 401(m). Under these tests, the ratio of employer matching contributions and employee after-tax contributions (as a percentage of each eligible employee's compensation) is computed. The average of these ratios for highly compensated employees cannot exceed the average of these ratios for all other eligible employees by more than the greater of

    • 125 percent, or

    • the lesser of (a) 200 percent, or (b) the percentage of all other eligible employees plus 2 percentage points.

For example, if the average of employee after-tax contributions and employer matching contributions to compensation for nonhighly compensated employees is 6 percent of compensation, the average for highly compensated employees can be up to 8 percent (6 percent plus 2 percent).

Administratively the employer must monitor the level of contributions made by nonhighly compensated employees, and then make sure that highly compensated employees do not exceed this level in order for the plan to remain qualified.

To meet this test, the employer may take into account 401(k) contributions to a plan maintained by the

Figure 34.1

THE FIVE STEP PROCEDURE

A summary of the procedure for determining an employee's
maximum salary reduction in a salary reduction-only TDA plan

1. Compute the employee's regular exclusion allowance under the procedure described in (1) under Tax Implications.

2. Compute the employee's Section 415 limit as described in (2) under Tax Implications.

3. Work out any catch up alternatives available to the employee. These are described in (3) under Tax Implications. If any of these provides a greater contribution than the lesser of the amount determined in Steps 1 and 2, the employee may want to make an election to use that alternative.

4. The limit so far is the greater of (i) Step 3 or (ii) the lesser of Steps 1 or 2. Compare this result with the $9,500 annual salary reduction limitation. If the result of the first 3 steps is more than $9,500, only $9,500 can be contributed, unless —

5. Determine if the "salary reduction catch up" described in Design Features above applies. If the employee has the required service and is employed by the right type of employer, the $9,500 limit can be raised to $12,500 or more (but never more than $15,000).

This five step procedure is just a simplified, schematic illustration of the computation procedure to show how the various limits interact. The actual annual calculation for each participant in a TDA plan is a complex, costly burden for the employer, and one that is full of possibilities for error. The planner who can develop a way to deliver this administrative service to client tax exempt organizations can get a considerable edge on the competition for selling investment products to the plan.

---

employer, or employer contributions to which the 401(k) vesting and withdrawal restrictions apply.

"Highly compensated employee" is defined as it is for virtually all employee benefit purposes. In summary (the details are in Appendix A) a highly compensated employee is an employee who

- was at any time a more than 5 percent owner of the employer

- received compensation from the employer over $75,000

- received compensation over $50,000 and was in the highest-paid 20% of the employer's employees

- was an officer and received compensation over 50% of the defined benefit dollar limitation (i.e., 50% of $94,023 in 1988)

The $50,000 and $75,000 limits are indexed annually. (See Appendix A.)

6. Distributions from the plan must follow the rules for qualified plan distributions. Certain premature or excessive distributions are subject to penalties. The distribution rules are discussed in Appendix B.

7. Distributions from the plan to employees are subject to income tax when received. Single sum distributions are *not* eligible for the special 5-year or 10-year averaging computations applicable to qualified plan distributions.

ERISA REQUIREMENTS

In general, ERISA applies to a TDA plan to the same extent it applies to a qualified plan. The reporting and disclosure requirements discussed in Appendix D therefore apply to a TDA in most cases. In addition, a plan subject to ERISA must observe its other requirements, including fiduciary requirements and plan requirements protecting spousal benefits. However, TDAs may be subject to the ERISA exemption applicable to all governmental and church plans (see Appendix D). In addition, an ERISA exemption under Labor Department regulations applies to plans that are (1) funded purely through voluntary salary reductions by employees, and (2) not considered "established or maintained by the employer." This exemption permits only minimal employer involvement with the plan.

HOW TO INSTALL A PLAN

Installation of a TDA plan is not subject to the qualified plan rules. Furthermore, some employers having TDA plans are not subject to any provisions of ERISA (e.g., church or governmental organizations.) Government approval of a TDA plan is not necessary and is not generally sought by plan installers. However, a written plan document similar to a qualified plan document is required if ERISA applies to the plan, and should be adopted as a matter of good policy even where not required by law.

In addition, salary reduction forms must be completed by plan participants before the plan's effective date so that salary reduction elections will be immediately effective.

The success of a TDA plan in meeting the employer's objectives and the nondiscrimination tests depends on effective communication with employees. Effective employer-employee communication is always important in employee benefit plans. But it is particularly essential for a TDA plan because of the active role of employees in the plan.

WHERE CAN I FIND OUT MORE ABOUT IT?

1. McFadden, John J., *Retirement Plans for Employees*. Homewood, IL: Richard D. Irwin, 1988.

2. Gee, Judith Boyers, *Pensions in Perspective*, 2nd Ed. Cincinnati, OH: The National Underwriter Co., 1987.

3. Graduate Course: Advanced Pension and Retirement Planning I (GS 814), The American College, Bryn Mawr, PA.

QUESTIONS AND ANSWERS

Question — How can a planner determine if an employer organization meets the technical eligibility requirements in the Code?

Answer — Most organizations that are tax exempt under Section 501(c)(3) have obtained a government ruling letter to that effect. Also, organizations that have been ruled tax exempt are listed in a government publication available at libraries. Planners should ask the prospective TDA client for a copy of the ruling letter, if any, and keep it in their files. If there is no ruling letter, or if the organization is not a Section 501(c)(3) organization, the planner should at minimum obtain an attorney's or accountant's written opinion that the organization meets the TDA criteria. In large or questionable cases, an IRS ruling should be sought.

Question — Can TDA plans cover "independent contractors" — for example, anesthesiologists or radiologists associated with, but not formally employed by, hospitals?

Answer — No. TDA plan participants must be employees of the plan sponsor. The best way for a planner to verify this is to ask the sponsor how these individuals are treated by the sponsor for employment tax purposes — social security (FICA) and federal unemployment (FUTA). Employees and independent contractors are treated differently under these taxes (the employer pays no employment taxes for independent contractors) and the treatment of these individuals in the TDA plan should be consistent.

Question — Can a TDA plan participant make deductible IRA contributions as well as salary reductions under the TDA plan?

Answer — Yes. However, in a year in which an individual makes salary reduction contributions to a TDA plan or the employer contributes to his TDA account, the individual is considered an "active participant" under the IRA rules. IRA contributions are deductible only within the reduced deductible IRA limits allowed for active plan participants — see Chapter 17. No deduction is allowed for a year in which adjusted gross income on a joint basis is $50,000 or more ($35,000 for a single person), with reduced deductions for adjusted gross income between $40,000 and $50,000 joint ($25,000-$35,000 single).

Appendix A

QUALIFIED PENSION AND PROFIT-SHARING PLANS: GENERAL RULES FOR QUALIFICATION

The design of qualified pension and profit-sharing plans is a very complex subject, and the complete details are beyond the scope of this book. However, because of the great importance of these plans in an employer's benefit program and for individual financial and retirement planning, every planner should have a basic understanding of how these plans are structured and what they can do.

WHAT IS A QUALIFIED PLAN?

A qualified pension or profit-sharing plan is a plan by which part of the compensation an employee would otherwise receive currently is deferred (both actually and for tax purposes) and deposited into a trust fund or insurance contract for the benefit of the employee. Benefits from the fund are paid when the employee retires or terminates employment. Qualified pension and profit-sharing plans are therefore plans of deferred compensation. A qualified plan receives tax benefits that are not available for a nonqualified deferred compensation plan (a plan that does not meet the Code requirements for qualified plans described below). These tax benefits are:

1. Amounts paid into a qualified plan to finance future retirement benefits are deductible to the employer in the year for which they are made.

2. The employee is not taxed when the employer makes contributions to the plan fund, even if the employee is fully vested in the retirement benefit.

3. The tax on salary put into the plan is deferred to the time when benefits are received by the employee or the employee's beneficiary. Some lump sum benefits are eligible for a special 5-year (or 10-year) averaging tax computation. (See Appendix B.)

4. The plan fund is tax exempt; earnings therefore accumulate tax free to the plan itself and are not taxed to the employee or the employee's beneficiary until benefits are paid. This significantly increases the effective investment return.

Tax deferral of both plan contributions and plan earnings is a valuable tax benefit. This feature permits plan funds to build up much faster than comparable savings outside the plan in most cases.

TYPES OF QUALIFIED PLANS

Qualified plans are either defined contribution or defined benefit plans. As the names imply, this depends on whether the plan specifies an employer contribution rate on the one hand, or guarantees a specified benefit level on the other.

Defined Contribution Plans

In a defined contribution plan, the employer establishes and maintains an individual account for each plan participant. When the participant becomes eligible to receive benefit payments — usually at retirement or termination of employment — the benefit is based on the total amount in the participant's account. The account balance includes employer contributions, employee contributions in some cases, and earnings on the account over all the years of deferral.

The employer does not guarantee the amount of the benefit a participant will ultimately receive in a defined contribution plan. Instead, the employer must make contributions under a formula specified in the plan. There are three principal types of defined contribution plan formulas:

- *Money purchase pension plan.* Under a money purchase plan, the employer must contribute each year to each participant's account a percentage of the participant's compensation. This percentage is usually about 10 percent, although percentages up to 25 are possible. The money purchase plan is probably the simplest of all types of plans and is one of the most common.

- *Target benefit pension plan.* A target plan is similar to a money purchase plan in that the employer must make annual contributions to each participant's account under a formula based on compensation. In a target plan, however, the participant's age at plan entry is also taken into account in determining the contribution percentage. This is done on an actuarial basis so that older entrants can build up retirement accounts faster. The objective — the target — is to provide approximately the same benefit level (as a percentage of compensation) for each participant at retirement. The employer does not guarantee this level, however, and the employee bears the risk as well as reaps the benefit of varying investment results.

- *Profit-sharing plan.* A profit-sharing plan is a defined contribution plan under which the employer determines the amount of the contribution each year, rather than having a contribution obligation based on each employee's compensation. In a profit-sharing plan, the employer can decide not to contribute

183

to the plan at all in certain cases. Typically, plan contributions are based on the employer's profits in some manner. If a contribution is made, the total amount must be allocated to each participant's account using a nondiscriminatory formula. Such formulas are usually based on compensation, but service can be taken into account.

Profit-sharing plans often feature employee contributions, typically with an employer match. For example, the plan could provide that employees may contribute to the plan up to 6 percent of their compensation, with the employer contributing 50 cents for every $1 of employee contribution. This type of plan is referred to as a *thrift* or *savings* plan.

Another variation on the profit-sharing plan design is the *cash or deferred* or *Section 401 (k)* plan. Under this type of plan, employees can make tax deferred contributions by electing salary reductions, which are permitted up to $7,000 annually per employee, as indexed for inflation ($7,313 in 1988). Employers often match employee salary reductions in order to encourage employee participation in these plans.

All these types of plans are discussed in more detail in separate chapters of this book.

Defined Benefit Plans

Defined benefit plans provide a specific amount of benefit to the employee at normal retirement age. There are many different types of formula for determining this benefit, as discussed in Chapter 6 of this book. These formulas are typically based on the employee's earnings averaged over a number of years of service. The formula also can be based on the employee's service.

These plans are funded actuarially, which means that, for a given benefit level, the annual funding amount is greater for employees who are older at entry into the plan, since the time to fund the benefit is less in the case of an older entrant. This makes defined benefit plans attractive to professionals and closely held business owners; they tend to adopt retirement plans for their businesses when they are relatively older than their regular employees. A large percentage of the total cost for a defined benefit plan in this situation funds these key employees' benefits, as discussed further in Chapter 6.

QUALIFIED PLAN REQUIREMENTS

In order to obtain the tax advantages of qualified plans, complex Internal Revenue Code and IRS regulatory requirements must be met. The following will summarize these requirements as briefly as possible. These rules have many exceptions and qualifications that will not be covered in detail. The rules described here are those applicable after 1988.

Eligibility and Coverage

A qualified plan must cover a broad group of employees, not just key employees and business owners. Two types of rules must be satisfied: the "age and service" ("waiting period") requirements, and the "overall coverage" or "participation" requirements.

Minimum waiting period and age requirements are often used in plans to avoid burdening the plan with employees who terminate after short periods of service. However, the plan cannot require more than one year of service for eligibility, and any employee who has attained the age of 21 must be allowed to enter the plan upon meeting the plan's waiting period requirement. As an alternative, the plan waiting period can be up to 2 years if the plan provides immediate 100 percent vesting upon entry. No plan can impose a maximum age for entry. For eligibility purposes, a year of service means a 12-month period during which the employee has at least 1,000 hours of service.

A qualified plan must satisfy at least one of three coverage tests of the Code:

1. the plan must cover at least 70 percent of employees who are not highly compensated. This is the *percentage test*, or

2. the plan must cover a percentage of nonhighly compensated employees that is at least 70 percent of the percentage of highly compensated employees covered. This is the *ratio test*, or

3. the plan must meet the *average benefit test*. Under the average benefit test, the plan must benefit a nondiscriminatory classification of employees, and the average benefit, as a percentage of compensation, for nonhighly compensated employees must be at least 70 percent of that for highly compensated employees.

"Highly compensated" is a concept defined in detail in Code section 414(q) (see below).

In applying the above three coverage tests, certain employees are not counted, which means that they can effectively be excluded from the plan. In particular, employees included in a collective bargaining unit can be excluded if there was good faith bargaining on retirement benefits.

When the coverage rules are applied, all related employers must be treated as a single employer. Thus, an employer generally cannot break up its business into a number of corporations or other separate units to avoid covering rank-and-file employees.

However, if the employer actually has bona fide "separate lines of business," it is possible to apply the coverage test separately to employees in each line of business. This allows plans to be provided only to one line of business, or several different plans tailored to different lines of business.

An employer can meet the coverage tests with separate plans for different groups of employees if the plans are deemed to be *comparable* under IRS tests. However, each plan must cover the lesser of 50 employees or 40 percent of all employees on each day of the plan year.

Highly Compensated — Definition for Employee Benefit Purposes

A *highly compensated employee* is any employee who, during the year or the preceding year

(a) was at any time a 5-percent owner (as defined for top-heavy purposes);

(b) received compensation from the employer in excess of $75,000, as indexed for inflation ($78,353 in 1988);

(c) received compensation from the employer in excess of $50,000, as indexed for inflation ($52,235 in 1988), and was in the "top-paid group" for the year; or

(d) was at any time an officer and received compensation greater than 50 percent of the defined benefit plan dollar limit in effect for that year (50% of $94,023 in 1988).

An employee described in (b), (c), or (d) will not be treated as a highly compensated employee for the current year unless he also was described in (b), (c), or (d) for the prior year, or if he is also one of the 100 highest paid employees for the current year.

For purposes of these rules, the "top-paid group" of employees for a year is the group of employees in the top 20 percent, ranked on the basis of compensation paid for the year. For the purpose of determining the top-paid group, the following employees may be excluded: (1) employees with less than 6 months of service, (2) employees who normally work less than $17^1/_2$ hours per week, (3) employees who normally work during not more than 6 months in any year, (4) employees under the age of 21, (5) except as provided by regulations, employees covered by a collective bargaining agreement, and (6) nonresident aliens with no U.S. earned income. At the employer's election, a shorter period of service, smaller number of hours or months, or lower age than those specified in (1) through (4) may be used. (A simplified alternative definition of "highly compensated" may be elected by an employer who maintained significant business operations in at least 2 significantly separate geographic areas. Such an employer may elect to treat an employee earning $50,000 (indexed) as highly compensated without regard to whether he was a member of the top 20% of employees.)

No more than 50 employees (or, if fewer, the greater of 3 employees or 10 percent of the employees) need be treated as officers; however, at least one officer must be treated as such. If no officer of an employer has received compensation greater than 50 percent of the defined benefit plan dollar limit, the highest paid officer will, nevertheless, be treated as "highly compensated."

Any compensation paid to an employee who is a member of the family of a 5-percent owner, or of one of the 10 highly compensated employees paid the greatest compensation during the year, will be treated as paid to the 5-percent owner or highly compensated employee. Family members include spouses of an employee, the employee's lineal ascendants and descendants, and their spouses.

Former employees are treated as highly compensated employees if (1) they were highly compensated employees when they separated from service, or (2) they were highly compensated employees at any time after attaining age 55.

The controlled group, common control, affiliated service group, and employee leasing provisions of Section 414 are to applied before applying the highly compensated employee rules.

Nondiscrimination in Benefits and Contributions

Qualified plans may not discriminate in favor of highly compensated employees either in terms of benefits or in terms of employer contributions to the plan. Some nondiscriminatory formulas will, however, provide a higher benefit for highly compensated employees. Contributions or benefits can be based on compensation or years of service, for example. Also, qualified plan benefit or contribution formulas can be "integrated" with social security. In an integrated plan, greater contributions or benefits are provided for higher paid employees whose compensation is greater than an amount based on the social security taxable wage base.

Integration with Social Security

Since most employees will receive social security benefits when they retire, a calculation of an employee's retirement needs must take these into account. Since social security benefits are effectively paid out of employer compensation costs, it is appropriate, and permitted by law, to reflect social security benefits by "integrating" a qualified plan's benefit formula with social security benefits. However, the rules for doing so are quite complex. The details will not be discussed here, but the financial planner should be familiar with the basic rules for social security integration.

Social security integration benefits employers from a cost point of view since it effectively reduces the cost of the qualified plan. Also, since social security provides a higher retirement income, relatively speaking, for lower paid employees, social security integration of qualified plans permits such plans to provide relatively greater benefits for highly compensated employees, which is often an employer objective.

Defined benefit plans. There are two methods for integrating defined benefit formulas with social security: the "excess" method and the "offset" method.

Under the excess method of integration with social security, the plan defines a level of compensation called the integration level. The plan then provides a higher rate of benefits for compensation above the integration level. A plan's integration level is an amount of compensation specified under the plan by a dollar amount or formula. Benefits under the plan expressed as a percentage of compensation are lower for compensation below the integration level than they are for compensation above the integration level.

> *Example:* Plan A's integrated formula provides an annual benefit of 30 percent of final average annual compensation plus 25 percent of compensation above the plan's integration level. Labelle, a participant in plan A, retires in 1991. Labelle's final average compensation is $40,000. The integration level (covered compensation — see below) is $19,086 — for illustration round it down to $19,000. Labelle's annual retirement benefit is
>
> - 30 percent of final average compensation of $40,000, or $12,000, plus
>
> - 25 percent of $21,000 ($40,000 - $19,000) or $5,250.
>
> The total benefit is $17,250 ($12,000 plus $5,250).

The Code, and IRS regulations and rulings interpreting the Code provisions, provide various rules specifying what maximum integration level a plan can use, and how big the percentage spread above and below the integration level can be. As a general rule, a plan's integration level cannot exceed an amount known as "covered compensation," which is specified by the IRS in a table. Covered compensation is the average of the contribution and benefit base under the Social Security Act for each year during the 35-year period ending with the year in which an employee attains age 65. Therefore, the covered compensation amount for each employee depends upon the year when the employee retires (see Figure A.1).

The Code and IRS regulations also restrict the percentage spread between the benefit as a percentage of compensation above and below the integration level. The "base benefit percentage" is the percentage of compensation that the plan provides for compensation below the integration level, and the "excess benefit percentage" is the percentage of compensation above the integration level.

The excess benefit percentage cannot exceed the base benefit percentage by more than ³/₄ of one percentage point for any year of service, or participant's years of service up to 35.

For example, if a defined benefit plan provides a benefit of 1 percent of compensation below the integration level for each year of service, then it can provide not more than 1.75 percent

of compensation above the integration level for each year of service. Or, for a participant with 35 years of service, if the plan provides a benefit of 30 percent of final average compensation below the integration level, it cannot provide more than 56.25 percent of compensation above the integration level. (The spread of 26.25 percent is ³/₄ of one percentage point multiplied by 35 years of service.) The difference between the base and excess benefit percentages — the *maximum excess allowance* — can be no greater than the base percentage. Thus if a plan provides 10 percent of final average compensation below the integration level, it can provide no more than 20 percent of compensation above the integration level.

Under the offset method of integration, the plan formula is reduced by a fixed amount or a formula amount that is designed to represent the existence of social security benefits. There is no integration level in an offset plan. The Code and IRS rulings and regulations provide limits on the extent of an offset for social security. In particular, the rules provide that no more than half of the benefit provided under the formula without the offset may be taken away by an offset. For example, if a plan formula provides 50 percent of final average compensation with an offset, even the lowest paid employee must receive at least 25 percent of final average compensation from the plan.

Defined contribution plans. Defined contribution plans can be integrated only under the excess method. Generally, the integration level must (unless revised in future regulations) equal the social security taxable wage base in effect at the beginning of the plan year ($48,000 for plan years beginning in 1989). The difference in the allocation percentages above and below the integration level can be no more than the lesser of

(1) the percentage contribution below the integration level or

(2) the greater of (a) 5.7% or (b) the old age portion of the social security tax rate.

Thus, for a plan year beginning in 1989, an integrated plan must have an integration level of $48,000. If the plan allocated employer contributions plus forfeitures at the rate of 15.7 percent of compensation above the integration level, then it would have to provide at least a 10 percent allocation for compensation below the integration level (making the difference 5.7 percent).

Vesting

If a qualified plan provides for employee contributions, the portion of the benefit or account balance attributable to employee contributions must at all times be 100 percent vested (nonforfeitable). The portion attributable to employer contributions must be vested under a specified vesting schedule that is at least as favorable as one of two alternative minimum standards:

Figure A.1

Calendar Year of Attainment of Age 65	1988 Covered Compensation*	Calendar Year of Attainment of Age 65	1988 Covered Compensation*
1988	$16,692	2006	34,968
1989	17,640	2007	36,036
1990	18,528	2008	37,068
1991	19,356	2009	38,040
1992	20,124	2010	38,952
1993	20,856	2011	39,828
1994	21,552	2012	40,680
1995	22,692	2013	41,496
1996	23,844	2014	42,276
1997	24,996	2015	42,900
1998	26,148	2016	43,452
1999	27,288	2017	43,884
2000	28,440	2018	44,244
2001	29,592	2019	44,520
2002	30,684	2020	44,724
2003	31,788	2021	44,880
2004	32,844	2022	44,964
2005	33,912	2023	45,000

*For years beginning after 1988, comparable tables will refer to "Attainment of Social Security Retirement Age" as opposed to "Attainment of Age 65."

1. *5-year vesting*. A plan's vesting schedule satisfies this minimum requirement if an employee with at least 5 years of service is 100 percent vested. No vesting at all is required before 5 years of service.

2. *3- to 7-year vesting*. The plan must provide vesting that is at least as fast as the following schedule:

Years of Service	Vested Percentage
3	20
4	40
5	60
6	80
7 or more	100

Funding Requirements

Employer and employee contributions to a qualified plan must be deposited into an irrevocable trust fund or insurance contract that is for the "exclusive benefit" of plan participants and their beneficiaries. The *minimum funding standard* of federal law provides a mathematical calculation of the minimum amount that must be contributed to a qualified pension plan. Pension plans, both defined benefit and defined contribution, must meet these annual minimum funding standards or be subject to penalty. Profit-sharing plans are not subject to the minimum funding standards as such, but contributions must be "substantial and recurring" or the IRS can deem the plan to be terminated. Substantial and recurring is not clearly

defined in the law so that there is always some risk in repeatedly omitting contributions.

The minimum funding standards applicable to defined benefit plans are related to the method by which an annual cost for these plans is determined. As discussed below, this annual cost must paid in quarterly or more frequent installments. The annual cost is based on an *actuarial cost method*.

Actuarial cost methods. An actuarial cost method determines the employer's annual cost for a defined benefit plan. Actuaries use a number of different actuarial cost methods, which can be relatively complex mathematically. However, these methods are based on simple principles that should be understood by financial planners even though the computational complexities are left to the actuary. An actuarial cost method develops a series of annual deposits to the plan fund that will grow to the point where as each employee retires the fund is sufficient to fully fund the employee's retirement benefit. There are two basic ways of spreading these costs over future working careers of employees. Under the *projected benefit* or level funding method, the total cost is divided into equal deposits for each employee's benefit spread over the period remaining until the employee's retirement. With the *accrued benefit* method the annual deposit is based on the benefit accrued each year. The accrued benefit method produces a generally rising series of deposits for a given employee, because as retirement approaches there is less time to fund each additional piece of accrued benefit. The overall plan cost does not necessarily rise, however, with the accrued benefit method, because employees may enter and leave the plan from time to time.

If a defined benefit plan provides past service benefits, the cost of these can be made part of the annual cost using a projected benefit or accrued benefit method. Alternatively, the past service benefit can be funded separately by developing what is known as a *supplemental liability*. The supplemental liability is paid off through deposits to the plan fund over a fixed period of years, up to 30, regardless of actual retirement dates for employees. The use of a supplemental liability can provide additional funding flexibility in many cases.

Projected benefit actuarial cost methods can be either individual or aggregate. With the individual methods, a separate cost is determined for each employee, with the total employer deposit being the sum of all the separate pieces. With the aggregate method, the cost is developed for the employer's payroll as a whole and is expressed as a percentage of payroll.

Because there are so many different approaches in determining the annual cost using an actuarial cost method, there is no one single annual cost applicable to a given defined benefit plan for a given group of employees. Different actuarial methods should be developed giving a variety of annual cost approaches as part of the design stage for a defined benefit plan.

Actuarial assumptions. Actuarial cost methods depend on making assumptions about various cost factors, since actual results cannot be known in advance. The annual cost developed under an actuarial cost method depends significantly on these assumptions, and there is considerable flexibility in choosing assumptions. Under the Code, such assumptions must be reasonable, within guidelines developed by the IRS. Actuarial assumptions include

- investment return on the plan fund

- salary scale — an assumption about increases in future salaries; this is particularly significant if the plan uses a final average type of formula

- mortality — the extent to which some benefit will not be paid because of the death of employees before retirement

- annuity purchase rate — this determines the funds needed at retirement to provide annuities in the amount designated by the plan formula

- the annuity purchase rate in turn depends on assumptions about future investment return and postretirement mortality

- turnover — the extent to which employees will terminate employment before retirement and thereby receive limited or no benefit

Deduction limits. The minimum funding standards require *minimum* annual contributions to the plan to maintain the plan fund soundness from an actuarial viewpoint. However, the opposite issue also exists; some employers would like to overfund their plans in order to accelerate tax deductions. This is prevented by a series of deduction limits which disallow deductions above specified levels determining actuarially. Between the minimum funding requirements and the deduction limit, there may be comfortable levels of funding for the plan that can be varied to meet employer cost objectives.

Timing of contributions. Plan contributions must be paid at least quarterly. For a calendar year taxpayer, contributions are due April 15, July 15, October 15 and January 15 of the following year; corresponding dates apply to fiscal year taxpayers. A failure to make timely payments subjects the taxpayer to interest on the missed installment.

For 1992 and thereafter, each quarterly payment must be 25% of the lesser of (a) 90% of the annual minimum funding amount or (b) 100% of the preceding year's minimum funding amount. This requirement is phased in from 1989 through 1991, beginning with only 6.25% (instead of 25%) of the contribution due quarterly in 1989.

Fiduciary rules. There are strict limits on the extent to which an employer can exercise control over the plan fund. The plan trustee can be a corporation or an individual, even a company president or shareholder, but plan trustees are subject to stringent federal fiduciary rules requiring them to manage the fund solely in the interest of plan participants and beneficiaries. Loans to employees are permitted within limits (see Appendix B), but the employer is penalized for borrowing from the plan.

Limitations on Benefits and Contributions

To prevent a qualified plan from being used primarily as a tax shelter for highly compensated employees, there is a limitation on plan benefits or employer contributions.

Defined benefit limits. Under a defined benefit plan, the benefit at age 65 or the social security retirement age, if later, cannot exceed the lesser of

- 100 percent of the participant's compensation averaged over the 3 years of highest compensation, or

- $90,000 as indexed for inflation

The $90,000 limit is to be adjusted after 1987 under a cost-of-living indexing formula. (For 1988, the amount is $94,023.)

The $90,000 limit (as indexed) is adjusted actuarially for retirement ages earlier or later than the social security retirement age. The table below indicates social security retirement ages under current law. For a participant born before

1938 whose social security retirement age is 65, the following is the maximum dollar benefit available (the figures should be indexed upward for 1988 and later years):

Retirement Age	Maximum Dollar Benefit Limit
55	$ 42,400
60	61,419
62	72,000
65	90,000
70	155,843

SOCIAL SECURITY RETIREMENT AGE

Born in	Can Retire with Full Social Security Benefits at
1937 or earlier	65 years
1938	65 years, 2 months
1939	65 years, 4 months
1940	65 years, 6 months
1941	65 years, 8 months
1942	65 years, 10 months
1943 to 1954	66 years
1955	66 years, 2 months
1956	66 years, 4 months
1957	66 years, 6 months
1958	66 years, 8 months
1959	66 years, 10 months
1960 or later	67 years

Defined contribution limits. For a defined contribution plan, the "annual additions" (employer contributions, employee salary reductions, employee contributions, and plan forfeitures reallocated from other participants' accounts) to each participant's account is limited. This annual additions limit cannot exceed the lesser of

- 25 percent of the participant's annual compensation, or

- $30,000

The $30,000 limit is subject to indexing. This limit will be adjusted when the adjusted defined benefit dollar limit reaches $120,000. Thereafter, the defined contribution limit will be set at one-fourth of the defined benefit limit.

Where there is both a defined benefit and a defined contribution plan covering the same employee, the defined benefit and defined contribution limits are adjusted under a combined formula.

$200,000 compensation limit. A further limitation on plan benefits or contributions is that only the first $200,000 of

each employee's annual compensation can be taken into account in the plan's benefit or contribution formula. For example, if an employee earns $300,000 annually and the employer has a 10 percent money purchase plan, the maximum contribution for that employee is $20,000 (10% of $200,000). The $200,000 will be indexed for years after 1988. Any compensation paid to an employee who is a member of the family of a 5-percent owner, or of one of the 10 highly compensated employees paid the greatest compensation during the year, will be treated as paid to the 5-percent owner or highly compensated employee. For this purpose, family members include the spouse of an employee and the employee's lineal descendants who have not attained age 19 by the close of the year.

Top-Heavy Requirements

Plans for closely held businesses often predominantly benefit the business owners. A *top-heavy* plan is one that provides more than 60 percent of its aggregate accrued benefits or account balances to key employees. If a plan is top-heavy for a given year, it must provide more rapid vesting than generally required. The plan can either provide 100 percent vesting after 2 years of service, or 6-year graded vesting as follows:

Years of Service	Vested Percentage
2	20%
3	40
4	60
5	80
6 or more	100

In addition, a top-heavy plan must provide minimum benefits or contributions for nonkey employees.

For defined benefit plans the benefit for each nonkey employee must be at least 2 percent of compensation multiplied by the employee's years of service, up to 20 percent. The average compensation used for this formula is based on the highest 5 years of compensation.

For a defined contribution plan, employer contributions during a top-heavy year must be at least 3 percent of compensation.

Even more stringent rules apply if the plan is deemed to be *super top-heavy* — that is, provides more than 90 percent of its accrued benefits or account balances for key employees.

CONTENTS OF THIS APPENDIX

I. PLANNING RETIREMENT DISTRIBUTIONS

Distributions from qualified pension, profit-sharing, and employer stock plans and Section 403(b) tax deferred annuity plans are subject to numerous special rules and distinctive federal income tax treatment. Advance consideration of all the potential implications of plan distributions is an important part of overall plan design.

Furthermore, in advising clients who are plan participants, a clear understanding of the qualified plan rules is important. A qualified or Section 403(b) plan can allow employees to accumulate substantial retirement benefits. Even a middle-level employee may have an account balance of hundreds of thousands of dollars available at retirement or termination of employment. Careful planning is important in order to make the right choices of payment options and tax treatment for a plan distribution, in order to obtain the right result in financial planning for retirement, and also to avoid adverse tax results or even a tax disaster.

The retirement plan distribution rules are astonishingly complicated. They are a maze full of tax traps that have developed in the law over many years, with Congress and the IRS adding new twists and turns almost every year. This appendix is only a basic outline of these rules, but even this basic outline is quite complex.

One way to thread the maze and give some structure to the subject is to look at the issue from the standpoint of advice to a plan participant who is about to retire. What questions need to be asked and what decisions must be made? Typically, the process might proceed by asking and answering these questions —

1. What kinds of distributions does the plan itself allow? The retiree's adviser should review plan documents, particularly the summary plan description (SPD) to determine what options are available. Sections II and III of this appendix discuss the issues that arise here.

2. Should the distribution be in a lump sum or in a periodic payout? Section V of this Appendix discusses the basic tax tradeoffs.

   — If the plan provides only a lump sum option, are the rollover provisions available to provide periodic or deferred payout? (Section VIII.)

3. If a periodic payment is chosen, what kind of payment schedule is best?

   — Note the requirement of spousal consent for a payment option that "cuts out" the spouse. (Section II.)

   — Are the minimum distribution requirements satisfied? (Section VII.)

   — Is the payment subject to an 10% early distribution penalty? (Section VII.)

   — Is the payment subject to the 15% excess distribution penalty? (Section VII.)

   — How will the payments be taxed? (Section IV A and B.)

4. If a lump sum payment is chosen —

   — Is it eligible for 5-year or 10-year averaging? (Section IV A, C, and D.)

   — If eligible for 10-year averaging, is the election of 10-year averaging beneficial? (Section IV E.)

   — If the participant was in the plan before 1974, is election of capital gain treatment beneficial? (Section IV E.)

— How much tax is payable? (Section IV C, D, and E.)

— Is the distribution subject to the 15% excess distribution penalty tax? (Section VII.)

5. What are the potential future estate tax and excess accumulation tax consequences of the form of distribution chosen? (Sections IV G and VII.)

II. PLAN PROVISIONS — REQUIRED SPOUSAL BENEFITS

All qualified pension plans must provide two forms of survivorship benefits for spouses: (1) the "*qualified preretirement survivor annuity*" and (2) the "*qualified joint and survivor annuity*." Stock bonus plans, profit-sharing plans, and ESOPs generally need not provide these survivorship benefits for the spouse if the participant's nonforfeitable account balance is payable as a death benefit to that spouse.

Preretirement Survivor Annuity

Once a participant in a plan requiring these spousal benefits is vested, the nonparticipant spouse acquires the right to a preretirement survivor annuity, payable to the spouse in the event of the participant's death before retirement. This right is an actual property right created by federal law.

In a defined benefit plan, the survivor annuity payable under this provision of law is the amount that would have been paid under a qualified joint and survivor annuity if the participant had either (1) in the case of the participant dying after attaining the earliest retirement age under the plan, retired on the day before his or her death, or (2) in the case of the participant dying before attaining such age, separated from service on the earlier of the actual time of separation or death and survived to the plan's earliest retirement age, then retired with an immediate joint and survivor annuity. (The calculation of joint and survivor annuity amounts is discussed below.)

If the plan is a defined contribution plan, the qualified preretirement survivor annuity is an annuity for the life of the surviving spouse that is the actuarial equivalent of at least 50 percent of the participant's vested account balance as of the date of death.

The preretirement survivor annuity is an automatic benefit. If no other election is made, a preretirement survivor annuity is provided. If the plan permits, a participant can elect to receive some other form of retirement survivorship benefit, including no preretirement survivorship benefit at all, or survivorship benefits payable to a beneficiary other than the spouse. However, the spouse must understand the rights given up and must consent in writing to the participant's choice of another form of benefit.

The right to make an election of a benefit other than the preretirement survivor annuity must be communicated to all participants with a vested benefit who have attained age 32 or older. The participant can elect to receive some other benefit than the preretirement survivor annuity at any time after age 35. The participant can also change this election at any time before retirement.

Consideration of "electing" out of the preretirement survivorship benefit becomes more important as a participant nears retirement age. Electing out of the preretirement survivorship benefit will generally increase the participant's benefit after retirement, unless the plan specifically subsidizes the retirement benefit. Thus, a participant may want to elect out of the benefit to increase the size of the monthly check received during the postretirement period. Alternatively, the participant may wish to provide a preretirement survivorship benefit for a beneficiary other than the surviving spouse.

Such elections must be considered very carefully, particularly by the nonparticipant spouse. Generally a nonparticipant spouse would (and should) not agree to waive this benefit unless the couple's overall retirement planning provided some compensating benefit to the spouse. The existence and amount of any such compensating benefit to the spouse should be documented in connection with the spouse's benefit waiver.

Any benefit waiver is potentially subject to contest by the deprived spouse at some later time. For this reason, full disclosure — in writing — to the nonparticipant spouse must be made, and that spouse should be advised to obtain an independent legal (and possibly also financial) adviser in connection with the waiver. Any consent of the nonparticipant spouse to an optional benefit form selected by the participant should be notarized. For large benefits, this advice to the spouse is an extremely important consideration.

Qualified Joint and Survivor Annuity

A qualified joint and survivor annuity is a postretirement death benefit for the plan participant's spouse. If the plan is subject to the requirement, it must automatically provide, as a retirement benefit, an annuity for the life of the participant with a survivor annuity for the life of the participant's spouse. The survivor annuity must be (1) not less than 50 percent of nor (2) greater than 100 percent of, the annuity payable during the joint lives of the participant and spouse. For example, if $1,000 per month is payable during the joint lives, the annuity to the surviving spouse can be any specified amount from $500 per month to $1,000 per month. The spouse's annuity must be continued even if the spouse remarries.

As with the preretirement survivor annuity, a participant may elect to receive another form of benefit if the plan permits. However, as with a qualified preretirement survivor annuity, the spouse must consent in writing to the election. An election to waive the joint and survivor form must be made during the 90 day period ending on the "annuity starting date" — the date on which benefit payments should have begun to the participant, not necessarily the actual date of payment. The waiver can be revoked — that is, the participant can change the election during the 90 day period. Administrators of affected plans must provide participants with a notice of the election period and an explanation of the consequences of the election within a reasonable period before the annuity starting date.

Since the joint and survivor annuity must be the actuarial equivalent of other forms of benefit, the participant may wish to increase the monthly pension by waiving the joint and survivor annuity and receiving a straight life annuity or some other form of benefit. Because of the spouse's right to the benefit, as discussed earlier, it is extremely important that spouses are made aware of what they are giving up if they consent to some other benefit form. Communication of the consequences of waiver must be made in writing, the spouse should be advised by independent counsel, and any waiver should be notarized.

III. PLAN PROVISIONS — OTHER BENEFIT FORMS

A qualified plan can offer a wide range of distribution options. Participants benefit from having the widest possible range of options, because this increases their flexibility in personal retirement planning. However, a wide range of options increases administrative costs. Also, the IRS makes it difficult to withdraw a benefit option once it has been established. Consequently, most employers provide only a relatively limited "menu" of benefit forms for participants to choose from.

Defined Benefit Plan Distribution Provisions

Defined benefit plans must provide a married participant with a *joint and survivor annuity* as the automatic form of benefit, as described earlier. For an unmarried participant, the plan's automatic form of benefit is usually a *life annuity* — typically monthly payments to the participant for life, with no further payments after the participant's death.

Many plans allow participants to elect to receive some other form of benefit from a list of options in the plan. However, to elect any option that eliminates the benefit for a married participant's spouse, the spouse must consent on a notarized written form to waive the spousal right to the joint and survivor annuity. As discussed earlier, this is not just a legal formality; in consenting to another form of benefit, the spouse gives up important and often sizable property rights in the participant's qualified plan that are guaranteed under federal law.

Typically plans offer, as an option to the joint or single life annuity, a *period-certain* annuity. A period-certain annuity provides payments for a specified period of time — usually 10 to 20 years — even if the participant, or the participant and spouse, both die before the end of that period. Thus, the period-certain annuity makes it certain that periodic (usually monthly) benefits will continue for the participant's heirs

even if the participant and spouse die early. Because of this guarantee feature, the annual or monthly payments under a period-certain option are less than they would be under an option where payments end at death (see table).

MONTHLY PAYMENTS — VARIOUS ANNUITY FORMS

Assumptions: plan participant aged 65, spouse aged 62 lump sum equivalent at age 65 of $200,000

Form of annuity	Monthly benefit
Life	$1,818
Life — 10 years certain	1,710
Life — 20 years certain	1,560
Joint and survivor — 50 percent	1,696
Joint and survivor — 66²/₃ percent	1,626
Joint and survivor — 100 percent	1,504

As the above comparison indicates, a period-certain option should be chosen if the participant wants to make sure that his heirs are provided for in case both he and his spouse die shortly after retirement. The reduction in monthly income is relatively small, since it is based on the average life expectancy of all annuitants, and assumes that the average annuitant (male or female) lives about 20 years after attaining age 65. Thus, the participant and spouse should consider a period-certain option if they are both in poor health, or if they want to make sure that children (or other heirs) with large financial needs are provided for in the event of their deaths. On the other hand, if the participant wants the largest possible monthly income from the plan, a life annuity should be chosen.

Defined benefit plans may allow a participant to choose a joint annuity with a beneficiary other than a spouse — for example, an annuity for the life of a participant with payments continuing after the parent-participant's death to a son or daughter. Proposed tax regulations limit the amount of annuity payable to a much younger beneficiary in order to ensure that the participant personally receives (and therefore is taxed on) at least a minimum portion of the total value of the plan benefit and that plan payments are not unduly deferred beyond the participant's death. (See the minimum distribution rules discussed below in Section VII.) Thus, a much younger beneficiary (except for a spouse) generally would not be allowed to receive a 100 percent survivor annuity benefit.

Defined Contribution Plan Distribution Provisions

Defined contribution plans include such plans as profit-sharing, 401(k), and money purchase plans. Section 403(b) tax-deferred annuity plans also have distribution provisions similar to defined contribution plans. Some defined contribution plans provide annuity benefits like those in defined benefit plans. In fact, money purchase plans, target benefit plans and Section 403(b) tax deferred annuity plans subject to ERISA must meet the preretirement and joint and survivor annuity rules discussed above. Other defined contribution plans do not have to meet these rules if (1) there is no annuity option and (2) the plan participant's account balance is payable to the participant's spouse in the event of the participant's death. Avoiding the required joint and survivor provisions simplifies plan administration and therefore reduces the plan's cost.

Annuity benefits are computed by converting the participant's account balance in the defined contribution plan into an equivalent annuity. The TIAA/CREF plan for college teachers, for example, is a defined contribution plan that primarily offers annuity options. In some plans the participant can elect to have his account balance used to purchase an annuity from an insurance company. The same considerations in choosing annuity options then apply as have already been discussed. If the plan offers annuity options, the required joint and survivor provisions apply, as discussed earlier.

Defined contribution plans often provide a lump sum benefit at retirement or termination of employment. Defined contribution plans often also allow the option of taking out non-annuity distributions over the retirement years. That is, the participant simply takes out money as it is needed, subject to the minimum distribution requirements discussed later. Such distribution provisions provide much flexibility in planning.

IV. TAX IMPACT

For many plan participants retirement income adequacy is more important than minimizing taxes to the last dollar. Nevertheless, taxes on both the federal and state levels must never be ignored since they reduce the participant's "bottom line" financial security. The greater the tax on the distribution, the less financial security the participant has.

A qualified plan distribution may be subject to federal, state, and local taxes, in whole or in part. This section will focus only on the federal tax treatment. The federal tax treatment is generally the most significant because federal tax rates are usually higher than state and local rates. Also, many state and local income tax laws provide a full or partial exemption or specially favorable tax treatment for distributions from qualified retirement plans. Planners should check with tax services such as the National Underwriter's Advanced Sales Reference Service (ASRS) to better understand the impact of state taxes on plan distributions.

Nontaxable and Taxable Amounts

Qualified plans often contain after-tax employee money — that is, contributions that have already been taxed. These amounts can be received by the employee free of Federal income taxes, although the order in which they are recovered for tax purposes depends on the kind of distribution.

The first step in determining the tax on any distribution, then, is to determine the participant's cost basis in the plan benefit.

The participant's cost basis can include:

- the total after-tax contributions made by the employee to a contributory plan

- the total cost of life insurance actually reported as taxable income on federal income tax returns by the participant (the P.S. 58 costs) if the plan distribution is received under the same contract that provides the life insurance protection. (If the plan trustee cashes in the life insurance contract before distribution, this cost basis amount is not available. For a person who is now or was self-employed, no P.S. 58 costs are available.)

- any employer contributions previously taxed to the employee — for example, where a nonqualified plan later becomes qualified

- certain employer contributions attributable to foreign services performed before 1963

- amounts paid by the employee in repayment of loans that were treated as distributions.

In-service (Partial) Distributions. If a participant takes out a partial plan distribution before termination of employment (as is provided for in many savings or thrift plans), the distribution is deemed to include both nontaxable and taxable amounts; the nontaxable amount will be in proportion to the ratio of total after-tax contributions (i.e., the employee's cost basis) to the plan account balance (similar to the computation of the annuity exclusion ratio discussed below). Expressed as a formula it looks like this:

$$\text{nontaxable amount} = \text{distribution} \times \frac{\text{total after tax contributions}}{\text{total account balance}}$$

However, there is a "grandfather" rule for pre-1987 after-tax contributions to the plan. If certain previously existing plans include contributions made before 1987, it is possible to withdraw after-tax money first. That is, if a distribution from the plan is made (at any time, even after 1987) that is *less* than the total amount of pre-1987 after-tax contributions, the entire distribution is received tax free. Once a participant's pre-1987 amount (if any) has been used up, the regular rule applies.

A taxable in-service distribution may also be subject to the early distribution penalty discussed later.

Total Distributions. If the participant begins annuity payments based on the entire account balance, the nontaxable amount will be in proportion to the ratio of total after-tax contributions in the plan to the total annuity payments expected to be received (see below). If the participant withdraws his or her entire account balance, the distribution may be eligible for the lump sum distribution treatment discussed below. Total distributions may also be subject to the early distribution penalty discussed below.

Taxation of Annuity Payments

The annuity rules of Code section 72 apply to periodic plan distributions made over more than one taxable year of the employee in a systematic liquidation of the participant's benefit. Amounts distributed are taxable in the year received, except for a proportionate recovery of the cost basis. The cost basis is recovered as part of each benefit payment through the calculation of an *exclusion ratio* that is applied to each payment to determine the nontaxable amount.

The exclusion ratio is

$$\frac{\text{investment in the contract}}{\text{expected return}}$$

Basically, the "investment in the contract" is the participant's cost basis. In the case of a life annuity, the "expected return" is determined by multiplying the total annual payment by the participant's life expectancy. Life expectancies are determined under tables found in Treasury Regulations. One of these tables, Figure B-1 is a unisex table of life expectancies which can be used for single life annuities.

Example: Fred Retiree retires at age 65 with a pension of $500 per month for his life. Fred's cost basis in the plan is $20,000. Fred's exclusion ratio will be

$$\frac{\$\ 20,000}{\$120,000} = \frac{1}{6}$$

The numerator ($20,000) is Fred's cost basis; the denominator ($120,000) is Fred's annual pension of $6,000 multiplied by his life expectancy of 20 years from Table V (Figure B.1). Therefore, $1/6$ of each payment Fred receives will be nontaxable. The remaining $5/6$ of each payment is taxable as ordinary income.

Once the exclusion ratio is determined, it will continue to apply until the cost basis is fully recovered. Payments received subsequently are taxable in full. If the participant dies before the cost basis is fully recovered, the participant's estate is allowed an income tax deduction for the unrecovered basis.

Other tables are used for joint life expectancies and special computations may be necessary to determine expected return in some situations, e.g., where there is a period-certain guarantee.

IRS Notice 88-118 provides a simplified "safe harbor" method of computing the amount of each payment excluded from tax. The safe harbor applies only to payments from a qualified plan or Section 403(b) tax-deferred annuity plan which are to be paid for the life of the employee or the joint lives of the employee and beneficiary. Under this method, the employee's investment in the contract is divided by the num-

ber of expected monthly payments set out in the IRS table below. The number of payments is based on the employee's age at the annuity starting date and the same table is used for both single life and joint and survivor annuity payments. The resulting dollar amount is excluded from each payment until the cost basis is fully recovered.

Age	# of payments
55 and under	300
56-60	260
61-65	240
66-70	170
71 and over	120

Lump Sum Distributions

A lump sum distribution may be desirable for retirement planning purposes, but the participant may not want a lump sum if it is taxed in high tax brackets. In determining the tax on a lump sum distribution, the first step is to calculate the taxable amount of the distribution. The taxable amount consists of (a) the total value of the distribution less (b) after-tax contributions and other items constituting the employee's cost basis (see "Nontaxable and Taxable Amounts," above). If employer securities are included in the distribution, the net unrealized appreciation of the stock is generally subtracted from the value of a lump sum distribution (see Chapter 9).

For qualified plans only (total distributions from IRAs, SEPs, or TDA (Section 403(b)) plans are not technically "lump sum distributions") there is a limited relief from this result: a special one-time 5-year averaging tax computation that a participant may elect if (a) the lump sum distribution is received after age $59^{1}/_{2}$ *and* (b) meets the following 4 requirements:

- it is made in one taxable year of the recipient,

- it represents the entire amount of the employee's benefit in the plan,

- it is payable on account of the participant's death, attainment of age $59^{1}/_{2}$, separation from service (nonself-employed person) or disability (self-employed person only), and

- the employee participated in the plan for at least 5 taxable years prior to the tax year of distribution (a death benefit is exempted from this requirement)

In determining whether the distribution is a "total" distribution, all pension plans maintained by the same employer are treated as a single plan, all profit-sharing plans are treated as a single plan, and all stock bonus plans are treated as one plan.

If the distribution meets all of these qualifications, the taxable amount is eligible for 5-year averaging. The participant must elect this treatment; it is not automatic. Only one elec-

Figure B.1

Table V — Ordinary Life Annuities
One Life — Expected Return Multiples
(from Reg. Sec. 1.72-9)

Age	Multiple	Age	Multiple	Age	Multiple
5	76.6	42	40.6	79	10.0
6	75.6	43	39.6	80	9.5
7	74.7	44	38.7	81	8.9
8	73.7	45	37.7	82	8.4
9	72.7	46	36.8	83	7.9
10	71.7	47	35.9	84	7.4
11	70.7	48	34.9	85	6.9
12	69.7	49	34.0	86	6.5
13	68.8	50	33.1	87	6.1
14	67.8	51	32.2	88	5.7
15	66.8	52	31.3	89	5.3
16	65.8	53	30.4	90	5.0
17	64.8	54	29.5	91	4.7
18	63.9	55	28.6	92	4.4
19	62.9	56	27.7	93	4.1
20	61.9	57	26.8	94	3.9
21	60.9	58	25.9	95	3.7
22	59.9	59	25.0	96	3.4
23	59.0	60	24.2	97	3.2
24	58.0	61	23.3	98	3.0
25	57.0	62	22.5	99	2.8
26	56.0	63	21.6	100	2.7
27	55.1	64	20.8	101	2.5
28	54.1	65	20.0	102	2.3
29	53.1	66	19.2	103	2.1
30	52.2	67	18.4	104	1.9
31	51.2	68	17.6	105	1.8
32	50.2	69	16.8	106	1.6
33	49.3	70	16.0	107	1.4
34	48.3	71	15.3	108	1.3
35	47.3	72	14.6	109	1.1
36	46.4	73	13.9	110	1.0
37	45.4	74	13.2	111	.9
38	44.4	75	12.5	112	.8
39	43.5	76	11.9	113	.7
40	42.5	77	11.2	114	.6
41	41.5	78	10.6	115	.5

tion is permitted and the election is available only if the distribution is received on or after the employee attained age 59½.

Five-year averaging is not available to a recipient of a death benefit unless the deceased plan participant had attained age 59½. (If the recipient is a spouse, the distribution can be rolled over to an IRA — see "Rollovers," below.)

Five-year averaging is available to a spouse or former spouse of a participant who receives a total distribution of a plan interest under a qualified domestic relations order (QDRO) pursuant to a divorce or separation, if a total distribution would be eligible for five-year averaging if paid to the participant.

Amounts accumulated prior to 1974 are eligible for capital gain treatment at the participant's election. If the participant was in the plan before 1974, the distribution is separated into pre-1974 and post-1973 portions on the basis of months of plan participation before and after January 1, 1974. This capital gain treatment is phased out through 1991 as follows:

Tools and Techniques

Year	Percent of Pre-1974 Portion Eligible for 20 Percent Rate
1987	100%
1988	95
1989	75
1990	50
1991	25

This capital gain treatment is not mandatory; a pre-1974 plan participant can elect to simply treat the entire distribution under the 5-year averaging provision. And, any portion of the distribution not eligible for capital gain treatment is eligible for 5-year averaging.

For participants who had attained age 50 by January 1, 1986, some of the more liberal rules of prior law for averaging and capital gains treatment are preserved (see "Grandfather Rules," below).

Five-year averaging works as follows. First, a "minimum distribution allowance" is subtracted from the taxable amount. The minimum distribution allowance is the *lesser* of $10,000 or one-half of the total taxable amount *reduced by* 20 percent of the total taxable amount in excess of $20,000. In other words, if the taxable amount is $70,000 or more the minimum distribution allowance disappears. The remaining taxable amount after the minimum distribution allowance is divided by 5 and a separate tax is determined on this portion. The separate tax is based on the single taxpayer rate without any deductions or exclusions, but taking into account the phase-out of the 15% bracket amount. The tax determined in this manner is multiplied by 5.

Example: (Using 1988 tax rates)

1.	Total taxable amount	$ 40,000
2.	Minimum distribution allowance $10,000 - [20% × ($40,000 - $20,000)]	-6,000
3.	Balance	34,000
4.	1/5 of the balance	6,800
5.	Tax on line 4	1,020
6.	Total tax	$ 5,100

The taxpayer elects and reports this calculation on Form 4972 reproduced at the end of this Appendix (or Form 5544 in the case of multiple recipients other than trusts), which is filed with the tax return for the year. Form 4972 includes detailed instructions and a worksheet for making the calculation.

The plan administrator of a plan making a distribution must report it on Form 1099-R (for a total distribution) or Form W-2P (for a partial distribution). If the participant does not want tax withheld from the distribution, he or she must complete Form W-4P and file it with the employer. Copies of these forms are also included at the end of this Appendix.

"Grandfather" Rules

The tax break for lump sum distributions was 10-year averaging instead of 5-year averaging from 1974 through 1986. For an individual who attained age 50 before January 1, 1986, the 10-year averaging provision is "grandfathered" to a certain extent and can be elected even if the participant is not age 59 1/2 or older at the time of the distribution. Such an individual who receives a distribution in 1987 or later may elect to use 10-year averaging using the 1986 tax rates instead of 5-year averaging with current rates and taking into account the prior law zero bracket amount. This grandfathering provision will normally be elected if it produces a lower tax than using 5-year averaging.

A further grandfather rule retains the capital gain rate of 20% for the capital gain portion of distributions to participants who attained age 50 before January 1, 1986 and elect capital gain treatment. The phase-out of capital gain treatment does not apply to such a participant. The 20% rate applies even if the distribution occurs after 1987 or even after 1991. As under the regular rule, capital gain treatment is not mandatory.

When to Elect 10-year Averaging or Capital Gain

10-year Averaging. A plan participant is eligible to elect the 10-year averaging provision instead of 5-year averaging if he or she attained age 50 before January 1, 1986 (i.e., was born on or before January 1, 1936).

If the tax on distributions of various amounts is computed under both 5-year and 10-year averaging, assuming that 1988 tax rates continue in effect, 10-year averaging provides the lowest tax as long as the adjusted total taxable amount is less than or equal to $473,700. Above $473,700 of taxable income, the 5-year averaging is preferable. (Actually, at this level — in fact for any distribution over $447,800 — 5-year averaging is the same as a flat 28 percent tax on the entire amount, so it has no real effect.) Thus, clients who are eligible for 10-year averaging and have distributions of $473,700 or less will benefit from 10-year averaging.

It should also be noted that for a participant who attained age 50 before January 1, 1986, not only the 10-year averaging calculation but the other favorable lump sum rules of earlier law were grandfathered. Thus, 10-year averaging (but not 5-year averaging) can be elected for a distribution on separation from service prior to age 59 1/2, if the participant attained age 50 before January 1, 1986. In cases where these favorable provisions can be used, electing 10-year averaging will almost always be advantageous.

Capital Gains. As mentioned earlier, a plan participant who attained age 50 before January 1, 1986 (was born on or before January 1, 1936) can elect to treat pre-1974 plan accruals as long term capital gain (under pre-1987 law). Any amount taxed as capital gain is taxed at a rate no greater than 20 percent. Therefore, as a general rule, an eligible participant will save taxes by electing the capital gain treatment whenever the adjusted total taxable amount of a lump sum distribution, after subtracting the capital gain portion, is taxed at an effective rate of more than 20 percent.

197

For example, suppose a participant receives a taxable distribution of $160,000, of which $20,000 is capital gain. The participant is eligible to elect 10-year averaging. Under the applicable tax computation, any amount over $137,100 is taxed at a rate of 23 percent or higher. Thus, the participant should elect capital gain treatment. With capital gain treatment, the last $20,000 of the distribution — the capital gain amount — will be taxed at a rate of only 20 percent, instead of 23 percent or more.

A plan participant who is eligible for capital gain with phaseout — a participant who had not attained age 50 by January 1, 1986, but was in the plan before 1974 — is much less likely to benefit by electing capital gain. Unless the differential in rates between capital gain and ordinary income is reintroduced before 1990, there won't be much advantage to this election.

Taxation of Death Benefits

In general, the same income tax treatment applies to death benefits paid to beneficiaries as to lifetime benefits payable to participants. The special lump sum provision can be used by the beneficiary. However, 5-year averaging is available only if the distribution is received on or after the decedent employee attained age 59½. If the employee had attained age 50 before January 1, 1986, the beneficiary may elect 10-year averaging even if the participant was not 59½ or older at his or her death. For an annuity distribution, the beneficiary uses the same annuity rules described earlier.

There are also some additional income tax benefits available.

First, up to $5,000 of the death benefit may be excludable as an employer-paid death benefit. If the benefit is a lump sum distribution, the full exclusion is available. If the benefit is in the form of periodic payments, the $5,000 exclusion is available only to the extent the employee's benefit was nonforfeitable prior to the employee's death.

Second, if the death benefit is payable under a life insurance contract held by the qualified plan, the pure insurance amount of the death benefit is excludable from income taxation. The pure insurance amount is the difference between the policy's face amount and its cash value at the date of death.

Example: Ellen Employee, aged 62, dies in 1989 before retirement. Her beneficiary receives a lump sum death benefit of $100,000 from the plan. The $100,000 is the proceeds of a cash value life insurance contract; the contract's cash value at Ellen's death was $60,000. Ellen reported a total of $10,000 of P.S. 58 insurance costs for this contract on her income tax returns during her lifetime. The taxable amount of the $100,000 distribution to the beneficiary is $100,000 less the following items:

- the pure insurance amount of $40,000 ($100,000 less the cash value of $60,000),

- the $5,000 employee death benefit exclusion, and

- Ellen's cost basis of $10,000 of P.S. 58 costs.

The taxable amount of this benefit is therefore $45,000. The beneficiary is eligible for 5-year (or 10-year) averaging on this taxable amount, or capital gain treatment for at least a portion of any pre-1974 amounts.

A third factor in the treatment of death benefits involves rollovers to an IRA. A spouse can rollover the death benefit received from a participant to the spouse's IRA. However, a nonspouse beneficiary is not allowed to rollover the benefit.

Federal Estate Tax

The entire value of a qualified plan death benefit is subject to inclusion in the decedent's gross estate for federal estate tax purposes. However, only high-income plan participants will actually be subject to estate tax. First, there is a high minimum tax credit applicable to the estate tax which essentially eliminates estate taxes for gross estates less than $600,000. In addition, the unlimited marital deduction for federal estate tax purposes eliminates federal estate tax on property transferred at death to a spouse in a qualifying manner.

In some cases, however, avoiding federal estate tax can be significant. For example, the estate may be relatively large and the participant may be single or divorced or for whatever reason unwilling to pay the death benefit to the spouse. Therefore, the marital deduction would not be available. Also, even when the death benefit is payable to a spouse, federal estate tax is merely delayed and is not really avoided; a spouse is often about the same age as the decedent, and thus within a few years much of the property transferred to the spouse is potentially subject to federal estate tax at the surviving spouse's death.

Some authorities believe it is possible to design a qualified plan so that death benefits can be excluded from the participant's estate. Here is the rationale: The federal estate tax law provides that all of a decedent's property is includable in the estate unless there is a specific exclusionary provision. Qualified plan death benefits are not subject to any specific exclusion, so they are generally includable. There is, however, a specific provision in the estate tax law for life insurance — Section 2042. Life insurance proceeds are includable in a decedent's estate only if the decedent had "incidents of ownership" (some valuable property right) in the insurance policies (or if proceeds are payable to the decedent's estate).

An incident of ownership includes the right to designate the beneficiary as well as similar rights under the policy. Some planners have attempted to design qualified plan death benefits using life insurance policies in which the decedent has no incidents of ownership. Some methods for doing this include the use of separate trusts or subtrusts under the plan for holding insurance policies, together with irrevocable beneficiary designations.

At this point the law is not entirely clear on whether these provisions will in fact avoid incidents of ownership. A conservative view is that they will not. However, if the amount is large enough so that the participant is willing to incur the costs of drafting the subtrust arrangement and the potential court costs if the arrangement is challenged by the IRS, there may be little to lose in the use of this technique, since estate inclusion is certain without it.

V. LUMP-SUM VS. DEFERRED PAYMENTS — THE TRADEOFFS

Often plan participants have a choice between a single lump-sum plan distribution and a series of deferred payments. This requires a choice between competing advantages.

Advantages of a lump-sum distribution include

- 5-year (or 10-year) averaging tax treatment, if the distribution is eligible

- freedom to invest plan proceeds at the participant's — not the plan administrator's — discretion

The contrasting advantages of a deferred payout are

- deferral of taxes until money is actually distributed

- continued tax shelter of income on the plan account while money remains in the plan

- security of retirement income

There is not one single favored alternative but rather competing advantages. In a given situation, a lump sum distribution may save more taxes, and in others the deferred payment may be a better tax choice. And, taxes are not the only factor to consider.

A full analysis for an individual may be complex, considering all the factors involved. A complete analysis should certainly be done where very large sums are involved. In other cases, it may be adequate to make a good estimate of the result.

The factors involved in determining which alternative to choose include

- the age of the participant (or the participant and beneficiary, if a survivorship annuity is involved). This affects the expected number of years of payout.

- the health of the participant (and beneficiary), which also affects the expected number of payout years.

- the expected return on investment.

- the current and future expected tax rates for the participant. This involves estimating not only what the rates will be, but also what tax bracket the participant will be in — i.e., the amount of total taxable income the participant will have.

- the nontax aspects — the amounts of income needed and when it will be needed.

- the total amount of the benefit; if the amount is large enough, the effect of the 15% excess distribution/accumulation penalty tax must be taken into account (see below).

In a sense, it is impossible to make an exact determination of this issue; for example, we can never know exactly what future tax rates will be or the amount of investment earnings actually received in the future. However, by making reasonable assumptions in a given case, some conclusions can usually be drawn.

The following table shows the decision "break point" for certain assumptions. The table takes into account only tax and investment factors; it does not consider issues such as the need for money at a given time. The three right-hand columns indicate the break points — if the current value of the retirement benefit as a lump sum, before taxes, is less than this amount, lump sum tax treatment saves money as compared with periodic payments.

LUMP SUM VS. INSTALLMENT PAYMENT BREAK POINTS*

Taxable Income Before Installment Payout	Assumed Rate of Return		
	6%	8%	10%
	Retirement Benefit Break Points + (0% Capital-Gains Proportion)		
0	28	23	0
10	28	23	0
20	28	23	0
30	147	71	48
40	147	71	48
50	147	71	48
60	147	71	48
70	219	136	51
80	238	158	94
90	238	158	94
100	238	158	94
110	238	158	94
120	238	158	94
130	238	158	94
140	238	158	94
150	238	158	94
160	198	143	94
170	160	97	59
180 or more	147	71	48

* $000 omitted.

Source: This chart was prepared by Robert J. Doyle, Jr., Associate Professor of Finance at The American College, Bryn Mawr, PA, for the College's course HS 326, Pensions and Retirement Planning.

Assumptions:

1. Participant and spouse are both aged 65.

Tools and Techniques

2. Participant and spouse are in normal health.

3. Any lump sum is taxed under 10-year averaging with 1986 rates (no pre-1974 amounts eligible for capital gains).

4. The periodic payment option is a level annuity over the joint life expectancy of the participant and spouse (25 years).

5. Tax rates are those for 1988 and are assumed to continue in effect indefinitely.

6. No exposure to the 15% excess distribution accumulation tax.

Example: Retiree Sy expects a taxable income of $40,000 during retirement, not counting retirement benefits from his qualified plan. He expects a before-tax return of 8% on invested assets. Other assumptions are as indicated above. Sy should elect lump sum distribution treatment for his retirement plan benefit if the distribution is valued at less than $71,000. For amounts larger than this, periodic payout will give a better result.

Additional charts like that above can be created (and have been — see the source indicated for the chart above) for different assumptions, in order to provide some broader guidance in making this decision for differing client groups. And, a series of individual calculations for a given client can always be made if the amount involved justifies the cost.

Some general conclusions from calculation charts made on the basis of different assumptions are:

- if pre-1974 plan participation exists — with the possibility of capital gain treatment — the break points are higher than indicated in the above table. That is, lump sum treatment is favorable up to a higher benefit amount.

- if the participant or spouse are older than 65, break points are higher (lump sum treatment is favorable up to a larger amount).

- if the participant and spouse are in poor health (shorter than normal life expectancy), break points are higher.

- with a single life annuity payout, or survivor annuity less than 100 percent, break points are higher.

- if payout is deferred until age 70½, break points are lower (i.e., the lump sum option is favorable only for smaller distributions).

VI. LOANS

Because of the 10% penalty tax on "early" distributions from qualified plans (see below), a plan provision allowing loans to employees may be attractive. This allows employees access to plan funds without extra tax cost. However, a loan provision increases administrative costs for the plan and may deplete plan funds available for pooled investments.

For participants to borrow from a plan, the plan must specifically permit such loans. Any type of qualified plan or Section 403(b) annuity plan may permit loans. Loan provisions are most common in defined contribution plans, particularly profit-sharing plans. There are considerable administrative difficulties connected with loans from defined benefit plans because of the actuarial approach to plan funding. Loans from IRAs and SEPs are not permitted.

Loans from a qualified plan to the following types of employee are prohibited transactions subject to penalties:

- an owner-employee — a proprietor or more-than-10 percent partner in an unincorporated business

- an S corporation employee who is a more-than-5 percent shareholder in the corporation.

Under the Tax Reform Act of 1986, however, a plan may make a loan to such employees if the Secretary of Labor grants an administrative exemption from prohibited transaction treatment for such loans.

Loans to regular employees are prohibited transactions subject to penalties unless such loans (1) are exempted from the prohibited transaction rules by an administrative exemption or (2) meet the requirements set out in Code section 72(p).

Section 72(p) provides that aggregate loans from qualified plans to any individual plan participant cannot exceed the *lesser* of

- $50,000 reduced by the excess of the highest outstanding loan balance during the preceding one-year period over the outstanding balance on the date the loan is made, or

- one-half the present value of the participant's vested account balance (or accrued benefit, in the case of a defined benefit plan).

A loan of up to $10,000 can be made, even if this is more than one-half the participant's vested benefit. For example, a participant having a vested account balance of $17,000 could borrow up to $10,000.

Loans must be repayable by their terms within 5 years, except for loans used to acquire a principal residence of the participant. Loans must be made available to participants on a nondiscriminatory basis. They must be adequately secured and bear a reasonable rate of interest. Security for the loan is usually the participant's plan account balance, but a participant can and may want to offer other security instead.

Interest on a plan loan in most cases will be consumer interest that is not deductible by the employee as an itemized deduction unless the loan is secured by a home mortgage.

Even if the loan is secured by a home mortgage, however, interest deductions are specifically prohibited in two situations: (1) if the loan is to a key employee as defined in the Code's rules for top-heavy plans (Section 416), or (2) if the loan is secured by a Section 401(k) or Section 403(b) plan account based on salary reductions.

VII. PENALTY TAXES

In addition to the complicated regular tax rules, distributions must be planned so that recipients avoid — or at least are not surprised by — four types of tax penalties. These are summarized as follows.

Early Distribution Penalty

This is in effect a penalty for making distributions "too soon." Early distributions from qualified plans, 403(b) tax deferred annuity plans, IRAs and SEPs are subject to a penalty of 10% of the taxable portion of the distribution.

The penalty does *not* apply to distributions

- made on or after attainment of age 59½,

- made to the plan participant's beneficiary or estate on or after the participant's death,

- attributable to the participant's disability,

- that are part of a series of substantially equal periodic payments made at least annually over the life or life expectancy of the participant, or the participant and a designated beneficiary (separation from the employer's service is required, except for IRAs),

- made after separation from service after attainment of age 55 (not applicable to IRAs),

- made to a former spouse, child or other dependent of the participant under a qualified domestic relations order,

- certain tax credit ESOP dividend payments, or

- distributions to the extent of medical expenses deductible for the year under Code section 213, whether or not actually deducted (not applicable to IRAs).

In the case of the periodic payment exception, if the series of payments is changed before the participant reaches age 59½ or, if after age 59½, within 5 years of the date of the first payment, the tax which would have been imposed, but for the periodic exception, is imposed with interest in the year the change occurs.

Minimum Distribution Requirements and Penalty

Distributions from qualified plans, 403(b) tax deferred annuity plans, IRAs, SEPs, and Section 457 governmental deferred compensation plans must generally begin by April 1 of the calendar year after the participant attains age 70½.

- There is an annual *minimum* distribution required; if the distribution is less than the minimum amount required there is a penalty of 50 percent of the amount not distributed that should have been.

- The minimum initial annual distribution is determined by dividing the participant's account balance (as of the last plan valuation date prior to the year of attaining age 70½) by the participant's life expectancy (or the participant and designated beneficiary's joint life expectancy from IRS regulations). Payments can be stretched out by re-calculating life expectancy annually. (Other minimum limits may also apply.)

- If the beneficiary is not a spouse, the minimum distribution may be further increased (using a factor — the "incidental benefit factor" — in proposed IRS regulations) to insure that the participant's share of the benefit is at least a minimum amount of the expected total. This factor will come into effect where the beneficiary is considerably younger than the participant.

These rules are fully in effect for plan years beginning after 1988. For persons who reach age 70½ before then, certain transition rules apply.

Excess Distribution Penalty

In addition to regular income tax, there is a penalty tax of 15 percent on annual distributions exceeding the greater of (a) $112,500 as indexed for inflation ($117,529 in 1988), or (b) $150,000.

- This penalty applies to the total (aggregate) of all distributions to the individual in a year from all qualified plans, 403(b) tax deferred annuities, IRAs and SEPs.

- If the recipient elects lump sum treatment on the distribution, the limit is increased to five times the above limit, i.e., $562,500 as indexed ($587,645 in 1988) or $750,000.

- There are potentially favorable "grandfather" provisions for participants whose accrued plan benefit on August 1, 1986 exceeded $562,500. To take advantage of these provisions, an election must have been made on the participant's 1987 or 1988 tax return, before the due date of the return, including extensions.

Excess Accumulation Penalty

At a participant's death, remaining balances in qualified plans, 403(b) tax deferred annuities, IRAs and SEPs are aggregated; there is a 15 percent penalty on any excess of this total over the present value (at date of death) of an annuity of $150,000 per year over the participant's life expectancy at death. (The $150,000 will be replaced by the excess distribution amount of $112,500 when that amount, as indexed, is more than $150,000.)

For individuals who had accrued plan benefits or account balances on August 1, 1986, a potentially favorable "grandfather" rule may be available if an election was made on their tax return for 1988 or earlier.

This 15 percent tax penalty is *in addition* to any regular federal estate tax and cannot be reduced by the marital deduction, charitable deduction, or the estate tax unified credit (although the tax is deductible from the gross estate). To the extent that the excise tax reduces estate taxes, the effective rate of the excise tax is reduced. For example, if the 15 percent excise tax reduces a portion of the estate otherwise taxable at 50%, the effective rate of the excise tax is only 7.5% (15% × 50%).

If the participant's surviving spouse is the sole beneficiary (or beneficiary of all but a minimal amount) of the plan benefit, the spouse can elect to have the excise tax on excess accumulations not apply at the participant spouse's death and, instead, to treat the plan benefit as his or her own for purposes of the application of the excess distribution and excess accumulation tax.

VIII. RETIREMENT PLAN ROLLOVERS

Tax-free "rollovers" of distributions from qualified plans, IRAs and SEPs, and Section 403(b) tax deferred annuity plans are specifically allowed by the Internal Revenue Code. With a rollover, a distribution of money or property from a retirement plan can be transferred or "rolled over" to a special type of IRA — the rollover IRA. Alternatively, in some cases the distribution can be rolled over to another plan of the same type — for example, from a qualified plan of one employer to another employer's qualified plan.

If the rollover is made within 60 days of receipt of the distribution and follows statutory rules, the tax on the distribution is deferred, i.e., the receipt is not a taxable event to the participant.

When Are Rollovers Used?

1. When a retirement plan participant receives a large plan distribution upon retirement or termination of employment and wants to defer taxes (and avoid any early distribution penalties) on part or all of the distribution.

2. When an individual participates in a qualified retirement plan or a 403(b) annuity plan that is being terminated by the employer, will receive a large termination distribution from the plan, has no current need for the income, and wishes to defer taxes on it.

3. When a participant in a qualified plan, 403(b) annuity plan, or IRA would like to continue to defer taxes on the

money in the plan, but wants to change the form of the investment or gain greater control over it.

Tax Treatment of Rollovers

1. Rollovers are available only for the following types of distributions

   • total distributions from a qualified plan or Section 403(b) tax deferred annuity plan that are paid in a single taxable year of the participant upon (a) separation from service, (b) attainment of age 59½, (c) death, or (d) in the case of a self-employed person, disability.

   • partial distributions of at least 50 percent of the participant's plan balance in a qualified plan or Section 403(b) tax deferred annuity plan that (1) are paid on account of the participant's separation from service with the employer, death or disability and (2) are not one of a series of periodic payments.

   • total distributions of a participant's plan balance in a qualified plan that are paid to the participant on termination of the plan.

2. The amounts received from the qualified plan must be transferred to the rollover IRA not later than the 60th day after the distribution from the qualified plan. Failure to meet this requirement subjects the distribution to income taxes (although the participant may be eligible to elect special 5-year or 10-year averaging to cushion the blow if the distribution qualifies for averaging).

3. Distributions from the rollover IRA are not eligible for 5-year (or 10-year) averaging tax treatment.

4. Distributions from the rollover IRA are subject to the same rules and limitations as all IRA distributions, discussed in chapter 17. To summarize, distributions must: (a) begin no later than April 1 of the year after the participant attains age 70½, and (b) be made in minimum amounts based on a life or joint life payout. Distributions are fully taxable as ordinary income, without 5-year (or 10-year) averaging. Distributions prior to age 59½ are subject to the 10 percent early withdrawal penalty, with the exceptions discussed earlier in this Appendix. Also certain excess distributions may be subject to the 15% excise tax discussed earlier.

5. Loans from a rollover IRA, like loans from any other IRA, are not permitted.

6. If a participant dies before withdrawing all of the rollover IRA account, the death benefit is includable in the deceased participant's estate for federal estate tax purposes. If payable to the participant's surviving spouse in a qualifying manner, the marital exclusion will defer estate taxes. However, if the amount from the plan included in the estate — together with all other amounts

includable in the estate from qualified plans, TDA plans, or IRAs — exceeds $562,500, the 15 percent excess accumulation penalty tax may apply. This tax cannot be reduced by the marital exclusion or any other estate tax exclusion or credit. (See the discussion of the excess accumulation penalty above.)

7. An IRA can be used as a conduit to hold qualified plan funds for transfer from one qualified plan to another when an employee changes employers. The initial transfer from the qualified plan to the IRA is tax free if the amount is transferred within 60 days. If the IRA contains no assets other than those attributable to the distribution from the qualified plan, then the amount in the IRA may subsequently be transferred tax free to another qualified plan if that plan allows such transfers. The entire amount in the conduit IRA must be transferred to the new plan. Thus an existing IRA should not be used for conduit rollovers; a new one should be established.

An IRA can also be used as a conduit between two Section 403(b) annuity plans. However, conduit rollovers are not permitted between a qualified plan and a Section 403(b) annuity plan.

As an alternative to a conduit IRA, a qualified plan distribution can be rolled over directly within 60 days to another qualified plan covering the employee, without using an IRA. However, the second qualified plan must be in existence and must permit such rollovers.

Alternatives to Rollovers

In cases where the rollover IRA is an alternative to leaving the money in the existing qualified plan, it may be better — or no worse — to leave the money in the plan if the participant is satisfied with the qualified plan's investment performance and the payout options available under that plan meet the participant's needs.

Results similar to a rollover IRA can be achieved if the qualified plan distributes an annuity contract to a participant in lieu of a cash distribution. The annuity contract does not have to meet the requirements of an IRA, but the tax implications and distribution restrictions are generally similar.

If a participant's objective is to absorb an existing Keogh or other qualified pension or profit-sharing plan account to avoid continuing administrative requirements, there is an alternative to the rollover IRA or direct rollover from old plan to new plan. Simply transfer all the assets directly from the trustee of the old Keogh plan to the trustee of the new transferee plan. This can be advantageous because a distribution from the plan is then eligible for the 5-year (or 10-year) lump sum provision. However, there are potential tax traps in a trustee-to-trustee transfer, and it should be done only under the guidance of an experienced tax adviser.

WHERE CAN I FIND OUT MORE ABOUT RETIREMENT PLAN DISTRIBUTIONS?

1. *Tax Facts 1*, National Underwriter Co., Cincinnati, OH; revised annually.

2. IRS Publications 575, *Pension and Annuity Income,* and 590, *Rollover IRAs,* available from local IRS offices.

Qualified Retirement Plan Distributions

					OMB No. 1545-0193

Form **4972**

Department of the Treasury
Internal Revenue Service

Tax on Lump-Sum Distributions

(Use This Form Only for Lump-Sum Distributions From
Qualified Retirement Plans)

▶ Attach to Form 1040 or Form 1041.   ▶ See separate Instructions.

1988

Attachment
Sequence No. **28**

Name(s) as shown on return

Identifying number

Part I	**Complete this part to see if you qualify to use Form 4972**		Yes	No
1	Did you rollover any part of the distribution?	1		
	If "Yes," do not complete the rest of this form.			
2	Was the participant age 50 or older on January 1, 1986?	2		
3	Was this a lump-sum distribution from a qualifying pension, profit-sharing or stock bonus plan?	3		
	If you answered "No" to 2 **or** 3, do not complete the rest of this form.			
4	Was the employee a participant in the plan for at least 5 years before the year of the distribution?	4		
5	Is this a distribution paid to a beneficiary of an employee who died?	5		
	If you answered "No" to 4 **and** 5, do not complete the rest of this form.			
6	Did you quit, retire, get laid off, or get fired from your job before receiving the distribution?	6		
7	Were you self-employed or an owner-employee and became disabled? (See Instructions under Distributions That Qualify) . .	7		
8	Were you 59½ or older at the time of the distribution?	8		
	If you answered "No" to **all** questions 5 through 8, do not complete the rest of this form.			

If you qualify to use this form, you may elect to use Part II, Part III, or Part IV; or elect to use Part II and Part III, or Part II and Part IV.

Part II	**Complete this part to choose the 20% capital gain election (See Instructions for a different capital gain election.)**		
	Check this box to choose the 20% capital gain election . . . . ▶ ☐		
1	Capital gain part from Box 3 of Form 1099-R. If you did not check the box above, enter zero	1	
2	Multiply line 1 by 20% (.20) and enter here. If you do not elect to use Part III or Part IV, also enter the amount on Form 1040, line 39, or Form 1041, Schedule G, line 1b	2	

Part III	**Complete this part to choose the 5-year averaging method**		
1	Ordinary income from Form 1099-R, Box 2 minus Box 3. If you did not check the box in Part II, enter the amount from Box 2 of Form 1099-R (taxable amount)	1	
2	Death benefit exclusion (see Instructions)	2	
3	Subtract line 2 from line 1 (total taxable amount)	3	
4	Current actuarial value of annuity, if applicable (from Form 1099-R, Box 8).	4	
5	Add lines 3 and 4 (adjusted total taxable income). If this amount is $70,000 or more, skip lines 6 through 9, and enter this amount on line 10	5	
6	Multiply line 5 by 50% (.50), but do not enter more than $10,000 . . . [6]		
7	Subtract $20,000 from line 5. Enter difference. If line 5 is $20,000 or less, enter zero . . . [7]		
8	Multiply line 7 by 20% (.20) . . . . [8]		
9	Subtract line 8 from line 6 (minimum distribution allowance)	9	
10	Subtract line 9 from line 5	10	
11	Federal estate tax attributable to lump-sum distribution. Do not deduct on Form 1040 or Form 1041 the amount attributable to the ordinary income entered on line 1 (see Instructions)	11	
12	Subtract line 11 from line 10	12	
13	Multiply line 12 by 20% (.20)	13	
14	Tax on amount on line 13. Use Tax Rate Schedule X (for single taxpayers) in Form 1040 Instructions (see Instructions)	14	
15	Multiply line 14 by 5. If no entry on line 4, skip lines 16 through 21, and enter this amount on line 22	15	
16	Divide line 4 by line 5 and enter the result as a decimal (see Instructions)	16	
17	Multiply line 9 by the decimal amount on line 16	17	
18	Subtract line 17 from line 4	18	
19	Multiply line 18 by 20% (.20)	19	
20	Tax on amount on line 19. Use Tax Rate Schedule X (for single taxpayers) in Form 1040 Instructions	20	
21	Multiply line 20 by 5	21	
22	Subtract line 21 from line 15	22	
23	Tax on lump-sum distribution (add Part II, line 2, and Part III, line 22). Enter on Form 1040, line 39, or Form 1041, Schedule G, line 1b . . . . ▶	23	

For Paperwork Reduction Act Notice, see separate Instructions.

Form **4972** (1988)

Tools and Techniques

Part IV   Complete this part to choose the 10-year averaging method

1	Ordinary income part from Form 1099-R, Box 2 minus Box 3. If you did not check the box in Part II, enter the amount from Box 2 of Form 1099-R (taxable amount)	**1**	
2	Death benefit exclusion (see Instructions)	**2**	
3	Subtract line 2 from line 1 (total taxable amount) . . .	**3**	
4	Current actuarial value of annuity, if applicable (from Form 1099-R, Box 8)	**4**	
5	Add lines 3 and 4 (adjusted total taxable amount). If this amount is $70,000 or more, skip lines 6 through 9, and enter this amount on line 10	**5**	
6	Multiply line 5 by 50% (.50), but do not enter more than $10,000	**6**	
7	Subtract $20,000 from line 5. Enter difference. If line 5 is $20,000 or less, enter zero	**7**	
8	Multiply line 7 by 20% (.20)	**8**	
9	Subtract line 8 from line 6 (minimum distribution allowance)	**9**	
10	Subtract line 9 from line 5	**10**	
11	Federal estate tax attributable to lump-sum distribution. Do not deduct on Form 1040 or Form 1041 the amount attributable to the ordinary income entered on line 1 (see Instructions)	**11**	
12	Subtract line 11 from line 10	**12**	
13	Multiply line 12 by 10% (.10)	**13**	
14	Tax on amount on line 13. Use Tax Rate Schedule in Form 4972 Instructions	**14**	
15	Multiply line 14 by 10. If no entry on line 4, skip lines 16 through 21, and enter this amount on line 22 .	**15**	
16	Divide line 4 by line 5 and enter the result as a decimal (see Instructions)	**16**	
17	Multiply line 9 by the decimal amount on line 16	**17**	
18	Subtract line 17 from line 4	**18**	
19	Multiply line 18 by 10% (.10)	**19**	
20	Tax on amount on line 19. Use Tax Rate Schedule in Form 4972 Instructions	**20**	
21	Multiply line 20 by 10	**21**	
22	Subtract line 21 from line 15	**22**	
23	Tax on lump-sum distribution (add Part II, line 2, and Part IV, line 22). Enter on Form 1040, line 39, or Form 1041, Schedule G, line 1b . . . . ▶	**23**	

★U.S.GPO:1988-0-205-287

1988 Department of the Treasury Internal Revenue Service

Instructions for Form 4972
Tax on Lump-Sum Distributions

(Section references are to the Internal Revenue Code.)

General Instructions

Paperwork Reduction Act Notice.—We ask for this information to carry out the Internal Revenue laws of the United States. We need it to ensure that taxpayers are complying with these laws and to allow us to figure and collect the right amount of tax. You are required to give us this information.

The time needed to complete this form will vary depending on individual circumstances. The estimated average time is:

Recordkeeping . . . . 33 min.

Learning about the law or the form . . . . 18 min.

Preparing the form . . . . 1 hr., 19 min.

Copying , assembling, and sending the form to IRS . . . . 35 min.

If you have comments concerning the accuracy of these time estimates or suggestions for making this form more simple, we would be happy to hear from you. You can write to either **IRS** or the **Office of Management and Budget,** at the addresses listed in the instructions of the tax return with which this form is filed.

A Change to Note.— If you are a spouse or former spouse who received a distribution as an alternative payee under a qualified domestic relations order, you can choose 5- or 10-year averaging to figure the tax on that income. The distribution must meet the other rules listed under **Distributions That Qualify.** This change was made by the Technical and Miscellaneous Revenue Act of 1988, and applies to taxable years ending after December 31, 1984.

Purpose of Form.—If you received a lump-sum distribution and were age 50 or older on January 1, 1986, your tax will usually be less if you can use Form 4972. **If you were not age 50 or older on January 1, 1986, you cannot use this form.** (For lump-sum distributions paid after an employee's death, see below.) If you receive an early distribution (before age 59 ½) from a qualified retirement plan, you may have to pay an additional 10% tax. File **Form 5329,** Return for Individual Retirement Arrangement and Qualified Retirement Plans Taxes, unless the distribution meets one of the exceptions. See the Instructions for Form 5329 and **Pub. 575,** Pension and Annuity Income.

Form 4972 is for use with Form 1040 for an individual or with Form 1041 for an estate or trust. Form 4972 is used for three purposes:

(1) To choose the 20% capital gain method by checking the box and completing Part II;

(2) To choose the 5- or 10-year averaging method by completing Part III or Part IV;

(3) To figure tax with the 5- or 10-year averaging method. With these methods, the ordinary income part of the lump sum is taxed as if you received it in equal parts over 5 or 10 years.

If you use any method mentioned above, you must use it for all lump-sum distributions you receive in one tax year.

If you do not use the 5- or 10-year averaging method, report the ordinary income amount of the lump sum on Form 1040, line 17b, or on Form 1041, line 8. If you do not make either capital gain election (described under **Capital Gain Elections**), combine the capital gain with the ordinary income (Form 1099-R, Box 2). Do not put an amount on Form 1040, line 17b, or on Form 1041, line 8, that you use in any of the tax computations on Form 4972.

The payer should have given you a **Form 1099-R** or other statement that shows the separate parts of your distribution. The amounts you will use from Form 1099-R in filling out Form 4972 are capital gain (Box 3); ordinary income (Box 2 minus Box 3); total of ordinary income plus capital gain (Box 2); and, if it applies, the current actuarial value of an annuity (Box 8). If applicable, get

the amount of Federal estate tax paid attributable to the taxable part of the lump-sum distribution from the person administering the deceased employee's or self-employed individual's estate.

If you need more information, get Pub. 575.

Filing Form 4972 After Employee's Death.—If a lump-sum distribution is paid out after an employee's death, and the employee was age 50 or older on January 1, 1986, the recipient of the distribution can choose the 20% capital gain method, or the 5- or 10-year averaging method.

Distributions That Qualify.—For you to use the 5- or 10-year averaging method, you had to be age 50 or older on January 1, 1986, and the lump sum must have been distributed under **all** the following circumstances:

(1) It came from a qualified pension, profit-sharing, or stock bonus plan.

(2) It came from all the employer's qualified plans of one kind (pension, profit-sharing, or stock bonus) in which the employee had funds.

(3) It was for the full amount credited to the employee. For this purpose, the balance to the credit of the employee does not include the accumulated deductible employee contributions under the plan.

(4) It was paid within a single tax year.

(5) It was paid in **any** of the following cases provided the employee was age 50 or older on January 1, 1986:

   a. The employee died.

   b. The employee, who was a common-law employee, quit, retired, was laid off, or was fired from the job. A common-law employee is anyone who performs services that an employer has the right to control (what will be done and how) and whom the employer has the right to fire.

   c. The self-employed individual or owner-employee became disabled as defined in section 72(m)(7).

Distributions That Do Not Qualify.—The following distributions do not qualify for the 5- or 10-year averaging method:

(1) Employee was under age 50 on January 1, 1986;

(2) U.S. Retirement Bonds distributed with the lump sum;

(3) Any distribution made before the employee has been a participant in the plan for 5 tax years before the tax year of the distribution, **unless it was paid because the employee died;**

(4) The current actuarial value of any annuity contract included in the lump sum (the payer's statement should show this amount, which you should use only to figure tax on the ordinary income part of the distribution);

(5) Any distribution to a 5-percent owner which is subject to penalties under section 72(m)(5)(A);

(6) A distribution, described in section 402(a)(6)(E), from any other pension plan maintained by an employer, if the recipient elected after December 31, 1978, to roll over a total distribution from the employer's money purchase plan into an Individual Retirement Arrangement (IRA) or another qualified plan;

(7) A distribution from an Individual Retirement Arrangement (IRA);

(8) Redemption proceeds of bonds rolled over tax free to a qualified pension plan, etc., from a qualified bond purchase plan; and

(9) A distribution from a qualified pension or annuity plan when the employee or the employee's surviving spouse received a partial distribution from the same plan (or another plan of the employer required to be aggregated for the lump-sum distribution rules), and the proceeds of the previous distribution were rolled over tax free to an Individual Retirement Arrangement (IRA).

How Often You Can Choose.—If you make an election this year, you cannot make an election another year with respect to another lump-sum distribution. For example, if you elect the 5- or 10- year averaging method this year, you cannot make either capital gain election or choose 5- or 10- year averaging another year. Similarly, if you make either capital gain election, you cannot make a capital gain or 5- or 10- year averaging election in another year.

When You Can Choose.—If you choose the 20% capital gain method or the 5- or 10-year averaging method, the Form 4972 can be filed with either an original or an amended return. Generally, you have 3 years from the later of the due date of your tax return or the date you filed your return to choose any of the methods.

Tools and Techniques

Capital Gain Elections.—Only the amount applicable to pre-1974 participation can receive capital gain treatment. The amount that qualifies for capital gain treatment should be shown on Form 1099-R, Box 3. If your distribution includes capital gain, there are two choices you can make: (1) the 20% capital gain election in Part II of Form 4972, or (2) the long-term capital gain election on Schedule D (Form 1040), Part II. If you choose (2), enter 95% (.95) of the amount from Form 1099-R, Box 3, on Schedule D (Form 1040), Part II. The remaining part of your distribution (Form 1099-R, Box 2, minus the amount used on Schedule D) should be entered on Form 1040, line 17b, or Form 1041, line 8. However, if you were age 50 or older on January 1, 1986, you may use Part III or IV, Form 4972, instead of Form 1040, line 17b, or Form 1041, line 8.

Tax on Prior Year Lump-Sum Distributions.—If you received another lump-sum distribution or an annuity contract for any year after 1982 and before 1988, and used Form 4972 or Form 5544 for that year, add those distributions to your 1988 distribution and figure your tax on Form 4972 for 1988 using the combined distributions. From that result, subtract the tax you paid on the lump-sum distributions on Form 4972 or 5544 for the earlier years. Show the subtraction under the applicable line. For example, subtract the tax you paid for the earlier years from the tax reported on the combined distributions on Part III or Part IV, line 23.

Multiple Recipient of Lump-Sum Distribution.—If you shared a lump-sum distribution from a qualified retirement plan when not all recipients were trusts (a percentage will be shown in Box 9, Form 1099-R), figure your tax on Form 4972 as follows:

Step 1.—Complete Parts I and II of Form 4972.

Step 2.—On a separate sheet of paper, divide the amounts shown on Form 1099-R, Boxes 2 and 8, by your percentage of distribution shown on Form 1099-R, Box 9. Also subtract Box 3 from Box 2 and divide that amount by your percentage of distribution.

Step 3.—Complete Form 4972, Parts III or IV through line 22. However, where amounts from Boxes 2 and 8, or Box 2 minus Box 3, of Form 1099-R are requested, use the results obtained in step 2 for those amounts.

Step 4.—On a separate sheet of paper, multiply your percentage of distribution by line 22, Part III or IV, Form 4972.

Step 5.—Add the result of step 4 to line 2, Part II, and enter the total on line 23, Part III or IV.

Line-by-Line Instructions
In General

If you received more than one distribution, add them and figure the tax on the total amount.

If you and your spouse are filing a joint return and each has received a lump-sum distribution, complete and file a different Form 4972 for each spouse's election, and combine them on Form 1040, line 39.

If you are filing for a trust that shared the distribution only with other trusts, figure the tax on the whole lump sum first. The trusts then share the tax in the same proportion that they shared the distribution.

Part II

Line 1.—Enter **ZERO** if your distribution does not include capital gain, **OR** if you are not making the 20% capital gain election.

If you **MAKE** the 20% capital gain election but do not take a death benefit exclusion, enter the entire capital gain amount from Form 1099-R, Box 3.

If you checked the box above line 1, and you are taking the death benefit exclusion, figure the amount to enter on line 1 as follows:

Step 1.—On a separate sheet of paper, divide the capital gain amount from Form 1099-R, Box 3, by the amount from Form 1099-R, Box 2 (taxable amount). Enter the result as a decimal.

Step 2.—Multiply your death benefit exclusion amount by the decimal amount figured in Step 1.

Step 3.—Subtract the dollar amount figured in Step 2 from the capital gain amount from Form 1099-R, Box 3. Enter the result on line 1.

The balance of your allowable death benefit exclusion (see Instructions for Parts III and IV, line 2) should be entered on line 2, Part III or IV, if you choose the 5- or 10-year averaging method.

Page 2

If any Federal estate tax was paid on the lump-sum distribution, you must decrease the capital gain amount by the amount of tax applicable to it. To figure the amount, multiply the total Federal estate tax paid on the lump-sum distribution by the decimal amount from Step 1. The result is the portion of the Federal estate tax applicable to the capital gain amount. Subtract that amount from the capital gain amount from Form 1099-R, Box 3, and enter the answer on line 1. The remainder of the Federal estate tax goes on line 11, Part III or IV.

Note: *If you take the death benefit exclusion, AND Federal estate tax was paid on the capital gain amount, the capital gain amount must be reduced by both the above methods to figure the correct entry for line 1, Part II.*

Parts III and IV

Line 1.—Community property laws do not apply to figuring tax on the amount you report on line 1. You can elect to include certain net unrealized appreciation in employee securities in net income. To make this election, add the amount that is in Box 6 of Form 1099-R to line 1, and on the dotted line to the left of line 1, write "NUA" (for net unrealized appreciation) and the amount.

Line 2.—If you received the distribution because of the employee's death, you can exclude up to $5,000 of the lump sum from your gross income. If the trust for which you are filing shared the lump sum with other trusts, it will share the exclusion in the same proportion as it shared the distribution. This exclusion applies to the beneficiaries or estates of common-law employees, self-employed individuals, and shareholder-employees who owned more than 2% of an S corporation. Pub. 575 gives more information about the death benefit exclusion.

Line 11.—A beneficiary who receives a lump-sum distribution because of an employee's death must reduce the taxable part of the distribution by any Federal estate tax on the part included in the estate. The reduction is made by entering on line 11 the Federal estate tax attributable to the lump-sum distribution. However, see the Instructions for Part II, line 1.

Part III, Lines 14 and 20.—Use Tax Rate Schedule X (single taxpayers) in the Form 1040 Instructions to figure the tax on the amount on lines 13 and 19 even if you use another method to figure the tax on your other income. If the amount on line 13 or 19 is over $89,560, use the worksheet below the Tax Rate Schedules to figure the tax. Complete the worksheet through line 5 (using the amount for single taxpayers), entering on line 2 of the worksheet the amount from line 13 or 19 of Form 4972. Add the amounts on lines 1 and 5, and enter the total on Form 4972, Part III, line 14 or 20, whichever applies.

Parts III and IV, Line 16.—Decimals should be carried to five places and rounded to four places. Drop amounts 4 and under (.44454 becomes .4445). Round amounts 5 and over up to the next number (.44456 becomes .4446).

Part IV, Lines 14 and 20.—Use this tax rate schedule to complete Part IV, lines 14 and 20:

Form 4972 Tax Rate Schedule

If the amount on Part IV, line 13 or 19, is:		Enter on Part IV, line 14 or 20	
Over—	But Not Over—		of the amount over—
$-0-	$1,190	---------- 11%	$-0-
1,190	2,270	$130.90 + 12%	1,190
2,270	4,530	260.50 + 14%	2,270
4,530	6,690	576.90 + 15%	4,530
6,690	9,170	900.90 + 16%	6,690
9,170	11,440	1,297.70 + 18%	9,170
11,440	13,710	1,706.30 + 20%	11,440
13,710	17,160	2,160.30 + 23%	13,710
17,160	22,880	2,953.80 + 26%	17,160
22,880	28,600	4,441.00 + 30%	22,880
28,600	34,320	6,157.00 + 34%	28,600
34,320	42,300	8,101.80 + 38%	34,320
42,300	57,190	11,134.20 + 42%	42,300
57,190	85,790	17,388.00 + 48%	57,190
85,790	----------	31,116.00 + 50%	85,790

19**88** Form W-4P

 **Department of the Treasury**
Internal Revenue Service

What Is Form W-4P? This form is for recipients of income from annuity, pension, and certain other deferred compensation plans to tell payers whether income tax is to be withheld and on what basis. The options available to the recipient depend on whether the payment is periodic or nonperiodic (including a qualified total distribution) as explained on page 3.

Recipients can use this form to choose to have no income tax withheld from the payment (except for payments to U.S. citizens delivered outside the U.S.) or to have an additional amount of tax withheld.

What Do I Need To Do? Recipients who want no tax to be withheld can skip the Worksheet below and go directly to line 1 of the form. All others should complete lines A through E of the Worksheet. Many recipients can stop at line E.

Other Income? If you have a large amount of income from other sources not subject to withholding (such as interest, dividends, taxable social security), you should consider making estimated tax payments using **Form 1040-ES**, Estimated Tax for Individuals. Call 1-800-424-3676 (in Hawaii and Alaska, check your local telephone directory for the number) for copies of Form 1040-ES, and

Publication 505, Tax Withholding and Estimated Tax.

When Should I File? File as soon as possible to avoid underwithholding problems.

Multiple Pensions? More Than One Income? To figure the number of allowances you may claim, combine allowances and income subject to withholding from all sources on one worksheet. You can file a Form W-4P with each pension payer, but do not claim the same allowances more than once. Your withholding will usually be more accurate if you claim all allowances on the largest source of income subject to withholding.

W-4P Worksheet To Figure Your Withholding Allowances

A Enter "1" for **yourself** if no one else can claim you as a dependent . . . . **A** _____

B Enter "1" if:
1. You are single and have only one pension; or
2. You are married, have only one pension, and your spouse has no income subject to withholding; or
3. Your income from a second pension or a job or your spouse's pension or wages (or the total of all) is $2,500 or less.
. . . . **B** _____

C Enter "1" for your **spouse**. But you may choose to enter "0" if you are married and have either a spouse who has income subject to withholding or you have more than one source of income subject to withholding. (This may help you avoid having too little tax withheld.) . . . . **C** _____

D Enter number of **dependents** (other than your spouse or yourself) whom you will claim on your return . . . . **D** _____

E Add lines A through D and enter total here . . . . ▶ **E** _____

For accuracy, do all worksheets that apply.
- If you plan to **itemize or claim other deductions** and want to reduce your withholding, turn to the Deductions and Adjustments Worksheet on page 2.
- If you have **more than one source of income subject to withholding or a spouse with income subject to withholding** AND your combined earnings from all sources exceed $25,000, or $40,000 if you are married filing a joint return, turn to the Multiple Pensions/More Than One Income Worksheet on page 2 if you want to avoid having too little tax withheld.
- If **neither** of the above situations applies to you, **stop here** and enter the number from line E on line 2 of Form W-4P below.

- - - - - - - - - - **Cut here and give the certificate to the payer of your pension or annuity. Keep the top portion for your records.** - - - - - - - - - - -

Form **W-4P**

Department of the Treasury
Internal Revenue Service

Withholding Certificate for Pension or Annuity Payments

OMB No. 1545-0415

19**88**

Type or print your full name	Your social security number
Home address (number and street or rural route)	Claim or identification number (if any) of your pension or annuity contract
City or town, state, and ZIP code	

Complete the following applicable lines:

1 I elect not to have income tax withheld from my pension or annuity. (Do not complete lines 2 or 3.) . . . . ▶ ☐

2 I want my withholding from each **periodic** pension or annuity payment to be figured using the number of allowances and marital status shown. (You may also designate an amount on line 3.) . . . . ▶ _____ (Enter number of allowances.)

☐ Single ☐ Married ☐ Married, but withhold at higher Single rate

3 I want the following additional amount withheld from each pension or annuity payment. **Note:** *For periodic payments, you cannot enter an amount here without entering the number (including zero) of allowances on line 2* . . . . ▶ $ _____

Your signature ▶ _____   Date ▶ _____

Tools and Techniques

Deductions and Adjustments Worksheet

NOTE: *Use this Worksheet only if you plan to itemize deductions or claim adjustments to income on your 1988 tax return.*

1. Enter an estimate of your 1988 itemized deductions. These include: qualifying home mortgage interest, 40% of personal interest, charitable contributions, state and local taxes (but not sales taxes), medical expenses in excess of 7.5% of your income, and miscellaneous deductions (most miscellaneous deductions are now deductible only in excess of 2% of your income) . . . . **1** $ _____

2. Enter: { $5,000 if married filing jointly or qualifying widow(er)
$4,400 if head of household
$3,000 if single
$2,500 if married filing separately } . . . . **2** $ _____

3. **Subtract** line 2 from line 1. If line 2 is greater than line 1, enter zero . . . . **3** $ _____

4. Enter an estimate of your 1988 adjustments to income. These include alimony paid and deductible IRA contributions. **4** $ _____

5. **Add** lines 3 and 4 and enter the total . . . . **5** $ _____

6. Enter an estimate of your 1988 income not subject to withholding (such as dividends or interest income) . . **6** $ _____

7. **Subtract** line 6 from line 5. Enter the result, but not less than zero . . . . **7** $ _____

8. **Divide** the amount on line 7 by $2,000 and enter the result here. Drop any fraction . . . . . **8** _____

9. Enter the number from Form W-4P Worksheet, line E, on page 1 . . . . **9** _____

10. **Add** lines 8 and 9 and enter the total here. If you plan to use the Multiple Pensions/More Than One Income Worksheet, also enter the total on line 1, below. Otherwise **stop here** and enter this total on Form W-4P, line 2 on page 1 . . . . **10** _____

Multiple Pensions/More Than One Income Worksheet

NOTE: *Use this Worksheet only if the instructions under line E on page 1 direct you here. This applies if you (and your spouse if married filing a joint return) have more than one source of income subject to withholding (such as more than one pension, or a pension and a job, or you have a pension and your spouse works).*

1. Enter the number from line E on page 1 (or from line 10 above if you used the Deductions and Adjustments Worksheet) . . . . **1** _____

2. Find the number in **Table 1** below that applies to the **LOWEST** paying pension or job and enter it here . . . **2** _____

3. If line 1 is **GREATER THAN OR EQUAL TO** line 2, **subtract** line 2 from line 1. Enter the result here (if zero, enter "0") and on Form W-4P, line 2, page 1. **Do not** use the rest of this worksheet . . . . **3** _____

4. If line 1 is **LESS THAN** line 2, enter "0" on Form W-4P, line 2, page 1, and enter the number from line 2 of this worksheet . . . . **4** _____

5. Enter the number from line 1 of this worksheet . . . . **5** _____

6. **Subtract** line 5 from line 4. . . . . **6** _____

7. Find the amount in **Table 2** below that applies to the **HIGHEST** paying pension or job and enter it here . . . . **7** $ _____

8. **Multiply** line 7 by line 6 and enter the result here . . . . **8** $ _____

9. **Divide** line 8 by the number of pay periods in each year. (For example, divide by 12 if you are paid every month.) Enter the result here and on Form W-4P, line 3, page 1. This is the additional amount to be withheld from each payment . . . . **9** $ _____

Table 1: Multiple Pensions/More Than One Income Worksheet

Married Filing Jointly		All Others	
If amount from **LOWEST** paying pension or job is—	Enter on line 2, above	If amount from **LOWEST** paying pension or job is—	Enter on line 2, above
0 - $4,000	0	0 - $4,000	0
4,001 - 8,000	1	4,001 - 8,000	1
8,001 - 18,000	2	8,001 - 13,000	2
18,001 - 21,000	3	13,001 - 15,000	3
21,001 - 23,000	4	15,001 - 19,000	4
23,001 - 25,000	5	19,001 and over	5
25,001 - 27,000	6		
27,001 - 32,000	7		
32,001 - 38,000	8		
38,001 - 42,000	9		
42,001 and over	10		

Table 2: Multiple Pensions/More Than One Income Worksheet

Married Filing Jointly		All Others	
If amount from **HIGHEST** paying pension or job is—	Enter on line 7, above	If amount from **HIGHEST** paying pension or job is—	Enter on line 7, above
0 - $40,000	$300	0 - $23,000	$300
40,001 - 80,000	550	23,001 - 48,000	550
80,001 and over	650	48,001 and over	650

Paperwork Reduction Act Notice.—This information is required to carry out the Internal Revenue laws of the United States.

Withholding From Pensions and Annuities.—Generally, withholding applies to payments made from pension, profit-sharing, stock bonus, annuity, and certain deferred compensation plans, from individual retirement arrangements (IRAs), and from commercial annuities. The method and rate of withholding depends upon the kind of payment you receive.

Periodic payments from all of the items above are treated as wages for the purpose of withholding. A periodic payment is one that is includible in your income for tax purposes and that you receive in installments at regular intervals over a period of more than one full year from the starting date of the pension or annuity. The intervals can be annual, quarterly, monthly, etc.

You can use Form W-4P to change the amount of tax to be withheld by using lines 2 and 3 of the form, or to exempt the payments from withholding by using line 1 of the form. This exemption from withholding does not apply to certain recipients who have payments delivered outside the United States. See *Exemption From Income Tax Withholding* later.

Caution: *Remember that there are penalties for not paying enough tax during the year, either through withholding or estimated tax payments. New retirees, especially, should see Publication 505. It explains the estimated tax requirements and penalties in detail. You may be able to avoid quarterly estimated tax payments by having enough tax withheld from your pension or annuity using Form W-4P.*

Unless you tell your payer otherwise, tax must be withheld on **periodic** payments as if you are married and claiming three withholding allowances. This means that tax will be withheld if your pension or annuity is more than $741.67 a month ($8,900 a year).

There are some kinds of periodic payments for which you **cannot** use Form W-4P since they are already defined as wages subject to income tax withholding. Retirement pay for service in the Armed Forces of the U.S. generally falls into this category. Certain deferred compensation plans also fall into this category. Your payer should be able to tell you whether Form W-4P will apply. Social security payments are not subject to withholding but may be includible in income.

For periodic payments, your certificate stays in effect until you change or revoke it. Your payer must notify you each year of your right to elect to have no tax withheld or to revoke your election.

Nonperiodic payments will have income tax withheld at a flat 10% rate unless the payment is a qualified total distribution. Tax will be withheld from a qualified total distribution using tables furnished payers and prescribed by the Treasury Department. Distributions from an IRA that are payable upon demand are treated as nonperiodic payments. You can elect to have no income tax withheld from a nonperiodic payment by filing Form W-4P with the payer and checking the box on line 1. Generally, your election to have no tax withheld will apply to any later payment from the same plan. You cannot use line 2 to change the way tax is withheld. But you may use line 3 to specify that an additional amount be withheld.

Exemption From Income Tax Withholding.— The election to be exempt from income tax withholding does not apply to any periodic payment or nonperiodic distribution which is delivered outside the United States to a U.S. citizen.

Other recipients who have these payments delivered outside the U.S. can elect exemption only if they certify to the payer that they are not: (1) a U.S. citizen who is a bona fide resident of a foreign country, or (2) an individual to whom section 877 of the Internal Revenue Code applies (concerning expatriation to avoid tax). The certification can be made in a statement to the payer under the penalties of perjury.

Caution: *Congress is currently considering legislation that would prohibit resident aliens receiving payments outside the U.S. from claiming this exemption. It would also treat U.S. possessions as if they were part of the U.S.*

Revoking the Exemption From Withholding.—If you want to revoke your previously filed exemption from withholding for periodic payments, file another Form W-4P with the payer. If you want tax withheld at the rate set by law (married with three allowances), write the word "Revoked" by the checkbox on line 1 of the form. If you want tax withheld at any different rate, complete line 2 on the form.

If you want to revoke your previously filed exemption for nonperiodic payments, write the word "Revoked" by the checkbox on line 1 and file Form W-4P with the payer.

Statement of Income Tax Withheld From Your Pension or Annuity.—By January 31 of next year, you will receive a statement from your payer showing the total amount of your pension or annuity payments and the total income tax withheld during the year.

Copies of Form W-4P will not be sent to IRS by the payer, regardless of the number of allowances claimed on line 2 of Form W-4P.

Tax Law Changes Effective for 1988

The Tax Reform Act of 1986 (the Act) made changes in the law that may affect your 1988 tax liability, including changes to your personal exemption and certain itemized deductions.

You may use your 1987 tax return as a guide in figuring your estimated taxes, but be sure to consider the tax law changes noted in this section. Where possible, we have included references to lines on the 1987 Form 1040 that are affected by the new law. If you filed Form 1040A, refer to the equivalent line, if any, on that form.

Itemized Deductions

- State and local sales taxes are no longer deductible.
- For 1988, only 40% of personal interest (such as interest on car loans or credit card balances) is deductible (lines 12a and 12b).

Standard Deduction

The standard deduction has been increased for all taxpayers. (For 1987 only, the elderly or blind were able to use the higher 1988 amount. Filers who claimed an additional withholding allowance based on the increased amount should check that their withholding is sufficient for 1988.) For 1988, the amounts are:

Filing Status	Standard Deduction
Married filing joint return and qualifying widow(er)	$5,000*
Head of household	$4,400*
Single	$3,000*
Married filing separately	$2,500*

*To this amount, add the Additional Amount below if you are elderly or blind.

Additional Amount for the Elderly or Blind.—An additional standard deduction amount of $600 is allowed for a married individual (whether filing jointly or separately) or for a qualifying widow(er) who is 65 or over or blind ($1,200 if the individual is both 65 or over and blind, $2,400 on a joint return if both spouses are 65 or over and blind). An additional standard deduction amount of $750 is allowed for an unmarried individual (single or head of household) who is 65 or over or blind ($1,500 if both 65 or over and blind).

Personal Exemption

The amount of the personal exemption has increased to $1,950 for the individual, the spouse, and for each dependent.

Tax Rates

For 1988, the tax rates have been reduced to 2 brackets, 15% and 28%, with the 15% rate being phased out for certain high income filers.

Caution: *As this form went to print, Congress was considering legislation concerning catastrophic health care insurance protection that would impose a supplemental medicare premium payable on your Federal income tax return. It would be imposed on individuals who are eligible for Part B Medicare benefits. If this legislation is passed, the IRS will use various means to alert taxpayers and furnish details on the subject. You may then want to increase your withholding by claiming fewer allowances or by asking for an additional amount of tax to be withheld from your payments.*

★U.S.GPO:1987-0-183-054

Qualified Retirement Plan Distributions

9898 ☐ VOID ☐ CORRECTED For Official Use Only

Type or machine print PAYER'S name, street address, city, state, and ZIP code	1 Gross distribution $	OMB No. 1545-0119	Total Distributions From Profit-Sharing, Retirement Plans, Individual Retirement Arrangements, Insurance Contracts, Etc.
	2 Taxable amount $	19 88	
	3 Amount in Box 2 eligible for capital gain election	Statement for Recipients of	
PAYER'S Federal identification number	RECIPIENT'S identification number	4 Federal income tax withheld $	Copy A For Internal Revenue Service Center
Type or machine print RECIPIENT'S name (first, middle, last)	5 Employee contributions or insurance premiums $	6 Net unrealized appreciation in employer's securities $	For Paperwork Reduction Act Notice and instructions for completing this form, see Instructions for Forms 1099, 1098, 5498, 1096, and W-2G.
Street address	7 Category of distribution		
City, state, and ZIP code	8 Other $ %	9 Your percentage of total distribution %	
Account number (optional)	10 State income tax withheld $	11 Payer's state number	

Form **1099-R**

Do NOT Cut or Separate Forms on This Page   Department of the Treasury - Internal Revenue Service

9898 ☐ VOID ☐ CORRECTED For Official Use Only

Type or machine print PAYER'S name, street address, city, state, and ZIP code	1 Gross distribution $	OMB No. 1545-0119	Total Distributions From Profit-Sharing, Retirement Plans, Individual Retirement Arrangements, Insurance Contracts, Etc.
	2 Taxable amount $	19 88	
	3 Amount in Box 2 eligible for capital gain election	Statement for Recipients of	
PAYER'S Federal identification number	RECIPIENT'S identification number	4 Federal income tax withheld $	Copy A For Internal Revenue Service Center
Type or machine print RECIPIENT'S name (first, middle, last)	5 Employee contributions or insurance premiums $	6 Net unrealized appreciation in employer's securities $	For Paperwork Reduction Act Notice and instructions for completing this form, see Instructions for Forms 1099, 1098, 5498, 1096, and W-2G.
Street address	7 Category of distribution		
City, state, and ZIP code	8 Other $ %	9 Your percentage of total distribution %	
Account number (optional)	10 State income tax withheld $	11 Payer's state number	

Form **1099-R**

Do NOT Cut or Separate Forms on This Page   Department of the Treasury - Internal Revenue Service

9898 ☐ VOID ☐ CORRECTED For Official Use Only

Type or machine print PAYER'S name, street address, city, state, and ZIP code	1 Gross distribution $	OMB No. 1545-0119	Total Distributions From Profit-Sharing, Retirement Plans, Individual Retirement Arrangements, Insurance Contracts, Etc.
	2 Taxable amount $	19 88	
	3 Amount in Box 2 eligible for capital gain election	Statement for Recipients of	
PAYER'S Federal identification number	RECIPIENT'S identification number	4 Federal income tax withheld $	Copy A For Internal Revenue Service Center
Type or machine print RECIPIENT'S name (first, middle, last)	5 Employee contributions or insurance premiums $	6 Net unrealized appreciation in employer's securities $	For Paperwork Reduction Act Notice and instructions for completing this form, see Instructions for Forms 1099, 1098, 5498, 1096, and W-2G.
Street address	7 Category of distribution		
City, state, and ZIP code	8 Other $ %	9 Your percentage of total distribution %	
Account number (optional)	10 State income tax withheld $	11 Payer's state number	

Form **1099-R**

Department of the Treasury - Internal Revenue Service

1 Control number	55555	For Official Use Only ▶ OMB No. 1545-0008	
2 Payer's name, address, and ZIP code		**3** Payer's Federal identification number	**4** Payer's state I.D. number
		5 State income tax withheld	**6** Name of state
		7 Tax amt not determined ☐ Deceased ☐ Legal rep. ☐	Subtotal ☐ Void ☐
8 Recipient's social security no.	**9** Gross annuity, pension, etc.	**10** Taxable amount	**11** Federal income tax withheld
12 Recipient's name (first, middle, last)		**13**	**14** Distribution code
		For Paperwork Reduction Act Notice, see the back of Copy D.	
15 Recipient's address and ZIP code		**Copy A—For Social Security Administration** See Instructions for Forms W-2 and W-2P and back of Copy D.	

Form **W-2P 1988**   **Statement for Recipients of Annuities, Pensions, Retired Pay, or IRA Payments**   Department of the Treasury Internal Revenue Service

Do NOT Cut or Separate Forms on This Page

1 Control number	55555	For Official Use Only ▶ OMB No. 1545-0008	
2 Payer's name, address, and ZIP code		**3** Payer's Federal identification number	**4** Payer's state I.D. number
		5 State income tax withheld	**6** Name of state
		7 Tax amt not determined ☐ Deceased ☐ Legal rep. ☐	Subtotal ☐ Void ☐
8 Recipient's social security no.	**9** Gross annuity, pension, etc.	**10** Taxable amount	**11** Federal income tax withheld
12 Recipient's name (first, middle, last)		**13**	**14** Distribution code
		For Paperwork Reduction Act Notice, see the back of Copy D.	
15 Recipient's address and ZIP code		**Copy A—For Social Security Administration** See Instructions for Forms W-2 and W-2P and back of Copy D.	

Form **W-2P 1988**   **Statement for Recipients of Annuities, Pensions, Retired Pay, or IRA Payments**   Department of the Treasury Internal Revenue Service

Do NOT Cut or Separate Forms on This Page

1 Control number	55555	For Official Use Only ▶ OMB No. 1545-0008	
2 Payer's name, address, and ZIP code		**3** Payer's Federal identification number	**4** Payer's state I.D. number
		5 State income tax withheld	**6** Name of state
		7 Tax amt not determined ☐ Deceased ☐ Legal rep. ☐	Subtotal ☐ Void ☐
8 Recipient's social security no.	**9** Gross annuity, pension, etc.	**10** Taxable amount	**11** Federal income tax withheld
12 Recipient's name (first, middle, last)		**13**	**14** Distribution code
		For Paperwork Reduction Act Notice, see the back of Copy D.	
15 Recipient's address and ZIP code		**Copy A—For Social Security Administration** See Instructions for Forms W-2 and W-2P and back of Copy D.	

Form **W-2P 1988**   **Statement for Recipients of Annuities, Pensions, Retired Pay, or IRA Payments**   Department of the Treasury Internal Revenue Service

Instructions

Please use this form to report payments under a retirement plan. Examples are pensions, retainer pay, annuities under a purchased contract, and payments from individual retirement accounts or annuities. See separate **Instructions for Forms W-2 and W-2P** for more information on how to complete Form W-2P.

Use Form W-2 to report payments that are subject to social security tax.

You need not file Form W-2P for the following cases: (a) You paid retirement benefits that are exempt from tax such as Veterans Administration payments. (b) You made payments as a fiduciary, filed Form 1041, and gave each beneficiary a Schedule K-1 (Form 1041). (c) You made total distributions reported on Form 1099-R.

Paperwork Reduction Act Notice.—We ask for this information to carry out the Internal Revenue laws of the United States We need it to ensure that taxpayers are complying with these laws and to allow us to figure and collect the right amount of tax. You are required to give us this information.

Instructions

Please use this form to report payments under a retirement plan. Examples are pensions, retainer pay, annuities under a purchased contract, and payments from individual retirement accounts or annuities. See separate **Instructions for Forms W-2 and W-2P** for more information on how to complete Form W-2P.

Use Form W-2 to report payments that are subject to social security tax.

You need not file Form W-2P for the following cases: (a) You paid retirement benefits that are exempt from tax such as Veterans Administration payments. (b) You made payments as a fiduciary, filed Form 1041, and gave each beneficiary a Schedule K-1 (Form 1041). (c) You made total distributions reported on Form 1099-R.

Paperwork Reduction Act Notice.—We ask for this information to carry out the Internal Revenue laws of the United States. We need it to ensure that taxpayers are complying with these laws and to allow us to figure and collect the right amount of tax. You are required to give us this information.

Instructions

Please use this form to report payments under a retirement plan. Examples are pensions, retainer pay, annuities under a purchased contract, and payments from individual retirement accounts or annuities. See separate **Instructions for Forms W-2 and W-2P** for more information on how to complete Form W-2P.

Use Form W-2 to report payments that are subject to social security tax.

You need not file Form W-2P for the following cases: (a) You paid retirement benefits that are exempt from tax such as Veterans Administration payments. (b) You made payments as a fiduciary, filed Form 1041, and gave each beneficiary a Schedule K-1 (Form 1041). (c) You made total distributions reported on Form 1099-R.

Paperwork Reduction Act Notice.—We ask for this information to carry out the Internal Revenue laws of the United States. We need it to ensure that taxpayers are complying with these laws and to allow us to figure and collect the right amount of tax. You are required to give us this information.

19**88**

**Department of the Treasury
Internal Revenue Service**

Instructions for Forms W-2 and W-2P

Highlights

If possible, please file Forms W-2 and W-2P either alphabetically by employees' last name or numerically by employees' SSN. This will help the Social Security Administration locate specific forms if there is trouble processing your submission.

General Instructions

(Section references are to the Internal Revenue Code, unless otherwise noted.)

A. Who Must File Forms W-2 and W-2P.—

*(1) Form W-2, Wage and Tax Statement.—*To be filed by employers. (See **Circular A,** Agricultural Employer's Tax Guide, or **Circular E,** Employer's Tax Guide. Household employers, see Form 942 instructions.)

*(2) Form W-2P, Statement for Recipients of Annuities, Pensions, Retired Pay, or IRA Payments.—*To be filed by employees' trusts or funds; Federal, state, or local government systems; life insurance companies; and other payers who make such payments.

B. When to File.—File Forms W-2 and W-2P with accompanying **Forms W-3,** Transmittal of Income and Tax Statements, by February 28, 1989.

If you need an extension of time to file Forms W-2, see the Instructions for Form W-3 under "When To File."

C. Where to File.—See Form W-3.

D. Calendar Year Basis.—You must base entries on Forms W-2 and W-2P on a calendar year.

E. Taxpayer Identification Numbers.—We use them to check the payments you report against the amounts shown on the employees' tax returns. Be sure to show the right social security number on the Forms W-2 or W-2P, or on magnetic media.

Persons in a trade or business use an employer identification number (00-0000000). This includes employee trusts, retirement systems, and so forth. Individuals use a social security number (000-00-0000). When you list a number, please separate the nine digits properly to show the kind of number.

Sole proprietors who are payers should show their employer identification number on the statements they prepare. But if you prepare a statement showing payment *to* a sole proprietor, give the proprietor's social security number in Box 8 of Form W-2 or Form W-2P.

Please show the full name, address, and identification number of the payer and the recipient on the form. If you made payments to more than one individual, show on the first line **ONLY** the name of the recipient whose number is on the statement. Show the other names on the second line. If the recipient is **NOT** an individual and the name runs over the first line, you may continue on the second and following lines.

F. Statements to Income Recipients.—You may give statements to income recipients on government-printed official forms or on privately printed substitute forms.

A Revenue Procedure titled "Specifications for Private Printing of Forms W-2, W-2P, and W-3" and reprinted as **Publication 1141,** explains the format that must be used on all substitute paper forms. You can get a copy from any Internal Revenue Service Center or district office.

*(1) Form W-2 Recipients.—*Generally, give statements to employees by January 31, 1989. If employment ends before December 31, 1988, you may give copies any time after employment ends. If the employee asks for Form W-2, give him or her the completed copies within 30 days of the request or the final wage payment, whichever is later.

*(2) Form W-2P Recipients.—*Generally, you should give statements to income recipients by January 31, 1989.

G. Corrections.—Use **Form W-2c,** Statement of Corrected Income and Tax Amounts, to correct errors in previously filed Forms W-2 and W-2P. Use **Form W-3c,** Transmittal of Corrected Income and Tax Statements, to transmit the W-2c forms to the Social Security Administration (SSA). Instructions are on the forms. If an employee (or recipient) loses a statement, write "REISSUED STATEMENT" on the new copy, but **do not send Copy A of the reissued statement to SSA.**

H. Sick Pay.—If you had employees who received sick pay in 1988 from an insurance company or other third-party payer, and the third party notified you of the amount of sick pay involved, you must report the following on the employees' W-2s:

(a) in Box 9, the amount (if any) of income tax withheld from the sick pay by the third-party payer;

(b) in Box 10, the amount the employee must include in income;

(c) in Box 11, the employee social security tax withheld by the third-party payer;

(d) in Box 13, the amount of sick pay that is subject to employer social security tax; and

(e) in Box 16, the amount (if any) not includible in income because the employee contributed to the sick pay plan.

You can include these amounts in the Forms W-2 you issue the employees showing wages, or you can give the employees separate W-2s and state that the amounts are for third-party sick pay. In either case, you must show in Box 21 of Form W-3 the total amount of income tax withheld by third-party payers, even though the amounts are includible in Box 9.

I. Penalties.—You may be assessed a $50 per document penalty if you:

● fail to file a timely Form W-2 with SSA or give the employee a copy;

● fail to file on magnetic media, if required; or

● fail to file paper forms with SSA that are machine readable.

If you fail to file a timely Form W-2P, you may be assessed a $25 per day penalty, up to $15,000 ($50 per failure for IRA information reporting).

There is also a penalty if you fail to include correct information on a statement.

How to Complete Form W-2

Copy A of Forms W-2 and W-2P is printed with three forms to an unperforated page. Send the whole page even if one or two of the forms are blank or void. If you are sending 42 or more Forms W-2, please show subtotals on every 42nd form for the preceding 41 forms to permit checking the transmittal totals. Since this form is processed by optical scanning machines, please type the entries, if possible, using black ink. Please do not make any erasures, whiteouts, or strikeovers on Copy A. Make all dollar entries without the dollar sign but with the decimal point (000.00).

The instructions below are for boxes on Form W-2. If an entry does not apply, leave it blank.

Box 1—Control number.—You may use this to identify individual Forms W-2. *You do not have to use this box.*

Box 3—Employer's identification number.—Show the number assigned to you by IRS (00-0000000). Do not use a prior owner's number.

Box 4—Employer's state I.D. number.—You do not have to complete this box, but you may want to if you use copies of this form for your state return. The number is assigned by the individual states.

Box 5.—Check the boxes that apply.

*Statutory employee.—*Check this box for statutory employees whose earnings are subject to social security tax but **NOT** subject to Federal income tax withholding. (See Circular E for more information on statutory employees.)

*Deceased.—*Check this box if the employee is now deceased.

*Pension plan.—*Check this box if the employee was an active participant (for any part of the year) in a retirement plan (including a simplified employee pension (SEP) plan) maintained by you. See IRS Notice 87-16, published in Internal Revenue Bulletin 1987-5, dated February 2, 1987, for definition of an active participant.

*Legal representative.—*Check this box when the employee's name is the only name shown but is shown as a trust account (e.g., John Doe Trust), or another name is shown in addition to the employee's name and the other person or business is acting on behalf of the employee.

Representatives are identified by words such as "custodian," "parent," or "attorney"; sometimes the employee is identified as a minor, child, etc. Do **NOT** check this box if the address is simply in care of someone other than the employee (John Doe, c/o Jane Smith).

*942 employee.—*For household employers only. See Form 942 instructions for information on when to check this box.

*Subtotal.—*If you are submitting **42 or more** Forms W-2 or W-2P, please give subtotal figures for every 41 individual forms. Check the "Subtotal" box on the form that shows the subtotal dollar amounts for the preceding 41 forms. Void statements are counted in order with good statements (*but do not include the money amounts from the void statements in the subtotal figures*). Subtotal statements should always be the last completed form on a page. The subtotal amounts to be shown are:

Form W-2—Boxes 6, 7, 9, 10, 11, 13, and 14
Form W-2P—Boxes 9, 10, and 11

Example: *An employer with Forms W-2 for 86 employees should show a subtotal on the 42nd statement, the 84th statement (showing the subtotal for statements 43 through 83), and the 89th statement (showing the subtotal for statements 85 through 88).*

*Deferred compensation.—*Check this box if you made contributions on behalf of the employee to a section 401(k), 403(b), 408(k)(6), 457, or 501(c)(18)(D) retirement plan. See also instruction "(d)" under Box 16.

*Void.—*Put an X in this square when an error has been made. (**Be sure the amounts shown on void forms are NOT included in your subtotals.**)

Box 6—Allocated tips.—If you are a large food or beverage establishment, show the amount of tips allocated to the employee. (See the instructions for **Form 8027,** Employer's Annual Information Return of Tip Income and Allocated Tips.) Do **NOT** include this amount in Box 10 (Wages, tips, other compensation) or Box 14 (Social security tips).

Box 7—Advance EIC payment.—Show the total amount paid to the employee as advance earned income credit payments.

Box 8—Employee's social security number.—Give the number shown on the employee's social security card. If the employee does not have a number, he or she should apply for one at any SSA office.

Box 10—Wages, tips, other compensation.—Show, before any payroll deductions, the total of:

(1) wages paid,

(2) noncash payments (including fringe benefits),

(3) tips reported, and

(4) all other compensation (including certain scholarships and fellowship grants, payments for moving expenses and reimbursements for employee business expenses if the employee does not account to you for those expenses.). Other compensation is what you pay the employee but do not withhold Federal income tax on. If you prefer not to include it in the total, you may show it on a separate Form W-2.

Note: *Payments to statutory employees, that are subject to social security tax but not subject to Federal income tax withholding, must be shown in Box 10 as other compensation. (See Circular E for definition of a statutory employee.)*

Box 11—Employee social security tax withheld.—Show the total employee social security tax (not your share) deducted and withheld or paid by you for the employee. (But if there was an adjustment in 1988 to correct the tax for a prior year, enter the amount withheld in 1988 increased by the adjustment for an overcollection or decreased by the adjustment for an undercollection.)

Example: *Employee A earned $26,000 in 1987. You withheld $1,759 in employee social security taxes. You should have withheld $1,859 ($26,000 x 7.15%). To correct this, you withheld extra tax in 1988 until you made up the $100. At the end of 1988 your books show $2,052.60 withheld ($1,952.60 ($26,000 x 7.51%) plus $100 to make up the 1987 error). To show the correct tax withheld for 1988, subtract the $100 from $2,052.60 and show $1,952.60 in Box 11 of Form W-2. Please note: You must file* **Form 941c,** *Statement to Correct Information Previously Reported on the Employer's Federal Tax Return, with your* **Form 941,** *Employer's Quarterly Federal Tax Return, in the quarter you find the error and issue the employee a Form W-2c for 1987.*

Box 12—Employee's name.—Enter the name as shown on the employee's social security card. If the name has changed, have the employee get a corrected card from any SSA office. Use the name on the original card until you see the corrected one.

Box 13—Total social security wages.—Show the total wages paid (before payroll deductions) subject to employer social security tax (but **NOT** including allocated tips). Generally, noncash payments are considered wages. Include employer contributions to certain qualified cash or deferred compensation arrangements, even though the contributions are not includible in Box 10 as wages, tips, and other compensation. (See Circular E for more information.) Include any employee social security tax and employee state unemployment compensation tax you paid for your employee rather than deducting it from wages (see Revenue Procedure 81-48, 1981-2 C.B. 623, for details). Do not enter more than $45,000 (the maximum social security wage base for 1988) in Box 13.

Box 14—Social security tips.—Show the amount the employee reported even if you did not have enough employee funds to collect the social security tax for the tips. When tips and wages subject to employee social security taxes amount to $45,000 **do NOT** show any additional tips in this box. But show all tips reported in Box 10 along with wages and other compensation.

Box 15—Employee's address and ZIP code.—This box has been combined with Box 12 (employee's name) on all copies except Copy A to allow employees' copies to be mailed in a window envelope or as a self-mailer.

Box 16—Employer's use.—Complete and label this box if (a), (b), (c), (d), (e), or (f) apply.

(a) You did **not** collect employee social security tax on all the employee's tips. Show the amount of tax that you could not collect because the employee did not have enough funds to deduct it from. Do not include this amount in Box 11.

(b) You provided your employee more than $50,000 of group-term life insurance. Show the cost of coverage over $50,000. Also include it in Box 10 and Box 13.

(c) You are reporting sick pay. Show the amount of any sick pay **NOT** includible in income because the employee contributed to the sick pay plan. Label it as nontaxable. If you issue a separate W-2 for sick pay, use Box 16 to label the W-2 as "Sick pay."

(d) You made contributions to a section 401(k) cash or deferred arrangement, to a section 403(b) salary reduction agreement to purchase an annuity contract, to a section 408(k)(6) salary reduction SEP, to a section 457 deferred compensation plan for state or local goverment employees, or to a section 501(c)(18)(D) tax-exempt organization plan. Check the "Deferred compensation" checkbox in Box 5, enter the elective deferral in Box 16, and label it "401(k)," "403(b)," etc.

(e) You are a Federal, state, or local agency with employees paying the 1.45% medicare portion of the social security tax. For these employees, write "Medicare qualified government employment" in Box 16, and show the social security wages and 1.45% tax withheld in Boxes 13 and 11, respectively.

(f) You made excess "golden parachute" payments to certain key corporate employees. If the excess payments are considered wages, the 20% excise tax is treated as income tax withholding. Include this tax in Box 9 and identify the amount as "EPP" in Box 16.

If none of the above apply, you may use Box 16 for any information you want to give the employee. Examples are union dues or health insurance premiums deducted, moving expenses paid, or reimbursements for employee business expenses included in Box 10.

Box 16a—Fringe benefits included in Box 10.—Show the total value of the taxable noncash fringe benefits included in Box 10 as other compensation. If you provided a vehicle and included 100 percent of the value in the employee's income, you must separately report this value to the employee in Box 16a or on a separate statement so the employee can compute the value of any business use of the vehicle.

Boxes 17 through 22—State or local income tax information.—You may use these to report state or local income tax information. You do not have to use them. But you may want to show the amounts on Copy A if you use copies of this form for your state or local tax returns or as recipients' statements.

How to Complete Form W-2P

The instructions below are for Form W-2P. If an entry does not apply, leave it blank. Use this form to report retirement payments other than total distributions that close an account. Examples are pensions, retired or retainer pay, annuities under commercial, individually purchased contracts, payments from individual retirement accounts or individual retirement annuities, and loans treated as distributions under section 72(p).

For treatment of repayments by recipients of erroneous pension benefits, see Circular E, Employer's Tax Guide.

Use Form W-2 to report payments from which you withheld social security tax.

Do **NOT** file Form W-2P for the following cases: (a) You paid retirement benefits that are exempt from tax such as Veterans Administration payments; (b) You made payments as a fiduciary, filed Form 1041, and gave each beneficiary a Schedule K-1 (Form 1041); or (c) You made total distributions reported on Form 1099-R.

Box 1—Control number.—You may use this to identify individual Forms W-2P. *You do not have to use this box.*

Box 3—Payer's Federal identification number.— Show the number assigned to you by the IRS (00-0000000).

Box 4—Payer's state I.D. number.—You do not have to complete this box, but you may want to if you use copies of this form for your state return. The number is assigned by the individual states.

Boxes 5 and 6—State income tax withheld and name of state.—You may use these to report state and local tax information if you use copies of this form for your state returns or as recipients' statements.

Box 7.—Check the boxes that apply.

*Taxable amount (Tax amt) **NOT** determined.*— Check this box if you are not able to figure the taxable amount of the annuity, pension, retirement pay, or IRA payment to report in Box 10:

Deceased.—Check this box if the recipient is now deceased.

Legal representative.—Check this box when the recipient's name is the only name shown but it is shown as a trust account (e.g., John Doe Trust), or when another name is shown as well as the recipient's name and the other person or business is acting on behalf of the recipient. Representatives are identified by words such as custodian, parent, or attorney; sometimes the recipient is identified as a minor, child, etc. Do **NOT** check this box if the address is simply in care of someone other than the recipient (such as John Doe c/o Jane Smith).

Subtotal.—If you are submitting **42 or more Forms W-2P**, please give subtotal figures for every 41 individual forms. See the W-2 instructions for Box 5 for details.

Void.—Put an X in this square when an error has been made. Forms W-2P should have no erasures, whiteouts, or strikeovers on Copy A. **(Be sure the amounts shown on void forms are NOT included in your subtotals.)**

Box 8—Recipient's social security number.—Give the number shown on the recipient's social security card. If the person does not have a number, he or she should apply for one at any SSA office.

Box 9—Gross annuity, pension, retired pay, or IRA payment.—Show total amount paid before income tax or other deductions were withheld. Do not include amounts exempt from tax as workmen's compensation under section 104. Include current insurance premiums (including "PS 58" costs) paid by the trustee or custodian, and loans treated as distributions under section 72(p).

Box 10—Taxable amount.—Show the amount the recipient should include in income (including "PS 58" costs). This often is the same as in Box 9. Also, the amount in Box 9 may include taxable earnings on an excess contribution while the excess contribution may be nontaxable. There may be some years in which none of the payments are taxable. You must make every effort to obtain the information necessary to compute the taxable amount. If you do not have the facts you need to figure the taxable amount, you may have to leave this box blank and check "Tax amt not determined" in Box 7.

For new rules on reporting the distribution of excess deferrals, excess contributions, and excess aggregate contributions, see IRS Notice 87-77, published in Internal Revenue Bulletin 1987-51, dated December 21, 1987.

Box 11.—Federal income tax withheld.

Box 12—Recipient's name.—Enter the name as shown on the recipient's social security card. If the name has changed, have the person get a corrected card from any SSA office. Use the name shown on the original card until you see the corrected one.

Box 13.—You may use Box 13 and the space below Boxes 13 and 14 for any other information that you want to give the recipient.

Box 14—Distribution code.—This box is used to identify distributions that may have special tax consequences. Use it to identify any distributions that are not normal retirement distributions. The code is a four-digit number starting with 555. The fourth digit identifies the type of distribution: 1—Premature distribution (other than codes 2, 3, 4, 8, or P); 2—Rollover; 3—Disability; 4—Death; 6—Other; 7—Normal IRA or SEP distribution; 8—Excess contributions/deferrals plus earnings taxable in 1988; "P"—Excess contributions/deferrals refunded in 1988 plus earnings taxable in the prior year (1987); 9—Current insurance premiums including PS 58 costs. (For example, 5553 for disability.) For code "P" distributions, you should advise the payee, at the time of the distribution, that the earnings are taxable in the prior year.

Box 15.—See Box 15, Form W-2 instructions.

★ U.S. GPO: 1988 - 203-842

Appendix C

INSTALLING A QUALIFIED RETIREMENT PLAN

This Appendix covers the complicated and distinctive steps involved in fact finding, designing, and installing a qualified retirement plan. Qualified plans comprise the following plans covered in this book:

Cash Balance Pension Plan	Chapter 3
Defined Benefit Pension Plan	Chapter 6
ESOP/Stock Bonus Plan	Chapter 9
HR 10 (Keogh) Plan	Chapter 15
Money Purchase Pension Plan	Chapter 23
Profit-Sharing Plan	Chapter 25
Savings Plan	Chapter 27
Section 401(k) Plan	Chapter 28
Target Benefit Pension Plan	Chapter 33

Three stages can be identified in the plan installation process: (I) Fact Finding; (II) Plan Selection and Design; and (III) Formal Installation Procedures.

I. FACT FINDING

A business planner or adviser must collect a significant amount of information about the business (1) first to determine if the business has a problem that can be solved, or a situation that can be improved, with a qualified plan; and (2) second, to decide what kind of plan or combination of plans is most appropriate for this purpose.

At the end of this Appendix is a detailed fact finding form that has been developed by The American College for its Advanced Pension and Retirement Planning courses. The information developed on this form can be used by the planner to determine if a qualified plan is appropriate — by reviewing it in light of the considerations discussed under "WHEN IS IT INDICATED?" in the chapters of this book that are listed above.

An experienced planner can often shortcut some of the information gathering stages by knowing intuitively when qualified plans are indicated in a particular business. However, even for experienced planners it often pays to fully document the formal fact finding process. This may help to uncover facts and ideas not previously considered. On the downside, it can also help the planner to justify his or her recommendations if the plan does not work out as well as expected. A systematic data gathering process is, therefore, a part of the professional planner's "due diligence" requirement.

II. PLAN SELECTION AND DESIGN

The next step in the process is to use the information determined in the fact finding process to make a systematic selection of the type of plan or plans that is most appropriate. The facts about the business should be reviewed in light of the criteria discussed in the "ADVANTAGES" and "DISADVANTAGES" sections in the chapters of this book devoted to qualified plans.

For example, if the information disclosed in the fact finding process indicates that the business has a history of fluctuation in earnings and cash flow, a plan with contribution flexibility such as a profit-sharing plan should be considered. Or, if the fact finding process indicates a need or desire to maximize plan contributions on behalf of a few older, highly compensated executives, the planner should consider a defined benefit plan. The process is not always clear cut, and often competing advantages must be weighed.

The fact finding form towards the end of this Appendix includes a section for recording plan specifications resulting from decisions made in the design and selection process. This section can be used by the plan drafter as a guide for producing the final legal documents.

III. FORMAL INSTALLATION PROCEDURES

Installing a plan involves various steps, some of which must comply with a fairly strict legal timetable. To help focus this discussion, an installation checklist for a typical qualified plan is set out in Figure C.1 for reference.

Plan Adoption

An employer must legally "adopt" a qualified plan during the employer's taxable year in which it is to be effective. (By contrast, a simplified employee pension (SEP) can be adopted as late as the tax filing date for the year — see Chapter 30.) The plan sponsor should adopt (and document the adoption of) the plan before the end of the year in which the plan is to become effective. The plan can be made effective to the beginning of the year of adoption. An adoption that is made later and reflected in "backdated" documents is not legally effective for purposes of the tax treatment of a qualified plan.

The reason for this requirement is basically one of tax accounting. An employer cannot obtain a deduction for an expense accrued during a year unless it meets the "all events" test for accrual. That is, all events that make the accrual a legally binding obligation of the employer must have occurred by the end of the tax year. Thus, a qualified plan

217

Tools and Techniques

Figure C.1

PLAN INSTALLATION CHECKLIST AND TIMETABLE

Assumptions: 1. Employer uses calendar year for tax reporting.
2. Plan is to be effective January 1, 1989.

Before December 31, 1989

1. Corporate board must pass a resolution adopting the plan. Plan document does not have to be in final form.
2. Trust agreement must be signed and trust established under state law; or application for group pension contract must be made and accepted by insurance company.
3. Plan must be "communicated to employees." This can be done orally at employee meetings or through a written communication. The summary plan description (SPD) can be used for this purpose simply by distributing it earlier than its regular due date (see below).

Before Employer's Tax Filing Date (March 15, 1990, with extensions to September 15, 1990 if applied for)

1. Plan should be drafted in final form and signed by plan sponsor and trustee.
2. Employer must make the 1989 contribution to the plan by this date in order for it to be deductible on the 1989 tax return.
3. Application for IRS determination letter should be filed before this date in order to extend the retroactive amendment period. However, there is no specific deadline for filing the application for determination.

Within 120 Days After Plan is Adopted (i.e., Board of Directors' resolution)

1. Furnish SPD to participants (see Appendix D of this book).
2. File SPD with Department of Labor.

Before Filing Application For Determination With IRS

1. Provide "Notice to Interested Parties" to employees as required by IRS regulations. This is a prescribed formal notice to employees of their rights in connection with the determination letter process. The notice must be provided 10 to 24 days before filing if the notice is mailed, and 7 to 20 days before filing if the notice is posted.

On or Before July 31, 1990 (and each July 31 thereafter)

1. File Annual Report (Form 5500 series) — see Appendix D.

On or Before September 30, 1990 (and each September 30 thereafter)

1. Furnish Summary Annual Report to participants (see Appendix D).

---

must have been legally adopted by the end of a particular tax year if the employer wishes to take a tax deduction for contributions to the plan for that year.

A corporation adopts a plan by a formal action of the corporation's board of directors. An unincorporated business should adopt a written resolution in a form similar to a corporate resolution. The plan does not have to be in final form in order to be legally adopted; the corporate resolution can simply set out the principal terms of the plan such as coverage, benefit formula, vesting, etc.

If the plan will use a trust for funding, a trust must be established before the end of the year of adoption that is valid under the law of the state in which it is established. A nominal plan contribution may be required for that purpose. If the plan is to be funded through an insurance contract, the insurer must accept the application for the contract before the end of the year, but the contract need not be formally adopted in final form at that time.

Advance Determination Letter

Because of the complexity of the qualified provisions, and the tax cost of having a plan considered "disqualified" by the IRS, most plan sponsors apply to the IRS for a ruling that the plan provisions meet Code requirements for favorable tax treatment as a qualified plan. This letter is generally referred to as a "determination letter."

Technically, a plan does not have to receive a favorable determination letter in order to be qualified. If the plan provisions in letter and in operation meet Code requirements, the plan is qualified and entitled to the appropriate tax benefits. However, without a determination letter, the issue of plan qualification for a given year does not arise until the IRS audits the employer's tax returns for that year. By that time, it is generally too late for the employer to amend the plan to correct any disqualifying provisions. So if the plan has a disqualifying provision or lacks an essential provision, the employer's tax deduction for the year being audited is lost. (In addition, the plan fund will lose its tax-exempt status and employees will become taxable on their vested benefits — a true all-around tax disaster.) A determination letter helps to avoid this problem since auditing agents generally will not raise the issue of plan qualification if the employer has a current determination letter — that is, one that shows the plan complies with current law.

Plans generally must be amended periodically to conform to changes in the law. Each time there is a significant amendment to the plan a new determination letter should be obtained.

It is always possible for the IRS to raise the issue that a plan is discriminatory *in operation* — as opposed to merely having discriminatory provisions on paper. A determination letter cannot prevent this. Fortunately such IRS attacks are relatively rare.

The Code contains a "retroactive amendment" procedure that allows plan sponsors to amend a plan retroactively to eliminate certain disqualifying provisions. Retroactive plan amendments may be made up to the employer's tax filing date for the year in question, including extensions. For example, if a corporate employer uses a calendar tax year, the tax filing date for the year 1988 is March 15, 1989, with possible extensions to September 15, 1989. A plan effective January 1, 1988 can be retroactively amended as late as September 15, 1989 under this provision.

An additional advantage of the determination letter procedure is that it can extend the time for retroactive amendments. If the determination letter request is filed before the tax filing date, retroactive amendments can be made as long as the determination letter request is still pending.

Determination letter requests are made on IRS forms of the 5300 series, depending on the type of plan. Copies of Form 5301, used for custom designed defined contribution plans, and Form 5307, used for master or prototype plans (see below) are reproduced at the end of this appendix.

The IRS once provided determination letters as a free service, but a fee schedule is now in effect. For a smaller employer, this fee can be a substantial factor in the cost of installing a plan. The fee currently is $400 for a custom designed plan with fewer than 100 participants, $600 for a plan with 100 or more participants, and $100 for a master or prototype plan. Form 8717 is filed along with the fee and the form from the appropriate member of the 5300 family.

Master and Prototype Plans

Custom design of a qualified plan can be costly because the plan document must be very lengthy to reflect all of the complex requirements of current law. The pension industry has developed methods to reduce the cost of plan drafting; these are particularly important to smaller employers, since the cost of installation must be spread over relatively few employees.

One of the most common methods of reducing drafting costs is to use a "master" or "prototype" plan offered by a financial institution as an inducement to use that institution's investment products to fund the plan. Insurance companies, banks, and mutual funds frequently offer master or prototype plans. These plans are standardized plans of various types — for example prototype profit-sharing or prototype money purchase — that use standardized language approved by the IRS. The plan sponsor has some degree of choice in basic provisions of the plan such as the vesting schedule, the contribution or benefit formula, etc.

A master plan is distinguished from a prototype in that a master plan usually refers to a plan under which various employers use a single financial institution for funding, while a prototype plan generally does not commit the plan sponsor to use any particular funding institution or medium.

The use of master or prototype plans greatly simplifies plan installation in many cases. The fee for adopting a master or prototype plan is usually much less than the cost of drafting a custom designed plan. The determination letter procedure is also simplified, because the "boilerplate" provisions of the plan have already been approved by the IRS. All the IRS has to do is determine whether the basic vesting schedule, contribution or benefit formula, etc., as applied to the employer in question, is nondiscriminatory.

The cost of drafting a custom designed plan has also been addressed by the pension industry. There are "document preparation services" that will generate documents from their central word processors based on a checklist of plan provisions submitted by the plan installer. Usually, the use of a document preparation service will speed IRS approval of a plan, because the IRS becomes familiar with the standard language used by various document preparers.

APP FORM 101

RETIREMENT PLAN DATA AND ABSTRACT FORM

Prepared for _____

By _____

Date_____

CONTENTS

CONTENTS (Continued)

CONTENTS (Continued)

SECTION I — RETIREMENT PLAN DATA

PART A — CLIENT PROFILE

A-1. Legal Name _____

Address _____

_____ Zip _____

Telephone Number _____

Contact _____

A-2. Employer (Taxpayer) Identification Number _____

A-3. Nature of Enterprise (Check Appropriate Line)

3.1 _____ Sole proprietorship   3.6 _____ Municipal corp. or government agency

3.2 _____ Partnership   3.7 _____ Professional corporation

3.3 _____ Business corporation   3.8 _____ Business or real estate trust

3.4 _____ S corporation   3.9 _____ Other: specify

3.5 _____ Exempt org. (Sec. _____)   _____

A-4. Nature of Business (Principal Business Activity)

_____

_____

A-5. Accounting Method (Check One)

_____ Cash   _____ Accrual

A-6. Fiscal Year Ends _____
                        (Month)   (Day)

A-7. Date of Incorporation or Establishment

_____ (Month and Year)

A-8. State of Incorporation or Domicile _____

A-9. Related Corporation or Unincorporated Entities, including Affiliated Service Groups (Names, Nature of Enterprises, Ownership Percentages of Related Enterprises)

_____

_____

_____

_____

_____

Tools and Techniques

A-10.   Predecessor Entities

    10.1 Name _____

    10.2 Nature of Entity _____

    10.3 Date of Establishment _____

    10.4 Date of Transfer _____

A-11.   What is the Approximate Rate of Employee Turnover as a Percent of the Active Group for the Past Five Years?

                            19 _____   _____ %

                            19 _____   _____ %

                            19 _____   _____ %

                            19 _____   _____ %

                            19 _____   _____ %

A-12.   Client Motives (For a New Benefit Program)

    _____

    _____

    _____

A-13.   Employee Groups under Consideration (For a New Benefit Program)

    13.1 _____ Salaried Employees

    13.2 _____ Hourly Employees

    13.3 _____ Collective-Bargaining Unit Employees

    13.4 _____ Leased Employees

    13.5 _____ Other

A-14.   Competitors in Industry (Details as to Their Compensation Programs)

    _____

    _____

    _____

A-15.   Local Nonindustry Employers (Details as to Their Compensation Programs)

    _____

    _____

    _____

    _____

PART B — FINANCIAL DATA

B-1.   **Attach Balance Sheets (Last Two or Three Years) and Summarize**

_____

_____

B-2.   **Attach Profit and Loss Statements and Summarize**

_____

_____

_____

_____

_____

_____

_____

B-3.   **Summarize Earnings Projections**

_____

_____

B-4.   **What Type of Cost Commitment Can Be Considered for a Pension or a Profit-Sharing Plan or Both?**

4.1 _____ % of payroll

4.2 _____ % of profit

4.3 _____ % of profit in excess of $ _____

4.4 $ _____ Flat dollar amount

4.5 Other _____

_____

PART C — CLIENT'S OTHER BENEFIT PROGRAMS

C-1.   Nonqualified Retirement Plans

   1.1   Plans of general application _____

   _____

   _____

   _____

   1.2   Personal plans (for individuals) _____

   _____

   _____

   _____

C-2.   Group Life Insurance

   2.1   How much _____

   2.2   Who is covered _____

   2.3   Beneficiary _____

   2.4   Premiums paid by

      (a) _____ Employer

      (b) _____ Employee

         _____ Payroll deduction

         _____ Other (specify) _____

   2.5   Carrier _____

C-3.   Accidental Death and Dismemberment

   3.1   How much _____

   3.2   Who is covered _____

   3.3   Beneficiary _____

   3.4   Premiums paid by

      (a) _____ Employer

      (b) _____ Employee

         _____ Payroll deduction

         _____ Other (specify) _____

   3.5   Carrier _____

   3.6   Workmen's compensation offset

      _____ Yes   _____ No   Explain _____

3.7   All accidents covered

_____ Yes   _____ No   Explain _____

C-4.   Long-Term Disability Coverage

      4.1   How much _____   How long _____

      4.2   Who is covered _____   Waiting period _____

      4.3   Premiums paid by

         _____ Employer

         _____ Employee

              _____ Payroll deduction

              _____ Other (specify) _____

      4.4   Carrier _____

      4.5   All causes

         _____ Yes   _____ No   Explain _____

      4.6   Offsets

         _____ Yes   _____ No   Explain _____

      4.7   Definition of disability _____

                               _____

                               _____

C-5.   Collectively Bargained or Other Qualified Retirement Plans (Complete Separately for Each Plan)

      5.1   Name _____

      5.2   Type of plan: _____ Pension _____ 401(K) _____ Profit-Sharing _____ Other.

      5.3   Contribution rate: By employer _____

                               By employee _____

      5.4   Benefit structure: _____

      5.5   Normal retirement benefit _____ At Age _____

      5.6   Early retirement benefit _____ At Age _____

      5.7   Death benefit _____

      5.8   Disability benefit _____

            Definition of disability _____

      5.9   Vesting rate _____

      5.10   Eligibility wait _____

      5.11   Number of client's employees covered _____

      5.12   Are there any employees who are covered by this plan to be covered by new plan? _____

           If so, are there to be offset provisions? _____

PART D — EMPLOYEE CENSUS DATA

Name	Sex	Date of Birth (or Age)	Date Hired (or Years of Service)	Position	Key Employee?	Percent of Voting Stock	Annual Nondeferred Compensation				Social Security Number
							Basic	Bonus	Overtime	Total	

SECTION II — RETIREMENT PLAN ABSTRACT

PART E — PLAN CHARACTERISTICS AND PROVISIONS

E-1.   Name of Plan _____

E-2.   Type of Plan

    2.1 _____ Defined-benefit: _____ Unit-benefit _____ Flat-benefit _____ Fixed-benefit

    2.2 _____ Defined-contribution money purchase

    2.3 _____ Target (assumed-benefit)

    2.4 _____ Profit-sharing

    2.5 _____ Thrift (savings)

    2.6 _____ Section 401(k)

    2.7 _____ Stock bonus

    2.8 _____ ESOP

    2.9 _____ Tax-deferred annuity (Section 403(b))

    2.10 _____ Other or combination of types (specify) _____

                       _____

                       _____

E-3.   Effective Date _____

E-4.   Anniversary Date _____

E-5.   Formal Name of Plan _____

E-6.   Eligibility Requirements

    6.1   Length of service _____

    6.2   Minimum age _____

    6.3   Entry dates (explain) _____

Tools and Techniques

6.4   Minimum salary or pay _____

6.5   Geographic location _____

6.6   Job classification _____

_____

_____

6.7   Collective-bargaining unit _____

_____

_____

6.8   Salaried only? (yes or no) _____

6.9   Line of business (explain) _____

6.10 Other (specify) _____

_____

_____

E-7.   Past Service: Is Past Service with Prior Employer(s) to Count as Service with Company for Eligibility Purposes?

_____

For benefit computation purposes? _____

If yes, name prior employer(s) _____

_____

_____

_____

E-8.   Integration (If Any)

8.1   _____ Social security (OASDI)

8.2   _____ Railroad retirement act

E-9.   Type of Integration

9.1   _____ Excess (stepped up)

9.2   _____ Offset

E-10. Integration Level

10.1 _____ Uniform integration break point $ _____

10.2 _____ Covered compensation table I

10.3 _____ Covered compensation table II

10.4 _____ Other _____

_____

E-11. Integration Benefit Formula _____

_____

_____

_____

E-12. Other Offsets: Indicate the Contributions to or Benefits from Other Plans Which Are to be Used as Offsets to This Plan and Whether or Not Such Other Plans Are Qualified Plans under the Internal Revenue Code.

_____

_____

_____

_____

E-13. Normal Retirement Benefit

    13.1 Formula

    13.2 Age _____

    13.3 Minimum years of service _____

    13.4 Minimum years of plan membership _____

    13.5 Other _____

E-14. Early Retirement Benefit

    14.1 Formula

    14.2 Age _____

    14.3 Minimum years of service _____

    14.4 Minimum years of plan membership _____

    14.5 Other _____

E-15. Deferred Retirement Benefit

    15.1 Formula

    15.2 Maximum age _____

    15.3 Minimum years of service _____

    15.4 Minimum years of plan membership _____

    15.5 Other _____

E-16. Disability Retirement

16.1 Formula

16.2 Minimum age _____

16.3 Minimum years of service _____

16.4 Minimum years of plan membership _____

16.5 Benefit commencement date _____

16.6 Definition of disability _____

   (a) _____ Disability for social security purposes

   (b) _____ Other (specify) _____

   _____

   _____

   _____

E-17. Death Benefits

17.1 **Preretirement** _____

   _____

   _____

17.2 **Postretirement** _____

   _____

   _____

E-18. Emergency Distributions _____

   _____

   _____

   _____

E-19. **Describe Deferral or Salary Reduction Option (Section 401(k) Plan)** _____

   _____

   _____

E-20. Withdrawal of Member Contributions

20.1 When _____

20.2 How much _____

20.3 Earnings on contributions _____

20.4 Penalty _____

_____

20.5 Notice requirement _____

E-21. Loans to members

21.1 Maximum _____

21.2 Minimum _____

21.3 Interest rate _____

21.4 Duration _____

E-22. Other Benefits (specify) _____

_____

_____

E-23. Contributions

23.1 Rate of employer contributions

(a) _____ Discretionary

(b) _____ As actuarially determined

(c) _____ Formula (state formula)

23.2 Rate of Member Contributions

(a) _____ Voluntary

Minimum _____

Maximum _____

(b) _____ Required

Amount or rate _____

Method of collection

_____ Payroll withholding

_____ Other (specify) _____

23.3 Employer Contributions To Be In

(a) _____ Cash

(b) _____ Stock

(c) _____ Other

Tools and Techniques

E-24. Use of Forfeitures (If Any)

    24.1 _____ To reduce subsequent employer contributions

    24.2 _____ Reallocated among plan members (defined-contribution only) state reallocation basis: _____

_____

E-25. Employer Contribution Allocation Formula

    25.1 _____ None. Unallocated funding

    25.2 _____ Prorate according to compensation

    25.3 _____ Prorate according to service

    25.4 _____ Prorate according to compensation and service

    25.5 _____ According to amounts contributed by employees

    25.6 _____ Other (specify) _____

_____

E-26. Vesting Schedule (Employer Contributions, Amounts Attributable to Employer Contributions, or Benefits Purchased with Employer Contributions)

    26.1 5-year vesting

    26.2 3- to 7-year vesting

    26.3 100% vesting with 2-year eligibility period

    26.4 Other basis (specify) _____

_____

    26.5 Set forth the vesting schedule in space below

_____

_____

_____

_____

_____

E-27. **Full and Immediate Vesting Is Required for Amounts, Earnings, and Benefits Derived from Employee Contributions.**

E-28. Special Provisions Relating to Vesting in Individual Insurance Contracts _____

_____

_____

_____

_____

E-29. **Definition of "Compensation" and "Hour of Service" for Plan Purposes (Indicate Status of Commissions, Bonuses, Overtime, etc., and for Defined-Benefit Plan Indicate Career Average, Final Average, or Other Basis for Determining Benefits)**

_____

_____

_____

_____

E-30. Definition of "Net Income" or "Net Profits" for Plan Purposes (If Applicable)

30.1 _____ Profits for federal income tax purposes, but prior to reduction for contributions under (a) _____ this plan or (b) _____ qualified plans including this plan, but excluding

_____

(state plans to be excluded) sponsored by employer

·30.2 _____ Other (specify) _____

_____

E-31. Beneficiary Designations

31.1 _____ None

31.2 _____ Automatic to spouse, if surviving, otherwise to estate of (a) _____ deceased member or (b) _____ deceased spouse

31.3 _____ Automatic to estate of deceased member

31.4 _____ As per designation by employee

E-32. Earmarking of Contributions (Directed Investments)

32.1 _____ Yes

32.2 _____ No

If yes, indicate investment options and limitations _____

_____

_____

_____

Tools and Techniques

E-33.   Mode of Distribution of Benefits (Normal Retirement)

    33.1 _____ Joint life, member and spouse (at least 50% to spouse)

    33.2 _____ Full range of options (see below)

    33.3 _____ Limited range of options (indicate which options are available below)

    33.4 _____ Range of options

        (a) _____ Life of member only

        (b) _____ Life of member, 5 years certain

        (c) _____ Life of member, 10 years certain

        (d) _____ Joint life, member and spouse (at least 50% to spouse)

        (e) _____ Joint life, member and dependent

        (f) _____ Joint life, member and designated joint annuitant

        (g) _____ Installments for 3 years

        (h) _____ Installments for 5 years

        (i) _____ Installments for 10 years

        (j) _____ Installments for 15 years

        (k) _____ Lump sum

        (l) _____ Other (specify) _____

        _____

    33.5 Method of determining actuarial equivalence _____

     _____

     _____

    33.6 How options are elected _____

     _____

E-34.   Timing of Distribution of Benefits

    34.1 Normal retirement benefits

        (a) _____ First day of month following normal retirement date

        (b) _____ Other (specify) _____

        _____

    34.2 Early Retirement Benefits

        (a) _____ First day of month following early retirement date

        (b) _____ First day of month following normal retirement date

        (c) _____ First day of any month after early retirement date but not later than first day of month following normal retirement date

        (d) _____ Combination of (b) & (c) above at employee's option

34.3 Disability benefits

    (a) _____ First day of month following disability

    (b) _____ First day of month following normal retirement date

    (c) _____ First day of month following early retirement date after disability and before normal retirement date

    (d) _____ Other (specify) _____

    _____

    (e) _____ Combination of (b) & (c) above at

    _____ Employee's option

34.4 Preretirement death benefits

    (a) _____ As promptly as practicable following death

    (b) _____ Other (specify) _____

    _____

34.5 Postretirement death benefits

    (a) _____ As promptly as practicable following death

    (b) _____ Pursuant to mode of retirement benefit election

    (c) _____ Other (specify) _____

    _____

34.6 Severance benefits

    (a) _____ As promptly as practicable following termination of employment (not later than 60th day after close of plan year)

    (b) _____ At normal retirement date

    (c) _____ 10 years after plan participation

    (d) _____ (a) or (c) at option of plan member

E-35. Plan Administration

35.1 **Plan administrator** _____

_____

35.2 **Plan administrator to have investment power?** _____ Yes _____ No

E-36. Insurance Provision and Restrictions _____

_____

_____

_____

E-37. Should There be Provisions in Plan and Trust Specifying That Insurance Company is Not a Party?

_____ Yes   _____ No

E-38. Other Special Features and Notes as to Plan Provisions (Attach Additional Sheets if Necessary)

_____

_____

_____

_____

_____

PART F — PLAN CENSUS DATA

Data for test under Section 410(b)(1) of the Internal Revenue Code

F-0.   Is this data being provided for a separate line of business under Code Sec. 414(r)?
        □ Yes, eligible (describe)   _____
        □ No, not eligible
        □ No separate line of business

F-1.   Total number of employees   _____

F-2.   Number of employees in collective-bargaining unit
        (retirement benefits were subject to good faith bargaining)
        (Code Sec. 410(b)(3)(A))   _____

F-3.   Number of employees who have not yet satisfied
        proposed plan eligibility waiting period* and
        minimum age requirements (Code Sec. 410(b)(4))   _____

F-4.   Number of employees excluded under Code Secs. 410(b)(3)(B)–(C)   _____

F-5.   Total Lines F-2 through F-4   _____

F-6.   Difference Line F-1 minus Line F-5   _____

F-6.1. Number of employees included in F-6 who are highly compensated
        (Code Sec. 414(q))   _____

        *NOTE: If plan excludes part-time or seasonal employees, defined as other than employment for fewer than
               1,000 hours per year, indicate here the definitions used in the plan

        _____

        _____

F-7.   Employees excluded from coverage*
        7.1   Ineligible due to being salaried   _____

        7.2   Ineligible due to being hourly paid   _____

        7.3   Ineligible due to job classification   _____

        7.4   Ineligible due to being covered in another   _____
              qualified plan

        7.5   Ineligible due to geographic location   _____

        7.6   Ineligible for other reasons (specify)   _____

                                                                          _____

              _____   _____

              _____   _____

        7.8   Total excluded under F-7   _____

        *NOTE: No excluded employee should be counted in more than one category above.

F-8.   Number of employees presently eligible to participate in plan
        (F-6 minus F-7.8)   _____

F-9.   Number of employees actually participating in plan   _____

F-10.   Number of plan participants who are highly compensated   _____

Tools and Techniques

Percentage test

F-11. Percentage of non-highly compensated employees participating—100 times

$$\left(\frac{\text{line F-9 minus line F-10}}{\text{line F-6 minus line F-6.1}} \right)$$

_____%*

Ratio test

F-12. Percentage of highly compensated employees participating—100 times
(line F-10 divided by F-6.1)

_____%

F-13. 0.7 times line F-11

_____%

F-14. Percentage of non-highly compensated employees participating—100 times

$$\left(\frac{\text{line F-9 minus line F-10}}{\text{line F-6 minus line F-6.1}} \right)$$

_____%

Average Benefits Test

F-15. Describe nondiscriminatory classification of employees _____

F-16. Average benefit percentage _____

_____

*If F-11 is 70 or greater, the plan's coverage meets the percentage test and no further computation is required.

PART G — FUNDING AND FIDUCIARY DETAILS

G-1.   Type of Instrument

　　　1.1　_____ Self-administered trust

　　　1.2　_____ Group DA

　　　1.3　_____ Group IPG

　　　1.4　_____ Group annuity

　　　1.5　_____ Individual policy (fully insured)

　　　1.6　_____ Individual policy and investment fund

　　　1.7　_____ Other (specify) _____ _____

　　　　　　　_____

G-2.   Actuarial Assumptions and Cost Method

　　　2.1　Actuarial assumptions

　　　　　(a) _____ Interest _____

　　　　　(b) _____ Turnover _____

　　　　　(c) _____ Annuity form to be funded _____

　　　　　(d) _____ Annuity purchase rate (dollar amount needed to purchase benefit of $10.00 per month at normal retirement)

　　　　　　　　Male _____　　　　　　　Female _____

　　　　　　　　　　　　　　　　　or

　　　　　　　(Dollar amount of monthly retirement income that can be purchased at normal retirement by $1,000)

　　　　　　　　Male _____　　　　　　　Female _____

　　　　　(e) _____ Preretirement mortality _____

　　　　　(f) _____ Salary scale _____

　　　　　(g) _____ Other (specify) _____

　　　　　　　_____

　　　2.2　Actuarial cost method _____

　　　　　_____

G-3.   Type of Fiduciary Arrangement

　　　3.1　_____ Bank trustee

　　　3.2　_____ Individual trustee(s)

　　　3.3　_____ Insurance or annuity contracts

　　　3.4　_____ Custodial account

　　　3.5　_____ U.S. retirement bonds

　　　3.6　_____ Other (specify) _____

　　　　　_____

Tools and Techniques

G-4.   Annual Asset Valuation Date _____

G-5.   Trust (or Other) Fiscal Year _____

G-6.   Fund (Trust, Custodial/Account, Annuity Plan) Identification Number _____

G-7.   SS-4 Needed?   _____ Yes   _____ No

G-8.   Full Name and Address of Trustee or Other Fiduciary (Named Fiduciary) _____

_____

_____

_____

G-9.   Is Trustee or Other Fiduciary Subject to Instruction by or Consent of Plan Committee, Advisor, or Other Party as to Acquisition, Retention, or Disposition of Investment Assets? _____

If so, specify name and address of party whose consent is needed and acts for which consent is needed

_____

_____

_____

G-10.   Situs of Trust _____

G-11.   Who Will Prepare and File Plan/Trust Returns and Reports with Internal Revenue Service and Department·of Labor?

11.1 Form 5500 (or 5500-C or 5500-R—indicate which)_____

11.2 Schedule A Form 5500_____

11.3 Schedule B Form 5500_____

11.4 Other reports_____

_____

_____

_____

G-12.   Unusual Trust Agreement Provisions (Or Unusual Provisions to Be Included in Agreements Used in Lieu of or in Addition to Trust Agreement) _____

_____

_____

_____

G-13.   Fiduciary Employer (Taxpayer) Identification Number _____

G-14.   Plan Administrator (If Other Than Employer) Identification Number _____

PART H — AGENCY FILING RECORDS

H-1. Internal Revenue Service

1.1 Who will file for "Letter of Determination" _____

_____

_____

_____

1.2 Indicate forms needed and date filed*

Needed	Form No.	Date Filed	Response Received
(a) _____	SS-4 (Employer)	_____	_____
(b) _____	SS-4 (Plan Administrator)	_____	_____
(c) _____	2848 or 2848-D	_____	_____
(d) _____	4578	_____	_____
(e) _____	5300	_____	_____
(f) _____	5301	_____	_____
(g) _____	5302	_____	_____
(h) _____	5303	_____	_____
(i) _____	5307	_____	_____
(j) _____	5309	_____	_____
(k) _____	5310	_____	_____

*Form Index:

(a), (b) SS-4—Application for employer (taxpayer) or plan administrator identification number

(c) 2848 or 2848-D—Power of attorney or authorization and declaration

(d) 4578—Application for approval of bond purchase plan

(e) Form 5300—Application for determination for defined-benefit plan

(f) 5301—Application for determination for defined-contribution plan

(g) 5302—Employee census

(h) Form 5303—Application for determination for collectively bargained plan

(i) Form 5307—Short form application for determination for employee benefit plan

(j) 5309—Application for determination of employee stock ownership plan

(k) 5310—Application for determination upon termination—notice of merger, consolidation or transfer of plan assets or liabilities

Where Letters of Determination are issued, indicate date of issuance and symbols in "response received" column.

Tools and Techniques

H-2.   State Government Filings (Preempted by Federal Law in Most Cases)

Filings Required	Forms to Be Submitted	Parties to Do Filing	Dates of Filing	Responses Received

H-3.   Securities and Exchange Commission _____

H-4.   Other _____

PART I — OTHER PROFESSIONALS
(Insert Names and Addresses)

I-1. Company's Accountant _____

_____

_____

_____

I-2. Company's Counsel _____

_____

_____

_____

I-3. Actuary _____

_____

_____

_____

I-4. Consultant _____

_____

_____

_____

I-5. Fiduciary _____

_____

_____

_____

I-6. Insurance Consultants (Indicate Lines of Coverage) _____

_____

_____

_____

I-7. Union Representatives _____

_____

_____

_____

Tools and Techniques

I-8.   Others (Specify) _____

_____

_____

_____

| Form **5300** (Rev. August 1988) Department of the Treasury Internal Revenue Service | **Application for Determination for Defined Benefit Plan** For Pension Plans Other Than Money Purchase Plans (Under sections 401(a) and 501(a) of the Internal Revenue Code) | OMB No. 1545-0197 Expires 6-30-91 **For IRS Use Only** File folder number ▶ Case number ▶ |

▶ Church and governmental plans not subject to ERISA need not complete lines 10, 11, 12b, 12c, and 15.

▶ **Caution:** All other plans must complete all lines except as indicated on specific lines. For example, if you answer "No" to line 7, you need not complete lines 7a and 7b since they require responses only if you answer "Yes" to line 7. N/A is only an acceptable answer if an N/A block is provided. All applications are now computer screened, therefore it is important that you provide all the information requested and have the application signed by the employer, plan administrator, or authorized representative. Otherwise, we may need to correspond with you or return your application for completion, which will delay its processing.

1 a Name of plan sponsor (employer if single employer plan)	**1 b** Employer identification no.
Address (number and street)	**1 c** Employer's tax year ends Month ☐ N/A
City or town, state, and ZIP code	Telephone number ( )

2 Person to be contacted if more information is needed (see Specific Instructions). If same as 1a, enter "same as 1a."

Name	Telephone number ( )
Address	

3 a Determination requested for (check applicable box(es)): See Instruction B. "What To File."

    (i) ☐ Initial qualification—Date plan signed _____ Date plan effective _____

    (ii) ☐ Amendment after initial qualification—Is plan restated? ☐ Yes ☐ No   Date amendment signed_____

                       Date amendment effective _____ Date plan effective_____

    (iii) ☐ Affiliated service group status (section 414(m))— Date effective _____ Date plan effective _____

    (iv) ☐ Partial termination— Date effective _____ Date plan effective _____

  b Enter IRS file folder number shown on the last determination letter issued to the plan sponsor _____ ☐ N/A

  c Is this application also expected to satisfy the notice requirement for this plan for merger, consolidation, or transfer of plan assets or liabilities involving another plan? See Specific Instructions. . . . . ☐ Yes ☐ No

  d Were employees who are interested parties given the required notification of the filing of this application? . . . . ☐ Yes ☐ No

  e Is this plan or trust currently under examination, or is any issue related to this plan or trust currently pending before the Internal Revenue Service, the Department of Labor, the Pension Benefit Guaranty Corporation, or any court?. . . . . . ☐ Yes ☐ No If "Yes," attach explanation.

4 a Name of plan	**b** Plan number ▶ _____
	c Plan year ends ▶ _____

5 Are there other qualified plans? (Do not consider plans that were established under union-negotiated agreements that involved other employers.) . . . . ☐ Yes ☐ No

If "Yes," enter for each other qualified plan you maintain:

  a Name of plan ▶ _____

  b Type of plan ▶ _____

  c Rate of employer contribution ▶ _____ ☐ N/A

  d Allocation formula ▶ _____ ☐ N/A

  e Benefit formula or monthly benefit ▶ _____ ☐ N/A

  f Number of participants ▶

6 Type of entity (check only one box). (If **b**, **c**, or **d** is checked, see instructions.):

  a ☐ Corporation   **b** ☐ Subchapter S corporation   **c** ☐ Sole proprietor   **d** ☐ Partnership

  e ☐ Tax exempt organization   **f** ☐ Church   **g** ☐ Governmental organization

  h ☐ Other (specify) ▶

7 Is this an adoption of a master or prototype plan? . . . . ☐ Yes ☐ No If "Yes," complete **a** and **b**.

a Name of plan	**b** Notification letter no.

8 a Type of plan: (i) ☐ Fixed benefit (ii) ☐ Unit benefit (iii) ☐ Flat benefit (iv) ☐ Other (specify) ▶	**b** Does plan provide for variable benefits?. . . . ☐ Yes ☐ No

  c Is this a defined benefit plan covered under the Pension Benefit Guaranty Corporation insurance program? . . . . ☐ Yes ☐ No ☐ Not determined

Under penalties of perjury, I declare that I have examined this application, including accompanying statements, and to the best of my knowledge and belief, it is true, correct, and complete.

Signature	Title	Date

For Paperwork Reduction Act Notice, see page 1 of the instructions.   Form **5300** (Rev. 8-88)

Tools and Techniques

Form 5300 (Rev. 8-88) Page **2**

(Section references are to the Internal Revenue Code, unless otherwise noted.)

Where applicable, indicate the article or section and page number of the plan or trust where the following provisions are contained. N/A (not applicable) is an appropriate response only if an "N/A" block is provided.

		Section and Page Number
9 a	General eligibility requirements: (Check box (i), (ii), (iii), or (iv), and complete (v), (vi), and (vii).) (i) ☐ All employees (ii) ☐ Hourly rate employees only (iii) ☐ Salaried employees only (iv) ☐ Other (specify) ▶ .... (v) Length of service (number of years) ▶ .... ☐ N/A (vi) Minimum age (specify) ▶ .... ☐ N/A (vii) Maximum age (specify) ▶ .... ☐ N/A	
b	Does any plan amendment since the last determination letter change the method of crediting service for eligibility? . . . . ☐ Yes ☐ No ☐ N/A	

10	Participation (see Specific Instructions):	Yes	No	Not certain
a	(i) Is the employer a member of an affiliated service group? . . . . If your answer is "No," go to 10b.			
	(ii) Did a prior ruling letter rule on what organizations were members of the employer's affiliated service group, or did the employer receive a determination letter on this plan that considered the effect of section 414(m) on this plan?			
	(iii) If (ii) is "Yes," have the facts on which that letter was based materially changed?			
b	Is the employer a member of a controlled group of corporations or a group of trades or businesses under common control?			

11	Coverage of plan at (give date) .... (Attach Form(s) 5302 as necessary—see instructions.) (If the employer is a member of an affiliated service group, controlled group of corporations, or a group of trades or businesses under common control, employees of all members of the group must be considered in completing the following schedule.)	**Number** Enter "0" if N/A
a	Total employed (see Specific Instructions) (include all self-employed individuals)	
b	Statutory exclusions under this plan (do not count an employee more than once):	
	(i) Number excluded because of age or years of service required	
	(ii) Number excluded because of employees included in collective bargaining . .	
	(iii) Number of other employees excluded (specify)	
c	Total statutory exclusions under this plan (add lines b(i) through (iii))	
d	Employees not excluded under the statute (subtract line c from line a)	
e	Other employees ineligible under terms of this plan (do not count an employee included in line b)	
f	Employees eligible to participate (subtract line e from line d)	
g	Number of employees participating in this plan	
h	Percent of nonexcluded employees who are participating (divide line g by line d) . . . . . % If line h is 70% or more, go to line k.	
i	Percent of nonexcluded employees who are eligible to participate (divide line f by line d) . . . %	
j	Percent of eligible employees who are participating (divide line g by line f) . . . . % If lines h and i are less than 70% or line j is less than 80%, see Specific Instructions and attach schedule of information.	
k	Total number of participants in this plan (include certain retired and terminated employees (see Specific Instructions))	
l	Has a plan amendment since the last determination letter resulted in exclusion of previously covered employees? . . . . ☐ Yes ☐ No ☐ N/A	

12	Does the plan define the following terms:	Yes	No	N/A	**Section and Page Number**
a	Compensation (earned income if applicable)?				
b	Break in service?				
c	Hour of service (under Department of Labor Regulations)?				
d	Joint and survivor annuity?				
e	Normal retirement age?				
f	Year of service?				
g	Entry date?				

	Yes	No	N/A	Section and Page Number
13 Employee contributions:				
a (i) Does the plan document allow voluntary deductible employee contributions?			▨	
(ii) If "Yes," are the voluntary deductible employee contributions appropriately limited? . .			▨	
b Are voluntary nondeductible contributions limited for all qualified plans to 10% or less of compensation?				
c Are employee contributions nonforfeitable?				
14 Integration:			▨	
Is this plan integrated with social security or railroad retirement?				
If "Yes," attach a schedule of compliance with Rev. Rul. 71-446 (see Specific Instructions).	▨	▨	▨	
15 Vesting:				
a Are years of service with other members of a controlled group of corporations, trades or businesses under common control, or an affiliated service group counted for vesting and eligibility to participate?				
b Is employee's right to normal retirement benefits nonforfeitable on reaching normal retirement age as defined in section 411(a)(8)?			▨	
c Does any amendment to the plan decrease any participant's accrued benefit?				
d Does any amendment to the plan directly or indirectly affect the computation of the nonforfeitable percentage of a participant's accrued benefit?				
e Does the plan preclude forfeiture of an employee's vested benefits for cause?			▨	

f Check only one of these boxes to indicate the vesting provisions of the plan:

- (i) ☐ Full and immediate.
- (ii) ☐ Full vesting after 10 years of service, i.e., no vesting for the first 9 years, 100% vesting after 10 years (section 411(a)(2)(A)).
- (iii) ☐ 5- to 15-year vesting (section 411(a)(2)(B)).
- (iv) ☐ Rule of 45 (section 411(a)(2)(C)).
- (v) ☐ 4/40 vesting (Rev. Procs. 75-49 and 76-11).
- (vi) ☐ 10% vesting for each year of service (not to exceed 100%).
- (vii) ☐ Other (specify—see Specific Instructions and attach schedule).

16 Administration:

a Type of funding entity:

- (i) ☐ Trust (benefits provided in whole from trust funds).
- (ii) ☐ Custodial account described in section 401(f) and not included in (iv) below.
- (iii) ☐ Trust or arrangement providing benefits partially through insurance and/or annuity contracts.
- (iv) ☐ Trust arrangement providing benefits exclusively through insurance and/or annuity contracts.
- (v) ☐ Other (specify) ▶ ....

	Yes	No	N/A	
b Does the trust agreement prohibit reversion of funds to the employer (Rev. Rul. 77-200)? . .			▨	
17 Benefits and requirements for benefits:				
a Normal retirement age is ▶ .... If applicable, years of service/participation required	▨	▨	▨	
b Does the plan contain an early retirement provision?				
If "Yes," (i) Early retirement age is ▶	▨	▨	▨	
(ii) Years of service/participation required ▶	▨	▨		
c Does the plan provide for payment of benefits according to section 401(a)(14)?			▨	
d Method of determining accrued benefit ▶...	▨	▨		
(i) Benefit formula at normal retirement age is ▶..	▨	▨		
(ii) Benefit formula at early retirement age is ▶...	▨	▨		
(iii) Normal form of retirement benefits is ▶..	▨	▨		
e Does the plan comply with the payment of benefits provisions of section 401(a)(11)? . . .			▨	
f Are benefits under the plan definitely determinable at all times (section 401(a)(25))? . . .			▨	
g Are benefits computed on the basis of total compensation?			▨	
If "No," see instructions and attach schedule.				
h If participants may withdraw their mandatory contributions or earnings, may withdrawal be made without forfeiting vested benefits based on employer contributions?	▨	▨	▨	

Page **4**

		Yes	No	N/A	**Section and Page Number**
17	Benefits and requirements for benefits—*(Continued)*				
i	Does the plan disregard service attributable to a distribution in computing the employer-derived accrued benefit?			▨	
j	If line i is "Yes," does the plan contain provisions that satisfy Regulations section 1.411(a)-7(d)(4) or (6)?				
k	Are distributions limited so that no more than incidental death benefits are provided? . . .			▨	
l	Does the plan provide for maximum limitation under section 415?			▨	
m	Does the plan meet the requirements of section 401(a)(12)?			▨	
n	Does the plan prohibit the assignment or alienation of benefits?			▨	
o	Does the plan prohibit distribution of benefits except for retirement, disability, death, plan termination, or termination of employment?			▨	
p	As a result of a plan amendment, has the amount of benefit or rate of accrual of the benefit been reduced?			▨	
18	Termination of plan or trust:			▨	
a	Are the participants' rights to benefits under the plan nonforfeitable (to the extent funded) on termination or partial termination of the plan?			▨	
b	Has the early termination rule been included in the plan (Regulations section 1.401-4(c))?.			▨	

Form 5300 (Rev. 8-88)   Page **5**

Caution: The following Procedural Requirements Checklist identifies certain basic data that will facilitate the processing of your application. While no response is required to the questions, you may find that answering them will ensure that your application is processed without the need for contact to obtain missing information. If the answer to any of the questions is "No," your application is incomplete. Incomplete applications are identified through a computer screening system for return to the applicant. **This checksheet should be detached before submitting the application.**

Procedural Requirements Checklist

		Yes	No	N/A
1	General requirements			
a	If this application is made by a representative on behalf of the employer or plan administrator, has a current power of attorney been submitted with this application (see "Signature" under General Information)?			
b	If notices or other communications are to be sent to someone other than the employer, have you provided proper authorization by attaching a completed **Form 2848**, Power of Attorney and Declaration of Representative, or by attaching a statement that contains all the information required (see Specific Instructions)?			
c	Have you completed and attached Form(s) 5302?			▨
d	Have you signed the application?			▨
e	Have you completed and attached Schedule T (Form 5300)?			▨
2	Specific requirements			
a	If this is a request for a determination letter on initial qualification of the plan, have the following documents been attached:			
	(i) Copies of all instruments constituting the plan?			
	(ii) Copies of trust indentures, group annuity contracts, or custodial agreements?			
b	If this is a request for a determination letter on the effect of an amendment on the plan after initial qualification, have the following documents been attached:			
	(i) A copy of the plan amendment(s)?			
	(ii) A description of the amendment covering the changes to the plan sections?			
	(iii) An explanation of the plan sections before the amendment?			
	(iv) An explanation of the effect of the amendment on the provisions of the plan?			
c	If this is a request for a determination letter on the qualification of the entire plan, as amended after initial qualification, have the following documents been included:			
	(i) A copy of the plan incorporating all amendments made to the date of the application?			
	(ii) A statement indicating that the copy of the plan is complete in all respects and that a determination letter is being requested on the qualification of the entire plan?			
	(iii) A copy of trust indentures, group annuity contracts, or custodial agreements if there has been any change since copies were last furnished to IRS?			
d	For partial termination:			
	(i) Have you completed line 3a according to the Specific Instructions?			
	(ii) Have you attached the information requested for a partial termination in General Instruction B?			
e	For a plan adopted by one or more members of a controlled group:			
	(i) Have you attached the statements requested in the Specific Instructions for line 10b?			
	(ii) Have you completed line 11 according to General Instruction B and the Specific Instructions?			
f	For a multiple-employer plan that does not involve collective bargaining:			
	(i) Have you submitted one fully completed application (Form 5300 or 5301, whichever is appropriate) for all adopting employers?			
	(ii) Have you attached a Form 5300 or 5301 (as applicable) with only lines 1 through 11 completed, and a Form 5302 for each employer who adopted the plan?			
g	For a plan that contains a cash or deferred arrangement, have you submitted the appropriate information requested for line 11?			
h	For governmental and church plans, have you completed Form 5300 or 5301 according to General Instruction B?			
i	For notice of merger, consolidation, or transfer of plan assets or liabilities, have you submitted the information requested in the Specific Instructions for line 3c?			
j	For a plan that is or may be sponsored by a member of an affiliated service group:			
	(i) Have you completed lines 3a, 10, and 11 according to the Specific Instructions?			
	(ii) Have you attached the information requested in the Specific Instructions for lines 10a(ii) and (iii)?			▨
3	Miscellaneous requirements:			
a	Have you entered the plan sponsor's 9-digit employer identification number on line 1b?			▨
b	If a determination letter was previously issued to this sponsor for any plan, have you entered the file folder number on line 3b?			
c	Have you answered line 3d?			▨
d	If this plan has been amended at least four times since the last determination letter on the entire plan was issued, have you attached a copy of the plan that includes all amendments made to the plan since that determination letter was issued?			
e	Have you entered the effective date of the plan in the space provided by the block you checked for line 3a?			▨
f	If applicable, have you attached schedules or other documentation required by:			
	(i) Form 5300, lines 2, 3e, 6, 11j, 14, 15f(vii), and 17g?			
	(ii) Form 5301, lines 2, 3e, 11j, 14, 15f(viii), 17k, 17l, 17m, and 17s?			

☀ U.S. Government Printing Office: 1988-523-199/00336

Tools and Techniques

Form **5301** (Rev. August 1988) Department of the Treasury Internal Revenue Service	**Application for** **Determination for Defined Contribution Plan** For Profit-sharing, Stock Bonus and Money Purchase Plans (Under Sections 401(a), 401(k), and 501(a) of the Internal Revenue Code)	OMB No. 1545-0197 Expires 6-30-91 **For IRS Use Only** File folder number ▶ Case number ▶

Caution: Church and governmental plans not subject to ERISA need not complete items 10, 11, 12b, 12c, 15, 17g, 17l, and 18b. All other plans must complete all items except as indicated on specific lines. For example, if you answer "No" to line 7, you need not complete lines 7a and 7b since they require responses only if you answer "Yes" to line 7. N/A is only an acceptable answer if an N/A block is provided. All applications are now computer screened, therefore it is important that you provide all the information requested and have the application signed by the employer, plan administrator, or authorized representative. Otherwise, we may need to correspond with you or return your application for completion, which will delay its processing.

1 a Name of plan sponsor (employer if a single employer plan)

1b Employer identification number

Address (number and street)

1c Employer's tax year ends
Month ☐ N/A

City or town, state and ZIP code

Telephone number ( )

2 Person to be contacted if more information is needed (If same as 1a, enter "same as 1a"). (See Specific Instructions.)

Name

Telephone number ( )

Address

3 a Determination requested for (check applicable boxes): (See Instruction B. "What To File.")

(i) ☐ Initial qualification—Date plan signed _____ Date plan effective _____

(ii) ☐ Amendment after initial qualification—Is plan restated? ☐ Yes ☐ No   Date amendment signed _____

Date amendment effective _____ Date plan effective _____

(iii) ☐ Affiliated service group status (section 414(m))—Date effective _____ Date plan effective _____

(iv) ☐ Partial termination—Date effective _____ Date plan effective _____

b Enter IRS file folder number shown on the last determination letter issued to the plan sponsor _____ ☐ N/A

c Is this application also expected to satisfy the notice requirement for this plan for merger, consolidation, or transfer of plan assets or liabilities involving another plan? (See Specific Instructions.) . . . . ☐ Yes ☐ No

d Were employees who are interested parties given the required notification of the filing of this application? . . ☐ Yes ☐ No

e Is this plan or trust currently under examination or is any issue related to this plan or trust currently pending before the Internal Revenue Service, the Department of Labor, the Pension Benefit Guaranty Corporation, or any court? . . . . ☐ Yes ☐ No
If "Yes," attach explanation.

f Does your plan contain cash or deferred arrangements described in section 401(k)? . . . . ☐ Yes ☐ No
If "Yes," is a determination also requested on the qualification of those provisions? (See Instruction B.) . . . ☐ Yes ☐ No

4 a Name of Plan

b Plan number ▶ _____

c Plan year ends ▶ _____

5 Are there other qualified plans? (Do not consider plans that were established under union-negotiated agreements that involved other employers.) . . . . ☐ Yes ☐ No

a Name of plan ▶ _____

b Type of plan ▶ _____

c Rate of employer contribution ▶ _____ ☐ N/A

d Allocation formula ▶ _____ ☐ N/A

e Benefit formula or monthly benefit ▶ _____ ☐ N/A

f Number of participants ▶

6 Type of entity (check only one box):

a ☐ Corporation   **b** ☐ Subchapter S corporation   **c** ☐ Sole proprietor   **d** ☐ Partnership

e ☐ Tax exempt organization   **f** ☐ Church   **g** ☐ Governmental organization

h ☐ Other (specify) ▶

7 Is this an adoption of a master or prototype plan? ☐ Yes ☐ No. If "Yes," complete **a** and **b**

a Name of plan

b Notification letter no.

8 Type of plan: **a** ☐ Profit-sharing   **b** ☐ Stock bonus   **c** ☐ Money purchase   **d** ☐ Target benefit

e ☐ Other (specify) ▶

Under penalties of perjury, I declare that I have examined this application, including accompanying statements, and to the best of my knowledge and belief, it is true, correct, and complete.

Signature ▶ _____   Title ▶ _____   Date ▶ _____

For Paperwork Reduction Act Notice, see page 1 of the instructions.   Form **5301** (Rev. 8-88)

(Section references are to the Internal Revenue Code, unless otherwise noted.)

Where applicable, indicate the article or section and page number of the plan or trust where the following provisions are contained. N/A (not applicable) is an appropriate response only if an N/A block is provided.

9 a General eligibility requirements: (Check box (i), (ii), (iii) or (iv), and complete (v), (vi) and (vii).)	**Section and Page Number**

(i) ☐ All employees   *(ii)* ☐ Hourly rate employees only   *(iii)* ☐ Salaried employees only

(iv) ☐ Other (specify) ▶ ....

(v) Length of service (number of years) ▶ .... ☐ N/A

(vi) Minimum age (specify) ▶ .... ☐ N/A

(vii) Maximum age (specify) ▶ .... ☐ N/A

b Does any plan amendment since the last determination letter change the method of crediting service for eligibility? . . . . ☐ Yes ☐ No ☐ N/A

		Yes	**No**	**Not Certain**
10	Participation (see Specific Instructions):			
a	*(i)* Is the employer a member of an affiliated service group?			
	If your answer is "No," go to 10b.			
	(ii) Did a prior ruling letter rule on what organizations were members of the employer's affiliated service group or did the employer receive a determination letter that considered the effect of section 414(m) on this plan?			
	(iii) If (ii) is "Yes," have the facts on which that letter was based materially changed?			
b	Is the employer a member of a controlled group of corporations or a group of trades or businesses under common control?			

		Number
11	Coverage of plan at (give date) .... (attach Form(s) 5302—see instructions)	Enter "0" if N/A
	(If the employer is a member of an affiliated service group, a controlled group of corporations, or a group of trades or businesses under common control, employees of all members of the group must be considered in completing the following schedule.) If your plan contains cash or deferred arrangements described in section 401(k), see the Specific Instructions for line 11.	
a	Total employed (see Specific Instructions) (include all self-employed individuals)	
b	Statutory exclusions under this plan (do not count an employee more than once)	
	(i) Number excluded because of age or years of service required	
	(ii) Number excluded because of employees included in collective bargaining	
	(iii) Number of other employees excluded (specify).......................................	
c	Total statutory exclusions under this plan (add lines b(i) through (iii))	
d	Employees not excluded under the statute (subtract line c from line a)	
e	Other employees ineligible under terms of this plan (do not count an employee included in line b)	
f	Employees eligible to participate (subtract line e from line d)	
g	Number of employees participating in this plan	
h	Percent of nonexcluded employees who are participating (divide line g by line d) . . . . . %	
	If line h is 70% or more, go to line k.	
i	Percent of nonexcluded employees who are eligible to participate (divide line f by line d) . . . . . %	
j	Percent of eligible employees who are participating (divide line g by line f) . . . . . %	
	If lines h and i are less than 70% or line j is less than 80%, see Specific Instructions and attach schedule of information.	
k	Total number of participants (include certain retired and terminated employees (see Specific Instructions)).	
l	Has a plan amendment since the last determination letter resulted in exclusion of previously covered employees? . . . . ☐ Yes ☐ No ☐ N/A	

		Yes	**No**	**N/A**	**Section and Page Number**
12	Does the plan define the following terms—				
a	Compensation (earned income if applicable)?				
b	Break in service?				
c	Hour of service (under Department of Labor Regulations)?				
d	Joint and survivor annuity?				
e	Normal retirement age?				
f	Year of service?				
g	Entry date?				
13 a	Employee contributions:				
	(i) Does the plan allow voluntary deductible employee contributions?				
	(ii) If "Yes," are the voluntary deductible employee contributions appropriately limited?. .				
	(iii) Are voluntary nondeductible contributions limited for all qualified plans to 10%, or less, of compensation?				
	(iv) Are employee contributions nonforfeitable?				

257

Tools and Techniques

		N/A	Section and Page Number
13	*(Continued)*		
b	Employer contributions: (Response required in either (i), (ii), (iii) or (iv).)		
	(i) Profit-sharing or stock bonus plan contributions are determined under: ☐ A definite formula ☐ An indefinite formula ☐ Both		
	(ii) Profit-sharing or stock bonus plan contributions are limited to: ☐ Current earnings ☐ Accumulated earnings ☐ Combination		
	(iii) Money purchase—Enter rate of contribution ▶ ----------------------------------		
	(iv) State target benefit formula, if applicable ▶		

		Yes	No	N/A	
14	Integration:				
	Is this plan integrated with social security or railroad retirement?				
	If "Yes" and this is a target benefit plan, attach a schedule of compliance with Rev. Rul. 71-446 (see Specific Instructions).				
15	Vesting:				
a	Are years of service with other members of a controlled group of corporations, trades or businesses under common control, or an affiliated service group counted for vesting and eligibility to participate?				
b	Are employee's rights to normal retirement benefits nonforfeitable on reaching normal retirement age as defined in section 411(a)(8)?				
c	Does any amendment to the plan decrease any participant's accrued benefit?				
d	Does any amendment to the plan directly or indirectly affect the computation of the non-forfeitable percentage of a participant's accrued benefit?				
e	Does the plan preclude forfeiture of an employee's vested benefits for cause?				
f	Check only one of the boxes to indicate the vesting provisions of the plan:				
	(i) ☐ Full and immediate.				
	(ii) ☐ Full vesting after 10 years of service; i.e., no vesting for the first 9 years, 100% after 10 years (section 411(a)(2)(A)).				
	(iii) ☐ 5- to 15-year vesting (section 411(a)(2)(B)).				
	(iv) ☐ Rule of 45 (section 411(a)(2)(C)).				
	(v) ☐ 4/40 vesting (Rev. Procs. 75-49 and 76-11).				
	(vi) ☐ 10% vesting for each year of service (not to exceed 100%).				
	(vii) ☐ 100% vesting within 5 years after contributions are made (class year plans only).				
	(viii) ☐ Other (specify—see Specific Instructions and attach schedule).				
16	Administration: **a** Type of funding entity:				
	(i) ☐ Trust (benefits provided in whole from trust funds).				
	(ii) ☐ Custodial account described in section 401(f) and not included in (iv) below.				
	(iii) ☐ Trust or arrangement providing benefits partially through insurance and/or annuity contracts.				
	(iv) ☐ Trust or arrangement providing benefits exclusively through insurance and/or annuity contracts.				
	(v) ☐ Other (specify) ▶ ------------------------------				
b	Does the trust agreement prohibit reversion of funds to the employer? (Rev. Rul. 77-200) . .				
c	Are limits placed on the purchase of insurance contracts?				
	If "Yes," complete (i), (ii) or (iii), below				
	(i) Ordinary life ▶ ------------------------------				
	(ii) Term insurance ▶ ------------------------------				
	(iii) Other (specify) ▶ ------------------------------				
d	If the trustees may earmark specific investments, including insurance contracts, are such investments subject to the employee's consent, or purchased ratably when employee consent is not required?				
e	Are loans to participants limited to their vested interests?				
17	Requirements for benefits—distributions—allocations:				
a	Normal retirement age is ▶ -------------------------------- If applicable, years of service/ participation required ▶				
b	Does the plan contain an early retirement provision?				
	If "Yes," (i) Early retirement age is ▶ --------------------------------				
	(ii) Years of service participation required ▶ --------------------				
c	Does the plan provide for payment of benefits according to section 401(a)(14)?				

Form 5301 (Rev. 8-88)

Page **4**

		Yes	No	N/A	Section and Page Number

17 *(Continued)*

d Distribution of account balances may be made in:
  (i) ☐ Lump sum   *(ii)* ☐ Annuity contracts
  (iii) ☐ Substantially equal annual installments—not more than ▶ .... years
  (iv) ☐ Other (specify) ▶ ....

e If distributions are made in installments, they are credited with:
  (i) ☐ Fund earnings
  (ii) ☐ Interest at a rate of ▶ .... % per year
  (iii) ☐ Other (specify) ▶ ....

f Does the plan comply with the payment of benefits provisions of section 401(a)(11)? . . .

g If this is a stock bonus plan, are distributions made in employer stock? . . . .

h If this is a pension plan, does it permit distribution only on death, disability, plan termination, or termination of employment? . . . .

i If this is a profit-sharing or stock bonus plan, what other events permit distributions? ....
....

j If participants withdraw their mandatory contributions or earnings, may withdrawal be made without forfeiting vested benefits based on employer contributions? . . . .

k Are contributions allocated on the basis of total compensation? . . . .
  If "No," see Specific Instructions and attach schedule.

l Are forfeitures allocated, in case of a profit-sharing or stock bonus plan, on basis of total compensation? If "No," explain how they are allocated . . . .

m Are trust earnings and losses allocated on the basis of account balances? . . . .
  If "No," explain how they are allocated.

n For target benefit or other money purchase plan, are forfeitures applied to reduce employer contributions? . . . .

o Does the plan provide for maximum limitation under section 415? . . . .

p Does the plan prohibit the assignment or alienation of benefits? . . . .

q Does the plan meet the requirements of section 401(a)(12)? . . . .

r Are trust assets valued at fair market value?. . . . .

s Are trust assets valued at least annually on a specific date? . . . .
  If "No," explain.

18 Termination of plan or trust:

a Are the participants' rights to benefits under the plan nonforfeitable (to the extent funded) upon termination or partial termination of the plan? . . . .

b Are employees' rights under the plan nonforfeitable on complete discontinuance of contributions under a profit-sharing or stock bonus plan? . . . .

Procedural Requirements Checklist

Caution: The following Procedural Requirements Checklist identifies certain basic data that will facilitate the processing of your application. While no response is required to the questions, you may find that answering them will ensure that your application is processed without the need for contact to obtain missing information. If the answer to any of the questions is "No," your application may be incomplete. Incomplete applications are identified through a computer screening system for return to the applicant. **This checksheet should be detached before submitting the application.**

		Yes	No	N/A
1	General requirements			
a	If this application is made by a representative on behalf of the employer or plan administrator, has a current power of attorney been submitted with this application (see "Signature" under General Information)?			
b	If notices or other communications are to be sent to someone other than the employer, have you provided proper authorization by attaching a completed **Form 2848,** Power of Attorney and Declaration of Representative, or by attaching a statement that contains all the information required (see Specific Instructions)?			
c	Have you completed and attached Form(s) 5302?			▨
d	Have you signed the application?			▨
e	Have you completed and attached Schedule T (Form 5300)?			▨
2	Specific requirements			
a	If this is a request for a determination letter on initial qualification of the plan, have the following documents been attached:			
	(i) Copies of all instruments constituting the plan?			
	(ii) Copies of trust indentures, group annuity contracts, or custodial agreements?			
b	If this is a request for a determination letter on the effect of an amendment on the plan after initial qualification, have the following documents been attached:			
	(i) A copy of the plan amendments?			
	(ii) A description of the amendment covering the changes to the plan sections?			
	(iii) An explanation of the plan sections before the amendment?			
	(iv) An explanation of the effect of the amendment on the provisions of the plan sections?			
c	If this is a request for a determination letter on the qualification of the entire plan, as amended after initial qualification, have the following documents been included:			
	(i) A copy of the plan incorporating all amendments made to the date of the application?			
	(ii) A statement indicating that the copy of the plan is complete in all respects and that a determination letter is being requested on the qualification of the entire plan?			
	(iii) A copy of trust indentures, group annuity contracts, or custodial agreements, if there has been any change since copies were last furnished to IRS?			
d	For partial termination:			
	(i) Have you completed line 3a according to the Specific Instructions?			
	(ii) Have you attached the information requested for a partial termination in General Instruction B?			
e	For a plan adopted by one or more members of a controlled group:			
	(i) Have you attached the statement requested in the Specific Instructions for line 10b?			
	(ii) Have you completed line 11 according to General Instruction B and the Specific Instructions?			
f	For a multiple-employer plan that does not involve collective bargaining:			
	(i) Have you submitted one fully completed application (Form 5300 or 5301, whichever is appropriate) for all adopting employers?			
	(ii) Have you attached a Form 5300 or 5301 (as applicable) with only line items 1 through 11 completed, and a Form 5302 for each employer who adopted the plan?			
g	For a plan that contains a cash or deferred arrangement, have you submitted the appropriate information requested for line 11?			
h	For governmental and church plans, have you completed Form 5300 or 5301 according to General Instruction B?			
i	For notice of merger, consolidation, or transfer of plan assets or liabilities, have you submitted the information requested in the Specific Instructions for line 3c?			
j	For a plan that is or may be sponsored by a member of an affiliated service group:			
	(i) Have you completed lines 3a, 10, and 11 according to the Specific Instructions?			
	(ii) Have you attached the information requested in the instructions for lines 10a(ii) and (iii)?			
3	Miscellaneous requirements—			▨
a	Have you entered the plan sponsor's 9-digit employer identification number in line 1b?			▨
b	If a determination letter was previously issued to this sponsor for any plan, have you entered the file folder number on line 3b?			
c	Have you answered line 3d?			▨
d	If this plan has been amended at least four times since the last determination letter on the entire plan was issued, have you attached a copy of the plan that includes all amendments made to the plan since that determination letter was issued?			
e	Have you entered the effective date of the plan in the space provided by the block you checked for line 3a?			▨
f	If applicable, have you attached schedules or other documentation as required by:			
	(i) Form 5301—Lines 2, 3e, 11j, 14, 15f(viii), 17k, 17l, 17m, and 17s?			
	(ii) Form 5300—Lines 2, 3e, 6, 11j, 14, 15f(viii), and 17g?			

✿U.S. Government Printing Office: 1988-523-207/00337

Employee Census

Form 5302
(Rev. November 1987)
Department of the Treasury
Internal Revenue Service

▶ **Attach to application for determination—defined benefit and defined contribution plans.** (Round off to nearest dollar)

Schedule of 25 highest paid participating employees for 12-month period ended ▶

OMB No. 1545-0416
Expires 11-30-90

This Form is NOT Open to Public Inspection

Name of employer

Employer identification number

Line no.	Participant's last name and initials (See instructions) (a)	Check		Age (d)	Years of service (e)	Annual Nondeferred Compensation			Employee contributions under the plan (i)	Defined Benefit		Defined Contribution			
		Officer, shareholder, or self-employed (b)	Percent of voting stock or business owned (c)			Used in computing benefits or employee's share of contributions (f)	Excluded (g)	Total (h)		Annual benefit expected under this plan (j)	Annual benefit under each other qualified defined benefit plan of deferred compensation (k)	Employer contribution allocated (l)	Number of units, if any (m)	Forfeitures allocated in the year (n)	Amount allocated under each other defined contribution plan of deferred compensation (o)
1															
2															
3															
4															
5															
6															
7															
8															
9															
10															
11															
12															
13															
14															
15															
16															
17															
18															
19															
20															
21															
22															
23															
24															
25															
Total for above															
Totals for all others (specify number ▶)															
Total for all participants															

For Paperwork Reduction Act Notice, see back of this form.

See instructions on the back of this form.

Form **5302** (Rev. 11-87)

Tools and Techniques

General Information

(Section references are to the Internal Revenue Code unless otherwise noted.)

Paperwork Reduction Act Notice.— We ask for this information to carry out the Internal Revenue laws of the United States. We need it to determine whether taxpayers meet the legal requirements for plan approval. If you want to have your plan approved by IRS, you are required to give us this information.

Purpose of Form.—This schedule is to be used by the Internal Revenue Service in its analysis of an application for determination as to whether a plan of deferred compensation qualifies under section 401(a) and 401(k), if applicable.

Public Inspection.—Section 6104(a)(1)(B) provides, generally, that applications filed for the qualification of a pension, profit-sharing, or stock bonus plan will be open to public inspection. However, section 6104(a)(1)(C) provides that information concerning the compensation of any participant will not be open to public inspection. Consequently, the information contained in this schedule will not be open to public inspection, including inspection by plan participants and other employees of the employer who established the plan.

General Instructions

Prepare the employee census for a current 12-month period. Generally the 12-month period should be the employer's tax year, a calendar year, or the plan year. If the actual information is not available, compensation, contributions, etc., may be projected for a 12-month period. However, such projection must be clearly identified.

Who Must File.—Every employer or plan administrator who files an application for determination for a defined benefit or a defined contribution plan is required to attach this schedule, complete in all details.

For collectively bargained plans a Form 5302 is required only if the plan covers employees of the representative labor union(s) or of any plan(s) for union members, and, if so, a separate Form 5302 is required for each such union or plan. For a plan, other than a collectively bargained plan, maintained by more than one employer (where all employers in each affiliated service group, controlled group of corporations, or group of trades or businesses under common control are considered one employer) a separate Form 5302 is required for each such employer.

Specific Instructions

Column (a), first list any participant who at any time during the 5-year period prior to the start of the current 12-month period owned directly or indirectly 10% or more of the voting stock or 10% or more of the business. Next, list the remaining participants in order of current compensation (see Note 2 and instructions for column (h), below) starting with the highest paid, followed by the next highest paid and so on. If there are fewer than 25 participants, list all the participants. Otherwise, only the first 25 who fall under the priorities listed above need be listed on lines 1 through 25.

Note 1: *For purposes of this form, "participant" means any employee who satisfies the participation requirements prescribed by the plan.*

Column (b), enter a check mark or an "X" to indicate that a participant is either an officer, a shareholder, or self-employed. If a participant is none of the above, enter N/A in this column for that participant.

Column (c), (i) enter the percentage of voting stock owned by a participant. For example, participant "P" owns 200 shares of voting stock of the employer's 5,000 shares outstanding. The percentage is 4% (200 ÷ 5,000). If a participant owns only nonvoting stock of the employer, make no entry in this column.

(ii) if an unincorporated business, enter the percentage of the business owned by the participant.

If a participant owns neither of the above, enter N/A.

Column (d), enter the attained age of each participant as of the end of the year for which this schedule applies. For example, if a participant's 47th birthday was on January 7, 1988, and the schedule covers the calendar year 1988, enter 47 for that participant.

Column (e), enter the number of full years of service each participant has been employed by the employer, and any prior employer if such employment is recognized for plan purposes.

Column (f), enter the amount of each participant's compensation that is recognized for plan purposes in computing the benefit (for a defined benefit plan) or in computing the amount of employer contribution that is allocated to the account of each participant (for a defined contribution plan). Do not include any portion of the employer contributions to this or any other qualified plan as compensation for any participant.

Column (g), enter the amount of compensation that is not recognized for purposes of column (f). For example, if a participant received $12,500 compensation for the year, $1,000 of which was a bonus and the plan does not recognize bonuses for plan purposes, enter $11,500 in column (f) and $1,000 in column (g).

Note 2: *"Compensation" for purposes of column (h) is defined as all amounts (including bonuses and overtime) paid to the participant for services rendered the employer. Do not enter employer contributions made to this or any other qualified plan.*

Column (h), enter the total amount of compensation for the year for each participant. The amount entered in this column will be the sum of the amounts entered in columns (f) and (g) for each participant.

Column (i), enter the total amount of mandatory and voluntary contributions made by each participant. If the plan does not provide for employee contributions of any kind, enter "N/A."

Column (j), enter the amount of benefit each participant may expect to receive at normal retirement age based on current information, assuming no future compensation increases. For example, under a 30% benefit plan, a participant whose benefit is based on annual compensation of $10,000 may expect an annual benefit of $3,000 ($10,000 × 30%) at retirement. In this case enter $3,000.

Column (k), enter the amount of benefit each participant may expect to receive under other qualified defined benefit plan(s) of deferred compensation of the employer.

Column (l), enter the amount of the employer's contribution that is allocated to the account of each participant.

Column (m), enter the number of units, if any, used to determine the amount of the employer contribution that is allocated to each participant.

Column (n), enter the amount of the forfeitures that is allocated to each participant, unless forfeitures are allocated to reduce employer contributions.

Column (o), enter the portion of the employer's contribution that is attributable to the cost for providing each participant's benefits under all defined contribution plans of the employer other than this plan.

Caution: *Before submitting this schedule, be sure that all relevant items are complete. Failure to meet this requirement may result in a request for the missing information or return of the schedule for completion, in which event there will be a delay in processing your application.*

☆ **U.S. Government Printing Office: 1987—201-993/60128**

Form 5307
(Rev. July 1987)

Department of the Treasury
Internal Revenue Service

Short Form Application for Determination for Employee Benefit Plan
(Other than Collectively Bargained Plans)
(Under sections 401(a) and 501(a) of the Internal Revenue Code)

OMB No. 1545-0200
Expires 5-31-90

File folder number ▶   **For IRS Use Only**
Case number ▶

Church and governmental plans not subject to ERISA need not complete items 16, 17, 18, 19, and 20.

All other plans must complete all items except as indicated on the specific lines. For example, if you answer "No" to line 16a(i), you need not complete lines 16a(ii) and (iii) since they require responses only if you answer "Yes" to line 16a(i). "N/A" is only an acceptable answer if an N/A block is provided. All applications are now computer screened; therefore, it is important that you provide all the information requested and have the application signed by the employer, plan administrator, or authorized representative. Otherwise, we may need to correspond with you or return your application for completion, which will delay its processing.

1 a Name, address, and ZIP code of sponsor (employer if single employer plan)

Telephone number ▶ (   )

2 a Employer identification number

b Employer's tax year ends
Month   ☐ N/A

3 Name, address, ZIP code, and phone number of person to be contacted if more information is needed. (See Specific Instructions.) (If same as 1a, enter "same as 1a.")

Name ▶   Telephone number ▶ (   )
Address ▶

4 Determination requested for—(Check applicable box):
a (i) ☐ Initial qualification—date plan adopted ▶
(ii) ☐ Amendment—date adopted ▶
(iii) If (ii) is checked, enter file folder number ▶
b Were employees who are interested parties given the required notification of the filing of this application? . . . ☐ **Yes** ☐ **No**

5 Check appropriate box to indicate the type of plan entity:
a ☐ Single employer plan
b ☐ Plan of controlled group of corporations, common control employers, or affiliated service group
c ☐ Multiple-employer plan
d ☐ Church plan
e ☐ Governmental plan
f ☐ Other (specify) ▶

6 a Name of plan
b Plan number ▶
c Plan year ends ▶

7 a This is a:
(i) ☐ Master or prototype plan
(ii) ☐ Field prototype plan
(iii) ☐ Uniform plan (see instructions)
b Letter serial number or notification letter number

8 a Is this a defined benefit plan? ☐ **Yes** ☐ **No**—If "Yes," indicate whether:
(i) ☐ Unit benefit
(ii) ☐ Fixed benefit
(iii) ☐ Flat benefit
(iv) ☐ Other (specify) ▶
b Is this a defined contribution plan? ☐ **Yes** ☐ **No**—If "Yes," indicate whether:
(i) ☐ Profit-sharing
(ii) ☐ Money purchase
(iii) ☐ Stock bonus
(iv) ☐ Target benefit
c (i) If 8a (i), (ii), (iii), or (iv) is checked, is this a defined benefit plan covered under the Pension Benefit Guaranty Corporation termination insurance program?
☐ **Yes** ☐ **No** ☐ **Not determined**
(ii) If 4a (ii) and 8b (i), (ii), (iii), or (iv) are checked and the plan was a defined benefit plan before the amendment, was the plan covered by the termination insurance program before the amendment?
☐ **Yes** ☐ **No** ☐ **N/A**

9 Effective date of plan
10 Effective date of amendment
☐ **N/A**

11 Date plan was communicated to employees ▶
How communicated ▶

12 Integration: Is this plan integrated with social security or railroad retirement (see instructions)? . . . . ☐ **Yes** ☐ **No**

13 Type of funding entity:
a ☐ Trust
b ☐ Custodial account
c ☐ Nontrusteed
d ☐ Trust with insurance contracts

14 a Does plan provide for maximum limitation under section 415 (see instructions)? . . . . ☐ **Yes** ☐ **No**
b Do you maintain any other qualified plan(s) (see instructions)? . . . . ☐ **Yes** ☐ **No**

Under penalties of perjury, I declare that I have examined this application, including accompanying statements, and to the best of my knowledge and belief it is true, correct, and complete.

Signature ▶   Title ▶   Date ▶

Signature ▶   Title ▶   Date ▶

For Paperwork Reduction Act Notice, see page 1 of the instructions.   Form **5307** (Rev. 7-87)

Tools and Techniques

15 Is any issue relating to this plan or trust currently pending before the Internal Revenue Service, the Department of Labor, the Pension Benefit Guaranty Corporation, or any court? . . . . ☐ Yes ☐ No
If "Yes," attach explanation.

			Yes	No	Not Certain
16 a	*(i)*	Is the employer a member of an affiliated service group? . . . . If there is uncertainty whether the employer is a member of an affiliated service group, check the "Not Certain" column.			
	(ii)	If 16a(i) is "Yes" or "Not Certain," did a prior ruling or determination letter rule on what organizations were members of the employer's affiliated service group? (See instructions.)			
	(iii)	If 16a(ii) is "Yes," have the facts on which that letter was based materially changed? (See instructions.)			
b		Is the employer a member of a controlled group of corporations or a group of trades or businesses under common control?			

Number
Enter "0" if N/A

17 Coverage of plan at (give date) ▶ --
  a Total employed
  b Exclusions under plan because of (do not count an employee more than once):
    (i) Minimum age (specify) ▶ ----------- ☐ N/A Years of service (specify) ▶ ----------- ☐ N/A
    (ii) Employees included in collective bargaining
    (iii) Nonresident aliens who receive no earned income from United States sources

  c Total exclusions (add b(i) through (iii)) . . . .
  d Employees not excluded under the statute (subtract c from a)
  e Ineligible under plan because of (do not count an employee included in b):

    (i) Minimum pay (specify) ▶ -------------------------------------- ☐ N/A

    (ii) Hourly-paid . . . . .

    (iii) Maximum age (specify) ▶ -------------------------------------- ☐ N/A

    (iv) Other (specify) ▶ -------------------------------------- ☐ N/A
  f Total employees ineligible (add e(i) through (iv)) . . . . .
  g Employees eligible to participate (subtract f from d) . . . . .
  h Number of employees participating in plan . . . . . .
  i Percent of nonexcluded employees who are participating (divide h by d) . . . . . . %
    If line i is 70% or more, go to line l.
  j Percent of nonexcluded employees who are eligible to participate (divide g by d) . . . . %
  k Percent of eligible employees who are participating (divide h by g) . . . . %
    If i and j are less than 70%, or k is less than 80%, see instructions.
  l Total number of participants, including certain retired and terminated employees (see instructions) . .

18 Vesting—Check only one of the boxes for the vesting provisions of the plan:
  a ☐ Full and immediate
  b ☐ Full vesting after 10 years of service (see instructions)
  c ☐ 5- to 15-year vesting, i.e., 25% after 5 years of service, 5% additional for each of the next 5 years, then 10% additional for each of the next 5 years (see instructions)
  d ☐ Rule of 45 (section 411(a)(2)(C)) (see instructions)
  e ☐ For each year of employment, beginning with the 4th year, vesting not less than 40% after 4 years of service, 5% additional for each of the next 2 years, and 10% additional for each of the next 5 years
  f ☐ Other (specify and see instructions) ▶

19 Complete only for a plan of more than one employer:
  a Total number of participants (including certain retired and terminated employees) . . . .
  b Participants whose benefits or accounts are fully vested
  c Number of contributing employers
20 Is the plan sponsor an S Corporation? . . . . ☐ Yes ☐ No

☆U.S. Government Printing Office: 1987—201-993/60056

Form **8717**	**User Fee for Employee Plan**	**For IRS Use Only**
(January 1988)	**Determination Letter Request**	Control number _____
Department of the Treasury	**Attach to determination letter applications.**	Amount paid _____
Internal Revenue Service		User fee screener

1 Sponsor's name	2 Sponsor's employer identification number

3 Plan name	4 Plan number

5 Type of request (check only one box and include a check or money order made payable to Internal Revenue Service for the   Fee
amount indicated)

a ☐ Form 5300 for plan with fewer than 100 participants . . . . $ 400

b ☐ Form 5301 for plan with fewer than 100 participants 400

c ☐ Form 5300 for plan with 100 or more participants 600

d ☐ Form 5301 for plan with 100 or more participants 600

e ☐ Form 5310 (for plan terminations only) with fewer than 100 participants 200

f ☐ Form 5310 (for plan terminations only) with 100 or more participants 350

Note: *For user fee purposes the total number of participants is the same number of participants entered on line 11k of Form 5300 or Form 5301 or on line 16(g) of Form 5310.*

g ☐ Form 5303 500

h ☐ Form 5307 100

i ☐ Form 6406 100

j ☐ Form 4461 or Form 4461-A (Uniform Plans only) 500

k ☐ Group trust 400

Instructions

The Revenue Act of 1987 requires payment of a user fee for determination letter requests submitted to the Internal Revenue Service. The fee must accompany each request submitted to a key district office with a postmark date or receipt date (if not mailed) after January 31, 1988.

The fee for each type of request for an employee plan determination letter is listed in item 5 of this form. Check the block that describes the type of request you are submitting, and attach this form to the front of your request form along with a check or money order for the amount indicated. Make the check or money order payable to the Internal Revenue Service.

Determination letter requests received with no payment or with an insufficient payment will be returned to the applicant and will have to be resubmitted with the proper fee.

To avoid delays in receiving a determination letter, please be sure that the proper application is sent to the appropriate address from the list shown below. Restated plans and plans amended to comply with the Tax Reform Act of 1986 will not be accepted on **Form 6406,** Short Form Application for Determination for Amendment of Employee Benefit Plan. Nor will a multiple plan (e.g., a profit-sharing and a money purchase plan) be accepted on one application form.

If entity is in this IRS District ▼	Send fee and request for determination letter or notification letter to this address ▼
Brooklyn, Albany, Augusta, Boston, Buffalo, Burlington, Hartford, Manhattan, Portsmouth, Providence	Internal Revenue Service EP/EO Division P. O. Box 1680, GPO Brooklyn, NY 11202
Baltimore, District of Columbia, Pittsburgh, Richmond, Newark, Philadelphia, Wilmington, any U.S. possession or foreign country	Internal Revenue Service EP/EO Division P. O. Box 17010 Baltimore, MD 21203
Cincinnati, Cleveland, Detroit, Indianapolis, Louisville, Parkersburg	Internal Revenue Service EP/EO Division P. O. Box 3159 Cincinnati, OH 45201
Dallas, Albuquerque, Austin, Cheyenne, Denver, Houston, Oklahoma City, Phoenix, Salt Lake City, Wichita	Internal Revenue Service EP/EO Division Mail Code 4950 DAL 1100 Commerce Street Dallas, TX 75242
Atlanta, Birmingham, Columbia, Ft. Lauderdale, Greensboro, Jackson, Jacksonville, Little Rock, Nashville, New Orleans	Internal Revenue Service EP/EO Division Room 1112 P. O. Box 941 Atlanta, GA 30301
Honolulu, Laguna Niguel, Las Vegas, Los Angeles, San Jose	Internal Revenue Service EP Application Receiving Room 5127 P. O. Box 536 Los Angeles, CA 90053-0536
Chicago, Aberdeen, Des Moines, Fargo, Helena, Milwaukee, Omaha, St. Louis, St. Paul, Springfield	Internal Revenue Service EP/EO Division 230 S. Dearborn DPN 20-6 Chicago, IL 60604
Sacramento, San Francisco	Internal Revenue Service EP Application Receiving Stop SF 4446 P. O. Box 36001 San Francisco, CA 94102
Anchorage, Boise, Portland, Seattle	Internal Revenue Service EP Application Receiving P. O. Box 21224 Seattle, WA 98111

Attach Check or Money Order Here

☆ U.S. Government Printing Office: 1988—201-993/60212

Form **8717** (1-88)

Tools and Techniques

Appendix D

ERISA REPORTING AND DISCLOSURE FOR PENSION AND WELFARE PLANS

The Employee Retirement Income Security Act of 1974 — ERISA — imposed extensive reporting and disclosure requirements on a broad range of employee benefit plans. These provisions require various forms and information to be disclosed to plan participants and/or filed with the IRS or the Department of Labor.

Under ERISA, employee benefit plans are divided into two types — *pension* plans and *welfare* plans. These definitions are broad enough that it generally makes sense to think of them in terms of their exceptions rather than their definitions. That is, an employee benefit plan should be considered covered by the provisions of ERISA unless there is a specific exemption in ERISA or the regulations interpreting ERISA.

A *pension plan* (as defined for ERISA purposes) includes all qualified pension, profit-sharing, stock bonus, and similar qualified plans. It also includes some nonqualified deferred compensation plans. (These may, however, be eligible for exemption from funding requirements and reporting and disclosure — see Chapter 24.) In general, an ERISA pension plan is any employee benefit plan that involves deferral of an employee's compensation to his or her retirement date or later.

A *welfare plan* (also called a welfare benefit plan) is defined in ERISA as any employee benefit plan providing medical, surgical, or hospital care or benefits, or benefits in the event of sickness, accident, disability, death or unemployment, or vacation benefits, apprenticeship or other training programs, or day care centers, scholarship funds, or prepaid legal services. Certain other plans described in federal labor law are also included.

Reporting and Disclosure for Pension Plans

Pension plans must meet the reporting and disclosure requirements described in the chart at the end of this Appendix, with certain exceptions.

The first exception is an exception from most or all parts of ERISA, including the reporting and disclosure requirements, for certain types of employer plans. These ERISA-exempt employer plans are:

- plans of state, federal, or local governments or governmental organizations.

- plans of churches, synagogues, or related organizations. (These plans, however, can elect to be covered under ERISA.)

- plans maintained outside the United States for non-resident aliens.

- unfunded excess benefit plans (these are one type of nonqualified deferred compensation plan, as discussed in Chapter 24).

- plans maintained solely to comply with workers' compensation, unemployment compensation, or disability insurance laws.

In addition to these exemptions in ERISA itself, federal regulations have been issued that give partial exemption or special treatment to a number of other types of pension plans. These special regulatory exemptions are

- A *severance pay plan* is not treated as a pension plan if

  (1) payments do not depend directly on the employee's retiring;

  (2) total payments under the plan are less than twice the employee's annual compensation during the year immediately preceding the separation from service; and

  (3) all payments to any employee are completed within 24 months of separation from service.

  A severance pay plan meeting these criteria need not comply with the reporting and disclosure requirements for pension plans, but must meet the more limited reporting and disclosure requirements for welfare plans discussed below. For example, welfare plans with fewer than 100 participants need not file an annual report (Form 5500 series) if benefits are fully insured or are paid by the employer out of its general assets.

- *Supplemental payment plans* that provide extra benefits to retirees to counteract inflation are exempt from numerous ERISA requirements under Department of Labor Regulations.

- *Employer-sponsored IRAs, simplified employee pensions (SEPs), and Section 403(b) TSA plans* are subject to reduced ERISA reporting and disclosure requirements in some cases. See Chapters 17, 30 and 34 for discussion.

At the end of this Appendix is a compliance chart indicating the major reporting and disclosure requirements of

Tools and Techniques

ERISA and the timetables for filing or reporting. Copies of the Form 5500 annual report forms are also included.

The following brief explanation of the most important of these reporting and disclosure requirements for pension plans should be helpful in interpreting the significance of these requirements. The major elements of reporting and disclosure are as follows.

1. The *Summary Plan Description* (SPD). The SPD is intended to describe the major provisions of the plan to participants in plain language. An SPD must be furnished automatically to participants within 120 days after the plan is established and to new participants within 90 days after entering the plan. The SPD must also be filed with the Department of Labor within 120 days after a new plan is adopted. If plan provisions change, supplements to the SPD must be provided to participants. The contents of the SPD are prescribed by Labor Department regulations, but there is no government form for SPDs.

2. The *Annual Report* (Form 5500 series). This annual financial reporting form must be filed with the IRS each year by the end of the seventh month after the plan year ends. In addition to balance sheets and income statements, an actuary's report (Schedule B, Form 5500) must be included if the plan is a defined benefit plan, and information about any insurance contracts held by the plan must be included on Schedule A, Form 5500.

   The annual report forms are simpler for plans covering fewer than 100 participants. These plans file the simplified Form 5500-C, and have the option of filing an even simpler form, Form 5500-R in two out of every three years.

3. *Summary Annual Report*. The summary annual report is a brief summary of financial information from the Annual Report (Form 5500 series) that must be provided to plan participants each year within nine months of the end of the plan year. Labor regulations have essentially reduced this report to a formality. Participants have a right to see the full Annual Report if they need information about the plan's financial status.

4. *Individual Accrued Benefit Statement*. If a plan participant requests a statement of his or her individual benefits under the plan, the plan administrator must provide it within 30 days. Only one such statement each year needs to be provided to a participant. However, it is good policy to provide an annual individual benefit statement to plan participants, since this helps to communicate the plan's benefits and give them greater impact.

Reporting and Disclosure for Welfare Plans

The same list of ERISA-exempt plans (government plans, church plans, etc.) described above applies to welfare plans as well as to pension plans. Thus, such plans are exempt from virtually all ERISA requirements, whether they are pension or welfare plans.

For welfare plans there are also numerous regulatory exemptions and limitations. The following employment practices and benefits have been declared by regulation to be exempt from ERISA reporting and disclosure requirements:

- overtime pay, shift pay, holiday premiums, and similar compensation paid for work done other than under normal circumstances.

- compensation for absence from work due to sickness, vacation, holidays, military duty, jury duty, or sabbatical leave or training programs, if paid out of the general assets of the employer (i.e., not funded in advance).

- recreational or dining facilities or first aid centers on the employer's premises.

- holiday gifts.

- group insurance programs offered to employees by an insurer under which no contribution is made by the employer, participation is voluntary, and the program is not actively sponsored by the employer.

- unfunded tuition reimbursement or scholarship programs (other than Section 127 educational assistance plans — see Chapter 8) that are paid out of the employer's general assets.

All other welfare plans are subject to the ERISA reporting and disclosure requirements. However, in general, these are less onerous than those applicable to pension plans. For example, welfare plans with fewer than 100 participants need not file an annual report (Form 5500 series) if they are fully insured or are paid out of the general assets of the employer on a pay-as-you-go basis.

In addition to ERISA, certain welfare plans are subject to a reporting requirement under Section 6039D of the Internal Revenue Code. These plans may be required to file the Form 5500 series of annual reports even though they are not subject to ERISA. This is explained further in the instructions to these forms, reproduced at the end of this Appendix.

At the end of this Appendix there is a compliance chart indicating forms that must be filed with the IRS or Department of Labor or disclosed to participants. Copies of the current government forms of the 5500 series with instructions are also included. Current versions of these forms may be obtained from the local IRS office.

Figure D.1

REPORTING AND DISCLOSURE FOR PENSION PLANS

I. Government Filings

Form	Description	Who Must File	When to File	Where to File
5500	Annual Return/Report of Employee Benefit Plan (with 100 or more participants at beginning of plan year).	Plan administrator.	On or before last day of seventh month after close of plan year. ($2^{1}/_{2}$ month extension available — file Form 5558).	IRS Service center indicated in instructions to Form 5500.
5500-C	Return/Report of Employee Benefit Plan (with fewer than 100 participants at beginning of plan year).	Plan administrator.	Same as Form 5500.	Same as Form 5500.
5500-R	Registration Statement of Employee Benefit Plan (with fewer than 100 participants at beginning of plan year).	Optional alternative to Form 5500-C if Form 5500-C has been filed for one of the prior two plan years.	Same as Form 5500.	Same as Form 5500.
5500EZ	Annual Return of One-Participant (Owners and Their Spouses) Plans.	May be filed for plans that cover only an individual or an individual and spouse who are the owners of a business. May also be filed for partnership plans that cover only partners or partners and their spouses.	Same as Form 5500.	Same as Form 5500.
Schedule A (Form 5500 Series)	Insurance Information.	Plan administrator, where any plan benefits are provided by an insurance company or similar organization. (Schedule A not necessary with Form 5500EZ.)	Attachment to Form 5500 series.	Same as Form 5500.
Schedule B (Form 5500 Series)	Actuarial Information.	Plan administrator of defined benefit plan subject to minimum funding standards.	Attachment to Form 5500 series.	Same as Form 5500.
Schedule P (Form 5500 Series)	Annual Return of Fiduciary of Employee Benefit Trust.	Trustee or custodian of qualified trust or custodial account. (Begins running of statute of limitations.)	Attachment to Form 5500 series.	Same as Form 5500.

Tools and Techniques

Figure D.1 (cont)

Form	Description	Who Must File	When to File	Where to File
Schedule SSA (Form 5500 Series)	Annual Registration Statement Identifying Separated Participants with Deferred Vested Benefits.	Plan administrator, if plan had participants who separated with deferred vested benefits during the plan year.	Attachment to Form 5500 Series.	Same as Form 5500.
PBGC Form 1-ES	Estimated Premium Payment (Base premiums for plans with 500 or more participants).	Plan administrator or sponsor of defined benefit plan subject to PBGC provisions.	Within two months after the end of the prior plan year.	Pension Benefit Guaranty Corporation P.O. Box 105655 Atlanta, GA 30348-5655
PBGC Form 1	Annual Premium Payment (Base premiums for plans with fewer than 500 participants and variable rate premiums).	Plan administrator or sponsor of defined benefit plan subject to PBGC provisions.	Within 8½ months after the end of the prior plan year.	Pension Benefit Guaranty Corporation P.O. Box 105655 Atlanta, GA 30348-5655
Summary Plan Description	Summary of the provisions of the plan in plain language; includes statement of ERISA rights.	Plan administrator.	Within 120 days after the plan is adopted. New SPD must be filed once every 5 years after the initial filing date if the plan is amended; otherwise, must be filed every 10 years.	SPD, Room N-5644 Pension and Welfare Benefits Administration U.S. Department of Labor 200 Constitution Ave. NW Washington, DC 20210
Summary of Material Modifications	Summary of any material modification to the plan and any change in summary plan description.	Plan administrator.	Within 210 days after the close of the plan year in which the modification was adopted unless changes or modifications are described in timely filed summary plan description.	SMM, Room N-5644 Pension and Welfare Benefits Administration U.S. Department of Labor 200 Constitution Ave. NW Washington, DC 20210

II. Disclosure to Pension Plan Participants

Item	Description	Who Must Provide	When Provided
Summary Plan Description	Summary of the provisions of the plan in plain language; includes statement of ERISA rights.	Plan administrator.	New plans: within 120 days after effective date. Updated SPD must be furnished within 210 days of every fifth plan year for plans that have been amended; otherwise SPD must be redistributed every 10 years. New participants: within 90 days after becoming a participant or benefits commence (in the case of beneficiaries).
Summary of Material Modification	Summary of any material modification to the plan and any change in summary plan description.	Plan administrator.	Within 210 days after the close of the plan year in which the modification was adopted unless changes or modifications are described in a timely distributed summary plan description.

Figure D.1 (cont)

Item	Description	Who Must Provide	When Provided
Summary Annual Report	Summary of annual report Form 5500 series. (Form 5500-R may be distributed for plans filing that form.)	Plan administrator.	Nine months after end of plan year, or within two months after close of extension period for filing annual report, if applicable.
Notice of Preretirement Survivor Benefit	Written explanation of preretirement survivor annuity, participant's right to make an election (or revoke election), to waive the annuity, spouse's rights, and effect of election or revocation.	Plan administrator of plan required to provide (see Appendix B).	Within period beginning on first day of plan year in which participant attains age 32 and ending with close of plan year in which participant attains age 34. Election must be made within the period beginning on the first day of the plan year in which the participant attains age 35 and ending with the participant's death. For individuals who become participants after age 32, plan must provide explanation within three years of first day of plan year they become participants.
Notice of Joint and Survivor Benefit	Written explanation of joint and survivor annuity, right to make election, waive the right to coverage, or revoke waiver, effect of election or revocation, and rights of the spouse.	Plan administrator of plan required to provide (see Appendix B).	Within reasonable period before annuity starting date. Election must be made no sooner than 90 days before the annuity starting date.
Notice to Terminated Vested Participants	Same information as provided to IRS on Schedule SSA (Form 5500 series) concerning participant's accrued benefit. Statement must include notice if certain benefits may be forfeited if the participant dies before a particular date.	Plan administrator.	No later than due date for filing Schedule SSA (Form 5500 series).
Individual Accrued Benefit Statement	Statement of participant's benefit accrued to date based on the latest available data. Statement must include notice if certain benefits may be forfeited if the participant dies before a particular date.	Plan administrator.	Within 30 days of participant's request. Need not be provided more than once in a 12-month period.

Tools and Techniques

Figure D.2

REPORTING AND DISCLOSURE FOR WELFARE PLANS

I. Government Filings

Form	Description	Who Must File	When to File	Where to File
5500	Annual Return/Report of Employee Benefit plan (with 100 or more participants at beginning of plan year).	Plan administrator.	On or before the last day of the seventh month after the close of the plan year. (2½ month extension available — file Form 5558.	IRS service center indicated in instructions to Form 5500.
5500-C	Return/Report of Employee Benefit Plan (with fewer than 100 participants at beginning of plan year).	Plan administrator. Need not file if plan benefits paid solely from the general assets of the plan sponsor, or if plan is fully insured.	Same as Form 5500.	Same as Form 5500.
5500-R	Registration Statement of Employee Benefit Plan (with fewer than 100 participants at the beginning of the plan year).	Optional alternative to Form 5500-C if Form 5500-C has been filed for one of the prior two plan years.	Same as Form 5500.	Same as Form 5500.
Schedule A (Form 5500 series)	Insurance information.	Plan administrator, where any benefits under the plan are provided by insurance company or similar organization.	Attachment to Form 5000 series.	Same as Form 5500.
Summary Plan Description	Summary of the provisions of the plan in plain language; includes statement of ERISA rights.	Plan administrator of a welfare plan except for unfunded or fully insured welfare plans with fewer than 100 participants.	Within 120 days after the plan is adopted. A new SPD must be filed once every five years after the initial filing date if the plan is amended; otherwise, must be filed every 10 years.	SPD, Room N-5644 Pension and Welfare Benefits Administration U.S. Department of Labor 200 Constitution Ave. NW Washington, DC 20210
Summary of Material Modifications	Summary of any material modification to the plan and any change in summary plan description.	Plan administrator of a welfare plan except for unfunded or fully insured welfare plans with fewer than 100 participants.	Within 210 days after the close of the plan year in which the modification was adopted unless changes or modifications are described in a timely filed summary plan description.	SMM, Room N-5644 Pension and Welfare Benefits Administration U.S. Department of Labor 200 Constitution Ave. NW Washington, DC 20210

Figure D.2

II. Disclosure to Welfare Plan Participants and Beneficiaries

Item	Description	Who Must Provide	When Provided
Summary Plan Description	Summary of the provisions of the plan in plain language; includes statement of ERISA rights.	Plan administrator.	New plans: within 120 days after effective date. Updated SPD must be furnished within 210 days of every fifth plan year for plans that have been amended. Otherwise, SPDs must be redistributed every 10 years. New participants: within 90 days after becoming a participant or benefits commence (in the case of beneficiaries).
Summary of Material Modifications	Summary of any material modification to the plan and any change in summary plan description.	Plan administrator.	Within 210 days after the close of the plan year in which the modification was adopted unless changes or modifications are described in a timely distributed summary plan description.
Summary Annual Report	Summary of annual report Form 5500 or 5500-C (Form 5500-R may be distributed for plans filing that form.)	Plan administrator.	Nine months after end of plan year or within two months after close of extension period for filing annual report, if applicable.

Tools and Techniques

Form **5500**	**Annual Return/Report of Employee Benefit Plan (With 100 or more participants)**	OMB No. 1210-0016
Department of the Treasury Internal Revenue Service	This form is required to be filed under sections 104 and 4065 of the **Employee Retirement Income Security Act of 1974 and sections 6039D, 6057(b) and 6058(a) of the Internal Revenue Code, referred to as the Code.**	**19ⓑ7**
Department of Labor Pension and Welfare Benefits Administration		**This form is open to public inspection.**
Pension Benefit Guaranty Corporation	▶ **For Paperwork Reduction Act Notice, see page 1 of the instructions.**	

For the calendar plan year 1987 or fiscal plan year beginning _____ , 1987, and ending _____ , 19___ .

Type or print in ink all entries on the form, schedules, and attachments. If an item does not apply, enter "N/A." File the originals.

If *(i)* through *(iii)* do not apply to this year's return/report, leave the boxes unmarked. This return/report is:
(i) ☐ the first return/report filed for the plan; *(ii)* ☐ an amended return/report; or *(iii)* ☐ the final return/report filed for the plan.
▶ Welfare benefit plans, including those described in Code section 6039D, need only complete certain items—see the instructions "What To File."
▶ Keogh (H.R. 10) plans must check the box in item 5a(iii).
▶ If you have been granted an extension of time to file this form, you must attach a copy of the approved extension to this form.
Check this box if an extension of time to file this return is attached ▶ ☐

Use IRS label. Other- wise, please print or type.	**1a** Name of plan sponsor (employer if for a single-employer plan)	**1b** Employer identification number
	Address (number and street)	**1c** Telephone number of sponsor ( )
	City or town, state, and ZIP code	**1d** If plan year changed since last return/report, check here . . . ▶ ☐

2a Name of plan administrator (if same as plan sponsor, enter "Same")	**1e** Business code number ▶
Address (number and street)	**2b** Administrator's employer identification no.
City or town, state, and ZIP code	**2c** Telephone number of administrator ( )

3 Is the name, address, and employer identification number (EIN) of the plan sponsor and/or plan administrator the same as they appeared on the last return/report filed for this plan? ☐ Yes ☐ No. If "No," enter the information from the last return/report in a and/or b.
a Sponsor ▶ _____ EIN _____
b Administrator ▶ _____ EIN _____
c If a indicates a change in the sponsor's name and EIN, is this a change in sponsorship only? (See specific instructions for definition of sponsorship.) ☐ Yes ☐ No

4 Check appropriate box to indicate the type of plan entity (check only one box):
a ☐ Single-employer plan   **c** ☐ Multiemployer plan   **e** ☐ Multiple-employer plan (other)
b ☐ Plan of controlled group of corporations or common control employers   **d** ☐ Multiple-employer-collectively-bargained plan   **f** ☐ Group insurance arrangement (of welfare plans)

5a *(i)* Name of plan ▶ _____	**5b** Effective date of plan
(ii) ☐ Check if name of plan changed since last return/report *(iii)* ☐ Check this box if this is a Keogh (H.R. 10) plan.	**5c** Enter three-digit plan number . . ▶

6a Welfare benefit plan (Plan numbers 501 through 999) must complete (i) through (vii) and 6c:
   (i) ☐ Health insurance   *(ii)* ☐ Life insurance   *(iii)* ☐ Supplemental unemployment
   (iv) ☐ Other (specify) ▶ _____
   (v) ☐ Code section 120 (group legal services plan)   *(vi)* ☐ Code section 125 (cafeteria plan)
   (vii) ☐ Code section 127 (educational assistance program)
   If you checked (v), (vi), or (vii) check if: ☐ **funded** or ☐ **unfunded.**
b Pension benefit plan (Plan numbers 001 through 500) must complete (i) through (vii) and 6c through 6f:
   (i) Defined benefit plan—(Indicate type of defined benefit plan): (A) ☐ Fixed benefit   (B) ☐ Unit benefit
      (C) ☐ Flat benefit   (D) ☐ Other (specify) ▶ _____
   (ii) Defined contribution plan—(indicate type of defined contribution): (A) ☐ Profit-sharing   (B) ☐ Stock bonus
      (C) ☐ Target benefit (D) ☐ Other money purchase   (E) ☐ Other (specify) ▶ _____
   (iii) ☐ Defined benefit plan with benefits based partly on balance of separate account of participant (Code section 414(k))
   (iv) ☐ Annuity arrangement of certain exempt organizations (Code section 403(b)(1))
   (v) ☐ Custodial account for regulated investment company stock (Code section 403(b)(7))
   (vi) ☐ Pension plan utilizing individual retirement accounts or annuities (described in Code section 408) as the sole funding vehicle for providing benefits
   (vii) ☐ Other (specify) ▶

Under penalties of perjury and other penalties set forth in the instructions, I declare that I have examined this return/report, including accompanying schedules and statements, and to the best of my knowledge and belief, it is true, correct, and complete.

Date ▶ _____ Signature of employer/plan sponsor ▶ _____
Date ▶ _____ Signature of plan administrator ▶ _____

Tools and Techniques

Form 5500 (1987)   Page **2**

6c Other plan features: *(i)* ☐ Thrift-savings   *(ii)* ☐ Participant-directed account plan   *(iii)* ☐ Pension plan maintained outside the United States

    (iv) ☐ Master trust (see instructions) ▶ _____

    (v) ☐ 103-12 investment entity (see instructions) ▶ _____

		Yes	No
d Single-employer plans enter the tax year end of the employer in which this plan year ends ▶ Month ____ Day ____ Year ____			
e Is the employer a member of an affiliated service group?			
f Does this plan contain a cash or deferred arrangement described in Code section 401(k)?			

7 Number of participants as of the end of the plan year (welfare plans complete only a(iv), b, c, and d):

a Active participants: *(i)* Number fully vested	**a(i)**	
(ii) Number partially vested	**(ii)**	
(iii) Number nonvested	**(iii)**	
(iv) Total	**(iv)**	
b Retired or separated participants receiving benefits	**b**	
c Retired or separated participants entitled to future benefits	**c**	
d Subtotal (add a(iv), b, and c)	**d**	
e Deceased participants whose beneficiaries are receiving or are entitled to receive benefits	**e**	
f Total (add d and e)	**f**	

		Yes	No
g *(i)* Was any participant(s) separated from service with a deferred vested benefit for which a Schedule SSA (Form 5500) is required to be attached to this form?	**g (i)**		
(ii) If "Yes," enter the number of separated participants required to be reported ▶			

8 Plan information—You must complete a, c, d   **a** Was any amendment to this plan adopted in this plan year?

		Yes	No
8 a (above)	**8a**		
b If "Yes," *(i)* And if any amendments have resulted in a change in the information contained in a summary plan description or previously furnished summary description of modifications—			
(A) Have summary descriptions of the change(s) been sent to participants?	**b(i)A**		
(B) Have summary descriptions of the change(s) been filed with DOL?	**(i)B**		
(ii) Does any amendment result in the reduction of the accrued benefit of any participant under the plan?	**(ii)**		
c Enter the date the most recent amendment was adopted ▶ Month ____ Day ____ Year ____			
d *(i)* Has a summary plan description been filed with DOL for this plan?	**d**		
(ii) If (i) is "Yes," what was the employer identification number and the plan number used to identify it? Employer identification number ▶ Plan number ▶			

		Yes	No
9a Was this plan terminated during this plan year or any prior plan year? If "Yes," enter year ▶ _____	**9a**		
b Were all plan assets either distributed to participants or beneficiaries, transferred to another plan, or brought under the control of PBGC?	**b**		
c Was a resolution to terminate this plan adopted during this plan year or any prior plan year?	**c**		
d If a or c is "Yes," have you received a favorable determination letter from IRS for the termination?	**d**		
e If d is "No," has a determination letter been requested from IRS?	**e**		
f If a or c is "Yes," have participants and beneficiaries been notified of the termination or the proposed termination?	**f**		
g If a is "Yes," and the plan is covered by PBGC, is the plan continuing to file a PBGC Form 1 and pay premiums until the end of the plan year in which assets are distributed or brought under the control of PBGC?	**g**		
h During this plan year, did any trust assets revert to the employer for which the Code section 4980 excise tax is due?	**h**		
i If h is "Yes," enter the amount of section 4980 tax paid with your Form 5330 ▶			

		Yes	No
10a In this plan year, was this plan merged or consolidated into another plan(s), or were assets or liabilities transferred to another plan(s)?	**10a**		

If "Yes," identify other plan(s):

b Name of plan(s) ▶	**c** Employer identification number(s)	**d** Plan number(s)

e Has Form 5310 been filed? .... ☐ Yes ☐ No

11 Indicate a funding arrangement in **a** through **e** and complete **f** if applicable: **a** ☐ Trust (benefits provided in whole from trust funds)

  b ☐ Trust or arrangement providing benefits partially through insurance and/or annuity contracts

  c ☐ Trust or arrangement providing benefits exclusively through insurance and/or annuity contracts

  d ☐ Custodial account described in Code section 401(f) and not included in **c** above

  e ☐ Other (specify) ▶ _____

  f If b or c is checked, enter the number of Schedules A (Form 5500) which are attached .... ▶

12a Has the plan used the services of a contract administrator (see instructions)? .... ☐ Yes ☐ No

If "Yes," you must complete line (1) of the schedule below.

b Did any other person who rendered services to the plan receive, directly or indirectly, compensation from the plan in the plan year? ☐ Yes ☐ No

If "Yes," furnish the following information starting on line (2):

(a) Name	**(b)** Employer identification number (see instructions)	**(c)** Official plan position	**(d)** Relationship to employer, employee organization, or person known to be a party-in-interest	**(e)** Gross salary or allowances paid by plan	**(f)** Fees and commissions paid by plan	**(g)** Nature of service code (see instructions)
(1)		Contract admin.				13
(2)						
(3)						

13 Plan assets and liabilities at the beginning and the end of the plan year (list all assets and liabilities at current value). A fully insured welfare plan or a pension plan with no trust and which is funded entirely by allocated insurance contracts which fully guarantee the amount of benefit payments should check the box and not complete the rest of this item ▶ . . . . ☐

Note: *Include all plan assets and liabilities of a trust or separately maintained fund. (If more than one trust/fund, report on a combined basis.) Include all insurance values except for the value of that portion of an allocated insurance contract which fully guarantees the amount of benefit payments. Round off amounts to the nearest dollar. Trusts with no assets at the beginning and the end of the plan year enter zero on line 13h.*

Assets		(a) Beginning of year	(b) End of year
a Cash: *(i)* On hand	a(i)		
(ii) In bank: (A) Certificates of deposit	(ii)(A)		
(B) Other interest bearing	(ii)(B)		
(C) Noninterest bearing	(ii)(C)		
(iii) Total cash (add (i) and (ii))	(iii)		
b Receivables: *(i)* Employer contributions	b(i)		
(ii) Employee contributions	(ii)		
(iii) Other	(iii)		
(iv) Reserve for doubtful accounts	(iv)		
(v) Net receivables (subtract (iv) from the total of (i), (ii), and (iii))	(v)		
c General investments other than party-in-interest investments:			
(i) U.S. Government securities: (A) Long term	c(i)(A)		
(B) Short term	(i)(B)		
(ii) State and municipal securities	(ii)		
(iii) Corporate debt instruments: (A) Long term	(iii)(A)		
(B) Short term	(iii)(B)		
(iv) Corporate stocks: (A) Preferred	(iv)(A)		
(B) Common	(iv)(B)		
(v) Shares of a registered investment company	(v)		
(vi) Real estate	(vi)		
(vii) Mortgages	(vii)		
(viii) Loans other than mortgages	(viii)		
(ix) Value of interest in pooled fund(s)	(ix)		
(x) Value of interest in master trust	(x)		
(xi) Value of interest in 103-12 investment entities	(xi)		
(xii) Other investments	(xii)		
(xiii) Total general investments (add (i) through (xii))	(xiii)		
d Party-in-interest investments:			
(i) Corporate debt instruments	d(i)		
(ii) Corporate stocks: (A) Preferred	(ii)(A)		
(B) Common	(ii)(B)		
(iii) Real estate	(iii)		
(iv) Mortgages	(iv)		
(v) Loans other than mortgages	(v)		
(vi) Other investments	(vi)		
(vii) Total party-in-interest investments (add (i) through (vi))	(vii)		
e Buildings and other depreciable property used in plan operation	e		
f Value of unallocated insurance contracts (other than pooled separate accounts):			
(i) Separate accounts	f(i)		
(ii) Other	(ii)		
(iii) Total (add (i) and (ii))	(iii)		
g Other assets	g		
h Total assets (add a(iii), b(v), c(xiii), d(vii), e, f(iii), and g)	h		
Liabilities			
i Payables: *(i)* Plan claims	i(i)		
(ii) Other payables	(ii)		
(iii) Total payables (add (i) and (ii))	(iii)		
j Acquisition indebtedness	j		
k Other liabilities	k		
l Total liabilities (add i, j, and k)	l		
m Net assets (subtract l from h)	m		
n During the plan year what were the:			
(i) Total costs of acquisitions of common stock?	n(i)		
(ii) Total proceeds from dispositions of common stock?	(ii)		

14 Plan income, expenses and changes in net assets for the plan year.

Note: *Include all income and expenses of a trust(s) or separately maintained fund(s) including any payments made for allocated insurance contracts. Round off amounts to nearest dollar.*

Income

		(a) Amount	(b) Total
a Contributions received or receivable in cash from—			
(i) Employer(s) (including contributions on behalf of self-employed individuals)	a(i)		
(ii) Employees	(ii)		
(iii) Others	(iii)		
b Noncash contributions (specify nature and by whom made) ▶	b		
c Total contributions (add total of a(iii) and b)	c		
d Earnings from investments—			
(i) Interest	d(i)		
(ii) Dividends	(ii)		
(iii) Rents	(iii)		
(iv) Royalties	(iv)		
e Net realized gain (loss) on sale or exchange of assets—			
(i) Aggregate proceeds	e(i)		
(ii) Aggregate costs	(ii)		
f Other income (specify) ▶	f		
g Total income (add c through f)	g		

Expenses

		(a) Amount	(b) Total
h Distribution of benefits and payments to provide benefits—			
(i) Directly to participants or their beneficiaries	h(i)		
(ii) To insurance carrier or similar organization for provision of benefits	(ii)		
(iii) To other organizations or individuals providing welfare benefits	(iii)		
i Interest expense	i		
j Administrative expenses—			
(i) Salaries and allowances	j(i)		
(ii) Fees and commissions	(ii)		
(iii) Insurance premiums for Pension Benefit Guaranty Corporation	(iii)		
(iv) Insurance premiums for fiduciary insurance other than bonding	(iv)		
(v) Other administrative expenses	(v)		
k Other expenses (specify) ▶	k		
l Total expenses (add h through k)	l		
m Net income (expenses) (subtract l from g)	m		

		(a) Amount	(b) Total
n Changes in net assets —			
(i) Unrealized appreciation (depreciation) of assets	n(i)		
(ii) Net investment gain (loss) from all master trust investment accounts	(ii)		
(iii) Net investment gain (loss) from all 103-12 investment entities	(iii)		
(iv) Other changes (specify) ▶	(iv)		
o Net increase (decrease) in net assets for the year (add m and n)	o		
p Net assets at beginning of year (line 13m, column (a))	p		
q Net assets at end of year (add o and p) (equals line 13m, column (b))	q		

15 All plans complete a, b, and c. Plans funded with insurance policies or annuity contracts also complete d and e:

			Yes	No
a During this plan year, was there a termination in the appointment of any person listed in b below?		a		
b If a is "Yes," check the appropriate box(es) and provide the name, position, address, and telephone number of the person(s) whose appointment has been terminated and an explanation for the termination:				

    (i) ☐ Trustee   *(ii)* ☐ Accountant   *(iii)* ☐ Insurance carrier   *(iv)* ☐ Enrolled actuary

    (v) ☐ Administrator   *(vi)* ☐ Investment manager   *(vii)* ☐ Custodian ▶

			Yes	No
c Have there been any outstanding material disputes or matters of disagreement concerning the above termination? See instructions		c		
d Have any insurance policies or annuities been replaced during this plan year?		d		

If "Yes," explain the reason for the replacement ▶

e At any time during the plan year was the plan funded with:

    (i) ☐ Individual policies or annuities,   *(ii)* ☐ Group policies or annuities, or   *(iii)* ☐ Both.

Form 5500 (1987)

Page **5**

	Yes	No

16 Bonding:

a Was the plan insured by a fidelity bond against losses through fraud or dishonesty? . . . .   **a**

If "Yes," complete b through f; if "No," complete only g.

b Indicate the number of plans covered by this bond ▶ _____

c Enter the maximum amount of loss recoverable ▶ _____

d Enter the name of the surety company ▶ _____

_____

e Does the plan, or a known party-in-interest with respect to the plan, have any control or significant financial interest, direct or indirect, in the surety company or its agents or brokers? . . . .   **e**

f In the current plan year was any loss to the plan caused by the fraud or dishonesty of any plan official or employee of the plan or of any other person handling funds of the plan? . . . .   **f**

If "Yes," see specific instructions.

g If the plan is not insured by a fidelity bond, explain why not ▶ _____

_____

17 Information about employees of employer at end of the plan year:

a Does the plan satisfy the percentage tests of Code section 410(b)(1)(A)? If "No," complete only b below and see Specific Instructions . . . .   **a**

b Total number of employees . . . .   **b**

c Number of employees excluded under the plan because of:

    (i) Minimum age or years of service . . . .   **c(I)**

    (ii) Employees on whose behalf retirement benefits were the subject of collective bargaining . .   **(II)**

    (iii) Nonresident aliens who receive no earned income from United States sources . . . .   **(III)**

    (iv) Total excluded (add (i), (ii), and (iii)) . . . .   **(Iv)**

d Total number of employees not excluded (subtract c(iv) from b) . . . .   **d**

e Employees ineligible (specify reason) ▶ _____   **e**

f Employees eligible to participate (subtract e from d) . . . .   **f**

g Employees eligible but not participating . . . .   **g**

h Employees participating (subtract g from f) . . . .   **h**

	Yes	No

18 Is this plan an adoption of any of the plans below? (If "Yes," check appropriate box and enter IRS serial number):   **18**

a ☐ Master/prototype plan, or   **b** ☐ Uniform plan

Enter the eight-character IRS letter serial number (see instructions) ▶

19 **a** Is it intended that this plan qualify under Code section 401(a)? . . . .   **a**

b Have you requested or received a determination letter from the IRS for this plan? . . . .   **b**

c *(i)* Is this a plan with Employee Stock Ownership Plan features? . . . .   **c(I)**

    (ii) If "Yes," were all valuations of employer stock, for the plan year covered by this return/report, made by an independent appraiser? . . . .   **(II)**

20 **a** If plan is integrated, check appropriate box:

    (i) ☐ Social security   *(ii)* ☐ Railroad retirement   *(iii)* ☐ Other

b Does the employer/sponsor listed in item 1a of this form maintain other qualified pension benefit plans? . .   **b**

If "Yes," list the number of plans including this plan ▶

21 **a** If this is a defined benefit plan, is it subject to the minimum funding standards for this plan year? . . . .   **a**

If "Yes," attach Schedule B (Form 5500).

b If this is a money purchase or target benefit plan, is it subject to the minimum funding standards? (If a waiver was granted, see instructions.) . . . .   **b**

If "Yes," complete (i), (ii), and (iii) below:

    (i) Amount of employer contribution required for the plan year under Code section 412 . . . .   **(I)**

    (ii) Amount of contribution paid by the employer for the plan year . . . .   **(II)**

    Enter date of last payment by employer . . . ▶ Month _____ Day _____ Year _____

    (iii) If (i) is greater than (ii), subtract (ii) from (i) and enter the funding deficiency here; otherwise enter zero. (If you have a funding deficiency, file Form 5330.) . . . .   **(III)**

Tools and Techniques

Form 5500 (1987)

Page **6**

22 Answer questions a, b, and c relating to the plan year. If a(i), (ii), (iii), (iv), or (v) is checked "Yes," schedules of those items in the format set forth in the instructions are required to be attached to this form.

		Yes	No
a *(i)* Did the plan have assets held for investment?	a(i)		
(ii) Did any nonexempt transaction involving plan assets involve a party known to be a party-in-interest? . . .	(ii)		
(iii) Were any loans by the plan or fixed income obligations due the plan in default as of the close of the plan year or classified during the year as uncollectable?	(iii)		
(iv) Were any leases to which the plan was a party in default or classified during the year as uncollectable? . .	(iv)		
(v) Were any plan transactions or series of transactions in excess of 3% of the current value of plan assets? . .	(v)		
b Is this plan exempt from the requirement that an accountant's opinion must be attached to this form?	b		

c If b is "No," attach the accountant's opinion to this form and check the appropriate box. This opinion is:

(i) ☐ Unqualified

(ii) ☐ Qualified/disclaimer per Department of Labor regulations 29 CFR 2520.103-8 and/or 2520.103-12(d)

(iii) ☐ Qualified/disclaimer other

(iv) ☐ Other (explain) ▶

	Yes	No
d If b is "No," do the financial statements or notes to the financial statements attached to this report disclose: *(i)* A loss contingency indicating that assets are impaired or liability incurred; *(ii)* Significant real estate or other transactions in which the plan and (A) the sponsor, (B) plan administrator, (C) the employer(s), or (D) the employee organization(s) are jointly involved; *(iii)* That the plan has participated in any related party transactions; or, *(iv)* Any unusual or infrequent events or transactions occurring subsequent to the plan year-end that might significantly affect the usefulness of the financial statements in assessing the plan's present or future ability to pay benefits?	d		

23 **a** Is the plan covered under the Pension Benefit Guaranty Corporation termination insurance program? . . . . ☐ Yes ☐ No ☐ Not determined

b If a is "Yes," or "Not determined," enter the employer identification number and the plan number used to identify it.
Employer identification number ▶   Plan number ▶

		Yes	No
24 **a** Is this plan a top-heavy plan within the meaning of Code section 416 for this plan year?	a		
b If a is "Yes," complete (i), (ii), and (iii) below:			
(i) Has the plan complied with the vesting requirements of Code section 416(b)?	(i)		
(ii) Has the plan complied with the minimum benefit requirements of Code section 416(c)?	(ii)		
(iii) Has the plan complied with the limitation on compensation of Code section 416(d)?	(iii)		
25 Have any individuals performed services as leased employees for any employer covered by this plan or for any other employer who is aggregated with any employer covered by this plan under section 414(b), (c), or (m)? . . If "Yes," see instructions for completing item 17.	25		
26 **a** If the plan distributed any annuity contracts this year, did these contracts contain a requirement that the spouse consent before any distributions under the contract are made in a form other than a qualified joint and survivor annuity?	a		
b Did the plan make distributions to participants or spouses in a form other than a qualified joint and survivor annuity (a life annuity if a single person) or qualified preretirement survivor annuity (exclude deferred annuity contracts)?	b		
c Did the plan make distributions or loans to married participants and beneficiaries without the required consent of the participant's spouse?	c		
d Upon plan amendment or termination, do the accrued benefits of every participant include the subsidized benefits that the participant may become entitled to receive subsequent to the plan amendment or termination? .	d		
27 Were distributions made in accordance with the requirements of Code section 417(e) (see instructions)? . . .	27		
28 Have any contributions been made or benefits accrued in excess of the Code section 415 limits, as amended by the Tax Reform Act of 1986?	28		
29 Has the plan made the required distributions in 1987 under Code section 401(a)(9)?	29		

SCHEDULE A
(Form 5500)
Department of the Treasury
Internal Revenue Service

Department of Labor
Pension and Welfare Benefits Administration

Pension Benefit Guaranty Corporation

Insurance Information
This schedule is required to be filed under section 104 of the
Employee Retirement Income Security Act of 1974.

▶ **File as an Attachment to Forms 5500, 5500-C, or 5500-R.**

▶ Insurance companies are required to provide this information
as per ERISA section 103(a)(2).

OMB No. 1210-0016

1988

**This Form Is
Open to Public
Inspection**

For calendar year 1988 or fiscal plan year beginning | , 1988 and ending | , 19

▶ **Part I must be completed for all plans required to file this schedule.**
▶ **Part II must be completed for all insured pension plans.**
▶ **Part III must be completed for all insured welfare plans.**

▶ Enter master trust or 103-12 IE name in place of "sponsor" and specify investment account or 103-12 IE in place of "plan" if filing with DOL for a master trust or 103-12 IE.

Name of plan sponsor as shown on line 1a of Form 5500, 5500-C, or 5500-R | **Employer identification number**

Name of plan | Enter three-digit plan number ▶

Part I **Summary of All Insurance Contracts Included in Parts II and III**
Group all contracts in the same manner as in Parts II and III.

1 Check appropriate box: **a** ☐ Welfare plan **b** ☐ Pension plan **c** ☐ Combination pension and welfare plan

2 Coverage: (a) Name of insurance carrier	(b) Contract or identification number	(c) Approximate number of persons covered at end of policy or contract year	Policy or contract year	
			(d) From	(e) To

3 Insurance fees and commissions paid to agents and brokers:		(c) Amount of commissions paid	(d) Fees paid	
(a) Contract or identification number	(b) Name and address of the agents or brokers to whom commissions or fees were paid		Amount	Purpose
Total				

4 Premiums due and unpaid at end of the plan year ▶ $: Contract or identification number ▶

Part II **Insured Pension Plans** Provide information for each contract on a separate Part II. Where individual contracts are provided, the entire group of such individual contracts with each carrier may be treated as a unit for purposes of this report.

▶ Contract or identification number ▶

5 Contracts with allocated funds, for example, individual policies or group deferred annuity contracts:

  a State the basis of premium rates ▶

  b Total premiums paid to carrier .

  c If the carrier, service, or other organization incurred any specific costs in connection with the acquisition
    or retention of the contract or policy, other than reported in 3 above, enter amount .
    Specify nature of costs ▶

6 Contracts with unallocated funds, for example, deposit administration or immediate participation guarantee
  contracts. Do not include portions of these contracts maintained in separate accounts:

  a Balance at the end of the previous policy year .

  b Additions: *(i)* Contributions deposited during year

    (ii) Dividends and credits .

    (iii) Interest credited during the year .

    (iv) Transferred from separate account .

    (v) Other (specify) ▶

    (vi) Total additions .

  c Total of balance and additions, add **a** and **b**(vi) .

  d Deductions:

    (i) Disbursed from fund to pay benefits or purchase annuities during year .

    (ii) Administration charge made by carrier .

    (iii) Transferred to separate account .

    (iv) Other (specify) ▶

    (v) Total deductions .

  e Balance at end of current policy year, subtract **d**(v) from **c** .

7 Separate accounts: Current value of plan's interest in separate accounts at year end .

For Paperwork Reduction Act Notice, see page 1 of the Instructions for Form 5500 or 5500-C.

Schedule A (Form 5500) 1988

Tools and Techniques

Part III	**Insured Welfare Plans**

Provide information for each contract on a separate Part III. If more than one contract covers the same group of employees of the same employer(s) or members of the same employee organization(s), the information may be combined for reporting purposes if such contracts are experience-rated as a unit. Where individual contracts are provided, the entire group of such individual contracts with each carrier may be treated as a unit for purposes of this report.

8 **(a)** Contract or identification number	**(b)** Type of benefit	**(c)** List gross premium for each contract	**(d)** Premium rate or subscription charge

9 Experience-rated contracts: **a** Premiums: *(i)* Amount received . . . .

 (ii) Increase (decrease) in amount due but unpaid . . . . . .

 (iii) Increase (decrease) in unearned premium reserve . . . . .

 (iv) Premiums earned, add (i) and (ii), and subtract (iii)

 b Benefit charges: *(i)* Claims paid . . . .

 (ii) Increase (decrease) in claim reserves . . . .

 (iii) Incurred claims, add (i) and (ii) . . . . . .

 (iv) Claims charged . . . .

 c Remainder of premium: *(i)* Retention charges (on an accrual basis)—(A) Commissions .

 (B) Administrative service or other fees . . . . . .

 (C) Other specific acquisition costs . . . . . .

 (D) Other expenses . . . . . .

 (E) Taxes. . . . . . .

 (F) Charges for risks or contingencies . . . . . .

 (G) Other retention charges . . . . . .

 (H) Total retention . . . .

 (ii) Dividends or retroactive rate refunds. (These amounts were ☐ paid in cash, or ☐ credited.) . . . .

 d Status of policyholder reserves at end of year: *(i)* Amount held to provide benefits after retirement

 (ii) Claim reserves . . . .

 (iii) Other reserves . . . . . .

 e Dividends or retroactive rate refunds due (do not include amount entered in **c**(ii))

10 Nonexperience-rated contracts: **a** Total premiums or subscription charges paid to carrier . . . . . .

 b If the carrier, service, or other organization incurred any specific costs in connection with the acquisition or retention of the contract or policy, other than reported in 3 above, report amount . . . .

 Specify nature of costs ▶ --

If additional space is required for any item, attach additional sheets the same size as this form.

General Instructions

This schedule must be attached to Form 5500, 5500-C, or 5500-R for every defined benefit, defined contribution, and welfare benefit plan where any benefits under the plan are provided by an insurance company, insurance service, or other similar organization.

Specific Instructions

(References are to the line items on the form.)

Include only contracts with policy or contract years ending with or within the plan year (for reporting purposes a year cannot exceed 12 months). Data on Schedule A (Form 5500) should be reported only for such policy or contract years. **Exception:** *If the insurance company maintains records on the basis of a plan year rather than policy or contract year, data on Schedule A (Form 5500) may be reported for the plan year.*

Include only the contracts issued to the plan for which this return/report is being filed.

Plans Participating in Master Trust(s) and 103-12 IEs—See the Form 5500 or Form 5500-C instructions for "Reporting Requirements for Investment Arrangements Filing With DOL."

2(c).—Since the plan coverage may fluctuate during the year, the number of persons entered should be that which the administrator determines will most reasonably reflect the number covered by the plan at the end of the policy or contract year.

Where contracts covering individual employees are grouped, entries should be determined as of the end of the plan year.

2(d) and (e).—Enter the beginning and ending dates of the policy year for each contract listed under column (b). Where separate contracts covering individual employees are grouped, enter "N/A" in column (d).

3.—All sales commissions are to be reported in column (c) regardless of the identity of the recipient. Override commissions, salaries, bonuses, etc., paid to a general agent or manager for managing an agency, or for performing other administrative functions, are not to be reported.

Fees to be reported in column (d) represent payments by insurance carriers to agents and brokers for items other than commissions (e.g., service fees, consulting fees, and finders fees).

Note: *For purposes of this item, commissions and fees include amounts paid by an insurance company on the basis of the aggregate value*

(e.g., policy amounts, premiums) of contracts or policies (or classes thereof) placed or retained. The amount (or pro rata share of the total) of such commissions or fees attributable to the contract or policy placed with or retained by the plan must be reported in column (c) or (d), as appropriate.

Fees paid by insurance carriers to persons other than agents and brokers should be reported in Parts II and III on Schedule A (Form 5500) as acquisition costs, administrative charges, etc., as appropriate. For plans with 100 or more participants, fees paid by employee benefit plans to agents, brokers, and other persons are to be reported on Schedule C (Form 5500).

5a.—The rate information called for here may be furnished by attachment of appropriate schedules of current rates filed with appropriate state insurance departments or by a statement as to the basis of the rates.

6.—Show deposit fund amounts rather than experience credit records when both are maintained.

8(d).—The rate information called for here may be furnished by attachment of appropriate schedules of current rates or by a statement as to the basis of the rates.

SCHEDULE B
(Form 5500)
Department of the Treasury
Internal Revenue Service
Department of Labor, Pension and
Welfare Benefits Administration
Pension Benefit Guaranty Corporation

Actuarial Information

This schedule is required to be filed under section 104 of the Employee Retirement Income Security Act of 1974, referred to as ERISA, and section 6059(a) of the Internal Revenue Code, referred to as the Code.

▶ **Attach to Forms 5500, 5500-C, 5500-R, or 5500EZ if applicable.**

OMB No. 1210-0016

19**87**

This Form Is Open to Public Inspection

For calendar plan year 1987 or fiscal plan year beginning _____ , 1987, and ending _____ , 19 ___ .

▶ **Please complete every item on this form. If an item does not apply, enter "N/A."**

▶ **Round off amounts to nearest dollar.**

Name of plan sponsor as shown on line 1a of Form 5500, 5500-C, 5500-R, or 5500EZ	Employer identification number

Name of plan	Enter three-digit plan number ▶	Yes	No

1 Has a waiver of a funding deficiency for this plan been approved by the IRS? . . . .
If "Yes," attach a copy of the IRS approval letter.

2 Is a waived funding deficiency of a prior plan year being amortized in this plan year? . . . .

3 Have any of the periods of amortization for charges described in Code section 412(b)(2)(B) been extended by IRS? . . .
If "Yes," attach a copy of the IRS approval letter.

4 a Was the shortfall funding method the basis for this plan year's funding standard account computations? . . . .
   b Is this plan a multiemployer plan which is, for this plan year, in reorganization as described in Code section 418 or ERISA section 4241? . . . .
   If "Yes," you are required to attach the information described in the instructions.

5 Has a change in funding method for this plan year been made? . . . .
If "Yes," attach either a copy of the letter showing IRS approval or state applicable Revenue Procedure authorizing approval if used.

6 Operational information:
   a Enter most recent actuarial valuation date ▶ _____
   b Enter date(s) and amount of contributions received this plan year for prior plan years and not previously reported:
     Date(s) ▶ _____ , Amount ▶ |_____|
   c Current value of the assets accumulated in the plan as of the beginning of the plan year . . . . . .
   d Present value of vested benefits as of the beginning of the plan year:
     (i) For retired participants and beneficiaries receiving payments . . . .
     (ii) For other participants . . . .
     (iii) Total . . . .
   e Present value of nonvested accrued benefits as of the beginning of the plan year . . . .
   f Number of persons covered (included in the most recent actuarial valuation):
     (i) Active participants . . . .
     (ii) Terminated participants with vested benefits . . . .
     (iii) Retired participants and beneficiaries of deceased participants . . . .

7 Contributions made to the plan for the plan year by employer(s) and employees:

(a) Month Year	(b) Amount paid by employer	(c) Amount paid by employees	(a) Month Year	(b) Amount paid by employer	(c) Amount paid by employees
			Total . . .		

Statement by Enrolled Actuary (see instructions before signing):

To the best of my knowledge, the information supplied in this schedule and on the accompanying statement, if any, is complete and accurate, and in my opinion the assumptions used in the aggregate (a) are reasonably related to the experience of the plan and to reasonable expectations, and (b) represent my best estimate of anticipated experience under the plan.

_____	_____
Signature of actuary	Date
_____	_____
Print or type name of actuary	Enrollment number
_____	_____
Name and address	Telephone number (including area code)

For Paperwork Reduction Act Notice, see the instructions for this schedule.   ＊ U.S. GPO: 1987 — 183-273   **Schedule B (Form 5500) 1987**

Tools and Techniques

8 Funding standard account and other information:

   a Accrued liabilities as determined for funding standard account as of (enter date) ▶ _____

   b Value of assets as determined for funding standard account as of (enter date) ▶ _____

   c Unfunded liability for spread-gain methods with bases as of (enter date) ▶ _____

   d *(i)* Actuarial gains or (losses) for period ending ▶ _____

       (ii) Shortfall gains or (losses) for period ending ▶ _____

   e Amount of contribution certified by the actuary as necessary to reduce the funding deficiency to zero, from 9m or 10h (or the attachment for 4b if required) . . . .

9 Funding standard account statement for this plan year ending ▶ _____

   Charges to funding standard account:

   a Prior year funding deficiency, if any . . . .

   b Employer's normal cost for plan year as of mo. _____ day _____ yr. _____

   c Amortization charges

       (i) Funding waivers (outstanding balance as of mo. _____ day _____ yr. _____ ▶ $ _____)

       (ii) Other than waivers (outstanding balance as of mo. _____ day _____ yr. _____ ▶ $ _____)

   d Interest as applicable to the end of the plan year on a, b, and c

   e Total charges (add a through d) . . . .

   Credits to funding standard account:

   f Prior year credit balance, if any . . . .

   g Employer contributions (total from column (b) of item 7)

   h Amortization credits (outstanding balance as of mo. _____ day _____ yr. _____ ▶ $ _____)

   i Interest as applicable to end of plan year on f, g, and h . . . .

   j Other (specify) ▶ _____

   k Total credits (add f through j) . . . .

   Balance:

   l Credit balance: if k is greater than e, enter the difference . . . . .

   m Funding deficiency: if e is greater than k, enter the difference

10 Alternative minimum funding standard account (omit if not used):

   a Was the entry age normal cost method used to determine entries in item 9 above? . . . . ☐ Yes ☐ No

      If "No," do not complete b through h.

   b Prior year alternate funding deficiency, if any

   c Normal cost . . . .

   d Excess, if any, of value of accrued benefits over market value of assets

   e Interest on b, c, and d . . . .

   f Employer contributions (total from column (b) of item 7) . . . .

   g Interest on f . . . .

   h Funding deficiency: if the sum of b through e is greater than the sum of f and g, enter difference . . .

11 Actuarial cost method used as the basis for this plan year's funding standard account computation:

   a ☐ Attained age normal   **b** ☐ Entry age normal   **c** ☐ Accrued benefit (unit credit)

   d ☐ Aggregate   **e** ☐ Frozen initial liability   **f** ☐ Individual level premium

   g ☐ Other (specify) ▶

12 Checklist of certain actuarial assumptions:	**A** Used for item 6d and e— value of accrued benefits				**B** Used for item 8, 9 or 10— funding standard account			
	Pre-retirement		Post-retirement		Pre-retirement		Post-retirement	
	☐ Yes	☐ No	☐ Yes	☐ No	☐ Yes	☐ No	☐ Yes	☐ No
a Rates specified in insurance or annuity contracts . . .								
b Mortality table code:								
(i) Males								
(ii) Females								
c Interest rate	%		%		%		%	
d Retirement age								
e Expense loading	%		%		%		%	
f Annual withdrawal rate:	*Male*	*Female*			*Male*	*Female*		
(i) Age 25	%	%			%	%		
(ii) Age 40	%	%			%	%		
(iii) Age 55	%	%			%	%		
g Ratio of salary at normal retirement to salary at:								
(i) Age 25					%	%		
(ii) Age 40					%	%		
(iii) Age 55					%	%		
h Is a statement of actuarial assumptions, actuarial funding method, etc., attached?							☐ Yes	☐ No

SCHEDULE P
(Form 5500)

Department of the Treasury
Internal Revenue Service

Annual Return of Fiduciary
of Employee Benefit Trust

▶ File as an attachment to Form 5500, 5500-C, 5500-R, or 5500EZ.

OMB No. 1210-0016

1987

For trust calendar year 1987 or fiscal year beginning _____ , 1987, and ending _____ , 19____ .

Please type or print

1 a Name of trustee or custodian

b Address (number and street)

c City or town, state, and ZIP code

2 Name of trust

3 Name of plan if different from name of trust

4 Have you furnished the participating employee benefit plan(s) with the trust financial information required to be reported by the plan(s)? . . . . ☐ Yes ☐ No

5 Enter the plan sponsor's employer identification number as shown on the form to which this schedule is attached . . . . ▶

Under penalties of perjury, I declare that I have examined this schedule, and to the best of my knowledge and belief it is true, correct, and complete.

Date ▶ _____   Signature of fiduciary ▶ _____

Instructions

(Section references are to the Internal Revenue Code .)

Paperwork Reduction Act Notice.—We ask for this information to carry out the law as specified in ERISA. We need it to determine whether the plan is operating according to the law. You are required to give us this information if you want to start the running of the statute of limitations.

A. Purpose of Form
You may use this schedule to satisfy the requirements under section 6033(a) for an annual information return from every section 401(a) organization exempt from tax under section 501(a).

The filing of this form will also start the running of the statute of limitations under section 6501(a) for any trust described in section 401(a) which is exempt from tax under section 501(a).

B. Who May File
(1) Every trustee of a trust described in section 401(a) which was created as part of an employee benefit plan.
(2) Every custodian of a custodial account described in section 401(f).

C. How To File
File Schedule P (Form 5500) for the trust year ending with or within any participating plan's plan year as an attachment to the Form 5500, 5500-C, 5500-R, or 5500EZ filed by the plan for that plan year.

Schedule P (Form 5500) may be filed only as an attachment to a Form 5500, 5500-C, 5500-R, or 5500EZ.

A separately filed Schedule P (Form 5500) will not be accepted.

If the trust or custodial account is used by more than one plan, file only one Schedule P (Form 5500). It must be filed as an attachment to one of the participating plan's returns/reports. If a plan uses more than one trust or custodial account for its funds, file one Schedule P (Form 5500) for each trust or custodial account.

D. Signature
The fiduciary (trustee or custodian) must sign this schedule. If there is more than one fiduciary, one of them, authorized by the others, may sign.

E. Other Returns and Forms That May Be Required
(1) Form 990-T.—For trusts described in section 401(a), a tax is imposed on income derived from business that is unrelated to the purpose for which the trust received a tax exemption. Report such income and tax on Form 990-T, Exempt Organization Business Income Tax Return. (See sections 511 through 514 and related regulations.)
(2) Forms W-2P and 1099-R.—If you made payments or distributions to individual beneficiaries of a plan, report these payments on Forms W-2P or 1099-R. (See sections 6041 and 6047 and related regulations.)
(3) Forms 941 or 941E.—If you made payments of distributions to individual beneficiaries of a plan, you are required to withhold income tax from those payments unless the payee elects not to have the tax withheld. Report this withholding on Form 941 or 941E. (See Forms 941 or 941E and Circular E, Publication 15.)

☆ U.S. Government Printing Office: 1987—183-275 23-0916750

Schedule P (Form 5500) 1987

SCHEDULE SSA (Form 5500) Department of the Treasury Internal Revenue Service	**Annual Registration Statement Identifying Separated Participants With Deferred Vested Benefits** Under Section 6057(a) of the Internal Revenue Code ▶ **File as an attachment to Form 5500, 5500-C, or 5500-R.** ▶ **For Paperwork Reduction Act Notice, see page 1 of the instructions for Form 5500 or 5500-C.**	OMB No. 1210-0016 19**88** This Form Is NOT Open to Public Inspection

For the calendar year 1988 or fiscal plan year beginning _____ , 1988, and ending _____ , 19 ___

▶ **This form must be filed for each plan year in which one or more participants with deferred vested benefit rights separated from the service covered by the plan. See instructions on when to report a separated employee.**

1a Name of sponsor (employer if for a single employer plan)	**1b** Sponsor's employer identification number
Address (number and street)	**1c** Is this a plan to which more than
City or town, state, and ZIP code	one employer contributes? . . ☐ **Yes** ☐ **No**
2a Name of plan administrator (if other than sponsor)	**2b** Administrator's employer identification no.
Address (number and street)	
City or town, state, and ZIP code	

3a Name of plan	**3b** Plan number ▶

4 Have you notified each separated participant of his or her deferred benefit? . . . . ☐ **Yes** ☐ **No**

5 Separated participants with deferred vested benefits (if additional space is required, see instruction, "What To File"):

(a) Social Security Number	**(b)** Name of participant	Enter code for nature and form of benefit		Amount of vested benefit			**(h)** Plan year in which participant separated
		(c) Type of annuity	**(d)** Payment frequency	**(e)** Defined benefit plan—periodic payment	**(f)** Units or shares	**(g)** Total value of account	

The Following Information Is Optional (See Specific Instruction 6)

6 Use this item to report (i) separated participants with deferred vested benefits who were previously reported on Schedule SSA (Form 5500) and who have received part or all of their vested benefits or who have forfeited their benefits during the plan year for which this form is being filed, and (ii) to delete participants erroneously reported on a prior Schedule SSA (Form 5500):

Note: *Participants listed in this item, because they have received part of their vested benefits, must also be reported in item 5 above listing their remaining vested benefits.*

(a) Social Security Number	**(b)** Name of participant	Enter code for nature and form of benefit		Amount of vested benefit			**(h)** Plan year in which participant separated
		(c) Type of annuity	**(d)** Payment frequency	**(e)** Defined benefit plan—periodic payment	**(f)** Units or shares	**(g)** Total value of account	

Under penalties of perjury, I declare that I have examined this report, and to the best of my knowledge and belief, it is true, correct, and complete.

------------------------   --   ------------------------
Date   Signature of plan administrator

Tools and Techniques

General Instructions

Note: *Please type or print all information and submit original copy only.*

Who Must File.—The plan administrator must file this form for any plan year for which a separated plan participant is reported under "When To Report a Separated Participant" below.

What To File.—File this schedule and complete all items. If you need more space, use additional copies of Schedule SSA, completing only items 1, 3, 5, and 6 of the additional copies.

A machine-generated computer listing showing the information required in items 5 and 6 may be submitted in lieu of completing items 5 and 6 on the schedule. Complete items 1 through 4 on Schedule SSA and enter in items 5 and 6 a statement that a list is attached. On each page of the computer list, enter the name of the sponsor, the EIN, the plan name, and the plan number. The list must be in the same format as items 5 and 6.

How To File.—File as an attachment to Form 5500, 5500-C, or 5500-R.

When To Report a Separated Participant.—

In general, *for a plan to which only one employer contributes,* a participant must be reported on Schedule SSA if:

(1) The participant separates from service covered by the plan in a plan year, and

(2) The participant is entitled to a deferred vested benefit under the plan.

The separated participant must be reported no later than on the Schedule SSA filed for the plan year following the plan year in which separation occurred. The participant may be reported earlier (i.e., on the Schedule SSA filed for the plan year in which separation occurred). Once separated participants have been reported on a Schedule SSA they should not be reported on a subsequent year's Schedule SSA.

However, a participant is not required to be reported on Schedule SSA if, before the date the Schedule SSA is required to be filed (including any extension of time for filing), the participant:

(1) Is paid some or all of the deferred vested retirement benefit,

(2) Returns to service covered by the plan, or

(3) Forfeits all of the deferred vested retirement benefit.

In general, *for a plan to which more than one employer contributes,* a participant must be reported on Schedule SSA if:

(1) The participant incurs two successive one-year breaks in service (as defined in the plan for vesting purposes) in service computation periods, and

(2) The participant is (or may be) entitled to a deferred vested benefit under the plan.

The participant must be reported no later than on the Schedule SSA filed for the plan year in which the participant completed the second of the two consecutive one-year breaks in service. The participant may be reported earlier (i.e., on the Schedule SSA filed for the plan year in which he or she separated from service or completed the first one-year break in service).

However, a participant is not required to be reported on Schedule SSA if, before the date the Schedule SSA is required to be filed (including any extension of time for filing), the participant:

(1) Is paid some or all of the deferred vested retirement benefit,

(2) Accrues additional retirement benefits under the plan, or

(3) Forfeits all of the deferred vested retirement benefit.

Cessation of Payment of Benefits.—As described above in "When To Report a Separated Participant," a participant is not required to be reported on Schedule SSA if, before the date the Schedule SSA is required to be filed, some of the deferred vested benefit to which the participant is entitled is paid to the participant. If payment of the deferred vested benefit ceases before all of the benefit is paid to the participant, the benefit to which the participant remains entitled must be reported on the Schedule SSA filed for the plan year following the last plan year within which any of the benefit was paid to the participant. However, a participant is not required to be reported on Schedule SSA on account of a cessation of payment of benefits if, before the date the schedule is required to be filed (including any extension of time for filing), the participant:

(1) Returns to service covered by the plan,

(2) Accrues additional retirement benefits under the plan, or

(3) Forfeits the remaining benefit.

Separation of a Re-employed Employee.— The deferred vested benefit reported on the current Schedule SSA for a re-employed employee who is again separated from service must include only the benefit not previously reported in or for prior years. Generally, the benefit to be shown on the current filing will be the benefit earned during the re-employment period.

Caution: *A penalty may be assessed if Schedule SSA (Form 5500) is not timely filed.*

Specific Instructions

4. Check "Yes" if you have complied with the requirements of Code section 6057(e). The notification to each participant must include the information set forth on this schedule and the information with respect to any contributions made by the participant and not withdrawn by the end of the plan year. Any benefits that are forfeitable if the participant dies before a certain date must be shown on the statement.

5(a). Please be careful to enter the exact social security number of each participant listed.

If the participant is a foreign national employed outside of the United States who does not have a social security number, enter the participant's nationality.

5(b). Enter each participant's name exactly as it appears on the participant's social security card or the employer's payroll records for purposes of reporting to the Social Security Administration.

5(c). From the following list, select the code that describes the type of annuity that will be provided for the participant. The type of annuity to be entered is the type that normally accrues under the plan at the time of the participant's separation from service covered by the plan (or for a plan to which more than one employer contributes at the time the participant incurs the second consecutive one-year break in service under the plan).

A A single sum

B Annuity payable over fixed number of years

C Life annuity

D Life annuity with period certain

E Cash refund life annuity

F Modified cash refund life annuity

G Joint and last survivor life annuity

M Other

5(d). From the following list, select the code that describes the benefit payment frequency during a 12-month period.

A Lump sum

B Annually

C Semiannually

D Quarterly

E Monthly

M Other

5(e). For a defined benefit plan, enter the amount of the periodic payment that a participant would normally be entitled to receive under 5(c), commencing at normal retirement age. However, if it is more expedient to show the amount of periodic payment the participant would be entitled to receive at early retirement date, enter that amount.

For a plan to which more than one employer contributes, if the amount of the periodic payment cannot be accurately determined because the plan administrator does not maintain complete records of covered service, enter an estimated amount and add the letter "X" in column 5(c) in addition to the annuity code to indicate that it is an estimate. If, from records maintained by the plan administrator, it cannot be determined whether the participant is entitled to any deferred vested benefit, but there is reason to believe he or she may be entitled, leave column 5(e) blank and enter "Y" in column 5(c) in addition to the annuity code.

5(f). For a defined contribution plan, if the plan states that a participant's share of the fund will be determined on the basis of units, enter the number of units credited to the participant.

If, under the plan, participation is determined on the basis of shares of stock of the employer, enter the number of shares and add the letter "S" to indicate shares. A number without the "S" will be interpreted to mean units.

5(g). For defined contribution plans, enter the value of the participant's account at the time of separation.

6. If, after a participant has been reported on Schedule SSA, the participant:

(1) is paid some or all of the deferred vested retirement benefit, or

(2) forfeits all of the deferred vested retirement benefit,

the plan administrator may, at its option, request that the participant's deferred vested benefit be deleted from Social Security Administration's records. Information reported in item 6, columns (a) through (g), is to be the exact information previously reported on Schedule SSA for the participant.

If this option is chosen because the participant is paid some of the deferred vested benefit, the reporting requirements described in "Cessation of Payment of Benefits" above apply if payment of the benefit ceases before all of the benefit is paid to the participant.

Also, if a person was erroneously reported on a prior Schedule SSA, use item 6 to delete this information from Social Security Administration's records.

Signature.—This form must be signed by the plan administrator. If more than one Schedule SSA is filed for one plan, only page one should be signed.

Form **5500-C**	**Return/Report of Employee Benefit Plan**	OMB No. 1210-0016
Department of the Treasury Internal Revenue Service	**(With fewer than 100 participants)**	**1987**
Department of Labor Pension and Welfare Benefits Administration	This form is required to be filed under sections 104 and 4065 of the Employee Retirement Income Security Act of 1974 and sections 6039D, 6057(b) and 6058(a) of the Internal Revenue Code, referred to as the Code.	**This Form is Open to Public Inspection**
Pension Benefit Guaranty Corporation		

For the calendar plan year 1987 or fiscal plan year beginning , 1987, and ending , 19 .

Type or print in ink all entries on the form, schedules, and attachments. If an item does not apply, enter "N/A." File the originals.

If (i) through (iii) do not apply to this year's return/report, leave the boxes unmarked. This return/report is:

(i) ☐ the first return/report filed for the plan; (ii) ☐ an amended return/report; or (iii) ☐ the final return/report filed for the plan.

▶ Welfare benefit plans, including those described in Code section 6039D, need only complete certain items or may not be required to file—see instructions "What To File."

▶ Keogh (HR 10) plans must check the box in item 5a(iii).

▶ One-participant plans file Form 5500EZ for 1987 (see page 1 of the instructions).

▶ If you have been granted an extension of time to file this form, you must attach a copy of the approved extension to this form.

Check this box if an extension of time to file this return is attached ▶☐

Use IRS label. Otherwise, please print or type.	**1a** Name of plan sponsor (employer, if for a single employer plan)	**1b** Employer identification number
	Address (number and street)	**1c** Telephone number of sponsor ( )
	City or town, state, and ZIP code	**1d** If plan year changed since last return/report, check here . . . ▶☐
	2a Name of plan administrator (if same as plan sponsor, enter "Same")	**1e** Business code number
	Address (number and street)	**2b** Administrator's employer identification no.
	City or town, state, and ZIP code	**2c** Telephone number of administrator ( )

3 Is the name, address, and employer identification number (EIN) of plan sponsor and/or plan administrator the same as they appeared on the last return/report filed for this plan? ☐ Yes ☐ No If "No," enter the information from the last return/report in a and/or b.

a Sponsor ▶ _____ EIN _____

b Administrator ▶ _____ EIN _____

c If 3a indicates a change in the sponsor's name and EIN, is this a change in sponsorship only? (See specific instructions for definition of sponsorship.)
☐ Yes ☐ No

4 Check box to indicate the type of plan entity (check only one box):

a ☐ Single-employer plan

b ☐ Plan of controlled group of corporations or common control employers

c ☐ Multiemployer plan

d ☐ Multiple-employer-collectively-bargained plan

e ☐ Multiple-employer plan (other)

5a (i) Name of plan ▶ _____

(ii) ☐ Check if name of plan changed since the last return/report.

(iii) ☐ Check this box if this is a Keogh (HR 10) plan.

5b Effective date of plan

5c Enter three-digit plan number . . . . ▶

6a Welfare benefit plan (Plan numbers 501 through 999) must check applicable items (i) through (vii) and 6c:

(i) ☐ Health insurance (ii) ☐ Life insurance (iii) ☐ Supplemental unemployment (iv) ☐ Other (specify) ▶ _____

(v) ☐ Code section 120 (group legal services plan) (vi) ☐ Code section 125 (cafeteria plan)

(vii) ☐ Code section 127 (educational assistance program)

If you checked (v), (vi), or (vii), check if: ☐ funded, or ☐ unfunded.

b Pension benefit plan (Plan numbers 001 through 500) must check applicable item in (i) through (vii) and answer 6c through 6f:

(i) Defined benefit plan—(indicate type of defined benefit plan below):

(A) ☐ Fixed benefit (B) ☐ Unit benefit (C) ☐ Flat benefit (D) ☐ Other (specify) ▶ _____

(ii) Defined contribution plan—(Indicate type of defined contribution plan): (A) ☐ Profit-sharing (B) ☐ Stock bonus

(C) ☐ Target benefit (D) ☐ Other money purchase (E) ☐ Other (specify) ▶ _____

(iii) ☐ Defined benefit plan with benefits based partly on balance of separate account of participant (Code section 414(k))

(iv) ☐ Annuity arrangement of certain exempt organizations (Code section 403(b)(1))

(v) ☐ Custodial account for regulated investment company stock (Code section 403(b)(7))

(vi) ☐ Pension plan utilizing individual retirement accounts or annuities (described in Code section 408) as the sole funding vehicle for providing benefits

(vii) ☐ Other (specify) ▶

Under penalties of perjury and other penalties set forth in the instructions, I declare that I have examined this return/report, including accompanying schedules and statements, and to the best of my knowledge and belief it is true, correct, and complete.

Date ▶ _____ Signature of employer/plan sponsor ▶ _____

Date ▶ _____ Signature of plan administrator ▶ _____

For Paperwork Reduction Act Notice, see page 1 of the Instructions. Form **5500-C** (1987)

Tools and Techniques

Form 5500-C (1987)   Page **2**

6c Other plan features: *(i)* ☐ Thrift-savings   *(ii)* ☐ Participant-directed account plan

(iii) ☐ Pension plan maintained outside the United States (see instructions)   *(iv)* ☐ Master trust (see instructions) ▶ ....

(v) ☐ 103-12 investment entity (see instructions) ▶ ....

		Yes	No
d Single-employer plans enter the tax year end of the employer in which this plan year ends ▶ Month...... Day...... Year......			
e Is the employer a member of an affiliated service group?	**6e**		
f Does this plan contain a cash or deferred arrangement described in Code section 401(k)?	**f**		

7a Total participants: *(i)* Beginning of plan year ▶ .... *(ii)* End of plan year ▶ ....

b *(i)* Was any pension benefit plan participant(s) separated from service with a deferred vested benefit for which a Schedule SSA (Form 5500) is required to be attached?	**7b**		
(ii) If "Yes," enter the number of separated participants required to be reported . . . . . . ▶			

8 Plan information. You must complete a, c and d (welfare plans do NOT complete b(ii)):

a Were any plan amendments to this plan adopted since the end of the plan year covered by the last return/report Form 5500 or 5500-C, which was filed for this plan (or during this plan year if this is the initial return/report)?	**8a**		
b If "Yes," *(i)* And if any amendments have resulted in a change in the information contained in a summary plan description or previously furnished summary description of modifications:			
(A) Have summary descriptions of the changes been sent to participants?	**b(i)(A)**		
(B) Have summary descriptions of the changes been filed with DOL?	**(i)(B)**		
(ii) Does any such amendment result in the reduction of the accrued benefit of any participant under the plan?	**(ii)**		
c Enter the date the most recent amendment was adopted . . . . . ▶ Month .... Day .... Year			
d *(i)* Has a summary plan description been filed with DOL for this plan?	**d**		
(ii) If (i) is "Yes," what was the employer identification number and the plan number used to identify it? Employer identification number ▶ Plan number ▶			

9 Plan termination information:

a Was this plan terminated during this plan year or any prior plan year? If "Yes," enter year ▶	**9a**		
b If "Yes," were all trust assets either distributed to participants or beneficiaries, transferred to another plan, or brought under the control of the Pension Benefit Guaranty Corporation (PBGC)?	**b**		
c If a is "Yes" and the plan is covered by PBGC, is the plan continuing to file a PBGC Form 1 and pay premiums until the end of the plan year in which assets are distributed or brought under the control of PBGC?	**c**		
d During this plan year, did any trust assets revert to the employer for which the Code section 4980 excise tax is due?	**d**		
e If d is "Yes," enter the amount of tax paid with your Form 5330 ▶			

10a Was this plan merged or consolidated into another plan, or were assets or liabilities transferred to another plan since the end of the plan year covered by the last return/report Form 5500 or 5500-C which was filed for this plan (or during this plan year if this is the initial return/report)? . . . . `10a`

If "Yes," identify the other plan(s):   **c** Employer identification number(s)   **d** Plan number(s)

b Name of plan(s) ▶ .... | .... | ....

.... | ....

e Has Form 5310 been filed? . . . . ☐ Yes ☐ No

11 Indicate funding arrangement:

a ☐ Trust   **b** ☐ Fully insured   **c** ☐ Combination   **d** ☐ Other (specify) ▶ ....
e If b or c is checked, enter the number of Schedules A (Form 5500) which are attached . . . . ▶

12a Is the plan covered under the Pension Benefit Guaranty Corporation termination insurance program? . . . . ☐ Yes ☐ No ☐ Not determined

b If a is "Yes" or "Not determined," enter the employer identification number and the plan number used to identify it.
Employer identification number ▶   Plan number ▶

13 Complete both 13a and b:

		Yes	No
a Is the plan insured by a fidelity bond?	**13a**		
(i) If "Yes," enter name of surety company ▶			
(ii) Amount of bond coverage ▶			
b Was any loss discovered since the last return/report Form 5500 or 5500-C was filed for this plan (or during this plan year if this is the initial return/report) ?	**b**		

14a If this is a defined benefit plan, is it subject to the minimum funding standards for this plan year? . . . . . . | **14a** | | |
If "Yes," attach Schedule B (Form 5500).

b If this is a money purchase or target benefit plan, is it subject to the minimum funding standards? (If a waiver was granted, see instructions.) | **b** | | |

If "Yes," complete (i), (ii), and (iii) below:

(i) Amount of employer contribution required for the plan year	**b(i)**	$
(ii) Amount of contribution paid by the employer for the plan year	**(ii)**	$
Enter date of last payment by employer ▶ Month .... Day .... Year		
(iii) If (i) is greater than (ii), subtract (ii) from (i) and enter the funding deficiency here. Otherwise enter zero. (If you have a funding deficiency, file Form 5330.)	**(iii)**	$

15 Plan assets and liabilities at the beginning and end of the current plan year (list all assets and liabilities at current value). A fully insured welfare or a pension plan with no trust and which is funded entirely by allocated insurance contracts which fully guarantee the amount of benefit payments should check the box and **not** complete the rest of this item . . . . ▶ ☐

Note: *Include all plan assets and liabilities of a trust or separately maintained fund. If more than one trust/fund, report on a combined basis. Include all insurance values except for the value of that portion of an allocated insurance contract which fully guarantees the amount of benefit payments. Round off amounts to nearest dollar. If you have no assets to report enter "-0-" on line 15g.*

Assets

		(a) Beginning of year	**(b)** End of year
a Cash—			
(i) Interest bearing	**a (i)**		
(ii) Noninterest bearing	**(ii)**		
(iii) Total cash (add (i) and (ii))	**(iii)**		
b Receivables	**b**		
c Investments—			
(i) Government securities	**c (i)**		
(ii) Pooled funds/mutual funds	**(ii)**		
(iii) Corporate (debt and equity instruments)	**(iii)**		
(iv) Value of interest in master trust	**(iv)**		
(v) Value of interest in 103-12 investment entities	**(v)**		
(vi) Real estate and mortgages	**(vi)**		
(vii) Other	**(vii)**		
(viii) Total investments (add (i) through (vii))	**(viii)**		
d Building and other depreciable property used in plan operation	**d**		
e Unallocated insurance contracts	**e**		
f Other assets	**f**		
g Total assets (add a(iii), b, c(viii), d, e, and f)	**g**		

Liabilities and Net Assets

h Payables	**h**		
i Acquisition indebtedness	**i**		
j Other liabilities	**j**		
k Total liabilities (add h through j)	**k**		
l Net assets (subtract k from g)	**l**		

16 Plan income, expenses, and changes in net assets during the plan year. Include all income and expenses of a trust(s) or separately maintained fund(s), including any premium payments to insurance companies. Round off amounts to nearest dollar.

		(a) Amount	**(b)** Total
a Contributions received or receivable in cash from:			
(i) Employer(s) (including contributions on behalf of self-employed individuals)	**a (i)**		
(ii) Employees	**(ii)**		
(iii) Others	**(iii)**		
b Noncash contributions	**b**		
c Earnings from investments (interest, dividends, rents, royalties)	**c**		
d Net realized gain (loss) on sale or exchange of assets	**d**		
e Other income (specify) ▶ _____	**e**		
f Total income (add a through e)	**f**		
g Distribution of benefits and payments to provide benefits:			
(i) Directly to participants or their beneficiaries	**g (i)**		
(ii) To insurance carrier or similar organization for provision of benefits (including prepaid medical plans)	**(ii)**		
(iii) To other organizations or individuals providing welfare benefits	**(iii)**		
h Interest expense	**h**		
i Administrative expenses (salaries, fees, commissions, insurance premiums)	**i**		
j Other expenses (specify) ▶ _____	**j**		
k Total expenses (add g through j)	**k**		
l Net income (subtract k from f)	**l**		
m Changes in net assets:			
(i) Unrealized appreciation (depreciation) of assets	**m (i)**		
(ii) Net investment gain (or loss) from all master trust investment accounts	**(ii)**		
(iii) Net investment gain (or loss) from all 103-12 investment entities	**(iii)**		
(iv) Other changes (specify) ▶ _____	**(iv)**		
n Net increase (decrease) in net assets for the year (add l and m)	**n**		
o Net assets at beginning of year (line 15l, column (a))	**o**		
p Net assets at end of year (add n and o) (equals line 15l, column (b))	**p**		

Form 5500-C (1987)   Page **4**

			Yes	No

17 As of the end of the plan year:

a What percentage of plan assets are loaned to a party-in-interest? . . . . **a** _____ %

b What percentage of plan assets are invested in securities issued by a party-in-interest? . . . . . . **b** _____ %

c What percentage of plan assets are invested in real estate which is leased by a party-in-interest? . . . . . . **c** _____ %

18 Since the end of the plan year covered by the last return/report Form 5500 or 5500-C which was filed for this plan (or during this plan year if this is the initial return/report:

a Has there been a termination in the appointment of any person listed in b below? . . . . **a**

b If a is "Yes," check the appropriate box(es) and provide the name, address, and telephone number of the person(s) whose appointment has been terminated and an explanation for the termination (see instructions):

(i) ☐ Trustee   (ii) ☐ Accountant   (iii) ☐ Insurance carrier   (iv) ☐ Enrolled actuary   (v) ☐ Administrator

(vi) ☐ Investment manager   (vii) ☐ Custodian ▶ _____

c Have there been any outstanding material disputes or matters of disagreement concerning the above terminations? (See instructions.) . . . . . . **c**

d Has the plan used the services of a contract administrator? . . . . **d**

If "Yes," enter the contract administrator's name and employer identification number (see instructions) ▶ _____

e Indicate the amount of the plan's administrative expenses for the:

(i) Preceding year ▶ $ _____   (ii) Second preceding year ▶ $ _____

f Have any insurance policies or annuities been replaced? . . . . **f**

g Was the plan funded with: (i) ☐ Individual policies or annuities   (ii) ☐ Group policies or annuities   (iii) ☐ Both

19 Since the end of the plan year covered by the last return/report Form 5500 or 5500-C which was filed for this plan (or during this plan year if this is the initial return/report):

a Other than transactions described in the exceptions outlined in the instructions, were there any transactions, directly or indirectly, between the plan and a party-in-interest? . . . . **a**

If "Yes," see specific instructions.

b Has the plan granted an extension on any loan for which, before the granting of an extension, it has not received all the principal and interest payments due under the terms of the loan? . . . . **b**

c Has the plan granted an extension of time or renewal for the payment of any obligation owed to it which amounts to more than 10% of the plan assets? . . . . **c**

20 As of the end of any plan year since the end of the plan year covered by the last return/report Form 5500 or 5500-C which was filed for this plan (or as of the end of this plan year if this is the initial return/report):

a Did the plan have investments of the type reportable under item 15c(vi) or (vii) which in the aggregate in either category exceeded 15% of plan assets? . . . . **a**

b Did the plan have loans outstanding or investments in a single enterprise (other than the United States Government) which exceeded 15% of plan assets? . . . . **b**

21 During the plan year covered by this return:

a Did any plan fiduciary who is an officer or an employee of the plan sponsor receive compensation from the plan for his or her services to the plan? . . . . **a**

b Did the plan acquire any qualifying employer security or qualifying employer real property when immediately after such acquisition the aggregate fair market value of employer securities and employer real property held by the plan exceeded 10% of the fair market value of the plan assets? . . . . **b**

c Has any plan fiduciary had either a financial interest worth more than $1,000 in any party providing services to the plan or received anything of value from any party providing services to the plan? . . . . . . **c**

d Has any employer owed the plan contributions which were more than 3 months past due under the terms of the plan? . . . . . **d**

e Were any loans by the plan or fixed income obligations due the plan in default as of the close of the plan year, or classified as uncollectable? . . . . **e**

f Were any leases to which the plan was a party in default or classified as uncollectable? . . . . **f**

22 Who is the plan's designated agent for legal process? ▶

23 Give the name and address of each fiduciary (including trustees) to the plan ▶ _____

_____

_____

24 Is this plan an adoption of any of the plans below? (If "Yes," check appropriate box and enter IRS serial number) **24**

a ☐ Master/prototype, or   **b** ☐ Uniform

Enter the eight-character IRS letter serial number (see instructions)   ▶

25a Is this plan integrated with social security? . . . . **a**

b Is it intended that this plan qualify under Code section 401(a)? . . . . **b**

c If b is "Yes," has this plan received a determination letter from the IRS? . . . . **c**

d Does the employer/sponsor listed in item 1a of this form maintain other qualified pension benefit plans? . . . . . . **d**

If "Yes," list the number of plans including this plan ▶

			Yes	No

26 Information about employees of employer at end of the plan year:

a Does the plan satisfy the percentage tests of Code section 410(b)(1)(A)? If "No," complete only b below and see Specific Instructions . . . . . **a**

b Total number of employees . . . . . **b**

c Number of employees excluded under the plan because of: *(i)* Minimum age or years of service . . . . . **c(i)**

  (ii) Employees on whose behalf retirement benefits were the subject of collective bargaining . . . . . **(ii)**

  (iii) Nonresident aliens who receive no earned income from United States sources . . . . **(iii)**

  (iv) Total excluded (add (i), (ii), and (iii)) . . . . . **(iv)**

d Total number of employees not excluded (subtract c(iv) from b) . . . . . **d**

e Employees ineligible (specify reason) ▶ _____ **e**

f Employees eligible to participate (subtract e from d) . . . . . **f**

g Employees eligible but not participating . . . . . **g**

h Employees participating (subtract g from f) . . . . . **h**

27 Vesting (check only one box to indicate the vesting provisions of the plan):

a Full and immediate vesting, or full vesting within 3 years . . . . . **a**

b No vesting in years 1 through 9, and full vesting after the 10th year of service . . . . . **b**

c For each year of employment, beginning with the 4th year, vesting equal to 40% after 4 years of service, 5% additional for the next 2 years, and 10% additional for each of the next 5 years . . . . . **c**

d 100% vesting within 5 years after contributions are made (class year plan only) . . . . . **d**

e Other vesting _____ **e**

			Yes	No

28a Did the employer receive plan assets (including a return of contributions) since the last return/report Form 5500 or 5500-C which was filed for this plan (or during this plan year if this is the initial return/report)? **a**

b If this is a defined benefit plan which provides for annual automatic increases in the maximum dollar limitations under Code section 415, does the plan provide that any such increase is effective no earlier than the calendar year for which IRS determines that increase under Code section 415(d)? **b**

c *(i)* Is this a plan with Employee Stock Ownership (ESOP) features? **c(i)**

  (ii) If "Yes," were all valuations of employer stock, for the plan year covered by this return/report, made by an independent appraiser? **(ii)**

29 Have any individuals performed services as a leased employee for any employer covered by this plan or for any other employer who is aggregated under section 414(b), (c), or (m) with any employer covered by this plan? . . . **29**
If "Yes," see instructions for completing item 26.

30a Is this plan a top-heavy plan within the meaning of Code section 416 for this plan year? . . . **a**

b If a is "Yes," complete (i), (ii), and (iii) below:

  (i) Has the plan complied with the vesting requirements of Code section 416(b)? . . . **b(i)**

  (ii) Has the plan complied with the minimum benefit requirements of Code section 416(c)? . . . **(ii)**

  (iii) Has the plan complied with the limitation on compensation of Code section 416(d)? . . . **(iii)**

31a If the plan (including terminating plans) distributed any annuity contracts this year, did these contracts contain a requirement that the spouse consent before any distributions under the contract are made? **a**

b Did the plan make distributions to participants or spouses in a form other than a qualified joint and survivor annuity (a life annuity if a single person) or qualified preretirement survivor annuity or life annuity (exclude deferred annuity contracts)? . . . **b**

c Did the plan make distributions or loans to married participants and beneficiaries without the required consent of the participant's spouse? **c**

d Upon plan amendment or termination, do the accrued benefits of every participant include the subsidized benefits that the participant may become entitled to receive subsequent to the plan amendment or termination? . . . **d**

32 Were distributions made in accordance with the requirements of Code section 417(e)? (See instructions.) . . . **32**

33 Have any contributions been made or benefits accrued in excess of the Code section 415 limits, as amended by the Tax Reform Act of 1986? . . . **33**

34 Has the plan made the required distributions in 1987 under Code 401(a)(9)? . . . **34**

If additional space is required for any item, attach additional sheets the same size as this form.

★U.S.GPO:1987-0-183-277

The Top of the Pyramid:

LONG-TERM INCENTIVES

A Comparative Analysis

STOCK APPRECIATION RIGHT
(SAR)

Description & Common Features	Tax Treatment	Accounting Treatment
Rights normally granted in tandem with an option where the executive, in lieu of exercising the option, can receive a payment equal to the excess of the stock's market value at exercise over the option price. SARs may be attached to Incentive Stock Options or Non-Qualified Stock Options or may be granted on a "stand alone" basis without an option. Payment of rights may be in cash, stock or combination.	Executive: -Value of the rights is taxed in year of exercise as ordinary income and is subject to withholding. Company: -Tax deduction in the amount of the executive's income from exercise is allowed in year executive is taxed.	The assumption in most instances is that the SAR, not the stock option, will be exercised. As such, the value of the right, i.e., the excess of the market value of the stock over the option price (at the close of each accounting period) is a compensation expense that is accrued over the period the SAR is outstanding.

Insider Trading Considerations For Publicly Held Companies	Advantages	Disadvantages
Grant of a Right: will not be considered a "purchase" if the plan meets certain requirements relating to administration by disinterested parties, shareholder approval, limits on benefits and limits on transferability of the option and related right. Full or Partial Cash Payment: -Any payment of the SAR in cash is not a "purchase" and/or "sale" if the company files certain financial data with SEC and the plan requires a six-month holding period, is administered by disinterested parties, has shareholder approval and permits exercise only during a "window period."* -Exercise during "window period" is not required if exercise date is more than six months from date of grant and is fixed in advance or is outside the executive's control. Full Payment in Stock: any payment of the SAR in stock is a "purchase" and will be matched with any "sale" in the preceding or following six months. *Third through twelfth business day period following the release of quarterly or annual company financial statements.	Executive: -Possibility of large gains. -Avoids financing costs of options. -Non-insiders may choose timing of exercise to maximize gains. Insiders have less flexibility. -If paid in cash and insider trading rules are met, no risk of insider losing gain. Company: -Executive gains parallel shareholder gains. -Facilitates executive ownership of company stock if awards are paid in stock.	Executive: -Stock price changes may not parallel company/executive performance; no gain unless market value increases. -Gains may be capped by company-imposed maximums designed to limit accounting charges. -Insider trading rules may result in inability to optimize gains. Company: -Executive gains may not parallel company performance. -Accounting expenses are unknown in advance and open-ended. -Accounting expenses may not follow earnings performance and may fluctuate greatly between accounting periods.

May 1987

INCENTIVE STOCK OPTION
(ISO)

Description & Common Features	Tax Treatment	Accounting Treatment
Option to purchase shares of company stock at 100% or more of stock's fair market value on date of grant for a period of up to ten years and designed to meet statutory requirements such as an annual limit on the value of options that can become exercisable and holding periods before sale. Any option granted to a shareholder of 10% or more of company's voting stock must be priced at 110% or more of the stock's fair market value, with an option term of no more than five years. Options may be exercised by cash payment or by tendering previously owned shares of stock.	Executive: –At exercise, no regular income tax is owed. However, the excess of the stock's fair market value at exercise over the option exercise price--i.e., "spread"--is a tax preference item that may trigger a minimum tax obligation. If shares are held at least two years from date of grant and one year from exercise ("qualifying disposition"), tax on sale is payable at long-term capital gains rates on increase in stock's value from date of grant to date of sale. If holding period requirements are not met ("disqualifying disposition"), the gain to the extent realized from grant to exercise is ordinary income; remainder is capital gain. (Note: Under the Tax Reform Act of 1986, favorable tax treatment for long-term capital gains is eliminated after 1986, except that the maximum rate on such gains in 1987 will be limited to 28%.) Company: –No tax deduction at time of exercise; if executive subsequently makes a disqualifying disposition, company may take tax deduction in year of disposition equal to "spread" at exercise. No tax deduction is allowed if qualifying disposition is made.	No expense recognizable unless options are exercised by pyramiding. Dilution may occur since options are common stock equivalents. Option proceeds and any tax savings resulting from a disqualifying disposition are credited to paid-in capital. Pyramiding If options are exercised by tendering previously owned shares of stock that have not been held for at least six months (which would constitute a disqualifying disposition for tax purposes), the difference between the fair market value of the stock and the option price is expensed in the year of exercise.

Insider Trading Considerations For Publicly Held Companies	Advantages	Disadvantages
Grant of Option: will not be considered a "purchase" if the plan meets certain requirements relating to administration by disinterested parties, shareholder approval, limits on benefits and limits on transferability of the option. Exercise of Option: will be considered a "purchase" and will be matched with any "sale" in the preceding or following six months.	Executive: –No tax on exercise (other than possible minimum tax on tax preference); taxation delayed until stock is sold. –Possibility of large gains. –Because the company has no accounting expense for options, limits need not be set on executive gains. –Can choose timing of exercise to maximize gains. –SARs can be attached if they have the same terms as the underlying option. Company: –No charge on income statement. –Executive gains parallel shareholder gains. –Facilitates executive ownership of company stock. –Provides an increase in paid-in capital. –Less need to assist executives with financing option exercises, since tax not owed until stock is sold.	Executive: –Options granted prior to 12/31/86 must be exercised in order of grant. –Three-month exercise limitation on termination, including retirement but excluding death. –$100,000 limitation constrains maximum per-executive award opportunity. –Cannot be granted to an executive owning more than 10% of the voting power of all classes of stock before the option is granted unless option price is at least 110% of stock's fair market value and option expires within five years of grant. –Stock price changes may not parallel company/executive performance; no gain unless market value increases. –May need to borrow money to finance option exercise. –Flexibility of timing of exercise and stock sales by insiders is limited by six-month insider trading rule. Company: –No corporate tax deduction if executive makes qualifying disposition of shares. –Executive gains may not parallel company performance. –Opportunity cost: paid-in capital will be less than it would have been if the stock were sold on the open market at the time of exercise.

Tools and Techniques

PHANTOM STOCK

Description & Common Features	Tax Treatment	Accounting Treatment
Units analogous to company shares are granted to executives. The value of the units generally equals the appreciation in the market value of the stock underlying the units. Phantom units are valued at a fixed date. Typically, the valuation is at retirement or five to fifteen years after grant. Payment may be in cash or stock or both. Dividend equivalents may be accrued. Phantom stock mirrors tax, accounting and insider trading treatment for SARs.	Executive: -On Payment Date: value of the units is taxed as ordinary income and is subject to withholding. Company: -On Payment Date: tax deduction in the amount of the executive's taxable income from the units.	The excess of the stock's value (at the close of each accounting period) over its value at date of award is a compensation expense that is accrued over the period the units are outstanding.

Insider Trading Considerations For Publicly Held Companies	Advantages	Disadvantages
Grants of Units: will not be considered a "purchase" if the plan meets certain requirements relating to administration by disinterested parties, shareholder approval, limits on benefits and limits on transferability of the units. Full or Partial Cash Payment: -Any payment in cash is not a "purchase" and/or "sale" if the company files certain financial data with the SEC and the plan requires a six-month holding period, is administered by disinterested parties and has shareholder approval. -Exercise during "window period"* not required if exercise date is more than six months from date of grant and is fixed in advance or is outside the executive's control. Otherwise, exercise must occur during window period. Full or Partial Stock Payment: will not be considered a "purchase" if the plan meets certain requirements related to administration by disinterested parties, shareholder approval and limits on benefits and if the participant has no control over the timing of share receipts. *Third through twelfth business day period following the release of quarterly or annual company financial statements.	Executive: -Possibility of large gains. -Avoids financing costs of options. -If participants do not control the form or timing of the units' valuation or settlement, there are minimal insider trading implications. -Dividend equivalents may be accrued. Company: -Executive gains parallel shareholder gains. -Facilitates executive ownership of company stock if awards are paid in stock.	Executive: -Stock price changes may not parallel company/executive performance; no gain unless market value increases. -Gains may be capped by company-imposed maximums designed to limit accounting charges. -Generally no flexibility in choosing when to value award; valuation date may not come at opportune time. -If participants control the form or timing of the units' valuation or settlement, trading restrictions will apply to insiders. Company: -Executive gains may not parallel company performance. -Accounting expenses are unknown in advance and open-ended. -Accounting expenses may not follow earnings performance and may fluctuate greatly between accounting periods.

May 1987

RESTRICTED STOCK

Description & Common Features	Tax Treatment	Accounting Treatment
An award of stock with no or nominal cost to the executive that is nontransferable and subject to a substantial risk of forfeiture. These restrictions lapse over a period of years. Dividends are paid to participants as declared.	**Executive:** -Timing: executive may elect to pay tax at date of award. However, the elimination of favorable long-term capital gain tax treatment under the Tax Reform Act of 1986 lessens the need for such elections. If no election, then tax liability arises when stock is transferable or is no longer subject to substantial risk of forfeiture, whichever is earlier. -Amount: the excess of the stock's fair market value when the restrictions lapse (or at the award date if early taxation is elected) over the price, if any, paid by the executive is taxed as ordinary income and is subject to withholding. -Dividends: dividends treated as compensation income while restrictions are in force unless executive elects taxation at time of award. -Note: if executive elects to be taxed at time of award and subsequently forfeits the stock, taxes paid cannot be recovered. **Company:** -On Date Executive Is Taxed: tax deduction in the amount of the executive's income from the award. -Dividends: tax deduction for dividends paid while stock is subject to restrictions unless executive elects taxation at time of award.	The value of the stock at the time of award (ignoring restrictions) over the amount, if any, paid by the executive is charged as a compensation expense over the period for which the related service is performed (usually the restriction period). Unless restrictions are performance-based (i.e., their lapsing depends on factors other than the passage of time), no expense is charged for any post-grant stock appreciation. Any tax savings on such post-grant appreciation bypass the income statement and are posted directly to the additional paid-in capital account on the balance sheet. If performance-based restrictions are used (that affect the number of shares the executive will ultimately receive or the price, if any, to be paid for them), an expense is also charged (net of tax effects) for any stock appreciation that occurs during the performance period.

Insider Trading Considerations For Publicly Held Companies	Advantages	Disadvantages
Award and Receipt of Stock: will not be considered a "purchase" if the plan meets certain requirements related to administration by disinterested parties, shareholder approval and limits on benefits and if the participant has no control over the timing of share receipts.	**Executive:** -Possibility of large gains. -A decline in price probably will not wipe out the value of the award; gains will probably never be zero. -Executive gets company stock on very favorable terms, and typically receives dividends and voting rights immediately. -Tax election provides flexibility. **Company:** -Executive gains parallel shareholder gains. -Accounting expenses are known in advance and therefore are controllable. -Facilitates executive ownership of company stock. -Shares immediately assigned to executives, so identification with the company may be stronger than with other devices. -Forfeiture requirement aids in executive retention.	**Executive:** -Stock price changes may not parallel executive/company performance. -By definition, there must be restrictions against resale and a substantial risk of forfeiture. **Company:** -Executive gains may not parallel company performance. -May create adverse shareholder reaction due to "something for nothing" appearance. -Executive's election regarding tax liability affects timing and amount of company's tax deduction. -May increase corporate minimum tax exposure, since actual tax deduction may exceed the expense taken for accounting purposes.

May 1987

Tools and Techniques

PERFORMANCE UNIT/ PERFORMANCE CASH

Description & Common Features	Tax Treatment	Accounting Treatment
A performance award granted in the form of a contingent number of units or as a contingent cash award. Units may be granted with a fixed dollar payment value, with the number of units earned varying on the basis of performance achievements. Alternatively, a fixed number of units may be granted with the payment value of these units varying on the basis of performance achievements. Duration of performance cycle varies but is typically three to five years. Financial objectives may relate to such items as cumulative growth in EPS or improvement in ROI. Payment may be in cash and/or stock of equivalent value.	Executive: -On Payment Date: value of the award paid in cash or unrestricted stock is taxed as ordinary income and is subject to withholding. Company: -On Payment Date: tax deduction in the amount of the executive's taxable income from the award.	The value of the units is a compensation expense that is estimated and accrued over the period during which related services are performed.

Insider Trading Considerations For Publicly Held Companies	Advantages	Disadvantages
Award of Unit: none. Full or Partial Cash Payment: none. Full or Partial Stock Payment: will not be considered a "purchase" and/or "sale" if the plan meets certain requirements relating to administration by disinterested parties, shareholder approval and limits on benefits and if the executive has no control over the timing or form of share receipts.	Executive: -Reward is related to a measure (e.g., EPS) over which executive has more control than over stock price. -Avoids financing costs of options. Company: -Direct relationship between executive gains and company performance is established. -Maximum accounting expenses can be known in advance, and controlled, and will follow earnings performance. -Can link executive rewards to the planning process and attainment of strategic business goals. -Forfeiture requirement aids in executive retention. -Can facilitate executive ownership of company stock, if awards are paid fully or partially in stock.	Executive: -Gains could be zero if performance target is not met. Company: -Executive gains do not necessarily parallel stock price performance. -Choice and setting of financial targets may be difficult for some companies.

May 1987

 TPF&C

PERFORMANCE SHARE

Description & Common Features	Tax Treatment	Accounting Treatment
A performance award is contingently granted in the form of a fixed number of common shares at the beginning of a performance cycle. The number of shares payable at the end of the cycle depends upon the extent to which objectives have been achieved. The value received by the executive depends both on the number of shares earned and their market value at the time of payment. Duration of performance cycle varies but is typically three to five years. Financial objectives may relate to such items as cumulative growth in EPS or improvement in ROI. Payout may be in shares of stock and/or cash of equivalent value.	Executive: -On Payment Date: value of award paid in cash or unrestricted stock is taxed as ordinary income and is subject to withholding. Company: -On Payment Date: tax deduction in the amount of the executive's income from the award.	The value of the shares is a compensation expense that is estimated and accrued over the period during which related services are performed. Unlike a performance unit plan, changes in the market value of the stock are also reflected.

Insider Trading Considerations For Publicly Held Companies	Advantages	Disadvantages
Award of Performance Shares: will not be considered a "purchase" if the plan meets certain requirements relating to administration by disinterested parties, shareholder approval, limits on benefits and limits on transferability of performance shares. Full or Partial Cash Payment: none. Full or Partial Stock Payment: will not be considered a "purchase" and/or "sale" if the above conditions are met and if the executive has no control over the timing or form of receipt.	Executive: -Reward partially related to a measure (e.g., EPS) over which executive has more control than over the stock price. -Avoids financing costs of options. Company: -Executive gains related to both company performance and shareholder gains. -Can facilitate executive ownership of company stock, if awards are paid in stock. -Can link executive rewards to the planning process and attainment of strategic business goals. -Forfeiture requirement aids in executive retention.	Executive: -Gains could be zero if performance target is not met. -Gains may be capped by company-imposed maximums designed to limit accounting charges. -End of performance period may not be most advantageous timing in terms of stock price. Company: -Choice and setting of financial targets may be difficult for some companies. -Accounting expenses are unknown in advance and open-ended.

May 1987

Tools and Techniques

COMBINATION PERFORMANCE
UNIT AND OPTION

Description & Common Features	Tax Treatment	Accounting Treatment
The simultaneous grant of performance units and a non-qualified option granted at market value. Cash payout from units enables executive to pay taxes on option exercise or helps to finance the exercise. Options granted at a discount will affect tax and accounting treatment.	**Executive:** –On Payment of Units: value of award paid is taxed as ordinary income and is subject to withholding. –On Exercise of Option: at exercise the excess of the market value of the stock (if not restricted) over the option price is taxed as ordinary income and is subject to withholding. **Company:** –On Payment of Units: tax deduction for the amount of the executive's income from the units. –On Exercise of Option: tax deduction for the amount of the executive's income from the exercise at time executive is taxed.	Each part of the combination plan is accounted for separately, ignoring the existence of the other part. Units: value of the units is a compensation expense that is estimated and accrued over the period during which related services are performed. Options: no expense charged; the option proceeds and the tax savings are credited to paid-in capital.

Insider Trading Considerations For Publicly Held Companies	Advantages	Disadvantages
Award of Units: none. Full or Partial Cash Payment of Units: none. Full or Partial Stock Payment of Units: will not be considered a "purchase" and/or "sale" if the plan meets certain requirements relating to administration by disinterested parties, shareholder approval and limits on benefits and if the executive has no control over the timing or form of share receipts. Grant of Option: will not be considered a "purchase" if the plan meets certain requirements relating to administration by disinterested parties, shareholder approval, limits on benefits and limits on transferability of the option. Exercise of Option: will be considered a "purchase" and will be matched with any "sale" in the preceding or following six months.	**Executive:** –Reward is partially related to a measure (e.g., EPS) over which executive has more control than over the stock price. –Executive can benefit from either or both stock price growth or achievement of performance targets. –Because the company has no accounting expense associated with stock options, limits generally not set on executive gains. –Executive can use cash from performance units to cover option financing costs, which reduces need to sell stock. **Company:** –Executive gains parallel company performance. –No accounting expense for market appreciation of stock. –Can link executive rewards to the planning process and attainment of strategic business goals. –Forfeiture requirement aids in executive retention. –Facilitates executive ownership of company stock to the extent options are exercised or units are settled in stock.	**Executive:** –Gains could be zero when earnings targets are not met and stock price fails to rise. –May have to borrow money to finance option exercises if performance unit payouts are not sufficient. –Flexibility of timing of option exercises and stock sales by insiders is limited by six-month insider trading rule. **Company:** –Choice and setting of financial targets may be difficult for some companies. –Opportunity cost: paid-in capital will be less than it would have been if option shares were sold on the open market at the time of exercise.

May 1987

CAREER SHARE

Description & Common Features	Tax Treatment	Accounting Treatment
Executive is offered an opportunity to purchase a fixed number of book value shares--known as "career shares"--that are convertible, according to a predetermined ratio, into shares of the company's common stock. Normally, the executive must pay the full book value for the career shares at the time of purchase, and the conversion ratio is set according to the relative book-value-to-market ratio at the time the career share is issued. Although career shares are typically fully vested and convertible at the time of the executive's purchase, convertibility may be conditional upon continued employment and/or performance. The company normally agrees to repurchase outstanding career shares, at their then current book value at any time or after some designated period of time. Some plans grant options to purchase the career shares, rather than immediately selling the shares to executives. Deviations from these typical design features may affect the tax, accounting and SEC treatment.	Executive: -At Purchase: §83(b) election is taken. No tax is owed if executive pays at least the career shares' fair market value. -Dividends or Dividend Equivalents on Career Share or Common Stock: taxed as ordinary income when earned. -At Conversion to Common Stock: no tax. -At Sale of Common Stock or Career Share: difference between proceeds of sale of stock and purchase price of related career share is taxed as long-term capital gain. (Note: Under the Tax Reform Act of 1986, favorable tax treatment for long-term capital gains is eliminated after 1986, except that the maximum rate on such gains in 1987 will be limited to 28%.) Company: -Company gets no tax deduction.	No expense is charged unless the career shares' purchase price is below book value or the conversion ratio was not known at the date of purchase. Purchase price of career share is shown as a separate class of equity on company's balance sheet, which is reclassified as publicly traded stock at conversion.

Insider Trading Considerations For Publicly Held Companies	Advantages	Disadvantages
Purchase of Career Share: will be considered a "purchase" and will be matched with any career share "sale" during the preceding or following six months. Conversion of Career Share: will not be treated as a "purchase" and/or "sale." Sale of Stock: will be considered a "sale" and will be matched with any stock "purchase" during the preceding or following six months.	Executive: -Limited risk of loss since both book and market values would have to decline for executive to incur a loss. -Possibility for large gains if stock price rises. -No tax owed until stock is sold, provided the career share is not sold at a discount to the executive. Company: -No accounting expense required. -Source of paid-in capital. -Aligns executive and shareholder interest in increasing stock price.	Executive: -Can involve significant financing requirements unless loans are provided. Company: -No corporate tax deduction.

May 1987

TPF&C

Tools and Techniques

JUNIOR STOCK

Description & Common Features	Tax Treatment	Accounting Treatment
Executive is offered an opportunity to purchase junior stock shares for their fair market value, which will become convertible (at a 1:1 ratio) into regular common stock shares if specified performance goals are achieved. The fair "market" value of junior shares is considerably below that of the shares into which they could convert due to junior stock's non-assured conversion feature and inferior rights, e.g., voting and dividends. Junior stock is nontransferable: it can only be converted into common stock--if the performance conditions are achieved--or sold back to the issuing corporation, usually at the original purchase price. Junior stock may be sold at a discount from fair value or granted at no cost to the executive, but this would affect tax and accounting treatment.	**Executive:** -Purchase of Junior Stock: §83(b) election is taken. Executive is taxed on difference between fair value of junior stock and price paid (difference is typically zero because stock is sold at full fair value). -At Conversion: no tax. -At Sale of Common Stock: taxed-- as capital gain--on difference between original junior stock purchase price and common stock price at time of sale. **Company:** -No deduction if sold to executive at fair value. If the fair value of the junior stock exceeds the price paid, the company can take a deduction for the excess amount. -Note: the IRS is presently considering the tax consequences of junior stock transactions as described above.	The excess of common stock's fair market value when conversion occurs (or becomes "probable," if earlier) over the price paid for the junior stock is estimated and accrued as an expense between the purchase and conversion dates. The purchase price of the junior stock plus the amounts charged as an expense are treated as paid-in capital on the balance sheet.

Insider Trading Considerations For Publicly Held Companies	Advantages	Disadvantages
Original Purchase of Junior Stock: will be considered a "purchase" and will be matched with any "sale" of junior stock in the preceding or following six months. Conversion of Junior Stock to Common: will not be considered a "purchase" or "sale" according to Rule 16b-9.* Resale of Junior Stock to Company: will be considered a "sale" and will be matched with any "purchase" of junior stock during the preceding or following six months. *This treatment is currently under review by the SEC and conversion may be considered a "purchase" for purposes of §16(b).	**Executive:** -Possibility of large gains at low purchase price. -Delayed taxation since tax is typically not owed until common stock is sold. -Company repurchase provision limits downside risk. **Company:** -Facilitates executive ownership of company stock. -Can communicate the importance of strategic goals. -Can link executive rewards to the planning process.	**Executive:** -Performance goals may never be reached, resulting in an investment opportunity loss. -Inferior ownership rights, e.g., dividends, voting, liquidation, until conversion. -Up-front cost of junior stock. **Company:** -Opportunity cost: capital received will be less than if common stock were sold on the open market. -No tax deduction unless sold at a discount from fair value. -Establishing a plan can be expensive due to its complexity. -Open-ended accounting liability until conversion.

May 1987

NON-QUALIFIED STOCK OPTION
(NQSO)

Description & Common Features	Tax Treatment	Accounting Treatment
Option to purchase shares of company stock at a stated price over a given period of time, frequently ten years. Option price normally equals 100% of stock's fair market value on date of grant but may be set below this level. Options may be exercised by cash payment or by tendering previously owned shares of stock.	Executive: -At exercise the excess of the fair market value of the stock over the option price is taxed as ordinary income and is subject to withholding. Taxation for insiders is delayed until the end of the required six-month holding period, unless executive elects to be taxed at exercise. Company: -Tax deduction in the amount of the executive's income from exercise of the option is allowed in year executive is taxed if withholding requirements are met.	No expense recognizable if both the number and price of optioned shares are fixed at the date of grant and the option is not discounted or exercised by pyramiding. Dilution may occur, however, since options are common stock equivalents. The option proceeds and tax savings are credited to paid-in capital. Discounting If option price is less than stock's fair market value when the option is granted, that discount is accrued as an expense over the vesting period. Pyramiding If options are exercised by tendering previously owned shares of stock that have not been held for at least six months, the difference between the fair market value of the stock and the option price is expensed in the year of exercise.

Insider Trading Considerations For Publicly Held Companies	Advantages	Disadvantages
Grant of Option: will not be considered a "purchase" if the plan meets certain requirements relating to administration by disinterested parties, shareholder approval, limits on benefits and limits on transferability of the option. Exercise of Option: will be considered a "purchase" and will be matched with any "sale" in the preceding or following six months.	Executive: -Possibility of large gains. -Because the company usually has no accounting expense, limits need not be set on executive gains. -Can choose timing of exercise to maximize gains. -Non-insiders may immediately sell enough shares to cover financing and tax costs. -Exercise by stock-for-stock swap permitted. -SARs can be attached. -Exercise periods after retirement without limitation. Company: -No charge on income statement. -Executive gains parallel shareholder gains. -Facilitates executive ownership of company stock. -Provides an increase in paid-in capital.	Executive: -Stock price changes may not parallel company/executive performance; no gain unless market value increases. -Flexibility of timing of option exercise and stock sales by insiders is limited by six-month insider trading rule. -May need to borrow money to finance option exercise. Company: -Executive gains may not parallel company performance. -Opportunity cost: paid-in capital will be less than it would have been if the stock were sold on the open market at the time of exercise. -May increase corporate minimum tax exposure since actual tax deduction may exceed the expense taken for accounting purposes.

May 1987

Tools and Techniques

CONVERTIBLE DEBENTURE

Description & Common Features	Tax Treatment	Accounting Treatment
Executive is offered an opportunity to purchase unsecured corporate bonds (i.e., "debentures") that are convertible, according to a predetermined ratio, into shares of the company's common stock. Normally, the executive must pay the debenture's full fair market value at the time of purchase; the debenture's interest rate approximates a market rate, and the conversion ratio is set according to the relative fair market value of the debenture and the common stock when the debenture is issued. Any deviation from these typical features may cause adverse tax and accounting consequences. The debentures may be fully vested and convertible at the time of the executive's purchase. Alternatively, convertibility may be conditional upon continued employment and/or performance.	Executive: -At Purchase: no tax if executive pays at least the debenture's fair market value. -Interest on Debenture: taxed as ordinary income when earned. -At Conversion to Common Stock: no tax. -Dividends: taxed at ordinary income rates when earned. -At Sale of Common Stock: difference between proceeds from sale of stock and purchase price of related debenture is taxed as long-term capital gain. (Note: Under the Tax Reform Act of 1986, favorable tax treatment for long-term capital gains is eliminated after 1986, except that the maximum rate on such gains in 1987 will be limited to 28%.) -If Debenture Held to Maturity: no tax. Company: -No tax deduction except for interest paid on debenture.	At Purchase: no expense is charged unless purchased for less than the debenture's fair market value. Balance sheet reflects increased cash and long-term debt. At Conversion: no income statement impact, but debt is reclassified as equity on the balance sheet. Earnings per Share: not normally dilutive to primary earnings per share until converted, but may dilute fully diluted earnings per share as soon as debenture is issued.

Insider Trading Considerations For Publicly Held Companies	Advantages	Disadvantages
Purchase of Debenture: will be considered a "purchase" and will be matched with any debenture "sale" during the preceding or following six months. Conversion of the Debenture: will not be treated as a "purchase" and/or "sale." Redemption of Debenture at Maturity: will not be treated as a "purchase" and/or "sale."	Executive: -No risk of loss, even if stock declines, since debenture can be held to maturity. -Executive receives market rate of interest while holding debenture. -Possibility for large gains if stock price rises. -No tax owed until stock is sold. Company: -No accounting expense required. -Source of capital. -Aligns executive and shareholder interest in increasing stock price.	Executive: -Can involve significant financing requirements and costs. Company: -No corporate tax deduction (except on interest paid).

May 1987

BOOK VALUE STOCK PURCHASE

Description & Common Features	Tax Treatment	Accounting Treatment
Executive is offered opportunity to purchase shares of stock, the price of which is determined by reference to book value. Shares must be resold to the company at a later date at the then per share book value. Shares for a book value plan may be a separate, nonvoting class of stock. Holders of this class of stock could receive dividends as paid. Offer is usually for a limited amount of time. Commonly used in closely held companies. Book value may be used in lieu of market value in the design of stock options, stock appreciation rights and phantom stock plans. Shares granted at a discount from book value will affect tax and accounting treatment.	Executive: -At Purchase: no tax consequences. -At Sale: increase in book value from date of purchase is taxed as a long-term capital gain if held for required holding period; otherwise, it is taxed at ordinary income rates. However, after 1986, long-term capital gains will be taxed at essentially the same rate as ordinary income (but subject to a 28% limit in 1987). Company: -At Purchase, Sale or Payment of Dividends: company gets no tax deduction.	No expense recognizable, although this is an area of discussion among accountants. Amounts received from executives for purchase are credited to paid-in capital.

Insider Trading Considerations For Publicly Held Companies	Advantages	Disadvantages
Grant of Purchase Right: will not be considered a "purchase" if the plan meets certain requirements relating to administration by disinterested parties, shareholder approval, limits on benefits and limits on transferability of the option. Exercise of Purchase Right: will be considered a "purchase" and will be matched with any "sale" of book value shares in the preceding or following six months.	Executive: -Possibility of large gains. -Reward is related to a measure over which the executive has more control than over the stock price. Company: -Possibly no accounting expense. -Provides an increase in paid-in capital.	Executive: -Stock may be resold to the company only. -Lacks open-market stock price appreciation potential. -Financing costs could be significant. Company: -Because each dollar of net income (after any dividend) increases book value, executive could receive payouts when earnings are positive but falling. -Could lead to retention of low-earning assets and avoidance of risk investment. -No tax deduction.

Tools and Techniques

SECTION 89 RULES

Section 89 of the Internal Revenue Code imposes a variety of rules on employee benefit plans effective for plan years beginning in 1989.

There are two separate sets of rules in Section 89:

(a) the *nondiscrimination* rules; these impose a major substantive burden on employers in designing and maintaining the plan, and

(b) the *qualification* rules (Section 89(k)); a set of rules somewhat similar to those of ERISA (Appendix D) that are primarily "paperwork" requirements.

An employer's failure to comply with the nondiscrimination rules generally results in a loss of some tax benefits to highly compensated employees that would otherwise be available. For example, if a health insurance plan is discriminatory, the value of the *discriminatory portion* of the health insurance coverage will be taxable, but only to highly compensated employees.

If the plan fails to meet the qualification requirements, benefits are taxable to *all* employees or, in the case of group-term life insurance benefits, their beneficiaries. The amount taxable is the amount of benefit actually paid, not the value of coverage. For example, if a group-term life insurance plan fails to meet the Section 89(k) qualification requirements, a death benefit payable to an employee's beneficiary is taxable income to the beneficiary.

Technically, Section 89 directly affects only the taxation of employees, not the employer. The employer's deduction for contributions to an employee benefit plan is not denied simply because the plan fails to comply with Section 89. However, as discussed below, employers can't simply ignore Section 89 because they must report income and withhold tax required as a result of a non-complying plan.

SECTION 89 NONDISCRIMINATION RULES

What Plans are Subject to the Nondiscrimination Rules?

Plans of churches, synagogues, and related organizations are *not* subject to these provisions of Section 89. For all other employers, the following employee benefit plans are subject to the nondiscrimination rules of Section 89:

- group-term life insurance

- accident and health plans (these include employer-provided arrangements such as

  — health insurance,

  — HMO, PPO, or similar arrangements,

  — ancillary health coverage such as dental, prescription, or vision plans,

  — medical reimbursement plans,

  — plans providing regular physical examinations, or

  — any other plan providing benefits that are excludable from the employee's income under Code section 105.

- dependent care plans under Section 129, *if* the employer elects to use the Section 89 rules as an alternative to the nondiscrimination rules in Section 129 (in some cases, the Section 89 rules might be easier to meet)

- group legal plans (Section 120) and educational assistance plans (Section 127), if the employer elects. Note, however, that as of this writing these plans expire at the end of 1988.

How are the Tests Applied?

If an employer provides a benefit plan for any highly compensated employee, that plan must be tested under the nondiscrimination rules in order to avoid full or partial loss of the plan's tax benefits for the highly compensated employee. The highly compensated employee must pay tax on any portion of the benefits that is deemed discriminatory under the tests described below.

The employer has an obligation to report nonqualifying benefits as taxable income on the highly compensated employee's Form W-2 for the year and withhold income tax. If the employer does not do this, the employer is liable for a penalty tax plus any under-withholding penalties. Thus, the employer does not have the option of simply ignoring Section 89 and letting the employee worry about whether or not plan benefits are taxable.

Some smaller employers may benefit from a rule that an employer that has only highly compensated employees need not comply with the Section 89 nondiscrimination rules.

"Highly compensated" is defined as it is for qualified plans under Code section 414(q) — Appendix A discusses the complete definition, which is both precise and complicated.

Eligibility Requirements. The plan's *eligibility* provisions must meet all of the following three requirements —

1. The 90%/50% test. This test requires that at least 90% of all "nonexcludable" nonhighly compensated employees must be eligible to participate in some plan of the type being tested. (The definition of "nonexcludable" in these tests is discussed below.) Also, they must have available a benefit that has a value equal to at least 50% of the largest employer-provided benefit under the plan available to any highly compensated employee. As a simple if unrealistic example, if the company president is eligible for company reimbursement of 100% of her medical expenses, a nonhighly compensated employee can't be considered as a plan participant in the 90% test unless that employee is eligible for company reimbursement of at least 50% of his medical expenses.

In performing the 90%/50% test, all plans of the employer of the same type are considered in the aggregate. That is, in testing a given health plan, all the employer's health plans are aggregated. Under certain circumstances, benefits funded through employee salary reductions can be treated as employer-provided benefits to help meet the tests.

2. The 50% eligibility test. This requires that at least 50% of employees eligible for the plan are *not* highly compensated. The requirement is deemed met if the percentage of highly compensated eligible employees is no greater than the percentage of nonhighly compensated eligible employees.

In applying the 50% eligibility test, "comparable" plans of an employer can be aggregated. The definition of comparable plan is discussed below.

3. The discriminatory provision test. Under this test, the plan must contain no provision relating to eligibility that discriminates in favor of highly compensated employees.

Benefit Requirements. For any testing year, the plan's *benefit* provisions are nondiscriminatory if the average employer-provided benefit received by nonhighly compensated employees is at least 75% of that received by highly compensated employees. The average employer-provided benefit for each of the two groups (highly and nonhighly compensated) is determined by dividing the aggregate employer-provided benefit received by the group by the number of nonexcludable employees in the group, whether or not they actually participate in the plan. In applying this test, all employer plans are aggregated.

Alternate 80% Test for Group-Term Life and Health Plans. Group-term life insurance plans under Section 79, and health plans (insured or noninsured) can comply with Section 89 by meeting a two-pronged alternate test (in lieu of the eligibility and benefit tests described above). Under this test, (a) the plan (or a group of comparable plans) must actually cover at least 80% of all non-excludable nonhighly compensated

employees, and (b) the discriminatory provision test (number 3 above) must be met. The 80% test can't be used for any plan that is part of a group of "comparable" plans (see below) unless the entire group of comparable plans meets the test.

Testing must be done on a "controlled group" basis, as in the case of qualified pension and profit-sharing plans. That is, all employees of a commonly controlled group of corporations or unincorporated businesses, or an affiliated service group, are treated as employed by a single employer for purposes of the Section 89 nondiscrimination rules. However, there are also rules under which the tests can be made separately for each of an employer's "separate lines of business" in certain circumstances.

What Employees are "Excludable"?

Section 89 allows certain employees to be excluded in applying the eligibility and benefit tests. The list of excludable employees is somewhat similar to the list of employees excludable in the qualified plan eligibility tests (see Appendix A) but it is not quite the same.

Section 89 excludable employees are

- employees who work fewer than the lesser of (a) 17 1/2 hours per week or (b) the fewest number of weekly hours required to participate in any plan of the type being tested (for purposes of the 80% test, there is a transition rule under which employers with fewer than 10 employees may exclude part-time employees who work more than 17 1/2 hours);

- employees who normally work during fewer than the lesser of (a) six months per year or (b) the fewest number of months per year required to participate in any plan of the type being tested;

- employees who have completed less than the lesser of (a) 12 months of service (6 months of service for core health benefits — definition below) or (b) the fewest number of months or days of service required to participate in any plan of the type being tested;

- employees who have not attained the lesser of (a) age 21 or (b) the youngest age required to participate in any plan of the type being tested;

- employees covered under a collective bargaining agreement if benefits of the type being tested have been the subject of good faith bargaining (however, this exclusion is severely restricted; see below);

- nonresident aliens with no U.S. source income;

- students employed by schools, colleges, and universities, if the employer is not required to withhold FICA from the students' wages and core health coverage is made available to them.

Section 89 provides that if any employee in an excludable category (except nonresident aliens) is covered under a plan of the type being tested, then no employees in that category can be excluded. For example, if an employer's collective bargaining unit employees have a health plan, the collective bargaining exclusion is unavailable in testing the employer's health plan. The collective bargaining exclusion would be available only if the bargaining unit had bargained on the issue and agreed *not* to have a health plan — a rare situation.

Another point to note in interpreting these exclusions is the prevalence of "lesser than" rules. Thus, for example if the employer has four health plans for its four divisions and one includes all part-time employees in that division (a "zero hour" participation requirement) then in testing any health plan, no part-timers can be excluded.

When are Plans "Comparable"?

The comparability criteria are complicated. The principal rules are:

- For purposes of the 50% test, plans are considered comparable if the smallest employer-provided benefit in the group to be aggregated is at least 95% of the largest employer-provided benefit in the group.

- For purposes of the alternative 80% test, plans are considered comparable if the smallest employer-provided benefit under any of the aggregated plans is at least 90% of the largest employer-provided benefit under these plans.

- For plans involving employee contributions, for purposes of both the 50% and 80% tests, plans are considered comparable if the annual cost difference to employees between plans is not more than $100, indexed for inflation.

The Exclusion for Core Health Benefit Coverage Under Another Plan

Employees often decline health coverage because they are covered under their employed spouse's plan. To deal with this situation equitably, an employer may exclude certain such employees for purposes of applying the benefits test and the 80% alternate test to health plans.

The employee may be excluded for this purpose *only* if the employee and his or her spouse and dependents are covered by a health plan providing "core benefits" maintained by another employer. Core benefits were defined in Congressional Committee Reports as health benefits other than dental, vision, orthodontia, psychological services, or elective cosmetic surgery. Employers may rely on employees' sworn statements as to the existence of such coverage.

SECTION 89 QUALIFICATION RULES

Code section 89(k) imposes a new set of rules applicable to welfare benefit plans in general. Some of these rules are similar to, or overlapping with, rules already applicable under ERISA. Although the penalties for noncompliance are severe, most properly-advised employers will have no difficulty in complying with most of these rules.

Section 89(k) requires the following of all affected welfare benefit plans:

- The plan must be in writing

- The employee's rights under the plan must be legally enforceable

- Employees must be provided reasonable notification of benefits available in the plan

- The plan must be maintained for the exclusive benefit of employees (this would appear generally to preclude, for example, covering non-employee shareholders under a corporate health plan)

- The plan must be established with the intention of being maintained for an indefinite period of time (this is similar to a rule applicable to qualified plans that imposes retroactive disqualification if a plan is terminated without a business reason after only a few years of operation).

Applicability. The qualification requirements of Section 89(k) apply to

- any "statutory employee benefit plan" (an accident or health plan covered under Code section 105(e) — most health plans are — and a group-term life insurance plan covered under Section 79)

- a qualified tuition reduction plan (Code section 117(d))

- a cafeteria plan (Section 125)

- a fringe benefit program providing no additional cost services, qualified employee discounts, or employer-operated eating facilities excludable from income under Section 132

- any plan operated through a VEBA (Section 501(c)(9) trust)

WHAT MUST THE EMPLOYER DO?

First, the employer must gather new types of data about its employees and plans in order to assess the impact of Section 89 and perform the statutory tests. Each benefit plan must be identified, and its eligibility, benefits, plan year, and other information tabulated.

An employee census must be developed to indicate compensation, hours worked, years of service, number of dependents, amounts contributed to employee plans (both salary reduction and after-tax), and other information necessary to identify highly compensated employees and perform the Section 89 tests. Many employers do not have all this information readily available from normal payroll records.

311

Then, after the tests have been made, the employer has two options with respect to the nondiscrimination requirements:

(1) modify noncomplying plans if the employer wants highly compensated employees to qualify for the available tax benefits, or

(2) leave the plan (or plans) as they are and simply report additional taxable income for highly compensated employees. The employer can then provide a compensating "bonus" to affected employees.

It is essential that both advisers and employers realize, however, that *neither* option can safely be selected until a full Section 89 analysis of the employer's plans is made.

With respect to the qualification requirements, the employer must identify all plans and determine which are subject to the requirements, collect the documentation for the plans, review them for clarity, and determine that employees are properly notified and that the other requirements are satisfied.

INDEX

Complete Your
LEIMBERG
LIBRARY

Use this handy postage-paid form to order additional copies of "The Tools and Techniques of Employee Benefit and Retirement Planning" or copies of

❏ "The Tools and Techniques of Estate Planning" - 7th edition
❏ "The Tools and Techniques of Financial Planning" - 3rd edition

PRICES*

The TOOLS AND TECHNIQUES OF EMPLOYEE BENEFIT AND RETIREMENT PLANNING

Single...$30.00 ea.
5 copies....................................$28.95 ea.
10 copies..................................$28.25 ea.
25 copies..................................$27.50 ea.

The TOOLS AND TECHNIQUES OF ESTATE PLANNING

Single...$35.00 ea.
5 copies....................................$33.25 ea.
10 copies..................................$31.50 ea.
25 copies..................................$30.00 ea.

The TOOLS AND TECHNIQUES OF FINANCIAL PLANNING

Single...$35.00 ea.
5 copies....................................$33.25 ea.
10 copies..................................$31.50 ea.
25 copies..................................$30.00 ea.

*Shipping & handling charges are additional.

To order use the
postage-free order cards
or
**CALL TOLL-FREE
1-800-543-0874**

2-2L

NATIONAL UNDERWRITER

The National Underwriter Co. • 420 East 4th St. • Cincinnati, OH 45202

Please send and bill me for:

_____ copies of The Tools and Techniques of Employee Benefit and Retirement Planning - new 1st edition (#271)
_____ copies of The Tools and Techniques of Estate Planning - 7th edition (#285)
_____ copies of The Tools and Techniques of Financial Planning - 3rd edition (#277)

(please print or type)

Name — Title	
Company	
Street Address	
City — State	Zip

2-2L

NATIONAL UNDERWRITER

The National Underwriter Co. • 420 East 4th St. • Cincinnati, OH 45202

Please send and bill me for:

_____ copies of The Tools and Techniques of Employee Benefit and Retirement Planning - new 1st edition (#271)
_____ copies of The Tools and Techniques of Estate Planning - 7th edition (#285)
_____ copies of The Tools and Techniques of Financial Planning - 3rd edition (#277)

(please print or type)

Name — Title	
Company	
Street Address	
City — State	Zip

2-2L

NATIONAL UNDERWRITER

The National Underwriter Co. • 420 East 4th St. • Cincinnati, OH 45202

Please send and bill me for:

_____ copies of The Tools and Techniques of Employee Benefit and Retirement Planning - new 1st edition (#271)
_____ copies of The Tools and Techniques of Estate Planning - 7th edition (#285)
_____ copies of The Tools and Techniques of Financial Planning - 3rd edition (#277)

(please print or type)

Name — Title	
Company	
Street Address	
City — State	Zip

BUSINESS REPLY MAIL

FIRST CLASS   **PERMIT NO. 68**   **CINCINNATI, OH**

POSTAGE WILL BE PAID BY ADDRESSEE

THE NATIONAL UNDERWRITER CO.
420 EAST FOURTH STREET
CINCINNATI, OHIO 45202-9960

BUSINESS REPLY MAIL

FIRST CLASS   **PERMIT NO. 68**   **CINCINNATI, OH**

POSTAGE WILL BE PAID BY ADDRESSEE

THE NATIONAL UNDERWRITER CO.
420 EAST FOURTH STREET
CINCINNATI, OHIO 45202-9960

BUSINESS REPLY MAIL

FIRST CLASS   **PERMIT NO. 68**   **CINCINNATI, OH**

POSTAGE WILL BE PAID BY ADDRESSEE

THE NATIONAL UNDERWRITER CO.
420 EAST FOURTH STREET
CINCINNATI, OHIO 45202-9960